Subprime Mortgage Credit Derivatives

The Frank J. Fabozzi Series

Subprime Mortgage Credit Derivatives

LAURIE S. GOODMAN
SHUMIN LI
DOUGLAS J. LUCAS
THOMAS A. ZIMMERMAN
FRANK J. FABOZZI

WILEY

John Wiley & Sons, Inc.

For general information on our other products and services or for technical support, please contact our Customer Care Department within the United States at (800) 762-2974, outside the United States at (317) 572-3993, or fax (317) 572-4002.

Wiley also publishes its books in a variety of electronic formats. Some content that appears in print may not be available in electronic books. For more information about Wiley products, visit our web site at www.wiley.com.

Library of Congress Cataloging-in-Publication Data:

Subprime mortgage credit derivatives / Laurie S. Goodman ... [et al.].
    p. cm.—(The Frank J. Fabozzi series)
    Includes index.
    ISBN 978-0-470-24366-4 (cloth)
        1. Mortgage loans—United States. 2. Mortgage loans—United
    States—Statistics. 3. Secondary mortgage market—United States. I.
    Goodman, Laurie S.
    HG2040.15.S825 2008
    332.63'244—dc22

                                    2008014507

Printed in the United States of America.

10 9 8 7 6 5 4 3 2 1

Contents

Preface

The purpose of this book is to explain subprime mortgage credit and its numerous derivative instruments. We cover the determinants of mortgage credit, mortgage securitization, and all the derivatives of mortgage credit (that is, credit default swaps, the ABX and TABX indices, and credit default swaps on mortgage-backed CDOs). Moreover, we provide methodologies for projecting losses for a pool of mortgage loans and present models for the valuation of mortgage securitizations and derivatives of mortgage securitizations.

The 13 chapters of this book are divided into five parts:

Part One: Mortgage Credit
Part Two: Mortgage Securitizations
Part Three: Credit Default Swaps on Mortgage Securities
Part Four: Loss Projection and Security Valuation
Part Five: The Subprime Meltdown

In Part One, we look at the underlying determinants of mortgage credit. This topic is essential for understanding the topics covered in the other four parts of the book. Chapter 1 provides an overview of the nonagency mortgage market. We look at the defining characteristics of jumbo prime, Alt-A, and subprime mortgages, describing how those characteristics have changed over time. In Chapter 2, we focus on first lien mortgages, paying particular attention to collateral characteristics. In addition, we describe the mortgage credit end game: The timeline from delinquency to foreclosure to real estate owned (REO) and the determination of loss severities. Our focus in Chapter 3 is on second lien mortgages where we provide intuition as to why the losses on such loans are so high.

In Part Two, we look at the structure of mortgage securitization. Credit support features (excess spread, overcollateralization, and subordination) are explained. This standard subprime structure is used in many Alt-A deals as well. In Chapter 5 we look at subprime triggers and stepdowns. These structural mechanisms make a substantial difference in determining the size and timing of cash flows to the various bond classes in a securitization transaction.

We devote Part Three to credit default swaps on mortgage securities. Chapter 6 provides an introduction to credit default swaps on asset-backed securities, describing the differences between credit default swaps on asset-backed securities (ABCDS) and credit default swaps on corporate bonds. Chapter 7 discusses the ABX and TABS indices. The importance of the ABX indices is hard to overstate; price transparency in these indices provides guidance for cash instruments. The relationships between cash bonds, ABCDS, and the ABX, including structural features and supply/demand technicals, are explored in Chapter 8. In Chapter 9, we explain credit default swaps on CDOs.

In Part Four we look at loss projection and securities valuation. The first step in valuing these securities is to estimate losses on the underlying collateral. In Chapter 10 we discuss loss projection methodologies for subprime, Alt-A, and second lien mortgages. In Chapter 11 we discuss ABX valuation using the loss projection methodology described in Chapter 10 and then extend the loss projection methodology to ABS CDOs in Chapter 12.

Part Five contains a single chapter: The great subprime meltdown of 2007. We discuss the roots of the market meltdown, as well as the future of the subprime market.

In this book, we refer to a number of data services. First American CoreLogic, LoanPerformance Data updates and maintains the database that provides the foundation for much of the quantitative work in this book. CPR & CDR Technologies, Inc. provides a front end for the LoanPerformance database. Intex Solutions, Inc. provides collateral data and deal modeling. Markit Group Limited provides pricing data for a variety of mortgage-related instruments.

We gratefully acknowledge the expertise and input of the following members of the UBS Securitized Products Research Group: James Bejjani, Christian Collins, Jeffrey Ho, Charles Mladinich, Trevor Murray, Laura Nadler, Danny Newman, Greg Reiter, Susan Rodetis, Dipa Sharif, Wilfred Wong, Victoria Ye, and Ke Yin. Their helpful discussions and ongoing support are appreciated. A special thanks is due Rei Shinozuka for his work in this area and for his significant contributions to this book.

Laurie S. Goodman
Shumin Li
Douglas J. Lucas
Tom Zimmerman
Frank Fabozzi

Laurie S. Goodman is co-head of Global Fixed Income Research and Manager of U.S. Securitized Products Research at UBS. Her Securitized Products Team is responsible for publications and relative value recommendations across the RMBS, ABS, CMBS and CDO markets. As a mortgage analyst, Dr. Goodman has long dominated *Institutional Investor's* MBS categories, placing first in five categories 40 times over the last 10 years. In 1993, she founded the securitized products research group at Paine Webber, which merged with UBS in 2000. Prior to that, she spent 10 years in senior fixed income research positions at Citicorp, Goldman Sachs, and Merrill Lynch, and gained buy-side experience as a mortgage portfolio manager. She began her career as a Senior Economist at the Federal Reserve Bank of New York. Dr. Goodman holds a BA in Mathematics from the University of Pennsylvania and both MA and Ph.D. degrees in Economics from Stanford University. She has published more than 170 articles in professional and academic journals.

Shumin Li is Executive Director of MBS/ABS Strategy and Research at UBS Investment Bank in New York. Prior to joining UBS in 2006, he worked at Credit Suisse and GMAC-RFC as a Vice President and Senior Analyst on residential mortgage-related research that includes prepayment and default modeling, structuring, and relative value analysis. From 2000 to 2004, Mr. Li worked at Fannie Mae as a Senior Financial Engineer where he was responsible for developing prepayment models of all mortgage products at the company. He started his career in the financial industry in 1998 working as a Quantitative Analyst at FleetBoston Financial Group in Providence, Rhode Island. Mr. Li has a master's degree in economics from Brown University and a bachelor's degree in economics from Peking University.

Douglas Lucas is an Executive Director at UBS and head of CDO Research. His team consistently ranks in the top three of *Institutional Investor's* fixed income analyst survey. His prior positions include head of CDO research at JPMorgan, co-CEO of Salomon Swapco, credit control positions at two boutique swap dealers, and structured products and security firm analyst at Moody's Investors Service. Mr. Lucas also served two terms as Chairman of The Bond Market Association's CDO Research Committee. While at Moody's from 1987 to 1993, he authored the rating agency's first default and rating transition studies, quantified the expected loss rating approach, and developed Moody's rating methodologies for collateralized debt obligations and triple-A special purpose derivatives dealers. He is also known for doing some of the first quantitative work in default correlation. Mr. Lucas has a BA *magna cum laude* in Economics from UCLA and an MBA with Honors from the University of Chicago.

Thomas A. Zimmerman is Managing Director and Head of ABS and mortgage credit research in the Securitized Products Strategy Group at UBS. Prior to joining UBS, he spent eight years at Prudential Securities, first as a Senior VP in the Mortgage Research Group and later as head of the ABS Research Department. Before that, he managed the MBS/ABS Research Group at Chemical Bank. Mr. Zimmerman started his research career as a Vice President in the Mortgage Research Department at Salomon Brothers. His research has appeared in numerous fixed income publications and industry reference works, including the *Handbook of Fixed Income Securities* and the *Handbook of Mortgage-Backed Securities*. He is a member of the UBS research team that consistently ranks in the top three of Institutional Investor's fixed income analyst survey. Mr. Zimmerman earned a BS in Management Science from Case Western Reserve University and an MS in Operations Research from the University of Southern California.

Frank J. Fabozzi is Professor in the Practice of Finance and Becton Fellow in the School of Management at Yale University. Prior to joining the Yale faculty, he was a Visiting Professor of Finance in the Sloan School at MIT. Professor Fabozzi is a Fellow of the International Center for Finance at Yale University and on the Advisory Council for the Department of Operations Research and Financial Engineering at Princeton University. He is an affiliated professor at the Institute of Statistics, Econometrics and Mathematical Finance at the University of Karlsruhe (Germany). He is the editor of the *Journal of Portfolio Management* and an associate editor of the *Journal of Fixed Income*. He earned a doctorate in economics from the City University of New York in 1972. In 2002, Professor Fabozzi was inducted into the Fixed Income Analysts Society's Hall of Fame and is the 2007 recipient of the C. Stewart Sheppard Award given by the CFA Institute. He earned the designation of Chartered Financial Analyst and Certified Public Accountant. He has authored and edited numerous books about finance.

Mortgage Credit

CHAPTER 1

Overview of the
Nonagency Mortgage Market

In this chapter we look at the major types of nonagency mortgage product, along with their defining characteristics and the variation in issuance volumes.

The value of residential 1–4 family real estate in the United States is $23 trillion. Against this, there is $10.7 trillion in mortgage debt, with the remaining 53% ($12.3 trillion) representing homeowner equity. That equity value is created because either a homeowner has no mortgage on their home, or the home's value exceeds the mortgage (via any combination of mortgage paydown, home price appreciation, or loan-to-value mortgage issuance).

Of the $10.7 trillion in residential mortgage debt, $6.3 trillion (58%) has been securitized. The securitized portion can be broken down into *agency mortgages* and *nonagency mortgages*. Agency mortgages are those guaranteed by either the Government National Mortgage Association (Ginnie Mae), a U.S. government agency, or one of the *government-sponsored enterprises* (GSEs), Fannie Mae or Freddie Mac. Nonagency mortgages are mortgages that, for a variety of reasons, do not meet underwriting criteria required by the agencies. Mortgages that fail to meet the underwriting standards of the agencies are said to be nonconforming mortgages.

Exhibit 1.1 shows that in 2007, agency mortgages represented approximately 66% of the securitized market, with the remaining 34% consisting of nonagency mortgages. The nonagency share contains jumbo prime (8% of the total), alternative-A or Alt-A (13%), and subprime (13%). While we will discuss in more detail later, jumbo prime mortgages are those whose are too large in size in qualify for Ginnie Mae, Fannie Mae, or Freddie Mac programs. Alt-A mortgages and subprime mortgages generally have more risk layering than standard agency *mortgage-backed securities* (MBS), while subprime borrowers are generally lower in credit quality than the borrowers backing agency MBS. On the nonsecuritized portion of the market, we do not have any information on the distribution of outstandings. (We do not know what percentage is prime, subprime, and Alt-A, which explains why market participants have seen widely divergent estimates on component sizes.)

EXHIBIT 1.1 Outstanding Mortgage Securities

Year	GNMA	FHLMC	FNMA	Total Agency	Nonagency	Total MBS	% of Total MBS		Value of residential 1–4 family real estate: $23 Trillion	
							% Agency	% Nonagency	1–4 Mtg. Outstanding	MBS as % of Total Mtg. Outstanding
1992	419,516	401,525	560,471	1,381,512	142,265	1,523,777	91%	9%	2,954,396	52%
1993	414,066	434,499	638,780	1,487,345	167,899	1,655,244	90%	10%	3,113,834	53%
1994	450,934	460,656	681,237	1,592,827	183,002	1,775,829	90%	10%	3,291,540	54%
1995	472,283	512,238	735,170	1,719,691	193,759	1,913,450	90%	10%	3,459,184	55%
1996	506,340	551,513	801,025	1,858,878	215,357	2,074,235	90%	10%	3,682,790	56%
1997	536,810	576,846	854,782	1,968,438	253,804	2,222,242	89%	11%	3,917,569	57%
1998	537,431	643,465	977,708	2,158,604	321,869	2,480,473	87%	13%	4,274,301	58%
1999	582,263	744,619	1,097,707	2,424,589	353,660	2,778,249	87%	13%	4,699,578	59%
2000	611,553	816,602	1,197,298	2,625,453	385,501	3,010,954	87%	13%	5,126,531	59%
2001	591,368	940,933	1,442,230	2,974,531	463,217	3,437,748	87%	13%	5,677,996	61%
2002	537,888	1,066,303	1,708,409	3,312,600	544,055	3,856,655	86%	14%	6,436,575	60%
2003	473,738	1,129,540	1,790,743	3,394,021	664,005	4,058,026	84%	16%	7,226,763	56%
2004	441,235	1,193,683	1,832,535	3,467,453	1,049,767	4,517,220	77%	23%	8,284,980	55%
2005	405,246	1,321,268	1,881,435	3,607,949	1,536,627	5,144,576	70%	30%	9,323,217	55%
2006	410,196	1,468,608	2,026,107	3,904,911	1,991,459	5,896,370	66%	34%	10,359,047	57%
2007-Q2	417,216	1,585,752	2,145,723	4,148,691	2,120,175	6,268,866	66%	34%	10,749,703	58%

Out of the 34% Nonagency	
Alt-A	13%
Prime	8%
Subprime	13%

Note: Estimates in italics.
Source: Inside MBS & ABS, LoanPerformance, and UBS.

ISSUANCE VOLUMES

Exhibit 1.2 shows the main sectors of MBS that we discuss and their respective issuance volumes from 1995 to the third quarter of 2007. Note that between 1995 and 2003, the agency share of mortgage issuance ranged from 75% to 85%. The nonagency share (15% to 25%) was comprised of jumbo, Alt-A, subprime, and "other," with the jumbo prime share the largest portion.

The agency share of issuance dropped to 54% in 2004, and then further to 45% in 2005 and 2006. The declining agency share during from 2004 to 2006 was accompanied by a large increase in subprime and Alt-A issuance. For example, the subprime share rose from 7% in 2003 to 19% to 22% in 2004 to 2006. The Alt-A share increased from 3% in 2003 to 15% to 18% in 2005 and 2006.

ROOTS OF THE 2007–2008 SUBPRIME CRISIS

Therein lies the roots of the subprime crises. The decline in agency issuance during 2004–2006, mirrored by a rise in subprime and Alt-A issuance, reflected the drop in housing affordability during this period. The reason for the drop in housing affordability was a rise in interest rates from their mid-2003 lows in conjunction with the continued rise in housing prices. Exhibit 1.3 shows the Freddie Mac Conventional Home Price Indices and the Case Shiller Home Price Indices. Notice the large run-up in *home price appreciation* (HPA) during 2003–2005; we clearly see that housing became less and less affordable.

The most commonly used measure of housing affordability is the National Association of Realtors Housing Affordability Index. This index, shown in Exhibit 1.4, measures the ability of a family earning the median income to buy a median-priced home. This calculation is critically dependent on three inputs: median family income, median home prices, and mortgage rates. It assumes a family earning the median family income buys the median priced home, puts down 20%, and takes out a 30-year conventional mortgage for the remaining 80% of the house value at prevailing interest rates.[1] If payments on a 30-year conventional mortgage consume 25% of a borrower's income, then the index has a value of 100. Our sample calculation consists of:

Median family income = $60,000 per year; $5,000 per month
Median priced home = $224,000
Downpayment = 20% × $224,000 = $44,800

[1] A *conventional mortgage* is one that is not guaranteed by an agency or government-backed insurance.

EXHIBIT 1.2 MBS Gross Issuance

Date	Agency ($ million)	Nonagency ($ million)				Total MBS ($ million)	% of Total					
		Alt-A	Jumbo	Subprime	Other		Agency	Alt-A	Jumbo	Subprime	Other	Nonagency
1995	269,132	498	25,838	17,772	4,818	318,058	84.6	0.2	8.1	5.6	1.5	15.4
1996	370,648	1,803	31,419	30,769	5,903	440,541	84.1	0.4	7.1	7.0	1.3	15.9
1997	367,884	6,518	49,975	56,921	5,719	487,016	75.5	1.3	10.3	11.7	1.2	24.5
1998	725,952	21,236	97,365	75,830	8,780	929,163	78.1	2.3	10.5	8.2	0.9	21.9
1999	685,078	12,023	74,631	55,852	5,394	832,977	82.2	1.4	9.0	6.7	0.6	17.8
2000	479,011	16,444	53,585	52,467	13,463	614,970	77.9	2.7	8.7	8.5	2.2	22.1
2001	1,087,499	11,374	142,203	87,053	26,691	1,354,819	80.3	0.8	10.5	6.4	2.0	19.7
2002	1,444,426	53,463	171,534	122,681	66,277	1,858,381	77.7	2.9	9.2	6.6	3.6	22.3
2003	2,131,953	74,151	237,455	194,959	79,653	2,718,170	78.4	2.7	8.7	7.2	2.9	21.6
2004	1,018,684	158,586	233,378	362,549	109,639	1,882,836	54.1	8.4	12.4	19.3	5.8	45.9
2005	964,697	332,323	280,704	465,036	113,247	2,156,007	44.7	15.4	13.0	21.6	5.3	55.3
2006	924,637	365,676	219,037	448,600	112,139	2,070,089	44.7	17.7	10.6	21.7	5.4	55.3
2007-9M	860,909	235,995	161,190	189,464	63,908	1,511,465	57.0	15.6	10.7	12.5	4.2	43.0
2007-Q1	265,208	96,873	60,333	88,554	26,148	537,116	49.4	18.0	11.2	16.5	4.9	50.6
2007-Q2	288,743	100,916	60,567	74,694	22,288	547,207	52.8	18.4	11.1	13.6	4.1	47.2
2007-Q3	306,958	38,206	40,290	26,216	15,472	427,142	71.9	8.9	9.4	6.1	3.6	28.1

Source: Inside MBS & ABS and UBS.

EXHIBIT 1.3   Home Price Indices

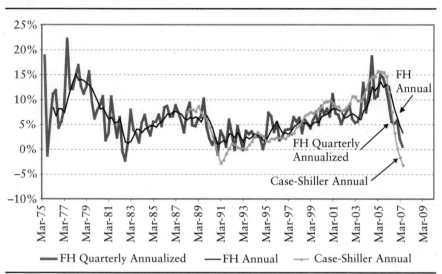

Note: Latest data: Q2 2007; quarterly FH annualized = 0.4%; FH annual = 3.3%; CS Annual = –3%.
Source: Freddie Mac.

EXHIBIT 1.4   Housing Affordability versus 30-year Mortgage Rates

Note: Latest is estimated: August 2007; housing affordability = 106.1; 30-year mortgage rate = 6.57%.
Source: National Association of Realtors and Freddie Mac.

Mortgage = 80% × $224,000 = $179,200
Mortgage rate = 6.50%
Mortgage payment 30-year fixed rate mortgage
    = $1,133 ($179,200 mortgage at 6.5%)

So the National Association of Realtors' calculation is:

25% of Median family income/Mortgage payment on median-priced home
= 25% × $5,000/$1,133 = 110.3

Home prices rose during the 2001–2003 period, but that rise was offset by the drop in interest rates, leaving housing affordability in the range of 129 to 146. However, mortgage rates rose from late 2003 through 2006, and housing values also rose, thus producing a sharp drop in housing affordability to a low of 99.6 by June 2006.

In order to maintain market share, originators began to relax origination standards. *Combined loan-to-value ratios* (CLTVs) rose (indicating a heavy use of second mortgages), the interest-only share rose, and documentation dropped. In the next section of this chapter, we examine the loan characteristics of jumbo, Alt-A, and subprime sectors, and quantify the drop in origination standards.

The fall in the agency share between 2004 and 2006 reflected that:

1. Fannie Mae and Freddie Mac were slow to embrace "affordability" products such as *interest-only loans* (IOs).
2. Both GSEs were reluctant to guarantee loans too far down the credit spectrum, and reluctant to guarantee mortgages with too much risk layering.
3. Even when agency execution was possible, agency risk-based pricing resulted in execution that was usually worse than nonagency execution.

Thus, most of the mortgage affordability products received nonagency execution. But subsequently in 2007 when nonagency execution channels became more costly, originators again sought agency execution.

The relaxation in origination standards was fine as long home prices were appreciating. When a borrower ran into difficulty, selling the home at a profit was a much better option than defaulting. However, in mid-2006 housing began to weaken. Existing home sales fell; home prices were stagnant and then began to decline. Vacant homes for sales hit a multiyear high and delinquencies began to rise.

In 2007, as the subprime crises emerged and intensified, the agency share rose, while subprime and Alt-A shares fell. During 2007, it had become very difficult to obtain a subprime or Alt-A mortgage. Origination capacity was cut considerably. Most subprime originators without deep-pocketed parent companies went out of business, and either ceased operations or were acquired. Moreover, even the remaining originators made very few subprime and Alt-A loans, as the securitized markets for these products had dried up. Investors who had historically purchased securities backed by pools of subprime and Alt-A mortgages were no longer willing to purchase the securities, at least not at rate levels that borrowers could afford to pay. Thus, originators had no one to sell the loans to and did not have the balance sheet capacity to warehouse these loans. As a result, many originators stopped making loans that did not qualify for agency guarantees and by mid-2007 the mortgage market was again dominated by the agencies.

DEFINING CHARACTERISTICS OF NONAGENCY MORTGAGES

Exhibit 1.5 presents the main characteristics of different sectors of the agency and nonagency market. It covers such loan and borrower characteristics as loan size, average FICO score, average LTV and CLTV, occupancy (owner versus investor), documentation (full versus nonfull), loan purpose (cash-out, cash-out refi, or rate refi), the percent in adjustable rate mortgages, the IO percent, and *debt-to-income* (DTI) ratio.

The nonagency sectors of the MBS market are defined by how they differ from agency collateral. *Jumbo prime mortgages* generally have higher FICO scores than agency mortgages. However, their main distinguishing characteristic is *size*; these loans exceed the conforming sized limit, $417,000 in 2007. The *Alt-A loans* may be conforming or nonconforming in terms of size. These mortgages tend to be of good credit as measured by their FICO score (approximately 710). Their distinguishing characteristic is the low percentage (23%) of borrowers who *fully document their income*. The distinguishing characteristic of *subprime* borrowers is their *FICO* score; averaging in the 620s, it is much lower than other borrower types.

LOAN CHARACTERISTICS

These loan characteristics collectively determine the prepayment and credit performance of each MBS deal. We now look at these characteristics in greater detail.

EXHIBIT 1.5   Loan and Borrower Characteristics by Product Type

	Agency	Jumbo Prime	Alt-A	Subprime
Lien	1st	1st	1st	1st
Loan limit	≤ Agency	> Agency	None	None
Average loan size	221,301	509,913	293,719	185,451
2006 Avg. loan size	230,403	577,022	320,828	210,472
Credit	Agency	A	A/A–	A–/C
Average FICO	725	739	712	628
2006 Avg. FICO	723	740	708	626
Average LTV	71	69	74	81
2006 Avg. LTV	73	71	75	81
Average CLTV	—	71	80	86
2006 Avg. CLTV	—	75	82	87
Occupancy (owner)	95%	99%	85%	95%
Full documentation	—	50%	23%	60%
Loan purpose				
Purchase	39%	46%	46%	40%
Cash out	59%	23%	36%	53%
Rate refi		30%	18%	7%
IO	9%	45%	43%	20%
ARMs	12%	52%	63%	73%
DTI	—	33%	36%	41%

Source: Fannie Mae, Freddie Mac, and LoanPerformance.

Combined Loan-to-Value Ratio

The CLTV ratio is the single most important factor determining credit performance on a loan. The *loan-to-value* (LTV) ratio refers to the loan amount divided by the value of a home. Thus, if there is a $160,000 loan (mortgage) on a $200,000 home, we would say the LTV ratio is 80% ($160,000/$200,000). The CLTV ratio is the sum of the first and second mortgages divided by the home's value. Thus, if there is a $160,000 first mortgage and a $30,000 second mortgage] against a $200,000 home value, we would say the borrower has a CLTV ratio of 95% ($190,000 mortgages/$200,000 value of home).

EXHIBIT 1.6 2006–2007 CLTV Distribution

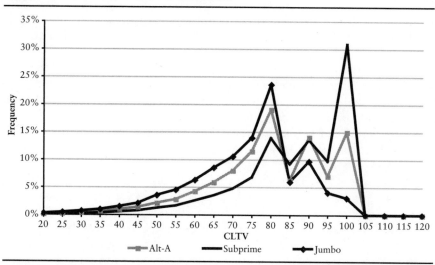

Source: LoanPerformance.

A high CLTV typically indicates that the buyer has stretched to buy a home, and could not put down as much as other borrowers. A high CLTV is often associated with a high DTI ratio as well as other weak credit indications.

In the agency world, any loan that exceeds 80% LTV requires *private mortgage insurance* (PMI). In the nonagency world, higher risk mortgages such as subprime and Alt-A typically have higher LTVs than is seen in agency pools. Exhibit 1.6 shows a distribution of the CLTVs on 2006 and 2007 jumbo, subprime, and Alt-A pools. Note that in both Alt-A and subprime pools there is a considerable percentage of loans with CLTVs in excess of 95%. Note also that this percentage is higher in subprime pools than in Alt-A pools.

Loans with higher CLTV ratios have higher delinquencies and higher loss severities. Those delinquencies and loss severities increase due to home price depreciation. Assume that a $200,000 house drops in value by 10% and is thus worth only $180,000. The borrower with a $160,000 first mortgage and a $30,000 second mortgage (mortgages total $190,000) will have little reason *not* to default on that home. The more the home depreciates in value, the higher the loss severity.

It is also important to realize that in a lower home price appreciation environment, loans with higher CLTV ratios will prepay more slowly, as they have fewer refinancing opportunities.

FICO Scores

Credit scores have been used in the consumer finance industry for several decades. Over the past decade, they have become an increasingly important part of assessing mortgage credit.

A credit score is an empirically derived quantitative measure of the likelihood that a borrower will repay a debt. Credit scores are generated from models that have been developed from statistical studies of historical data, and use as inputs details from the borrower's credit history. FICO scores are tabulated by an independent credit bureaus, using a model created by Fair Isaac Corporation (FICO). These scores range from 350 to 900, with higher scores denoting lower risk.

FICO scores have been shown to play an important role in determining both delinquencies and prepayment speeds. Lower FICO mortgages default at a much higher rate than their higher FICO counterparts, and exhibit much higher losses. On the prepayment side, it has historically been the case that lower FICO borrowers prepay much faster than higher FICO counterparts. That's because a low credit borrower who stays current on consumer and mortgage loans for a year may be able to refinance at a lower rate. Thus, refinancing due to "credit curing" has historically been the source of relatively high base-case speeds on subprime loans. In addition, many borrowers had refinanced as a way to tap into the equity on their home, which had increased in value. With the subprime crisis limiting the availability of credit to these borrowers, and home prices falling, voluntary prepayments fell sharply in 2007. Providing a modest cushion, involuntary prepayments (defaults are passed through as a prepayment) rose.

Moreover, lower FICO pools tend to be much less sensitive to changes in interest rates. This reflects the fact that in a refinancing, lower credit borrowers face higher closing costs and points.

Exhibit 1.5 shows that the average FICO scores are 725, 739, 712, and 628 for agency, jumbo, Alt-A, and subprime, respectively. It's important to realize that FICO scores alone do not sufficiently define a loan. This is clearly illustrated in Exhibit 1.7, which depicts the FICO distribution. Note that approximately 18% of subprime loans have FICO scores that exceed 680, while 27% of the Alt-A loans have FICO scores that fall below 680.

Documentation

Documentation is generally defined as either *full documentation* ("full doc") or *limited documentation*. Full documentation generally involves the verification of income (based on the provision of W-2 forms) and assets (from bank statements). With limited documentation, either income or as-

EXHIBIT 1.7 FICO Distribution

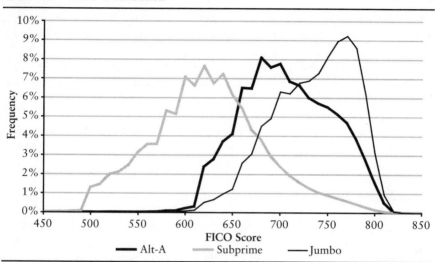

Source: LoanPerformance.

sets are not verified. Limited documentation can take many forms, including SISA (stated income, stated assets), NISA (no income (income not provided, stated assets), No Ratio (income not provided, assets verified). Each originator has its own definition of limited documentation. Moreover, originators differ considerably in the degree to which they attempt to ferret out stated income borrowers that are clearly lying. Some originators verify employment for stated income borrowers; others do not. Some originators go a step further and make sure the income is reasonable for the occupation specified; others do not perform that step.

Limited documentation is the key feature in defining Alt-A product. In fact, the Alt-A market originally arose to accommodate borrowers who owned their own business and lacked traditional documentation such as employment and income verification. Then, in the late 1990s, the agencies began to accept limited documentation for borrowers with higher FICO scores and lower LTVs, and the jumbo market followed suit. Note that the limited documentation was historically accompanied by compensating factors. However, from 2004 to 2006, documentation standards were relaxed considerably, without requiring any type of compensating factors.

Limited documentation loans tend to have higher default rates than full documentation loans. Moreover, limited documentation tends to be highly correlated with other risk factors (higher LTV, lower FICO, higher DTI). Documentation alone tends to be of secondary importance as a determinant of prepayment stability.

Loan Size

All agency loans for single family homes must be less than the conforming loan limit of $417,000.[2] The loan limit is reset annually, based on October-to-October changes, as measured by the Federal Housing Finance Board (FHFB). Even though the limit is $417,000, the average loan size is much smaller; by the third quarter of 2007 it was approximately $225,000 for new origination.

Loans carrying agency credit and meeting all other agency credit criteria except size are referred to as jumbo prime loans. (Often they are refereed to as either "jumbo" or "prime"). The average size of jumbo loans is $510,000. (However, that includes loans extended when the loan limit was smaller; e.g., the loan size limit in 2003 was $322,700. The average loan size for 2006 jumbo origination was $577,000.

Alt-A loans can be either conforming or nonconforming. Their average size of $294,000 falls midway between that of agencies and jumbos. Approximately 25% (as measured by number) of Alt-A mortgages issued in 2006, and 50% (as measured by balances) were nonconforming in terms of size.

Subprime loans are typically similar in size to agency loans. However, there is a substantial minority of loans that are nonconforming in terms of size. Thus, 6% of subprime mortgages issued in 2006 (measured by number) and 20% (measured by balances) were nonconforming in terms of size. This is clearly shown in Exhibit 1.8 which illustrates the size distribution of jumbo, Alt-A, and subprime loans.

Loan size is important in understanding both delinquency and prepayment characteristics. Note that smaller loans are less prepayment-sensitive than loans with larger balances. This reflects the fact that the fixed costs of refinancing have a larger impact on smaller mortgages. Smaller loans also tend to have higher losses than larger loans, reflecting the higher fixed costs of liquidation.

Loan Purpose

Loan purpose can take one of three forms: *purchase*, *refi*, or *cash-out refi*. Historically, loan purpose has not been that important in determining either default or prepayment behavior. However in the 2004–2006 period, purchase loans had much more risk layering than did either refi or cash-out refis. That is, borrowers stretched to buy their homes, and these purchase loans were far more apt to have higher DTI ratios, higher CLTVs, and higher proportions of second mortgages and interest-only or 40-year mortgages.

[2] The limit is greater for 2–4 unit homes, and single family homes located in Alaska, Hawaii, Guam, and the Virgin Islands.

EXHIBIT 1.8   Loan Size Distribution

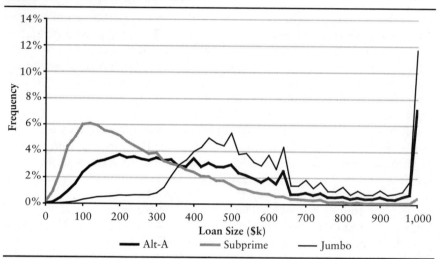

Source: LoanPerformance.

Debt-to-Income Ratio

While a borrower's FICO score is used as an indicator of an individual's *willingness* to repay their loan, DTI is used as a measure of their *ability* to repay it. Two DTI ratios are commonly used in mortgage underwriting: *front-end DTI* and *back-end DTI*. The front-end ratio divides a homeowner's housing payments (including principal, interest, real estate taxes, and home insurance payments) by gross income. A back-end ratio divides total monthly debt payments (including housing-related payments plus all credit card and auto debt, as well as child support payments) by gross income. In practice, FICO and DTI tend to be highly correlated. Exhibit 1.5 indicates that jumbo mortgages have an average FICO of 739 and a back-end DTI of 33%. Alt-A mortgages have an average FICO of 712 and a DTI of 36%, while subprime mortgages have an average FICO of 628 and an average DTI of 41%.

For mortgages guaranteed by Ginnie Mae, 31% is the maximum acceptable front-end ratio and 43% the maximum acceptable back-end ratio. Some exceptions may be made for compensating factors such as a low LTV ratio or sizable assets. For mortgages guaranteed by Fannie Mae and Freddie Mac, as well as for nonagency product, there are no absolute cutoffs because risk-based pricing is used.

High DTIs are one more indicator that borrowers stretched to buy their home, and are therefore at a higher risk of default than borrowers with low DTIs.

Adjustable Rate Mortgages

The standard *adjustable rate mortgage* (ARM) is fixed for a period of time, and floats thereafter. In agency, Alt-A, and jumbo lending, the standard ARM is fixed for 3, 5, 7, or 10 years, and resets annually thereafter. Five years is the most common time to reset, with both 7- and 10-year terms more popular than the three-year term. During the floating period, the loan is generally indexed to either one-year CMT (constant maturity Treasury) or one-year LIBOR (London Interbank Offer Rate). Thus, if the loan is indexed to one-year CMT, it will reset to 1-year CMT + a prespecified margin. These loans are often referred to as *hybrid ARMs*, or in the case of a mortgage with the rate fixed for five years, a 5/1 hybrid ARM. The 5 in this case refers to the initial rate lock period. The 1 refers to the fact that it resets annually thereafter.

It is important to realize that the mortgages have caps to control payment shock for the borrower. The most common cap on a 5/1 hybrid is a 5/2/5 cap. That is, the loan rate can rise 5% at the first reset, 2% at each subsequent reset, and is subject to a life cap of 5%.

Another type of ARM is the *option ARM*. Option ARMs generally have low initial payments, and the payment caps limit the amount the payments can be raised. These mortgages often accrue at a higher rate than the borrower is paying. Thus, the loans are experiencing negative amortization—that is, their balances are growing. At the end of 60 months, or when the loan reaches the negative amortization limit (110%, 115% or 125%), whichever comes first, the loan will recast and then will fully amortize over the remaining term.

In subprime, the most common ARMs are the 2/28 or 3/27. The 2/28 (3/27) has a rate fixed for a two-year (three-year) period, and then floats at a rate of approximately LIBOR + 600. The floating rate is readjusted every six months, subject to a 2% or 3% initial cap, a 1% cap at each reset, and a life cap of 6% over the initial rate. Let us assume the borrower took out a 2/28 mortgage at an initial rate of 8%, and LIBOR remained constant at 5%. Thus, the fully indexed rate would be 11% (5% LIBOR + 600). At the reset in two years, the rate would jump to 10% (it would hit its 2% cap); it would hit its fully indexed 11% rate at the second reset in 2.5 years.

Borrowers taking out ARMs are generally looking to lower their monthly payment. ARM borrowers generally have more risk layering than their fixed rate counterparts, and hence have higher defaults. They generally have higher CLTV ratios, leading to higher loss severity.

ARM borrowers have historically prepaid faster than their fixed rate counterparts, as many ARM borrowers have a shorter expected tenure in their home. They are willing to take a rate fixed for five years rather than 30 years, as they believe that in three to five years they will trade up to a larger home.

Interest-Only Mortgages an 40-Year Mortgages

Interest-only mortgages are mortgages in which the borrower does not pay principal for a period of time. For 30-year fixed rate mortgages, the interest-only period is generally 10 years; the borrower then pays off the principal over the remaining 20 years. For adjustable rate mortgages, the interest-only period is generally the same or longer than the initial fixed period. For example, a hybrid ARM with a 30-year mortgage term and an initial interest rate that is fixed for five years may have a 5-year interest-only period, a 7-year interest-only period; or a 10-year interest-only period. 40-year mortgages are mortgages with 40-year terms rather than the standard 30-year term.

Both interest-only mortgages and 40-year mortgages are *affordability products*—products designed to lower a borrower's monthly payment. The monthly payment on a $200,000 30-year fixed rate mortgage with a 6.5% interest rate would be $1,264. If the mortgage was interest-only for the first 10 years, the monthly payments during that time would be $1,083, which is $181 or 14.3% lower than on an amortizing mortgage. However, once the 10-year interest-only period ends, the payment jumps to $1,491, as the borrower must then pay down the principal over a 20-year period. Payments on a 40-year mortgage would be $1,171, which is $93 or 7.4% less than on a traditional 30-year mortgage.

Borrowers taking out interest-only mortgages or 40-year mortgages tend to have higher defaults than those who use conventional 30-year mortgages, as it is one more manifestation that the borrower is stretching to buy the house. Prepayment behavior on interest-only mortgages tends to be fairly similar to that on amortizing mortgages.

Occupancy

Pools of Alt-A mortgages tend to have a higher percentage of investor properties than do jumbo or agency pools. Subprime mortgages tend to have a higher percentage of investor properties than jumbo pools, but less investor properties than in Alt-A pools. In the 2004–2006 period, questions were raised about the accuracy of the percentage of investor properties in pools. It is widely believed that many investors stated that their properties were owner-occupied, when in fact they were not, causing an underestimate of investor share.

Occupancy is important in understanding credit performance. Loans with a higher percentage of investor properties tend to default more often, and they also experience higher loss severities when they default. Investor properties also tend to have somewhat more stable prepayment profiles. That is, as interest rates drop, they are slightly less apt to refinance.

Summary

While all the factors we discussed play some role in both credit performance and prepayment behavior, the three major determinants of credit performance are CLTV, FICO, and documentation. The the most important determinants of prepayment stability are loan size, FICO, and ARM versus fixed.

RISK LAYERING

We are now in a position to quantify the slip in origination standards that occurred during the 2002–2006 period. Exhibit 1.9 tells the story. The table shows ARMs in the top section (jumbo, Alt-A, subprime, and option ARMs), and fixed rate product in the bottom section (jumbo, Alt-A, subprime). Note that option ARMs are Alt-A in terms of credit quality. However, because these instruments can experience negative amortization, they have a lower initial CLTV than do more traditional Alt-A hybrid ARMs, so including them with more traditional Alt-A hybrid ARMs would produce a misleading comparison versus other products.

First look at subprime ARMs. Note that from 2002 to 2006, CLTVs rose from 81% to 88%. This reflected a rise from 4% to 34% for piggyback second mortgages. The percentage of loans with CLTVs in excess of 90% rose from 27% in 2002 to 56% in 2007. The increase in interest-only mortgages from 1% to 10% is quite substantial, as was the rise in 40-year mortgages from 0% to 31%. The increase in affordability products was, in part, an effort to offset the effect of the rise in interest rates and the increase in home prices. Many borrowers stretched to buy their home, as evidenced by an increase in the purchase share from 33% to 46% and an increase in the DTI from 40% to 42%. The current DTI is probably understated, as many of the DTI calculations were based on stated income. (The full documentation percentage dropped from 66% to 53% over this period.)

The increase in risk layering is by no means a subprime phenomenon. Look at the increased risk layering in Alt-A ARM product. Note that from 2002 to 2006, CLTVs rose from 74% to 85%, reflecting a rise in piggyback second mortgages, from 4% to 53%. The percentage of mortgages with CLTVs that exceed 90% shot up from 15% to 49%. The percentage of interest-only mortgages rocketed from 30% to 82%, while the full documentation percentage dropped from 30% to 20%. The FICOs were largely unchanged.

In fact, no matter which set of numbers one looks at, the increase in risk layering is apparent.

EXHIBIT 1.9 Collateral Characteristics

Product	Orig. Year	CLTV	% IO	% 40 Yr.	% Piggyback	% Purchase	% CLTV > 80	% CLTV ≥ 90	% Full Doc	FICO	DTI Back-end
Prime ARMs	2001	67	25	0	0	32	4	3	60	729	30
	2002	66	50	0	1	28	3	2	56	733	31
	2003	68	52	0	10	34	10	7	50	733	32
	2004	73	71	0	23	52	20	15	51	734	34
	2005	74	83	0	27	56	23	17	48	739	35
	2006	75	90	0	30	49	25	18	35	737	37
	2007	73	92	1	30	34	24	12	22	733	36
Alt-A ARMs	2001	74	17	0	2	47	22	16	32	704	35
	2002	74	30	0	4	46	21	15	30	707	34
	2003	78	57	0	24	50	34	27	28	708	35
	2004	83	76	0	39	61	47	40	33	709	36
	2005	84	83	0	48	64	52	45	28	713	37
	2006	85	82	2	53	60	56	49	20	710	38
	2007	84	85	3	47	49	54	47	15	712	39
Subprime ARMs	2001	81	0	0	4	34	45	25	71	598	40
	2002	81	1	0	4	33	47	27	66	605	40
	2003	84	6	0	11	35	56	38	63	613	40
	2004	85	21	0	20	40	61	45	59	619	41
	2005	87	33	8	29	46	64	51	55	626	41
	2006	88	20	31	34	46	69	56	53	623	42
	2007	85	19	28	20	34	64	49	57	618	42

EXHIBIT 1.9 (Continued)

Product	Orig. Year	CLTV	% IO	% 40 Yr.	% Piggyback	% Purchase	% CLTV > 80	% CLTV ≥ 90	% Full Doc	FICO	DTI Back-end
Option ARMs	2001	68	0	3	0	33	2	1	31	721	31
	2002	69	0	1	1	37	2	1	32	720	28
	2003	71	0	5	7	30	10	5	27	702	32
	2004	73	1	5	13	34	14	8	22	699	32
	2005	77	0	9	25	38	27	18	17	710	35
	2006	79	6	29	34	29	38	27	10	709	35
	2007	78	24	22	27	22	32	21	10	714	37
Prime Fixed	2001	69	0	0	0	36	5	3	78	730	31
	2002	65	0	0	1	27	3	2	75	735	32
	2003	64	0	0	7	21	5	2	56	740	31
	2004	67	2	0	10	40	7	5	55	740	34
	2005	71	21	0	19	48	15	10	54	742	34
	2006	75	27	0	26	56	22	15	52	743	37
	2007	76	41	1	33	53	30	20	45	744	38

EXHIBIT 1.9 (Continued)

Product	Orig. Year	CLTV	% IO	% 40 Yr.	% Piggyback	% Purchase	% CLTV > 80	% CLTV ≥ 90	% Full Doc	FICO	DTI Back-end
Alt-A Fixed	2001	77	0	0	2	46	26	20	32	703	35
	2002	74	1	0	3	43	22	16	34	711	36
	2003	72	3	0	8	33	23	17	33	712	34
	2004	76	11	0	16	47	30	24	36	711	36
	2005	77	34	0	28	46	33	27	35	715	37
	2006	80	38	3	37	48	42	36	22	708	38
	2007	78	44	4	30	38	36	30	22	714	39
Subprime Fixed	2001	78	0	0	1	21	42	22	74	622	38
	2002	79	0	0	1	19	42	25	67	635	39
	2003	79	0	0	3	18	45	27	67	640	39
	2004	80	2	0	6	22	46	30	69	640	39
	2005	82	6	3	9	26	53	38	68	638	40
	2006	84	6	14	11	30	58	45	67	633	41
	2007	80	5	18	6	16	50	33	70	622	41

Source: LoanPerformance.

Exhibit 1.9 also makes the point that the risk layering was much less in fixed rate mortgages than it was in ARMs. This is true across the credit spectrum in jumbo, Alt-A, and subprime paper. It is most easily seen by looking at 2006 production Alt-A ARMs versus fixed. Compare the CLTV of 85% on the Alt-A ARMS to the CLTV of 80% on Alt-A fixed from the same vintage. This reflects the situation that 53% of the Alt-A ARMs have piggyback second mortgages versus 37% of the fixed. The interest-only mortgage share on the ARMs is 82% versus the fixed at 38%. The purchase share on the ARMs is higher (60% versus 48%), while the FICO scores and full documentation percentages are very similar.

AGENCY VERSUS NONAGENCY EXECUTION

Now return to Exhibit 1.2. Note the rise in the agency share in 2007. Ginnie Mae has marginally relaxed its standards through the introduction of the FHASecure program. This program allows borrowers who are delinquent as a result of the reset, but who were current for the six months before the reset and can meet the FHA's other conditions (such as DTI), to possibly qualify for an FHA mortgage. However, only a relatively small subset of borrowers met the criteria. By contrast, in early 2007, Freddie Mac and Fannie Mae left their standards as to which mortgages qualified for agency execution unchanged. As the year wore on, and home price depreciation became a reality, Freddie and Fannie tightened their standards and raised their pricing. The large increase in agency volume in 2007 reflected the fact that with the subprime and Alt-A markets shut, agency execution was the only avenue for securitization available. In order to fully understand this, it is important to take a step back and look at GSE pricing.

Fannie Mae and Freddie Mac have a rate, negotiated with each originator, at which they guarantee prime mortgages. This originator-specific guarantee fee is in the range of 16 to 18 basis points, and is for all mortgages that meet "prime" standards. For mortgages not qualifying for "prime" designation, the GSEs use risk-based pricing. For example, Fannie Mae has three levels of risk-based pricing—Expanded Approval Levels 1–3 (EA1, EA2, EA3). It is important to realize that in early 2007, neither Fannie Mae nor Freddie Mac changed their criteria as to which loans would qualify for agency execution, but they both automated the process of getting a risk-based priced loan approved. By mid-2007, mortgage loans whose risk warranted EA3 execution would pay approximately 125 basis points over prime execution. This was increased still further late in the year. In addition, any mortgage over 80% LTV requires PMI. Fannie Mae and Freddie Mac, by charter, cannot take the first loss on a mortgage with an LTV in excess of 80%. The PMI companies have also been raising their rates. Moreover, depending on the risk level of the mortgage, Fannie and Freddie often require that PMI reduce LTV to 75%, or even 70%.

In 2006, a lender could offer a conforming sized subprime borrower several types of mortgages—a 7.5% mortgage, with the rate fixed for the first two years, and resetting to [LIBOR + a 600 margin] thereafter; or a 9.0% fixed-rate agency mortgage. The 7.5% mortgage resulted in much lower payments and were far more appealing to the borrower. In addition, in the subprime market, a borrower could take out a 99% LTV mortgage, which mortgage insurers charged dearly for. Thus, during the 2004–2006 period mortgages that could go agency or nonagency execution were executed through nonagency channels. During the course of 2007, it became very difficult to sell a subprime or Alt-A deal to investors. This fed back to the primary market, where originators were reluctant to extend mortgages that could not be securitized, and that they were unwilling to hold on balance sheet. Thus, there was only one channel of execution for subprime and Alt-A mortgages: agency execution. And this channel was not open to all borrowers in these markets. Subprime and Alt-A mortgages that did not qualify for agency execution were just not getting done.

Exhibit 1.10 shows the increased presence of loans with less than pristine credit in agency pools. Note that for 2006, 10% of the mortgages in fixed rate amortizing pools have LTVs greater than 80%, for September 2007 that proportion dropped to 26%. And interest-only mortgage pools with less than pristine credit have become even more common. In 2006, 3% of the 10/20s had LTVs that exceeded 80%, by September 2007 that was up to 27%. While there is much month-to-month variation, it is clear that the GSEs are guaranteeing more loans with less than pristine credit.

Looked at from the other angle, we estimate that approximately 68% of conforming Alt-A borrowers and 33% of conforming subprime borrowers would qualify for a mortgage from Fannie Mae or Freddie Mac. However, agency execution is not available, so does nothing for the 50% of Alt-A balances or 20% of subprime mortgages that are too large to qualify for a GSE guarantee. It also does nothing for the conforming-sized loans that cannot qualify for an agency mortgage.

SUMMARY

In this chapter, we discussed the characteristics of three major types of nonagency MBS: jumbo, Alt-A, and subprime. We have shown that jumbo prime mortgages are loans of very high quality that are above the GSE loan limit of $417,000. Alt-A loans tend to have limited documentation plus at least one other risk factor. Subprime mortgages are usually extended to low-

EXHIBIT 1.10   High LTV/Low FICO (% of issuance)

	Fixed 30	Fixed IO (10/20)	5/1 Hybrid	All Hybrid	Fixed 30	Fixed IO (10/20)	5/1 Hybrid	All Hybrid
	%LTV > 80				%LTV > 90			
2003	5%	0%	2%	2%	1%	0%	1%	1%
2004	9%	1%	5%	4%	2%	0%	2%	1%
2005	8%	2%	4%	4%	2%	0%	1%	1%
2006	10%	3%	2%	5%	2%	0%	0%	0%
Jan-07	9%	3%	2%	13%	2%	1%	0%	2%
Feb-07	9%	4%	1%	7%	3%	1%	0%	3%
Mar-07	9%	7%	3%	5%	3%	1%	0%	1%
Apr-07	13%	10%	2%	5%	4%	2%	0%	0%
May-07	16%	25%	2%	5%	4%	4%	0%	3%
Jun-07	21%	30%	8%	10%	6%	4%	5%	6%
Jul-07	21%	36%	11%	8%	6%	7%	8%	6%
Aug-07	22%	27%	6%	5%	7%	9%	5%	3%
Sep-07	26%	27%	14%	15%	5%	6%	7%	9%
	%FICO < 700 & LTV > 80				%FICO < 700 & LTV > 90			
2003	3%	0%	1%	1%	1%	0%	1%	0%
2004	7%	0%	3%	2%	2%	0%	2%	1%
2005	5%	1%	1%	1%	1%	0%	1%	1%
2006	5%	1%	1%	1%	1%	0%	0%	0%
Jan-07	5%	1%	0%	0%	2%	0%	0%	0%
Feb-07	5%	2%	0%	0%	2%	1%	0%	0%
Mar-07	5%	3%	1%	2%	2%	1%	0%	0%
Apr-07	7%	2%	0%	0%	3%	2%	0%	0%
May-07	10%	5%	0%	1%	3%	4%	0%	0%
Jun-07	14%	9%	3%	3%	5%	3%	2%	1%
Jul-07	14%	8%	5%	4%	5%	5%	5%	3%
Aug-07	14%	9%	4%	2%	5%	6%	3%	2%
Sep-07	13%	5%	5%	3%	3%	4%	4%	2%

EXHIBIT 1.10   (Continued)

	Fixed 30	Fixed IO (10/20)	5/1 Hybrid	All Hybrid	Fixed 30	Fixed IO (10/20)	5/1 Hybrid	All Hybrid
	%FICO < 700				%FICO < 660			
2003	10%	2%	3%	3%	2%	0%	0%	0%
2004	15%	9%	6%	5%	3%	0%	1%	1%
2005	12%	5%	4%	4%	3%	0%	1%	1%
2006	12%	8%	4%	3%	2%	1%	0%	0%
Jan-07	13%	10%	9%	7%	2%	0%	0%	0%
Feb-07	11%	6%	7%	7%	2%	0%	0%	0%
Mar-07	12%	7%	12%	12%	2%	0%	0%	0%
Apr-07	15%	6%	5%	5%	3%	1%	0%	0%
May-07	15%	9%	9%	9%	4%	1%	1%	1%
Jun-07	17%	10%	9%	9%	5%	0%	1%	1%
Jul-07	20%	11%	13%	11%	4%	0%	2%	2%
Aug-07	18%	11%	9%	6%	5%	1%	1%	1%
Sep-07	17%	6%	10%	7%	5%	0%	1%	0%
	%FICO < 660 & LTV > 80				%FICO < 660 & LTV > 90			
2003	1%	0%	0%	0%	0%	0%	0%	0%
2004	2%	0%	1%	1%	0%	0%	1%	0%
2005	1%	0%	0%	0%	0%	0%	0%	0%
2006	1%	0%	0%	0%	0%	0%	0%	0%
Jan-07	1%	0%	0%	0%	0%	0%	0%	0%
Feb-07	1%	0%	0%	0%	0%	0%	0%	0%
Mar-07	2%	0%	0%	0%	1%	0%	0%	0%
Apr-07	2%	0%	0%	0%	1%	0%	0%	0%
May-07	3%	0%	0%	0%	1%	0%	0%	0%
Jun-07	4%	0%	0%	0%	1%	0%	0%	0%
Jul-07	3%	0%	1%	0%	1%	0%	1%	0%
Aug-07	4%	1%	0%	0%	1%	0%	0%	0%
Sep-07	4%	0%	1%	0%	1%	0%	0%	0%

Source: Fannie Mae and Freddie Mac.

er quality borrowers, and often contain other risk factors. In this chapter, we also examine the factors that determine default and prepayment risk: CLTV, FICO scores, documentation, loan size, loan purpose, debt-to-income ratio, adjustable rate mortgages, interest-only, and 40-year mortgages.

We took this one step further and outlined the origins of the subprime crises, making it clear that during the 2004–2006 period, as housing became less affordable, origination standards were stretched. The stretching of affordability product occurred in Alt-A and jumbo loans as well as in subprime. The stretch in affordability standards would have been fine if home prices had continued to appreciate. But with home price appreciation turning to home price depreciation, defaults, and delinquencies rose across the board.

In the next chapter we discuss the relationship between risk characteristics and losses and delinquencies. We show that risk layering coupled with a weak housing market produces high delinquencies and defaults.

CHAPTER 2

First Lien Mortgage Credit

In this chapter, we take a detailed look at first lien mortgage credit. We focus primarily on subprime collateral, although we do compare with prime and Alt-A mortgages when it is necessary. Loan-level data from Loan-Performance are used throughout our analysis.

We hope to convey the message that our analysis is important not in terms of the magnitude or the historicalness of the recent credit performance. It is in our methodology and way of analyzing mortgage credit that we have made the biggest strides.

The chapter is divided into four sections. In the first section we discuss how to define and measure mortgage credit. We review various ways of analyzing delinquencies, discuss the usefulness of roll rates in monitoring short-term performance trends, and explain some common misconceptions about loss severities.

In the second section, we identify the collateral characteristics that drive mortgage credit performance. In doing so, we analyze the classic drivers of credit performance, namely, FICO score and *loan-to-value* (LTV) ratio. We highlight the role of deterioration of the four Cs in mortgage underwriting (i.e., credit, collateral, capacity, and character) in the subprime debacle.

The third section focuses on how recent foreclosure/REO timelines and severity compare with historical observations. We concentrate on the role of geography on timelines and severity. Geography affects timelines since different states have different foreclosure procedures. Geography is also important in determining severity due to the differences in home price appreciation and timelines.

In the final section, we discuss the role of the unobservable in the recent subprime debacle. We analyze the effect of changes of reported collateral characteristics. However, we strongly believe that, after taking *house price appreciation* (HPA) and collateral difference into account, 2006 origination still underperformed previous vintages by a large margin. We attribute the unexplained underperformance of the 2006 vintage to deteriorating underwriting practices that were not evident from the data reported on the typical term sheets.

CONCEPTS AND MEASUREMENTS OF MORTGAGE CREDIT

Before we present the fancy charts, we nail down some fundamentals in order to avoid confusion in our lengthy discussions of mortgage credit. The very first question that comes to mind is: What is mortgage credit? Does it mean delinquencies, roll rates, defaults or losses? Actually, it means all of the above and much more. We would argue that even prepayments should be considered as part of our broad discussion on mortgage credit since they are a major driver of cumulative loss.

Suppose we all agree that mortgage credit include delinquencies, roll rates, defaults, and losses, then how do we measure and analyze them? Let's start with delinquencies.

Mortgage Bankers Association versus Office of Thrifts Supervision

Two entities have specified two basic ways of measuring mortgage delinquency: the Mortgage Bankers Association (MBA) and the Office of Thrifts Supervision (OTS). The difference between the two standards to measure mortgage delinquency that they specify is essentially one day. For example, assume the mortgage payment is due January 1. If the servicer does no receive the payment on January 31, then the mortgage is considered 30-day delinquent (denoted "30DQ") by MBA standard. However, by the OTS standard, only if the payment is not received by February 1 would the mortgage be considered 30DQ. So if the payment arrives on February 1, then MBA would define the mortgage as 30DQ while OTS would define it as current.

For historical reasons, prime mortgages report delinquencies by MBA standard (the more stringent standard) while subprime mortgages report by OTS standard (the more lenient standard). What about Alt-A? The problem with Alt-A is that it covers a broad spectrum of mortgages with some being close to prime while others being close to subprime. How trustees or master servicers report Alt-A delinquencies is not uniform. Some report by OTS standard and others report by MBA standard.

How Do We Analyze Delinquencies?

The most common way of analyzing delinquencies is to look at the percentages of various delinquency buckets, namely the *percentage of outstanding balance* in 30DQ, 60DQ, 90+DQ, foreclosure and REO (real estate owned). Though the most common, it is not necessarily the best way to analyze delinquencies due to prepayment (we noted at the outset that prepayment should be considered part of mortgage credit) and the reduction of pool factor as collateral prepays. The problem is particularly pronounced for subprime

EXHIBIT 2.1 Subprime ARM First Lien 60+DQ% of Outstanding Balance by Vintage

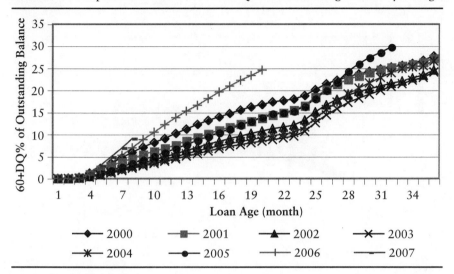

Source: LoanPerformance.

ARMs right after reset as illustrated in Exhibit 2.1. The increase of delinquency after month 24 is due to the rapid reduction in pool factor. Despite the fact that an increase of delinquency under any circumstances is not a good thing, delinquency measured as a percent of outstanding balance may not be a good predictor of life time cumulative losses. Come to think about it, would you rather have a pool with a pool factor of 50%, 25% of outstanding balance in 60+DQ, or a pool with a factor of 80% and 20% of outstanding in 60+DQ, assuming both pools have the same seasoning (age)?

On the other hand, delinquencies measured as a *percent of original balance* are more reflective of the overall credit performance since it takes prepayment and reduction of pool factors into consideration. Exhibit 2.2A and 2.2B show the delinquency (60+DQ) and cumulative loss seasoning curve of various vintages of subprime mortgages. The correlation between 60+DQ of original balance and cumulative loss is much stronger than the correlation between 60+DQ of outstanding balance and cumulative loss.

Both of the aforementioned delinquency measures are reported by the master seriver/trustee and quite easy to calculate. Multiply the delinquencies as a percent of outstanding balance by the pool factor gives us the delinquencies as a percent of original balance. However, neither of these two measures takes the losses (or loans that are already liquidated) into consideration, which for seasoned deals could be quite sizable. Nor do these delinquency measures capture the cumulative aspect of serious delinquency. For exam-

EXHIBIT 2.2

Panel A. Subprime First Lien 60+DQ% of Original Balance by Vintage

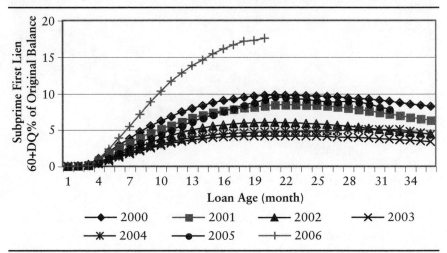

Panel B. Subprime First Lien Cumulative Loss by Vintage

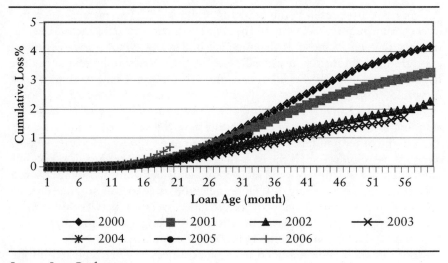

Source: LoanPerformance.

ple, if a loan cures from 60DQ to 30DQ (the borrower makes one extra payment) in a certain month, then it is not included in either of these two delinquency measures (whether it is percent of current balance or percent of original balance) since at that point in time, the loan is not 60DQ. And

EXHIBIT 2.3   Subprime First Lien Cumulative First Time 60+DQ% by Vintage

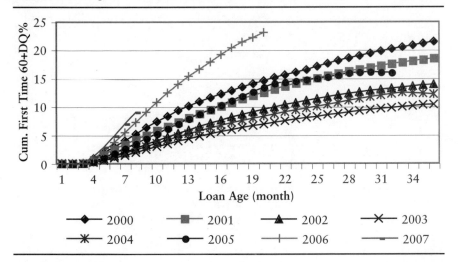

Source: LoanPerformance.

here lies the problem. To the extent that those cured loans will not become seriously delinquent (60DQ or worse) again, then either of these measures is fine. However, we know that is not the case. A loan cured from 60DQ has a high probability of becoming seriously delinquent again. It would be nice if we can have a sense of what we call *cumulative serious impairment* (CSI). We define CSI as cumulative first 60+DQ (technically a loan can go directly from 30DQ to foreclosure so our definition does include those rare situations). Think of a loan first time reaching 60+DQ as default (an extremely broad definition of default). Once a loan reaches default, it has a permanent mark on it. Exhibit 2.3 shows the CSI percent of various vintages of subprime mortgages. Unfortunately, for most people who do not have access to loan-level data, CSI is impossible to calculate and is not reported anywhere.

Roll Rates

It is important to realize that the usual delinquency statistics (such as 30- and 60-day delinquencies and so on) are relatively coarse and do not fully account for the behavior of delinquent loans—these statistics are snapshots, just like a balance sheet, and do not capture the dynamical aspects of delinquencies. Indeed, two similar pools might have the same proportion of loans 90+ days delinquent, but those loans might not have the same likelihood of defaulting or being cured. Besides, the distribution of delinquencies is impacted by the time spent by each loan in each stage of delinquency.

EXHIBIT 2.4   Historical Roll Rates: 2006 Origination

	Current	30DQ	60DQ	90+DQ	Foreclosure	REO	Payoff
Current	95.13	3.13	0.12	0.02	0.02	0.00	1.57
30DQ	21.53	26.01	44.69	0.88	4.93	0.01	1.94
60DQ	5.87	6.84	12.64	33.00	39.79	0.04	1.81
90+DQ	2.53	0.84	2.55	59.40	31.79	0.82	2.07
Foreclosure	1.91	0.35	0.51	5.03	81.54	8.56	2.10
REO	0.03	0.00	0.00	0.32	0.39	93.95	5.31

Source: LoanPerformance.

How do loans transit from one delinquent state to the other? A simple way to analyze delinquent loan behavior is to calculate *empirical transition matrices* using our loan-level data. Exhibit 2.4 is calculated on loans that were originated in 2006 and tells us how the loans' delinquency status evolved month-to-month. The columns are the states to which the loans transition, while the rows are the states from which the loans transitioned. For example, the first row tells us that in any given month, 95.13% of the volume of loans that were current (not delinquent) stayed current, and 3.13% became 30–59 days delinquent. The percentages also sum to 100% horizontally.

Roll rates can be very handy as a tracking and monitoring tool. Any significant movements of worsening transitions indicate problems ahead. Any significant lengthening of loans staying in foreclosure and REO may indicate potential servicing related issues or change of servicing practice.

Defaults, Losses, and Severity

There is no ambiguity in regard to cumulative loss. A dollar lost is a dollar lost. It is an objective measure. However, there is no universally agreed-upon definition of default. That is, default is a subjective measure. The subjectivity of default makes our conversations on severity-related issues quite challenging. Since losses do not change regardless of our definition, a broader definition of default necessarily reduces the severity (Losses = Defaults × Loss severity), which means that severity is also a subjective measurement.

Speaking of severity, there are several flavors as well. Since losses occur over time (periodic loss, we call it), there is the corresponding periodic severity. Then there is cumulative severity (cumulative loss divided by cumulative default) or lifetime severity. If this is not confusing enough, sometimes people define severity only for those loans that have incurred losses (severity given losses, rather than severity given defaults), which means that in order to have a complete grasp of losses and severity, we have to know the percent of loans that do not generate losses. Whenever we have a conversation on severity, we need to make sure we understand what the default definition is and what severity we are referring to.

The choice of default definition also affects the default timing. A broad definition tends to front load the default timing curve (a lot of defaults early on).

How Do We Look at Seasoning Curves?

The most popular way of looking at a delinquency seasoning curve is by vintage (and by other characteristics such as FICO, LTV, etc.). The problem is that the last (or most recent) data point only captures one month of originations. For example, in order for 2006 vintage to have an age of 20 months by September 2007, the loans can only be originated in January 2006. The second-to-last data point then has two months of originations: Age 19 captures how January 2006 originations performed in August 2007 and how February 2006 originations performed in September 2007, and so forth. The last few data points are not sufficiently representative of the entire vintage we are analyzing. The other problem is that for any given age, the data display behavior that took place in different calendar months. To put it differently, they are not truly reflective of what is happening *now*.

The other way to look at a seasoning curve is by sample period instead of by vintage, as seen in Exhibit 2.5. It shows how loans (for any given age, say 24-month old) performed in the last three months versus how they performed a year ago. It easily captures what is taking place now and compares with what took place some time ago. The disadvantage is that we cannot do the analysis by vintage since right now as of the most current month, the 24-month old loans were originated in late 2005 while the 12-month old loans were originated in late 2006, a mismatch of vintage.

Finally, to overcome the shortcomings of both these approaches, we can analyze time series (rather than seasoning curves) performance by vintage as seen in Exhibit 2.6. This way, we can eliminate the mismatch of vintages and observe the time series progression of performance. But do we lose the seasoning aspect of the analysis? The answer is no except that we have to define seasoning slightly differently. We call it *vintage age*. For example, for 2006 vintage, September 2007 corresponds to a vintage age of 9 if we consider the birth month of 2006 vintage to be December 2006 (the last month of origination for 2006 vintage). If we consider January 2006 as the birth month of 2006 vintage, then the vintage age would be 21 by September 2007.

In practice, we conduct our analysis using all three approaches in order to gain different perspectives.

EXHIBIT 2.5 Subprime First Lien 60+DQ% of Outstanding Balance by Observation Quarter

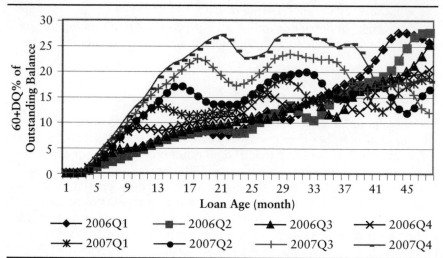

Source: LoanPerformance.

EXHIBIT 2.6 Subprime First Lien 60+DQ% of Outstanding Balance by Vintage

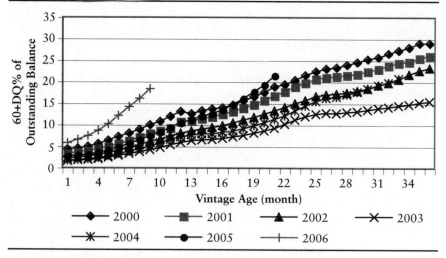

Source: LoanPerformance.

COLLATERAL CHARACTERISTICS AND MORTGAGE CREDIT: ASSAULT OF THE FOUR Cs IN 2006 (CREDIT, COLLATERAL, CAPACITY, AND CHARACTER)

Exhibit 2.3 shows the overall cumulative first time 60+DQ seasoning curve by different vintages (2000–2007 origination years). The sharp increase of delinquency of the 2006–2007 vintage has been well documented. What is the role of collateral deterioration in their performance? To answer this question, we will go step-by-step through the analysis of the two most fundamental mortgage credit variables—FICO and LTV. They are important in both mortgage underwriting and performance. Many originators use a matrix pricing approach (FICO by LTV grid) and then add on additional rates (in 25 to 50 bps interval) for other risk layering (various document deficiency, investor properties, and so on).

Credit: FICO Erosion (Dilution)

As the first C in the four Cs of mortgage underwriting (credit, collateral, capacity, and character), FICO is probably the most widely used underwriting variable in consumer credit lending, such as credit cards, autos, and mortgages. The predictive power is presented in Exhibit 2.7A through 2.7E, which shows the usual seasoning curve by loan age of first lien subprime mortgages of 2000–2004 vintage. Given the predictive power we see in these exhibits, no wonder lenders fell in love with FICO.

EXHIBIT 2.7

Panel A.   Subprime First Lien Cumulative First Time 60+DQ% by FICO: 2000 Vintage

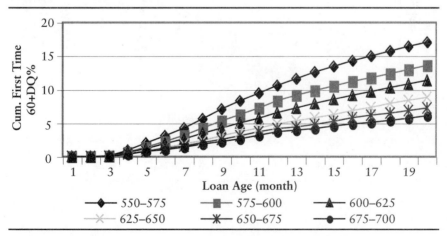

EXHIBIT 2.7 (Continued)

Panel B.   Subprime First Lien Cumulative First Time 60+DQ% by FICO: 2001 Vintage

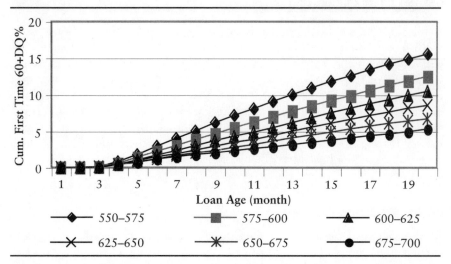

Panel C.   Subprime First Lien Cumulative First Time 60+DQ% by FICO: 2002 Vintage

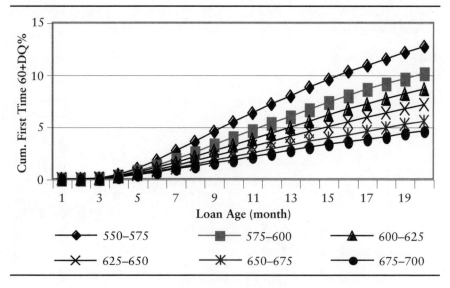

EXHIBIT 2.7   (Continued)
Panel D.   Subprime First Lien Cumulative First Time 60+DQ% by FICO: 2003 Vintage

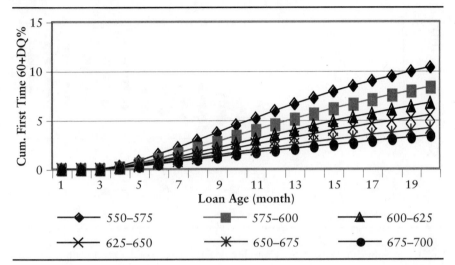

Panel E.   Subprime First Lien Cumulative First Time 60+DQ% by FICO: 2004 Vintage

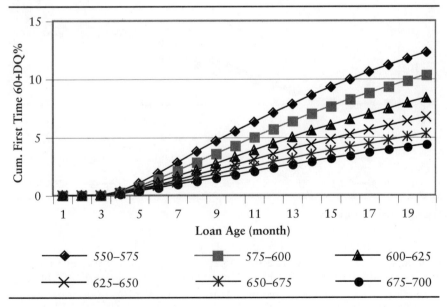

Source: LoanPerformance.

EXHIBIT 2.8

Panel A.   Subprime First Lien Cumulative First Time 60+DQ% by FICO: 2005 Vintage

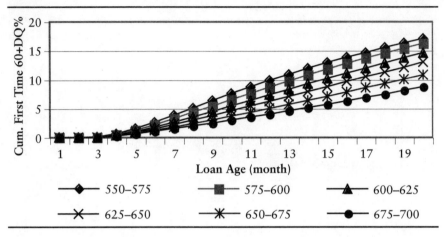

Panel B.   Subprime First Lien Cumulative First Time 60+DQ% by FICO: 2006 Vintage

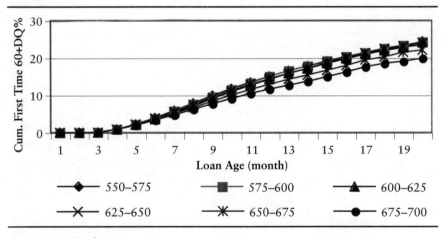

Source: LoanPerformance.

The relationship started to deteriorate for the 2005 vintage among all products, as seen in Exhibit 2.8A. That is, the predictive power of FICO became smaller. When it comes to 2006 vintage (see Exhibit 2.8B), FICO's predictive power is severely eroded. Among certain sub-populations within the 2006 vintage, FICO's predictive power has completely evaporated.

The wholesale erosion of the predictive power of FICO has many reasons. From the observable variables, Exhibit 2.9 summarizes the collateral characteristics across FICO buckets for 2006 subprime ARMs. The message cannot be clearer. That is, higher FICO loans consistently have other characteristics that are deemed risky, namely higher combined LTV (CLTV), lower percentage of full documentation loans, higher percentage of investor properties and purchase loans, and so on. The unobservable factors are numerous, such as commingling borrower and coborrower's FICO and income, thinly filed FICO (borrowers without much credit history), and massive FICO curing offered by brokers. Ironically, the widely publicized FICO awareness education may have produced a significant side effect and taught many borrowers to explore the loopholes in the FICO scoring system, which the credit bureaus have been slow to fix. FICO NextGen, the acclaimed new FICO score, is advertised as more consumer friendly and "relaxed minimum scoring criteria allows for more scorable files."

Some people argue that the deterioration of the housing market might have contributed to the FICO dilution. We call it the "blame-everything-on-HPA" syndrome. We believe it is the other way around. A booming housing market makes people take out risky loans that they would not take out in a normal housing market. In order to take out those loans, people tend to massage their FICOs as much as possible and lenders overly rely on FICO to make those loans. In a sense, housing bull market causes FICO dilution which contributes to the eventual collapse of the housing market.

Collateral: LTV, CLTV, and CLTV = 80, All in a Weak Housing Market

Now we are ready to move on to the second C, collateral. For first lien mortgages, why should we care about *combined LTV* (CLTV)? As long as the value is accurate (a big if), the fact that there is a second lien on the property should not really matter. It sounds logical, doesn't it? The fallacy ignores the fact that CLTV measures borrower's leverage to the housing market. The higher it is, the more leveraged the borrower is to the housing market, which means that as the housing market deteriorates, borrowers with higher CLTV will be more affected. There is no equity cushion, it has become more difficult to prepay the mortgage since CLTV is going higher and more importantly, since the borrowers have no skin in the game, becoming delinquent (or eventually handing in the keys) is a much easier decision.

We certainly agree that severity will be different. However, we feel that the existence of a second lien, in addition to indicating the higher leverage to the housing market, further demonstrates the willingness of the borrower to take advantage of easy access to subordinate financing and potentially may increase the likelihood of delinquency. Exhibit 2.10 summarizes the

EXHIBIT 2.9 Subprime First Lien ARMs 2006 Vintage

FICO	Low/No Doc and CLTV ≥ 100	Low/No Doc and CLTV ≥ 90	Purchase and CLTV = 100	Piggyback	Full Doc	Investor	CLTV	Purchase	IO
<550	0.005	0.02	0.02	0.04	0.69	0.021	75.90	0.12	0.01
550–575	0.008	0.05	0.04	0.06	0.66	0.029	80.25	0.21	0.03
575–600	0.019	0.09	0.18	0.20	0.68	0.033	85.27	0.35	0.12
600–625	0.095	0.21	0.28	0.33	0.61	0.042	89.01	0.45	0.20
625–650	0.235	0.36	0.36	0.44	0.47	0.057	91.22	0.54	0.25
650–675	0.317	0.45	0.41	0.50	0.38	0.070	92.23	0.61	0.30
675–700	0.361	0.50	0.44	0.53	0.34	0.088	92.74	0.66	0.34

Source: LoanPerformance.

EXHIBIT 2.10 Subprime First Lien ARMs >=100 CLTV

Orig. Year	Piggyback	Low/No Doc and CLTV ≥ 100	Low/No Doc and CLTV ≥ 90	Purchase and CLTV = 100	Full Doc	Purchase	IO	FICO
2005	No	0.269	0.27	0.75	0.73	0.76	0.29	651.00
2005	Yes	0.518	0.52	0.86	0.48	0.86	0.49	655.93
2006	No	0.368	0.37	0.75	0.63	0.76	0.15	645.50
2006	Yes	0.542	0.54	0.86	0.46	0.86	0.29	652.31

Source: LoanPerformance.

collateral differences of loans with the same CLTV (subprime ARM, greater than or equal to 100 CLTV), one with piggyback seconds versus the other without. The differences in full documentation loans, IO loans, and purchase percent are the highlights. Performance, as seen in Exhibit 2.11 clearly proves that our intuition is correct. For the highest CLTV bucket (greater than or equal to 100) among subprime ARMs originated in 2006, loans with piggybacks have CSIs 20% higher than loans without piggybacks.

Having settled the battle between piggybacks versus nonpiggybacks, we focus on the effect of CLTV on delinquency performance. Two things stand out from Exhibit 2.12A through 2.12D.

First, the effect of CLTV is highly vintage specific, or to put it differently, it is very HPA dependent. In a housing bull market, the effect of CLTV on delinquency is quite weak. In a housing bear market, CLTV has a much larger impact on delinquency performance as the higher leverage works as a double-edged sword.

Second, loans with CLTV exactly equal to 80 tend to perform worse than loans with CLTV between 80 and 90. In the case of 2006 vintage, 80-CLTV loans are only better than loans with CLTV greater than or equal to 100. The observation highlights what we have always suspected and known qualitatively (but not quantitatively). That is, loans with CLTV exactly equal to 80 are more than likely to have a second lien that is unknown and therefore not reported by the originator/servicer. Given the higher percentage of purchase loans among them, this observation hardly surprises anyone.

EXHIBIT 2.11   2006 Subprime ARM First Lien

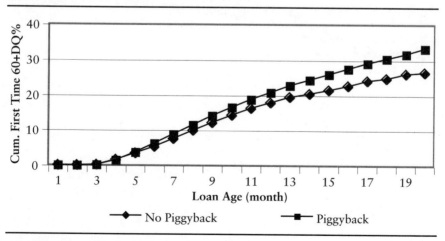

Source: LoanPerformance.

EXHIBIT 2.12

Panel A.   Subprime First Lien 2003 Vintage

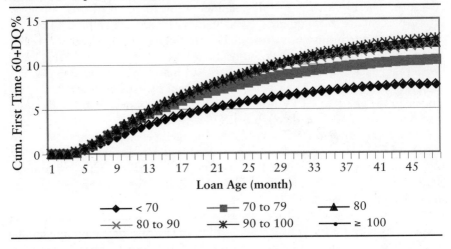

Panel B.   Subprime First Lien 2004 Vintage

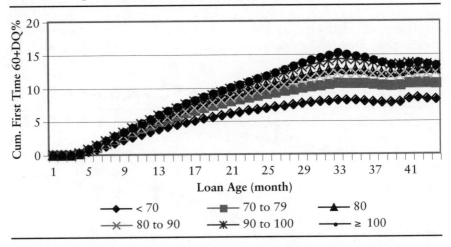

In the subprime world, the overall theme from the discussion above is that just as lenders overemphasized the importance of FICO in 2005–2006, they simultaneously underemphasized the effect of CLTV. When in previous years CLTV mattered very little while FICO clearly separated out the good versus bad loans, the reverse is stunningly true under the current regime. We do not like to call it *regime switching* since such a term will imply that the issues we are facing today are somehow impossible to predict and there is nothing we could have done to prevent this madness from happening. The

EXHIBIT 2.12   (Continued)
Panel C.   Subprime First Lien 2005 Vintage

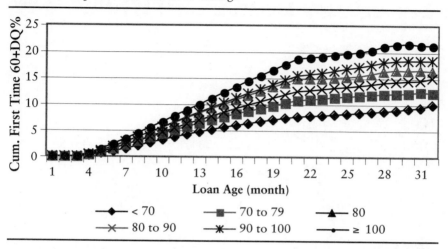

Panel D.   Subprime First Lien 2006 Vintage

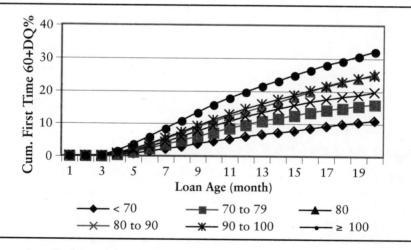

Source: LoanPerformance.

reality is that the writing has always been on the wall. For whatever reason, very few people paid attention to it.

Finally, one other question people like to ask is how reliable an appraisal is. Exhibit 2.13 summarizes the percentage of properties (weighted by the original amount) whose appraisal is exactly the same as sale price or higher. We will leave the readers to conclude on the reliability of the appraisal.

EXHIBIT 2.13   Subprime First Lien: Sale Price versus Appraisal

	Origination Year	Sale Price = Appraisal	Sale Price ≤ Appraisal
ARM	2007	53%	99%
ARM	2006	60%	99%
ARM	2005	60%	97%
ARM	2004	61%	97%
ARM	2003	61%	97%
ARM	2002	59%	97%
ARM	2001	53%	97%
ARM	2000	52%	97%

	Origination Year	Sale Price = Appraisal	Sale Price ≤ Appraisal
Fixed Rate	2007	53%	99%
Fixed Rate	2006	53%	98%
Fixed Rate	2005	51%	97%
Fixed Rate	2004	55%	96%
Fixed Rate	2003	54%	96%
Fixed Rate	2002	53%	97%
Fixed Rate	2001	47%	97%
Fixed Rate	2000	44%	96%

Source: LoanPerformance.

Capacity and Character: Debt-to-Income Ratio and Documentation

We believe that capacity is and only is about income. To the extent documentation of income is on shaky ground, capacity will be called into question. A simple math illustrates the problem. Assuming all mortgages pay interest-only payment, further assuming taxes, property insurance, second lien and other debt payment amount to $500 per month (an extremely low number and we are ignoring amortization), using the reported back-end *debt-to-income* (DTI) ratio in Exhibit 2.14, the derived income is $64,000 per year for 2006 subprime ARM borrowers. Exhibit 2.14 also lists a scenario under which we assume a $1,000 per month other payment, which gives us $79,000 per year, again for 2006 subprime ARM borrowers. Aside from the reasonableness of these income levels for an average subprime borrower, the increase between 2005 and 2006 is about 10%, which by itself was not credible since we know income growth is very small year over year.

EXHIBIT 2.14 Subprime First Lien: Derived Income

	Origination Year	Derived Income ($500 tax, insurance, second lien and other debt/month)	Derived Income ($1000 tax, insurance, second lien and other debt/month)
ARM	2007	$67,265	$82,994
ARM	2006	$64,001	$79,787
ARM	2005	$57,257	$73,505
ARM	2004	$55,226	$73,167
ARM	2003	$53,234	$70,020
ARM	2002	$54,175	$71,708
ARM	2001	$52,569	$69,458
ARM	2000	$51,755	$69,823

	Origination Year	Derived Income ($500 tax, insurance, second lien and other debt/month)	Derived Income ($1000 tax, insurance, second lien and other debt/month)
Fixed Rate	2007	$56,511	$73,094
Fixed Rate	2006	$54,762	$71,548
Fixed Rate	2005	$50,923	$68,206
Fixed Rate	2004	$51,028	$69,064
Fixed Rate	2003	$52,131	$70,586
Fixed Rate	2002	$53,548	$73,107
Fixed Rate	2001	$53,839	$74,627
Fixed Rate	2000	$46,985	$66,579

Source: LoanPerformance.

The reality is such that the actual DTI is much higher than the reported DTI and the corresponding mortgage and overall debt burden of these borrowers is, simply put, overwhelming.

Adding the four Cs (credit, collateral, capacity and character) together, we can see where the problem of 2006 origination comes from. They come from credit (FICO) dilution, collateral (appraisal) inflation, capacity (income) exaggeration, and lack of character (documentation). Put it more bluntly, underwriting of 2006 production was under assaults from all fronts. When the housing market turned, the ripple morphed into a tsunami.

THE END GAME: FORECLOSURE, REO TIMELINE, AND SEVERITY

What is the end game after loans have stayed in serious delinquency for a number of months? This section discusses foreclosure and REO timeline and loss severity, both historical and recent.

Foreclosure Process

Servicers typically send out a *notice of default* (NOD) or *notice of intent* (NOI) to foreclose letter to the borrower after the mortgage has been "X" days past due. The exact number of days depends on the state (some require servicers to record a NOD to begin the foreclosure process). There typically is a grace period that allows borrowers to cure and catch up on past due payments before the foreclosure process officially starts. Once a borrower fails to cure within the grace period, servicers can foreclose. Per the Freddie Mac seller/servicer guideline:

> Initiation of foreclosure is the submission of a Mortgage case and appropriate foreclosure documentation to litigation (foreclosure) counsel or trustee after taking all appropriate actions to accelerate the Mortgage. You are considered to have initiated foreclosure on the date you send the case to the foreclosure counsel or trustee.

Generally, foreclosure does not start until the loan is approximately 120-days past due. Servicers try to maximize the amount of time to work out delinquent loans. In a *judicial foreclosure*, servicers may have to demonstrate to the court that they have actively tried to work out delinquent loans. However, such an effort cannot last indefinitely. Again, per Freddie Mac seller/servicer guide:

> You must initiate foreclosure on a First-Lien Mortgage no later than 150 days from the Due Date of Last Paid Installment (DDLPI) (120th day of Delinquency) unless a workout or relief option has been approved or the property has one of the conditions in Section 66.12. However, if a Mortgage had been modified under our loan modification workout option, you must initiate foreclosure no later than 120 days from the DDLPI (90th day of Delinquency).

As a matter of fact, the latest recommended timeline between DDLPI and foreclosure sale is exactly 150 days for all states.

As part of the loss-mitigation strategies, third-party short sales (servicers accept a payment that is less than the full amount owed) may occur both prior to and during the foreclosure process. Servicers may accept a short sale based on a certain haircut to *broker price opinion* (BPO). Basically, the trade-off between foreclosure/REO and short sale is the haircut to BPO versus foreclosure/REO cost plus potential property value decline.

Foreclosures are typically categorized as either judicial or nonjudicial. Foreclosures on a mortgage without filing lawsuits or obtaining court orders are considered *nonjudicial*. This occurs because borrowers signed documents such as a deed of trust that gives the trustee right to sell property to pay off debt.

If a loan is not directly liquidated from foreclosure (either with or without a short sale), it then becomes REO (real estate owned). Depending on states, there may be a redemption period during which borrowers can pay the full amount and redeem the property. The presence of REO redemption is important since it can potentially further extend the REO-to-liquidation timeline. Within a given state, the right to redemption can also depend on whether the foreclosure is judicial and/or whether a deficiency judgment (a court judgment that the defaulting borrower owes to the lender after foreclosure) is waived or prohibited. Finally, deficiency is also highly state-dependent. For example, in California, the California Code of Civil Procedures states

> Lenders may not seek a deficiency judgment if (1) the foreclosure is non-judicial or if (2) foreclosure is on a purchase money obligation. The same rules do not apply to guarantee or later lien holders. The lenders may seize alternative collateral. If the lender forecloses by filing a lawsuit, then the lender can obtain both a foreclosure sale order and a judgment against the borrower for a deficiency after the court-ordered sale, but only for the difference between the judgment and the fair value of the security.

Next we analyze the foreclosure timeline by states (data are first-lien subprime mortgages from LoanPerformance). We choose not to analyze servicers for two reasons. First, LoanPerformance does not provide detailed information on foreclosure/REO, and servicers treat REO redemption periods differently when they report data to LoanPerformance, thus timelines may not be directly comparable across servicers. Second, portfolio attributes are quite different across servicers (thus a more problematic comparison).

Timeline by State and Liquidation/Payoff Year

Exhibit 2.15 tabulates the most recent (as of 7/1/2007) Freddie Mac foreclosure-to-REO timeline. We also list the judicial and nonjudicial foreclosure states. Note that ** in either of these two columns means that it is the primary method, although the other foreclosure method is also allowed. For any given state, if * is present in one column but not the other, it means that it is the only foreclosure method allowed in that particular state.

EXHIBIT 2.15   Freddie Mac Foreclosure to REO Timeline

State	Freddie Mac Foreclosure-to-REO Timeline (months)	Judicial	Nonjudicial
Alabama	2.83	*	**
Alaska	4.67	*	*
Arizona	4.17	*	*
Arkansas	4.33	*	*
California	4.50	*	**
Colorado	5.50	*	*
Connecticut	7.33	*	
DC	3.33		*
Delaware	8.33	*	
Florida	5.67	*	
Georgia	2.67	*	**
Hawaii	4.67	*	**
Idaho	6.33		*
Illinois	9.17	*	
Indiana	8.83	*	
Iowa	10.50	*	*
Kansas	6.00	*	
Kentucky	8.83	*	
Louisiana	7.33	*	
Maine	11.83	**	*
Maryland	2.83	*	
Massachusetts	4.50		*
Michigan	2.50	*	*
Minnesota	3.67	*	*
Mississippi	4.33	*	**
Missouri	2.83	*	**

EXHIBIT 2.15   (Continued)

State	Freddie Mac Foreclosure-to-REO Timeline (months)	Judicial	Nonjudicial
Montana	6.83	*	* *
Nebraska	5.17	*	
Nevada	5.17	*	* *
New Hampshire	3.67	*	* *
New Jersey	10.00	*	
New Mexico	8.33	*	
New York	9.33	*	
New York City	14.17	*	
North Carolina	4.00		*
North Dakota	6.33	*	
Ohio	8.83	*	
Oklahoma	8.33	* *	*
Oregon	6.00		*
Pennsylvania	10.00	*	
Rhode Island	2.83	*	*
South Carolina	7.17	*	
South Dakota	6.83	*	* *
Tennessee	3.00		*
Texas	3.00		*
Utah	5.50	*	*
Vermont	12.00	*	*
Virginia	2.00		*
Washington	5.33	*	* *
West Virginia	4.83		*
Wisconsin	10.33	*	
Wyoming	3.33	*	* *

Source: Freddie Mac and UBS.

Exhibit 2.16 shows the historical foreclosure to liquidation/payoff timeline. These are loans that bypass REO and go directly from foreclosure to liquidation. Not all foreclosed loans end up in REO. Historically, especially in states with large housing booms (such as California), many foreclosed

EXHIBIT 2.16 Foreclosure-to-Payoff Timeline

State	2007	2006	2005	2004	2003	2002	2001	2000
AK	4.6	4.5	3.3	6.0	3.3	3.4	3.2	2.7
AL	2.8	3.6	4.7	3.6	4.3	4.2	3.9	4.8
AR	5.0	5.3	7.9	5.6	5.7	4.4	3.0	4.4
AZ	3.1	2.8	3.6	4.3	4.5	3.8	3.2	3.3
CA	3.3	2.8	2.7	3.3	3.8	3.5	3.5	3.2
CO	4.0	3.6	4.4	4.3	4.4	4.1	3.8	3.4
CT	5.0	4.7	5.6	6.1	6.0	4.8	6.0	5.6
DC	3.6	3.8	4.2	5.6	6.0	4.4	5.5	5.5
DE	5.2	5.7	7.2	9.3	7.6	6.4	4.6	5.4
FL	3.9	4.0	5.1	5.8	5.7	4.8	4.8	5.2
GA	2.9	2.6	3.6	3.6	3.8	3.4	3.8	4.9
HI	4.0	3.8	5.1	6.9	5.5	8.9	6.3	5.5
IA	7.9	7.1	8.1	8.7	7.6	7.2	6.9	6.5
ID	4.2	4.2	6.2	5.4	5.9	5.2	4.3	4.4
IL	5.7	5.6	5.8	6.5	6.6	5.9	5.5	5.2
IN	7.4	6.7	8.0	7.8	8.4	7.5	7.5	6.7
KS	7.1	6.0	5.4	6.1	6.6	5.0	6.0	7.9
KY	8.0	7.7	9.9	10.3	10.2	7.4	6.8	6.2
LA	7.2	10.6	6.9	7.9	7.0	6.1	5.0	4.8
MA	3.8	3.8	3.8	4.3	4.7	4.1	3.3	4.1
MD	3.5	3.2	5.7	7.1	7.4	6.3	5.5	3.8
ME	6.0	5.5	7.3	6.4	6.6	6.5	4.7	3.7
MI	4.5	4.8	5.3	5.7	5.5	4.8	4.4	3.9
MN	3.9	4.2	4.5	5.1	4.9	4.5	4.3	4.4
MO	2.4	2.2	2.3	3.0	3.5	3.2	3.5	3.0
MS	4.7	6.4	4.4	6.1	6.0	5.2	3.6	4.4

loans never entered REO. Variations across states mostly reflect the differences in foreclosure process between judicial and nonjudicial foreclosures. HPA plays an important role in year-to-year variations within the same state. HPA also has some impact (though not as large as the effect of judicial versus nonjudicial) on variations across states. Servicers have a large impact on the timelines, as well, though we do not analyze the effects of servicer in

EXHIBIT 2.16 (Continued)

State	2007	2006	2005	2004	2003	2002	2001	2000
MT	3.7	4.1	6.3	4.7	5.5	4.4	5.8	4.6
NC	4.7	5.8	6.1	5.8	7.9	5.1	4.8	5.2
ND	5.5	6.0	9.7	3.6	5.2	4.2	2.5	1.0
NE	5.5	4.8	5.3	4.5	5.3	4.5	4.7	4.6
NH	3.3	2.9	3.5	3.3	5.0	3.2	2.9	3.8
NJ	5.1	4.9	5.7	6.2	6.7	6.8	7.4	6.2
NM	4.5	4.7	5.9	6.7	6.0	8.4	5.4	6.4
NV	3.5	3.1	3.4	4.5	4.4	4.4	3.6	3.4
NY	5.6	5.1	5.9	7.3	7.9	7.5	6.7	7.2
OH	8.7	9.9	10.4	10.2	9.9	7.5	8.0	6.6
OK	7.1	7.6	8.0	8.4	7.8	6.2	7.3	5.9
OR	4.1	4.3	4.9	5.3	5.5	5.1	4.6	4.9
PA	6.2	7.2	7.2	8.0	7.8	6.9	6.3	5.8
RI	3.2	3.6	3.6	4.2	5.0	4.9	3.7	4.6
SC	6.9	7.7	8.2	9.7	9.3	6.7	5.8	5.8
SD	5.6	5.5	6.6	6.4	3.5	3.3	6.1	
TN	2.8	2.6	3.0	3.2	4.3	3.1	4.3	2.8
TX	3.8	3.5	3.7	4.2	4.0	3.4	2.7	3.2
UT	3.9	4.3	4.7	4.9	4.6	4.1	4.3	3.9
VA	2.5	2.2	2.5	3.7	4.2	3.4	5.1	3.6
VT	6.4	5.9	6.4	6.0	4.3	4.3	4.4	1.5
WA	4.2	4.0	4.6	4.9	5.3	4.6	4.1	3.8
WI	6.8	8.2	8.4	8.6	8.1	7.2	7.6	5.7
WV	6.6	7.1	10.4	6.6	4.7	5.4	2.5	3.1
WY	4.6	2.8	4.4	3.2	2.7	2.9	1.8	1.5

Source: LoanPerformance.

this chapter. For some of the large states such as California, Florida, Illinois, New York, and Texas, foreclosure-to-liquidation timelines have been relatively stable since 2000, although California did show a slight lengthening of foreclosure-to-liquidation timeline.

Going forward, the foreclosure-to-liquidation timeline (the one without going through REO) is less important since we expect the majority of loans will first transition to REO before being liquidated. This is because in a depressed housing market, short sales have become increasingly unlikely, since potential property buyers tend to wait for property prices to drop further. To investors in the lower part of the capital structure (BBB– or BBB, for example), the important considerations are (1) how many loans will go through REO process, (2) REO timeline, and (3) how long will the servicer continue to advance. We address the REO timeline next.

Exhibit 2.17 shows the foreclosure-to-REO timeline, again by state and liquidation year. For the same state across the years, the pattern seems relatively stable. Comparing Exhibits 2.16 and 2.17, we see that the foreclosure-to-liquidation timeline is generally shorter than foreclosure-to-REO timeline. That is because borrowers can still pay in full while the mortgages are in foreclosure. Short sales can also take place in foreclosure.

EXHIBIT 2.17   Foreclosure-to-REO Timeline

State	2007	2006	2005	2004	2003	2002	2001	2000
AK	4.1	4.4	4.3	6.0	6.8	6.1	4.6	5.6
AL	2.6	2.6	2.7	3.2	3.5	4.9	6.5	4.7
AR	3.6	4.3	4.4	4.1	4.2	4.3	3.8	4.7
AZ	3.6	4.7	4.0	4.5	4.9	4.2	4.2	5.6
CA	4.2	4.1	4.0	4.7	4.9	4.4	4.1	4.2
CO	4.2	4.4	4.6	5.1	5.4	5.1	4.6	5.5
CT	5.7	5.8	6.7	6.9	6.1	6.5	6.6	5.8
DC	2.8	3.0	3.3	3.0	6.4	4.4	3.3	4.5
DE	8.1	9.3	10.6	10.2	9.6	8.3	9.6	9.5
FL	5.2	5.6	6.0	6.5	6.2	5.8	6.0	6.4
GA	2.4	2.5	2.6	3.3	3.0	3.2	3.7	3.6
HI	3.4	5.2	5.8	6.3	5.6	7.2	8.4	14.7
IA	8.9	8.7	9.2	10.9	10.3	8.6	9.3	8.0
ID	5.5	5.2	6.4	6.3	6.9	6.3	6.4	5.8
IL	7.7	8.0	8.6	9.3	8.9	8.7	8.1	7.8
IN	7.5	7.6	8.2	9.0	9.0	8.5	8.0	8.3
KS	5.2	6.3	6.8	8.2	7.7	7.4	6.5	6.2
KY	8.6	9.0	10.0	11.3	11.1	9.0	9.5	8.2
LA	7.9	8.1	6.2	6.6	6.6	5.9	4.6	5.7
MA	4.2	4.4	4.8	5.1	4.5	4.7	5.5	5.8

EXHIBIT 2.17 (Continued)

State	2007	2006	2005	2004	2003	2002	2001	2000
MD	2.7	2.8	4.0	6.1	5.5	5.1	4.8	5.9
ME	10.3	10.1	11.4	11.3	10.6	10.9	10.1	10.8
MI	3.8	4.3	5.0	6.4	6.6	6.3	6.2	6.6
MN	4.8	4.8	5.2	6.1	6.3	6.1	6.2	7.4
MO	2.0	2.2	2.5	3.0	3.1	3.1	2.9	2.9
MS	3.9	5.0	4.2	5.3	5.3	4.8	4.3	3.9
MT	4.9	7.2	6.0	6.4	7.1	7.3	9.1	5.6
NC	3.8	4.2	5.2	6.3	6.0	5.7	5.0	4.8
ND	7.7	8.2	8.0	16.6	6.2	8.0	5.3	9.0
NE	4.5	4.8	5.4	5.1	5.4	5.1	6.4	4.1
NH	2.7	2.5	3.0	4.0	6.0	3.3	2.4	3.5
NJ	7.9	7.7	7.7	8.2	8.6	8.7	9.8	8.1
NM	6.9	6.4	6.8	7.3	8.2	7.6	7.3	6.9
NV	4.2	4.2	3.9	5.0	5.1	4.7	4.0	4.5
NY	7.9	7.7	8.5	9.4	9.8	10.1	9.9	9.6
OH	9.2	10.2	11.3	11.9	11.2	10.0	8.6	8.6
OK	7.5	7.7	8.6	8.7	8.3	7.4	6.8	6.5
OR	5.0	5.3	6.1	5.8	6.0	6.0	5.7	5.4
PA	8.0	8.1	8.6	8.8	8.0	8.7	8.5	8.5
RI	3.4	3.3	3.7	4.9	5.0	3.5	4.6	5.1
SC	6.6	7.5	9.1	10.2	9.3	8.6	7.7	7.0
SD	6.9	6.1	8.2	10.3	9.5	9.0	4.7	13.0
TN	2.2	2.7	2.9	3.2	3.2	3.1	2.6	2.9
TX	2.9	3.3	3.3	3.7	3.6	3.2	3.1	3.5
UT	4.4	4.5	5.0	5.1	5.2	4.9	4.0	4.8
VA	1.9	2.2	3.0	3.5	3.0	3.1	2.9	3.7
VT	8.7	9.3	9.3	11.4	11.0	9.1	22.2	10.3
WA	4.7	5.0	5.1	5.2	6.0	5.2	4.9	4.8
WI	8.6	8.5	9.6	10.5	10.6	8.9	9.0	8.1
WV	3.1	4.5	6.8	5.5	5.7	4.9	3.0	2.7
WY	5.6	4.5	4.4	5.6	4.6	4.9	4.4	5.3

Source: LoanPerformance.

Exhibit 2.18 shows the historical REO-to-liquidation timeline. One thing stands out quite differently from what we saw in Exhibits 2.16 and 2.17. Across most states, REO-to-liquidation timeline has lengthened between 2006 and 2007. For example, in 2006, REO-to-liquidation timeline in California was 3.4 months, while in 2007 it was 5.1 months. We attribute this to HPA and the increasing backlog of REO loans. At the moment, most of the timelines in Exhibit 2.18 are still within the historical norm (the very short timeline in 2005 and 2006 in states such as California was due to high HPA and very few REO loans).

EXHIBIT 2.18   REO Liquidation Timeline

State	2007	2006	2005	2004	2003	2002	2001	2000
AK	5.8	6.2	5.5	10.0	10.1	7.6	6.5	5.1
AL	5.9	5.8	5.9	6.8	7.7	7.4	6.0	6.2
AR	5.6	5.4	6.5	7.0	7.4	7.1	7.0	6.0
AZ	4.6	4.2	5.2	5.3	5.3	5.4	5.0	4.5
CA	5.1	3.4	3.8	6.1	5.5	6.0	5.5	5.4
CO	6.9	6.2	6.2	6.6	6.3	5.5	4.7	4.3
CT	5.8	4.7	5.6	6.1	6.4	6.8	6.1	5.8
DC	5.5	6.8	2.7	8.8	9.5	9.5	7.1	6.2
DE	5.2	4.5	5.3	5.2	5.2	7.7	7.7	5.0
FL	5.1	4.2	4.0	4.6	4.7	5.2	4.8	4.4
GA	6.3	5.1	5.2	6.4	6.5	5.9	5.8	5.5
HI	5.6	4.2	13.1	11.6	10.5	8.5	8.6	6.5
IA	5.6	5.4	5.9	6.0	6.7	7.0	6.9	4.9
ID	4.9	5.7	4.9	6.2	7.3	6.0	5.8	5.4
IL	6.4	4.9	4.8	5.3	5.6	6.0	6.0	5.2
IN	5.2	4.6	4.8	5.7	5.5	6.1	5.5	5.3
KS	6.9	6.2	6.3	5.9	6.2	6.7	6.6	5.1
KY	5.8	5.8	6.2	5.9	6.6	7.0	5.5	4.7
LA	4.5	6.6	5.3	5.9	5.6	6.1	5.5	5.1
MA	7.1	5.5	4.8	6.1	7.8	8.2	7.1	6.0
MD	6.1	4.8	6.5	7.1	8.5	8.7	8.3	6.8
ME	5.9	6.0	5.3	7.1	7.4	7.4	5.7	5.8
MI	10.1	8.7	8.9	8.9	8.4	8.6	7.6	6.9

EXHIBIT 2.18 (Continued)

State	2007	2006	2005	2004	2003	2002	2001	2000
MN	9.3	8.1	6.9	6.6	6.7	6.5	5.1	5.1
MO	5.8	5.3	5.3	5.8	5.9	6.3	5.7	5.0
MS	5.4	5.8	6.1	6.8	7.0	6.9	7.0	4.9
MT	4.9	5.7	6.4	6.6	7.5	6.8	6.8	6.6
NC	5.0	4.9	5.8	7.1	7.1	7.1	6.9	6.5
ND	5.4	7.3	5.2	13.9	4.6	6.8	7.0	2.0
NE	5.2	5.4	5.4	6.4	5.5	6.3	5.1	5.2
NH	6.4	5.1	4.1	5.9	9.4	6.7	5.2	6.0
NJ	6.3	4.8	5.2	5.7	6.6	6.1	5.8	4.8
NM	6.1	6.3	6.0	6.8	6.4	6.6	6.3	6.1
NV	5.7	4.1	5.0	6.1	5.4	5.6	4.7	5.5
NY	6.1	5.4	6.4	7.3	7.9	8.4	6.8	5.6
OH	6.8	6.2	6.6	6.3	6.6	6.8	6.5	5.2
OK	5.5	5.1	5.5	6.0	6.3	6.0	6.3	5.1
OR	4.2	4.7	5.2	5.9	6.0	6.1	5.2	5.2
PA	6.0	6.0	6.5	6.8	7.8	7.5	7.6	7.1
RI	6.2	4.5	1.8	4.8	7.4	6.7	5.3	4.5
SC	5.0	5.1	6.4	7.7	7.8	7.1	6.6	5.8
SD	8.4	7.8	7.7	9.3	8.7	12.0	8.5	5.8
TN	5.2	4.9	5.8	6.9	6.6	6.6	6.3	5.8
TX	5.3	5.0	5.3	6.0	6.0	5.7	5.8	5.3
UT	4.9	3.7	4.2	4.8	5.3	5.7	4.8	4.4
VA	5.3	4.4	6.1	6.3	6.8	6.6	6.9	5.8
VT	6.4	5.3	7.1	6.6	7.4	10.2	4.8	4.7
WA	4.0	4.3	5.4	5.7	5.9	6.4	5.8	5.7
WI	5.5	5.0	4.9	5.1	5.2	6.3	5.6	4.6
WV	6.3	7.4	8.0	9.6	8.0	8.3	8.1	7.7
WY	6.1	6.9	6.5	6.6	7.6	5.2	7.4	5.1

Source: LoanPerformance.

EXHIBIT 2.19 REO-to-Liquidation Timeline

	AZ	CA	FL	IL	MA	MI	MN	OH
2005Q1	4.9	5.8	4.3	4.9	5.4	8.9	6.8	6.6
2005Q2	5.0	4.0	3.9	5.0	4.6	9.1	6.8	6.5
2005Q3	5.6	3.4	3.8	4.5	5.1	8.6	6.9	6.6
2005Q4	5.2	2.7	4.0	5.0	4.2	9.1	7.1	6.6
2006Q1	3.5	2.5	3.6	4.8	5.6	9.0	7.8	6.5
2006Q2	3.6	3.0	4.5	4.8	4.9	8.8	8.0	6.3
2006Q3	5.4	3.4	3.9	4.8	5.4	8.7	8.1	6.0
2006Q4	4.0	3.8	4.5	5.3	6.0	8.5	8.3	6.2
2007Q1	3.9	4.4	4.4	6.0	7.0	9.4	8.8	6.6
2007Q2	4.4	5.0	4.7	6.1	6.8	9.9	9.2	6.8
2007Q3	5.1	5.3	5.2	6.8	7.1	10.5	9.8	6.9

	AZ	CA	FL	IL	MA	MI	MN	OH
2005Q1	114	36	343	512	27	891	213	936
2005Q2	82	45	287	497	50	1051	257	1043
2005Q3	69	52	237	462	50	1006	196	1081
2005Q4	33	42	225	469	71	1083	209	1245
2006Q1	41	116	208	545	69	1378	298	1346
2006Q2	30	150	225	626	127	1586	362	1319
2006Q3	36	273	260	745	165	1620	378	1498
2006Q4	57	450	303	725	211	2096	469	1743
2007Q1	148	1048	466	916	332	2475	609	1830
2007Q2	278	2065	620	1092	461	3062	827	2222
2007Q3	368	3219	938	1125	542	3494	829	2406

Source: LoanPerformance.

In Exhibit 2.19, we show REO-to-liquidation timeline by liquidation quarter beginning from the first quarter of 2005. The top panel is the timeline; the lengthening of the timeline is quite visible across these states. The bottom panel is the number of subprime first lien loans (to the extent we can capture them in LoanPerformance) that were liquidated from REO in each quarter. The increase in REO liquidation is astounding! In California during the first quarter of 2005, only 36 loans were liquidated from REO, whereas in the third quarter of 2007 we had 3,219 loans liquidate, an almost 100-fold increase. Even in Rust Belt states such as Michigan and Ohio, the number of REO liquidations has risen three- to fourfold in from 2005 to 2007 from continuing worsening of the housing market and the employment situation there.

The rising number of loans going through REO and the lengthening of the REO timeline suggest that it will take longer before loans are eventually liquidated. Assuming servicers continue to advance (a big assumption), this should increase the value of the lower part of the capital structure, where bonds are currently priced based on their IO values.

Severity by State

Before we proceed with our analysis, we briefly discuss the components of severity. Age of delinquency (principal and interest advance, taxes, servicing fee) and property value drop are the most important drivers, accounting for most of the losses. Foreclosure costs (mostly legal) and repair costs can be several thousand dollars. Other costs are monthly utility, eviction and other miscellaneous expenses, which are typically a few hundred dollars per item.

There are many different ways of defining severity. Some people (including the authors) prefer to define default first, then calculate severity with the inclusion of all defaulted loans, regardless of losses. Some calculate severity on loans with losses only. Here we will present both flavors. For this chapter, we define default as any loans paid off with losses, or any loans paid off from 60+DQ, or any loans paid off from current or 30DQ but with prior REO history (the last category intends to capture REO redemption loans). Our default definition tries to capture as many loans as possible.

We also remind the reader that severity is a function of many variables: current LTV, loan size, note rate, delinquency status before liquidation, and of course, state. Since the focus of this section is "state," we do not discuss the other factors.

Exhibit 2.20 shows severity on subprime first lien loans with losses by state and liquidation year. States with the largest housing boom in 2003–2005 have all reverted back to, or close to, historical norms. For example, severity on California loans now stands at 23% (it was single digit in 2004–2006). The 23% is close to what we observed in 2000 and 2001 (30% and 26%, respectively). We observe similar patterns in Florida, Arizona, and Nevada, the previous "hot" real estate areas.

On the other hand, we see severity almost doubling in Michigan since 2000 (from 36% to 71%) due to the distressed economic and employment environment and long REO redemption period. Ohio, now with the highest severity in the country at 74%, has always had very high severity due to

EXHIBIT 2.20   Severity on Loans with Losses (by state and payoff year)

State	2007	2006	2005	2004	2003	2002	2001	2000
AK	23	22	31	35	34	21	47	54
AL	45	43	46	52	59	55	58	53
AR	45	48	54	51	55	58	56	56
AZ	23	15	19	22	24	23	28	26
CA	23	8	7	9	13	19	26	30
CO	35	30	26	26	25	22	21	23
CT	28	23	27	30	38	49	53	62
DC	29	32	11	26	31	43	44	46
DE	28	28	35	42	56	68	66	78
FL	34	24	22	27	35	36	38	42
GA	43	41	39	41	41	41	36	46
HI	15	10	14	19	24	41	37	26
IA	55	51	55	58	56	55	56	56
ID	21	24	26	37	43	44	42	43
IL	42	37	35	43	51	56	57	59
IN	69	64	63	69	72	72	73	70
KS	42	45	45	46	50	55	55	49
KY	52	48	52	55	57	61	52	47
LA	46	34	45	51	53	57	54	54
MA	34	25	16	19	23	27	35	39
MD	21	14	24	41	53	62	72	79
ME	43	38	40	43	59	66	54	58
MI	71	56	47	48	47	49	40	36
MN	42	31	24	25	23	24	34	36
MO	49	45	41	47	54	55	55	59
MS	55	51	55	62	63	63	65	54
MT	23	27	33	36	41	46	41	41
NC	38	40	47	55	50	50	46	42
ND	39	52	39	32	46	43	49	43
NE	42	40	41	41	43	44	43	36
NH	32	22	17	20	19	30	25	34

EXHIBIT 2.20 (Continued)

State	2007	2006	2005	2004	2003	2002	2001	2000
NJ	29	19	16	24	35	44	50	56
NM	34	37	41	49	50	53	55	51
NV	23	12	10	17	21	23	25	27
NY	35	36	42	46	60	58	55	61
OH	74	67	65	66	64	67	62	59
OK	47	45	47	52	55	58	57	54
OR	18	15	21	28	30	32	34	33
PA	56	61	62	68	73	73	75	76
RI	38	28	11	16	25	22	39	58
SC	46	49	60	70	65	65	64	56
SD	38	37	41	49	48	56	40	42
TN	42	41	44	48	49	48	49	51
TX	38	36	39	42	42	43	40	37
UT	19	19	24	29	32	35	34	30
VA	24	18	28	33	37	41	44	53
VT	35	36	43	29	57	54	63	77
WA	16	15	19	25	31	34	37	39
WI	46	39	37	39	47	50	51	57
WV	51	66	65	72	63	65	64	56
WY	24	20	27	25	34	37	53	38

Source: LoanPerformance.

long foreclosure/REO timeline, low HPA, and smaller loan size, although 2007 severity is still 10% higher than the last few years.

Not only is severity trending up, but also the percent of defaulted loans with losses is rising at the same time, as seen in Exhibit 2.21. States with both HPA and unemployment problems (such as Indiana, Michigan, and Ohio) have a very large percentage (in excess of 80%) of defaulted loans that incur losses. This is because many defaulted loans go through the entire foreclosure to REO to liquidation process instead of short sales. The economic environment in these Rust Belt states is such that there are very few (if any at all) property buyers at any price level.

On the other hand, the spike in percent of default loans with losses in Arizona, California, Florida, and Nevada is extremely disconcerting. The

EXHIBIT 2.21 Percent of Defaulted Loans with Losses (by state and payoff year)

State	2007	2006	2005	2004	2003	2002	2001	2000
AK	70	28	21	49	49	58	50	47
AL	71	55	64	72	77	82	70	70
AR	76	63	60	74	75	80	77	71
AZ	59	15	18	46	59	61	55	52
CA	61	15	7	11	18	27	40	48
CO	86	73	71	68	60	42	30	38
CT	53	28	24	37	42	50	58	63
DC	43	5	5	23	38	46	70	67
DE	38	28	30	47	63	61	66	59
FL	39	11	18	36	47	55	63	74
GA	80	72	66	71	73	68	63	60
HI	32	5	10	17	35	64	71	50
IA	81	72	73	75	74	78	65	69
ID	48	30	50	67	74	76	81	74
IL	62	41	39	52	57	60	61	59
IN	84	74	76	80	83	83	77	78
KS	84	72	72	70	78	73	65	70
KY	79	71	68	76	72	79	73	64
LA	49	32	51	71	77	78	68	70
MA	70	34	22	22	19	22	26	37
MD	44	15	19	37	51	67	81	81
ME	66	37	31	47	49	44	48	45
MI	86	75	68	71	72	66	60	53
MN	79	59	44	42	41	34	35	52
MO	84	72	69	75	76	79	77	75
MS	68	45	66	79	80	77	69	65
MT	42	30	48	57	61	64	62	63
NC	71	68	69	77	75	74	67	67
ND	76	55	65	17	78	73	87	53
NE	82	71	67	79	73	76	71	70
NH	73	49	35	21	44	36	44	48

EXHIBIT 2.21 (Continued)

State	2007	2006	2005	2004	2003	2002	2001	2000
NJ	40	20	19	25	33	45	55	50
NM	46	45	59	72	77	82	71	64
NV	71	28	14	24	52	57	56	70
NY	32	14	15	23	32	41	44	45
OH	83	76	72	77	79	78	75	68
OK	78	73	71	76	80	77	76	75
OR	33	21	36	54	64	69	68	66
PA	57	43	43	58	67	67	73	70
RI	73	33	14	12	20	43	51	66
SC	71	63	70	75	75	78	69	66
SD	63	62	55	75	70	58	74	41
TN	74	67	65	76	80	81	79	77
TX	80	69	70	73	72	66	61	61
UT	39	42	59	76	79	78	77	75
VA	69	26	25	39	54	62	67	67
VT	41	24	15	29	33	58	50	11
WA	38	22	34	53	64	67	66	60
WI	72	56	51	56	61	72	64	60
WV	61	55	57	65	73	82	75	74
WY	31	38	45	44	58	59	80	71

Source: LoanPerformance.

percentage has tripled or quadrupled in these states in a span of less than two years. Combining with the three- to fourfold increase of severity on loans with losses, overall severity (including all defaulted loans, regardless of losses) has increased in excess of tenfold in California since the beginning of 2006.

Not surprisingly, but again very alarmingly, if we evaluate the data by pay-off quarter or month, overall severity in California increased over twentyfold since mid-2006. As a matter of fact, in the first lien subprime mortgage universe in California, severity is currently the highest ever, and still trending up. For historical severities higher than the current level, we can only find negative amortization loans liquidated in the mid-1990s (there were no subprime loans then). Exhibit 2.22 shows California severity since January 1990 (there were not enough liquidated loans prior to that).

EXHIBIT 2.22   Subprime First Lien Severity

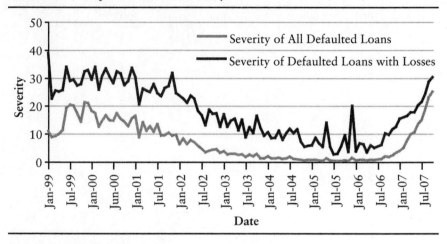

Source: LoanPerformance.

THE ROLE OF UNOBSERVABLE IN 2006 SUBPRIME MORTGAGE CREDIT

We conclude this chapter by looking at the role of unobservable variables in the 2006 subprime mortgage credit performance. Exhibit 2.23 summarizes the characteristics of observed variables. The deterioration in collateral characteristics is reflected by:

1. *Higher CLTV (combined LTV) and a larger share of purchase loans.* For example, CLTVs of subprime ARMs rose from 81 to 88 between 2001 and 2006, and the percentage of purchase loans rose from 34% to 46% over that same time. Besides higher average CLTV, we also observe larger shares of loans with CLTVs in excess of 80 and 90.
2. *A rising share of affordability products* (such as IO, 40-year, and loans with piggyback seconds). The popularity of these products coincided with the historical high HPA.
3. *A smaller share of loans with full documentation.* Again, using subprime ARMs as an example, the percent full documentation declined from 71% to 53% from 2001 to 2006.

In subsequent subsections, we focus on cohorts with the highest risk layering (CLTV exceeding 100, low doc, purchase); among 2/28s originated in California, they consistently rank in the top two in volume in every quarter of 2006 (see Exhibit 2.24).

EXHIBIT 2.23 Subprime Collateral Characteristics (by origination year)

Product	Orig. Year	Outstanding Balance ($)	CLTV	Percent IO	Percent 40 Yr.	Percent Piggyback	Percent Purchase	Percent CLTV > 80	Percent CLTV ≥ 90	Percent Full Doc	FICO
Subprime ARMs	2001	44,607,059,110	81	0	0	4	34	45	25	71	598
Subprime ARMs	2002	79,328,711,538	81	1	0	4	33	47	27	66	605
Subprime ARMs	2003	135,094,597,066	84	6	0	11	35	56	38	63	613
Subprime ARMs	2004	265,038,761,936	85	21	0	20	40	61	45	59	619
Subprime ARMs	2005	360,388,229,784	86	33	8	29	46	63	50	55	626
Subprime ARMs	2006	287,267,930,844	88	20	37	34	46	68	56	53	623
Subprime Fixed	2001	24,135,560,757	80	0	0	1	25	47	29	71	628
Subprime Fixed	2002	33,717,369,475	80	0	0	1	24	47	30	68	640
Subprime Fixed	2003	67,982,647,063	80	0	0	3	21	47	31	67	643
Subprime Fixed	2004	83,632,086,640	81	2	0	5	27	50	35	68	643
Subprime Fixed	2005	96,075,544,949	84	5	2	7	34	59	46	64	643
Subprime Fixed	2006	106,436,918,327	86	6	14	9	36	64	52	59	646

Source: LoanPerformance.

EXHIBIT 2.24   Cohorts with the Largest Dollar Amount (CA, 2/28s)

	CLTV	FICO	Doc	Purpose	Original Balance
2005Q1	≤ 100	≥ 650	Low	Purchase	$2,027,711,227
2005Q1	≥ 100	≥ 650	Full	Purchase	$1,033,769,278
2005Q1	80 to 90	≥ 650	Low	Purchase	$800,095,026
2005Q1	< 80	≤ 550	Full	Refi cash-out	$789,066,740
2005Q1	90 to 100	≥ 650	Low	Purchase	$583,905,885
2005Q2	≥ 100	≥ 650	Low	Purchase	$3,362,806,294
2005Q2	≥ 100	≥ 650	Full	Purchase	$1,370,129,858
2005Q2	80 to 90	≥ 650	Low	Purchase	$1,047,759,601
2005Q2	≥ 100	625–650	Low	Purchase	$875,024,478
2005Q2	90 to 100	≥ 650	Low	Purchase	$820,684,473
2005Q3	≥ 100	≥ 650	Low	Purchase	$3,835,905,218
2005Q3	80 to 90	≥ 650	Low	Purchase	$1,386,465,738
2005Q3	≥ 100	≥ 650	Full	Purchase	$1,372,715,239
2005Q3	≥ 100	625–650	Low	Purchase	$1,090,205,208
2005Q3	90 to 100	≥ 650	Low	Purchase	$961,273,853
2005Q4	≥ 100	≥ 650	Low	Purchase	$3,084,437,316
2005Q4	80 to 90	≥ 650	Low	Purchase	$1,112,020,233
2005Q4	≥ 100	≥ 650	Full	Purchase	$1,043,714,234
2005Q4	≥ 100	625–650	Low	Purchase	$938,696,706
2005Q4	< 80	≤ 550	Full	Refi cash-out	$670,940,998

What a Difference a Year Makes: 2005 versus 2006 Originations

Given the worsening collateral characteristics, we would expect 2006 production to perform worse, especially in a weak housing market. However, reading Exhibit 2.23 more carefully raises more questions. Specifically, focusing on the difference between 2006 and 2005 productions, we see:

- For ARMs, CLTV is 2 points higher, IO 13% lower, 40 year 29% higher, piggyback 5% higher, CLTV > 80 5% higher, CLTV ≥ 90 6% higher, and full documentation 2% lower for 2006 originations.
- For *fixed rate 2006 production*, CLTV is 2 points higher, IO 1% higher, 40 year 12% higher, piggyback 2% higher, purchase 2% higher, CLTV > 80 5% higher, CLTV ≥ 90 6% higher, and full documentation 5% lower.

EXHIBIT 2.24 (Continued)

	CLTV	FICO	Doc	Purpose	Original Balance
2006Q1	≥ 100	≥ 650	Low	Purchase	$2,308,029,244
2006Q1	≥ 100	625–650	Low	Purchase	$910,407,144
2006Q1	80 to 90	≥ 650	Low	Purchase	$869,706,828
2006Q1	≥ 100	≥ 650	Full	Purchase	$836,184,122
2006Q1	<80	≤ 550	Full	Refi cash-out	$536,762,514
2006Q2	≥ 100	≥ 650	Low	Purchase	$2,806,734,748
2006Q2	≥ 100	625–650	Low	Purchase	$1,069,053,285
2006Q2	≥ 100	≥ 650	Full	Purchase	$1,005,682,930
2006Q2	80 to 90	≥ 650	Low	Purchase	$547,436,810
2006Q2	≥ 100	625–650	Full	Purchase	$526,845,072
2006Q3	≥ 100	≥ 650	Low	Purchase	$2,745,564,279
2006Q3	≥ 100	625–650	Low	Purchase	$1,002,801,772
2006Q3	≥ 100	≥ 650	Full	Purchase	$859,229,036
2006Q3	≥ 100	625–650	Full	Purchase	$515,821,922
2006Q3	≥ 100	600–625	Full	Purchase	$491,152,141
2006Q4	≥ 100	≥ 650	Low	Purchase	$1,896,511,662
2006Q4	≥ 100	625–650	Low	Purchase	$638,867,162
2006Q4	≥ 100	≥ 650	Full	Purchase	$606,528,422
2006Q4	≥ 100	625–650	Full	Purchase	$416,359,879
2006Q4	≥ 100	600–625	Full	Purchase	$409,336,190

Source: LoanPerformance.

Clearly, 2006 collateral characteristics were worse than 2005 production. But do these differences justify the performance differences between the two vintages?

Exhibits 2.25A and 2.25B show performance of 2005 and 2006 first lien subprime ARM and fixed rate mortgages, via 60+DQ as a percent of remaining balance (including foreclosure, REO, bankruptcy). For both fixed rate mortgages and ARMs, 60+DQ% of 2006 production are currently running 75% to 100% higher than 2005 counterparts. The collateral difference itself doesn't seem capable of explaining such a larger variation. Anyone who has followed the recent developments in the mortgage market will immediately point out that 2005 and 2006 vintages experienced very different HPA—hence, the performance difference. We completely agree that

EXHIBIT 2.25

Panel A.   Subprime ARM First Lien

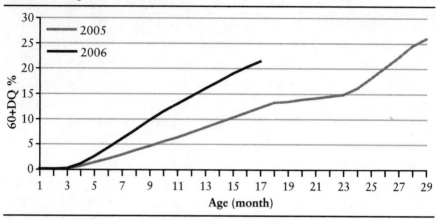

Panel B.   Subprime Fixed First Lien

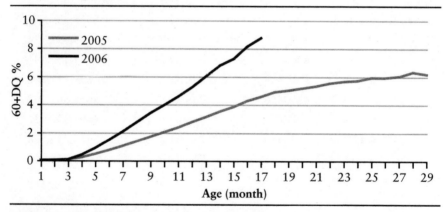

Source: LoanPerformance.

HPA played a very important role in the performance differences. However, in the following section, we argue that a significant portion of this cannot be easily explained by HPA.

How Much Does One Quarter's HPA Matter?

Exhibit 2.26 summarizes historical state-level HPA from OFHEO. We show both 2005 and 2006 annual HPA and annualized quarterly HPA. One thing that immediately jumps out is the HPA difference between 2005Q4 and 2006Q1 in states such as Arizona, California, Maryland, and Nevada. In California, annualized quarterly HPA decelerated from 20.5

EXHIBIT 2.26 HPA by State

State	2006	2005	2006				2005			
			Q4	Q3	Q2	Q1	Q4	Q3	Q2	Q1
AK	7.5	14.5	4.0	6.9	11.0	8.2	15.1	16.9	15.5	10.6
AL	8.5	8.7	8.4	8.2	8.9	8.2	9.7	8.9	10.1	6.1
AR	6.4	7.6	5.2	4.8	7.7	8.0	5.5	9.5	10.3	5.3
AZ	9.5	35.4	4.2	5.2	11.4	17.6	32.2	36.5	48.6	25.4
CA	4.6	21.4	−0.9	3.1	6.0	10.5	20.5	21.1	24.9	19.4
CO	3.2	5.8	4.2	3.5	4.6	0.5	4.9	5.7	7.6	5.1
CT	3.8	11.8	1.4	3.9	3.4	6.8	10.1	11.8	13.8	11.3
DC	7.6	23.5	8.6	5.6	7.5	8.5	25.4	25.6	25.5	17.7
DE	7.7	15.4	9.3	4.3	7.5	9.7	11.0	20.8	17.7	12.3
FL	9.6	27.8	3.6	5.7	10.3	19.5	25.0	30.3	33.1	22.9
GA	5.7	6.3	7.4	5.5	4.5	5.6	6.1	7.5	5.2	6.3
HI	7.2	24.5	−2.5	9.3	5.3	17.8	26.1	26.6	27.3	18.3
IA	3.1	5.9	4.1	5.0	4.1	−0.9	5.4	7.4	6.5	4.3
ID	14.7	18.7	10.7	12.8	19.2	16.2	21.3	25.9	17.7	10.4
IL	6.0	9.4	5.0	5.5	5.9	7.6	9.5	8.9	10.4	8.6
IN	2.6	4.1	4.3	4.7	0.6	0.9	2.3	6.5	4.5	3.0
KS	4.5	4.7	5.7	5.1	4.1	3.1	3.4	5.3	7.1	3.1
KY	4.2	4.8	5.6	3.4	3.5	4.4	3.2	6.8	6.3	2.9
LA	11.2	9.2	8.6	10.4	11.5	14.4	15.4	8.1	8.7	5.0
MA	0.1	7.7	3.3	−1.4	−2.9	1.6	4.9	6.7	10.1	9.3
MD	9.4	21.8	6.1	7.2	10.8	13.6	20.0	21.5	27.0	19.0
ME	5.0	10.4	9.8	4.3	−0.1	6.4	9.0	10.2	10.9	11.7
MI	−0.5	3.0	2.6	−1.1	−3.4	−0.1	0.8	4.1	3.2	3.8
MN	2.8	7.7	4.8	2.0	1.3	3.1	6.6	7.9	9.1	7.3
MO	4.8	6.9	6.2	4.8	3.0	5.2	6.4	7.3	6.9	6.9
MS	9.8	7.4	7.1	11.9	11.1	8.9	10.5	7.4	8.1	3.7
MT	10.9	14.2	7.6	13.7	15.0	7.5	17.2	11.7	18.4	9.6
NC	8.3	8.0	10.2	7.6	7.5	7.8	10.6	9.2	5.3	7.1
ND	5.6	8.1	−0.1	6.7	10.6	5.3	7.2	13.0	10.4	2.1
NE	2.6	3.9	0.5	3.4	5.0	1.5	0.8	5.7	6.7	2.6

EXHIBIT 2.26 (Continued)

			2006				2005			
State	2006	2005	Q4	Q3	Q2	Q1	Q4	Q3	Q2	Q1
NH	2.1	9.4	3.1	0.4	0.2	5.0	6.9	9.4	10.4	10.9
NJ	6.0	15.6	3.5	3.7	7.4	9.4	15.2	16.3	18.0	13.0
NM	13.2	14.9	10.0	13.1	16.6	13.0	14.6	16.8	18.7	9.6
NV	4.0	18.4	0.4	1.9	2.2	11.9	16.9	15.5	23.5	17.9
NY	5.4	13.0	6.9	1.4	3.4	10.1	12.8	12.9	14.7	11.8
OH	1.2	3.3	2.9	0.5	−0.4	1.9	0.9	4.5	4.1	3.9
OK	5.0	6.0	5.2	4.3	7.6	3.1	6.9	6.9	8.1	2.3
OR	13.7	20.0	7.9	12.4	18.4	16.4	20.7	23.3	23.5	12.7
PA	7.3	12.3	6.3	6.1	7.5	9.4	11.4	13.6	15.2	9.1
RI	2.8	10.6	2.0	−0.9	3.7	6.7	6.3	9.6	16.8	9.9
SC	8.5	8.9	10.5	7.8	7.2	8.5	9.1	11.2	7.0	8.3
SD	5.8	7.7	4.1	10.8	7.4	1.1	7.7	6.1	10.1	7.0
TN	8.3	7.8	9.2	6.9	9.9	7.3	6.7	9.4	9.0	6.1
TX	7.2	5.3	6.7	8.1	7.7	6.5	4.9	6.3	7.1	2.9
UT	18.0	13.1	16.9	20.6	20.4	14.3	15.3	15.1	14.5	7.6
VA	7.7	19.7	6.1	4.0	9.4	11.5	15.1	21.4	24.8	17.8
VT	7.5	13.2	6.1	3.2	11.4	9.3	9.6	15.5	17.2	10.6
WA	13.8	18.6	8.6	14.0	16.9	16.1	19.2	18.7	23.1	13.6
WI	4.2	7.7	6.5	3.8	1.8	4.5	6.3	8.7	8.0	7.8
WV	5.6	11.1	3.3	11.1	1.0	7.4	7.7	14.3	14.3	8.1
WY	14.0	12.8	13.9	17.6	11.0	13.5	13.1	17.1	11.8	9.2

Source: Office of Federal Housing Enterprise Oversight.

to 10.5, a full 10 percentage point drop on an annualized basis, or 2.5 percentage point drop nonannualized basis. Put differently, for mortgages originated in 2005, Q4 and 2006, Q1, the difference in their cumulative HPA should be about 2.5%.

Exhibits 2.27a and 2.27b compare 60+DQ% by origination quarter. Exhibit 2.27a shows 2/28 ARM, purchase, low doc loans originated in California, with CLTV ≥ 100, and FICO ≥ 650. In essence, we controlled for all major drivers of mortgage credit performance; namely, product, loan purpose, documentation level, geography, CLTV, FICO. Of the observed variables, we can only attribute the performance difference to 2.5% HPA.

EXHIBIT 2.27

Panel A. 60+DQ% of 2/28 ARM (CA, First Lien, Purchase, Low Doc, CLTV ≥ 100, FICO ≥ 650)

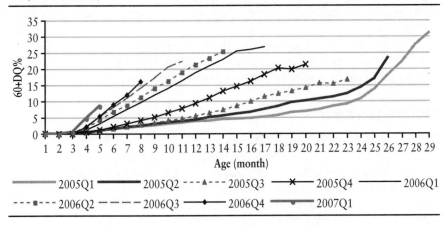

Panel B. 60+DQ% of 2/28 ARM (CA, First Lien, Purchase, Low Doc, CLTV ≥ 100, 625 ≤ FICO < 650)

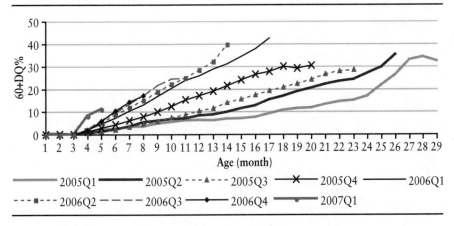

Source: LoanPerformance.

At Month 15, 60+DQ% of 2006Q1 origination is 26%, while it is 15% for 2005Q4 origination, again a difference greater than 70%. Put differently, if HPA were mostly responsible for the performance difference, then we would have to believe that a 2.5% HPA could worsen credit performance by a whopping 70%.

To further illustrate our point that HPA played a limited role in the performance differences between 2005 and 2006 vintage, we show in Exhibit

2.28a, the performance of similar loans from states that had not seen a lot of volatilities in HPA (namely, 2/28 first lien ARM, purchase, low doc, CLTV ≥ 100, and FICO ≥ 650).[1] The separation between 2005Q4 and 2006Q1 performance, though not as large as that we saw among CA loans, is clearly visible.

On the other hand, Exhibit 2.28b shows the performance of cash-out, full doc 2/28 loans from these same states, but with CLTV < 80 and FICOs of 575–600. There is very little performance difference.

If Not HPA, Then What?

We believe that neither underwriting variables we publicly observed (such as CLTV, FICO, documentation, loan purpose, and geography from Loan-Performance), nor HPA, is fully capable of explaining the historically bad performance of 2006 production. The main culprit, in our opinion, is the unobserved underwriting variables and the extent to which originators were willing to push the envelope in underwriting these mortgages.

In a booming housing market, loans leveraged to the hilt (CLTV ≥ 100, low doc, purchase) are most prone to being underwritten with the loosest

EXHIBIT 2.28

Panel A.   60+DQ% of 2/28 ARM (Stable HPA states, First Lien, Purchase, Low Doc, CLTV ≥ 100, FICO ≥ 650)

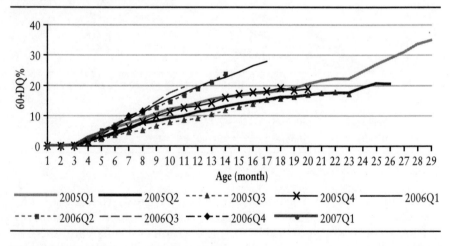

---

[1] We selected loans from the following states: Alabama, Arkansas, Georgia, Illinois, Kentucky, Missouri, Mississippi, North Carolina, North Dakota, New Mexico, Oklahoma, Oregon, Pennsylvania, South Carolina, South Dakota, Tennessee, Texas, Utah, Washington, and Wyoming.

EXHIBIT 2.28 (Continued)

Panel B. 60+DQ% of 2/28 ARM (Stable HPA states, First Lien, Cash-Out, Full Doc, CLTV < 80, 575 ≤ FICO < 600)

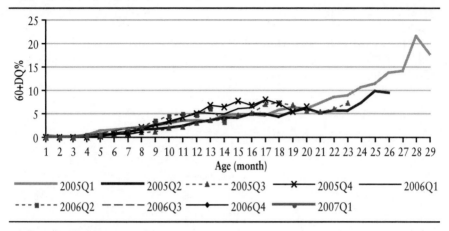

Source: LoanPerformance.

guidelines. But as housing turns, these loans will show the weakest performance. In such an environment, overreliance on FICO proves fatal, as it had become the last line of defense (and with loose underwriting, turned into a line of sand). So it is no surprise if many originators pushed the envelope on FICOs (e.g., thinly filed FICOs, comingling of borrower and co-borrowers' FICO and income). Such mortgages are also the most likely candidates for inflated appraisals. We suspect lenders loosened such secondary criteria as time on job, time in home, time since last bankruptcy, and so on, criteria that never makes into a term sheet. In essence, loans with seemingly similar or even identical reported characteristics would perform very differently in this environment.

To conclude, we show in Exhibits 2.29A and 2.29B the 60+DQ% of 2/28 (again from California), cash-out, full doc loans with CLTV < 80. Performance differences across different origination quarters are much less dramatic than in the previous section. The exhibits convey the same message: Mortgages with low leverage (low CLTV, full doc, cash-out) are much less likely impacted by loose underwritings.

EXHIBIT 2.29

Panel A. 60+DQ% of 2/28 ARM (CA, First Lien, Cash-Out, Full Doc, CLTV < 80, 600 ≤ FICO < 625)

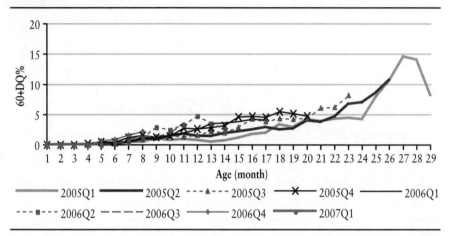

Panel B. 60+DQ% of 2/28 ARM (CA, First Lien, Cash-Out, Full Doc, CLTV < 80, FICO < 550)

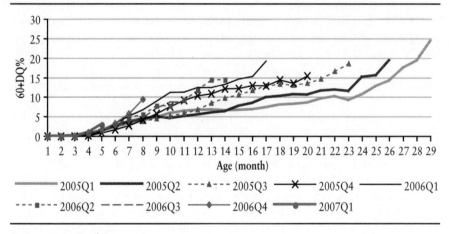

Source: LoanPerformance.

CHAPTER 3

Second Lien Mortgage Credit

In this chapter, we look at the performance of second lien mortgages (*seconds* or *second lien*). When the subprime market imploded in 2006 and 2007, seconds were one of the first sectors to exhibit unusually high defaults. By mid-2006, trading desks were punishing whole loan subprime packages that had a larger than average percentage of seconds. It appears that in a stressful environment, seconds are more vulnerable to the layered risks than are first lien mortgages.

This chapter starts off by comparing historical performances of seconds in *closed-end seconds* (CES, or *standalone seconds*) deals versus regular subprime deals that are mostly comprised of first lien mortgages. We then evaluate the recent performances of seconds in the context of the 2006–2007 subprime debacles. Our analyses indicate that the historically bad performance of recent seconds liens shares the same traits of first lien counterparts, which are highlighted by loose underwriting and collateral risk layering.

TWO TYPES OF SECONDS

Second liens occur in nonagency MBS in two forms: either as a small part of a first subprime deal, or in a standalone second deal. For historical reasons, seconds very rarely appear in prime or Alt-A deals, but have long played a role in subprime. In the early days of the "home equity" market (1991–1993), a substantial percentage of the loans were seconds. However, in the modern subprime world (i.e., post-1995), seconds have played only a minor role. As shown in Exhibit 3.1, the second lien percentage of subprime deals in the LoanPerformance database went from 6% to 7% in 1995–1997 to a low of 1.3% to 2.5% in 2000–2004, and then rose to over 4% in 2006. In the 1995–2002 period, few seconds came from piggyback originations, and few had *combined loan-to-value ratios* (CLTVs) of 100%. With the explosion of piggybacks in both Alt-A and subprime in 2003–2004, subprime deals began to contain a larger percentage of seconds.

EXHIBIT 3.1   Second Lien Percent Among Subprime Deals

	Total			Fixed Rate		ARM	
Orig. Year	Original Amount ($ billion)	Second Lien %	ARM %	Original Amount ($ billion)	Second Lien %	Original Amount ($ billion)	Second Lien %
1995	3.4	5.6	37.9	2.1	9.1	1.3	0.0
1996	9.4	7.0	33.4	6.2	10.6	3.1	0.0
1997	19.6	6.1	48.3	10.2	11.8	9.5	0.0
1998	37.5	3.8	47.4	19.7	7.2	17.7	0.0
1999	51.7	2.8	51.2	25.2	5.7	26.5	0.1
2000	48.0	2.5	64.1	17.2	6.9	30.8	0.0
2001	68.3	1.7	65.9	23.3	5.0	45.0	0.0
2002	115.3	1.6	70.5	34.0	5.4	81.3	0.0
2003	213.1	1.3	66.9	70.5	3.8	142.5	0.0
2004	355.5	2.0	77.2	80.9	8.5	274.6	0.0
2005	470.9	3.2	81.3	88.0	16.2	382.9	0.2
2006	392.9	4.2	77.3	89.2	18.4	303.7	0.0
2007	60.6	1.7	72.6	16.6	6.0	44.0	0.1

Source: LoanPerformance.

When we break down the percentage of second liens by fixed rate versus ARMs, we observe the following:

- Virtually all second liens in subprime deals are fixed rate mortgages (no surprise!).
- The decline of second lien percentage in subprime deals until 2004 was due to both an increasing percentage of ARMs in these deals and a declining share of second liens among fixed rate loans.
- Within the fixed rate subprime space, the percentage of second liens doubled from 2004 level (8.5%) to 16% to 18% in 2005 and 2006 (even higher than it was in 1995–1997).

The number of 100% second lien deals also rose sharply over the past few years. In Exhibit 3.2, we show the growth in the number and volume of second lien deals since 1995. (The data are from the Intex database, and is in rough agreement with data from Moody's.) Hence we believe the growth trend evident in Exhibit 3.2 gives a fair impression of how much this sector has expanded in recent years. There were only a handful of second lien deals

EXHIBIT 3.2   Number of Second Lien Standalone Deals

Issue Year	Deal Count	Original Balance (millions)
1995	1	84
1996	4	770
1997	4	916
1998	4	1,279
1999	8	2,605
2000	2	272
2001	9	2,740
2002	11	3,791
2003	29	7,993
2004	34	11,220
2005	55	24,319
2006	74	38,336

Source: Intex.

in 1999–2001, with a volume of approximately $2 billion per annum. By 2004, volume rose to $11 billion on 34 deals, and in 2006 reached $38 billion within 74 deals. This rapid expansion of closed-end second deals reflected the steep rise in the use of 80/20 loans in Alt-A and subprime sectors.

HIGHER RISKS IN SECONDS

By their very nature, seconds carry more risk than do first lien mortgages. If a foreclosure occurs, it is unlikely that the second lien holder will receive any proceeds (i.e., loss severities are typically almost 100%). In an exceptionally strong housing market it is possible that a default on a well-seasoned second may not result in a complete loss if the CLTV has been pushed well below 100. In contrast, in some recent subprime deals, loss severities on seconds have been greater than 100% (some in the 110% range). While there are situations where severities may be less than or greater than 100%, a 100% severity is the standard assumption, and is what the rating agencies use in setting credit enhancement levels.

If loss severities are typically higher on seconds than on firsts—what about default rates? In the "old" days, when many seconds were not piggybacks, CLTVs were in the high-80s to mid-90s, and there were not many deals with CLTVs in the high-90s. Nor were cumulative loss rates much greater on seconds than on firsts.

EXHIBIT 3.3 60+DQ% on Seconds in Subprime Deals (by origination year)

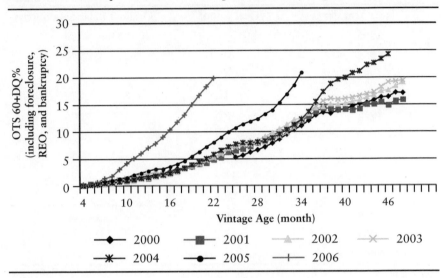

In Exhibits 3.3 and 3.4, we show performance data for subprime seconds that are included in traditional subprime deals for vintage years 2000–2006. Exhibit 3.3 depicts 60+ day delinquencies of outstanding balance; Exhibit 3.4 cumulative losses on these seconds. We show the performance by the age of a vintage (labelled "Vintage Age" on the horizontal axis). For example, for the 2005 vintage, a vintage age of 1 corresponds to January 2005. The advantage of analyzing data using vintage age is twofold. First, the last data point of each vintage corresponds to the most recent calendar month, and captures the performance of an entire vintage (versus the traditional seasoning curve, where the last data point of each vintage only captures one month of origination of a specific vintage). Second, we still preserve the capability of comparing performance across vintages, since at similar vintage age, the average loan age of each vintage is roughly equal.

As seen in Exhibit 3.4, cumulative losses on all of the well-seasoned vintage year seconds come in less than or equal to 6%. Cumulative losses on subprime firsts from those years max out at about 5%. That's not a great difference. If the cumulative losses are about the same and loss severities on seconds are about 100%, then cumulative defaults on seconds must have been less than on firsts. We do not know if in fact that was the case, because the data are very spotty, but one explanation could be that many of the seconds in those earlier deals were Alt-A. We note that data on seconds is notoriously poor compared to that on firsts, but even taking this into account, it appears that for 1998–2004, second liens did not perform much differently

EXHIBIT 3.4   Cumulative Loss on Seconds in Subprime Deals (by origination year)

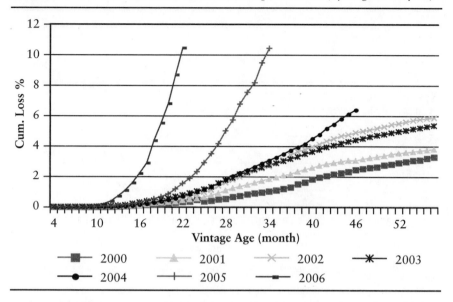

from first liens. This may have led to a false sense of security about how seconds would perform in more difficult environments.

How does the performance of seconds in traditional subprime deals compare to that of seconds in standalone second deals? In Exhibit 3.5 we show 60+-day delinquencies for standalone seconds; in Exhibit 3.6 we show cumulative losses for standalone seconds. In general, cumulative losses from standalone seconds (Exhibit 3.6) are lower than on seconds from traditional subprime deals (Exhibit 3.4). For vintage years 2002–2003, cumulative losses on standalone seconds deals were much lower 6%, whereas cumulative losses for 2002 and 2003 on seconds in traditional subprime deals hit that level.

Given the spotty data on cumulative losses on earlier (2000–2001) vintages from LoanPerformance (many CES deals of earlier vintages did not report loss information to LoanPerformance, which was why we did not show cumulative losses on CES deals for the 2000 and 2001 vintages), we turn to our favored measure of default for second liens to compare performance of second liens in subprime deals and CES deals. Exhibits 3.7 and 3.8 show the cumulative first time *60+-day delinquencies percentage* (60+DQ%). For second liens, we prefer to define defaults as loans reaching 60+DQ for the first time, since the likelihood of curing from 60+DQ is very remote for second liens. The conclusion we draw from these two exhibits is consistent with the picture on cumulative losses. That is, second liens in CES deals seem to perform better than their counterparts in subprime deals.

EXHIBIT 3.5   60+DQ% on CES Deals (by origination year)

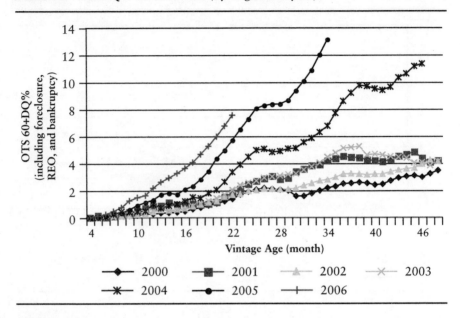

EXHIBIT 3.6   Cumulative Loss on CES Deals (by origination year)

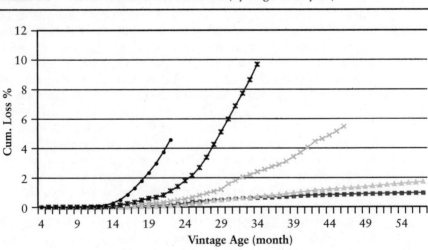

EXHIBIT 3.7 Cumulative First Time 60+DQ% on Seconds in Subprime Deals (by origination year)

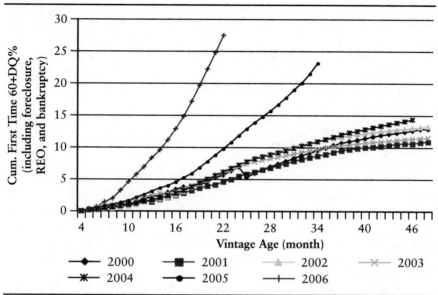

EXHIBIT 3.8 Cumulative First Time 60+DQ% on Seconds in Subprime Deals (by origination year)

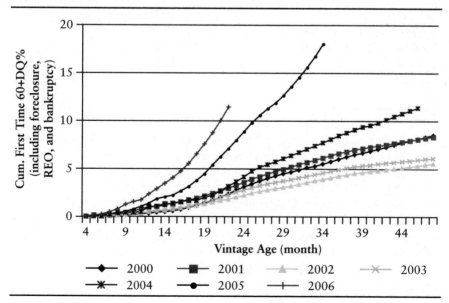

How good was the performance of second liens in the period 2000–2005? It's good enough that in early 2005, Moody's upgraded 40 tranches from 19 CES deals, reflecting among other things the fast prepayments and the low losses associated with a very high HPA environment. The same factors that led to superior performance in other mortgage sectors had led to a sterling performance in seconds. So it is easy to see why investors and rating agencies alike were taken by surprise when losses on 2005, and especially on 2006 deals, began to accelerate at historically fast rates.

RECENT PERFORMANCE

Now look at the recent vintages, 2005 and 2006. The data in both Exhibit 3.2 (seconds in traditional subprime deals) and Exhibit 3.6 (seconds in standalone second deals) show that the trajectories of 2005 and 2006 vintages are very different from those of earlier vintages. 2005 vintage loans are on a track to have considerably higher losses than the previous worst vintage (2000). Granted, second lien losses are front-loaded, and the 2005 loss line may stop climbing so rapidly when the loans are seasoned (i.e., the rate of advance may ease as it did in other vintages), but so far there is no sign of that. The same is true with the 2006 vintage; it shows losses far exceeding those on the 2000 and 2005 vintages. In fact, the 2006 vintage is exhibiting remarkably large losses for this early a stage. According to both the Intex and the LoanPerformance data, cumulative losses on 2006 vintage CES deals are already 4.5% when the vintage is 20-months old. If we look at 60+-day delinquencies in Exhibits 3.3 and 3.5, both 2005 and 2006 continue to track well above earlier years. This suggests that 2005 and 2006 cumulative loss curves will continue to climb sharply in 2008.

WHY HIGHER LOSSES?

The data we just examined make it clear that the 2005, and especially the 2006, vintage seconds are experiencing a much larger number of defaults and losses than earlier vintages. As in first lien subprime and other sectors of the mortgage market, the rise in losses can be traced to two factors—worse underwriting and a more difficult housing market. Until 2006, a strong housing market covered many sins, including some very poor underwriting of mortgage loans. Once housing slowed, the effect of the poor underwriting surfaced quickly—via a spike in EPDs and a surge in defaults on both first and second lien subprime loans. Since second liens are typically written off rather than foreclosed, losses in seconds shot up much faster than in the first lien sector. Of course, the delinquency pipeline on first liens also points to a very steep rise in losses at a later date.

We can gain some insight into what triggered the rise in losses by looking at the trend in second lien collateral characteristics. Exhibit 3.9 shows for our two sets of subprime seconds the collateral characteristics for the years 1998 to 2006. As in the traditional subprime and Alt-A markets the deterioration of credit standards is evident in the risk layering. Not one, but a number of collateral characteristics were loosened over the years, with the greatest changes occurring in the past three to four years. The changes include:

- DTI increasing from 36/37 to 40/42
- CLTV increasing from 85/86 to 97/98
- Full documentation percentage declining from 70/85 to 35/45
- Purchase loan percentage increasing from 15/30 to 75/80
- DTI greater than 45 increasing from 15/25 to 30/45
- Condo percentage increasing from 1/2 to 8.5/8.8

In looking at the data in Exhibit 3.9, it is hard to see that there was a sharp break beginning in 2005, a change great enough to have triggered the sharp increase in losses. Rather, it appears that the continuing deterioration of credit combined with a slowing of the housing market triggered the sharp deterioration observed in the data in Exhibits 3.3 to 3.8.

To further investigate the causes of the higher losses, we looked in detail at the characteristics of loans that caused the greatest amount of poor credit performance. We show that data in Exhibit 3.10, which covers seconds in traditional subprime deals (not from standalone second deals.) Not surprisingly, it shows that the loans with the greatest 60-day delinquencies are low doc/purchase loans. (If we had data on *first-time homeowners* (FTH), they would probably show that within this purchase subset, FTHs performed much worse than the average purchase loan in each bucket in Exhibit 3.10.) The best performing seconds were the refi and cash-out/full doc loans. It is noteworthy that the worst performing buckets had the higher FICO scores, while the best performing buckets had the lowest FICO scores. This is what we saw in the traditional subprime market. The high FICO scores that accompanied the layered risk loans were insufficient to offset the negative effect of several high risk elements in a single loan.

SUMMARY

Second lien mortgages originated in 2005 and 2006 have experienced a sharp acceleration in seriously delinquent loans and losses. The causes are

EXHIBIT 3.9 Loan Characteristics: Seconds in Traditional Subprime Deals versus Seconds in Standalone Second Deals

Panel A. Traditional Subprime Deals

Orig. Year	Balance	WAC	Loan Size	FICO	DTI	1st LTV	2nd LTV	CLTV	% CA	% FL	% Full Doc	% Condo	% Purchase	% DTI > 45
1998	1,442,677,146	11.19	33,205	646	37	61	26	84	15.3	9.5	89	1.2	3	14
1999	1,473,460,624	11.30	35,860	638	39	58	25	83	22.1	7.4	91	2.0	11	28
2000	1,195,424,507	12.27	38,127	619	40	62	24	81	20.9	7.2	84	2.5	8	34
2001	1,161,371,003	11.73	40,014	627	40	65	22	84	27.4	6.2	80	3.5	22	31
2002	1,836,493,565	11.54	39,953	646	41	75	20	94	42.4	4.6	66	6.0	58	35
2003	2,684,978,286	10.74	43,657	648	42	77	20	97	48.9	4.8	61	7.8	70	39
2004	6,992,318,635	10.30	49,229	655	41	78	20	98	46.2	5.7	54	8.4	77	36
2005	14,940,450,473	10.24	54,539	658	42	78	20	98	37.7	8.2	48	8.7	77	41
2006	16,540,581,725	11.31	59,299	653	42	79	20	99	34.0	10.9	45	8.4	78	43

EXHIBIT 3.9 (Continued)

Panel B. Standalone Second Deals

Orig. Year	$ Balance	WAC	Loan Size	FICO	DTI	1st LTV	2nd LTV	CLTV	% CA	% FL	% Full Doc	% Condo	% Purchase	% DTI > 45
1998	204,320,433	10.57	35,252	717	37	74	17	91	48.7	2.2	99	3.9	59.38	16.14
1999	69,025,595	10.79	36,310	701	37	71	18	90	44.1	3.6	92	3.6	37.52	16.78
2000	1,169,342,370	11.32	40,629	698	39	69	20	88	46.4	2.8	67	5.9	39.32	25.47
2001	3,054,618,873	11.09	39,061	696	39	73	19	92	44.9	3.6	72	6.4	59.32	25.66
2002	3,062,140,575	9.74	37,398	699	41	75	18	93	40.5	3.6	85	7.0	77.85	37.45
2003	3,601,582,758	9.65	42,439	685	41	79	18	97	49.2	3.8	53	8.7	78.94	34.21
2004	7,666,772,817	9.91	45,466	670	42	79	19	98	38.2	5.9	56	8.3	82.71	38.10
2005	15,442,166,102	10.33	51,737	676	41	78	20	98	30.7	9.2	39	8.8	82.55	32.66
2006	27,790,038,804	10.30	54,528	696	40	74	20	93	27.0	9.0	31	8.8	61.18	30.23

Source: LoanPerformance.

EXHIBIT 3.10 Characteristics Associated with Poor Credit Performance: Subprime Seconds, 2006 Vintage

Purpose	Occupancy	Document	Original Amount	60+ Day	1 Mo.	2 Mo.	3 Mo.	FICO	FICO < 600	CLTV
Purchase	Owner	Low	7,054,307,151	23.82	6.00	4.78	19.18	667	1.33	99.7
Cash-out	Owner	Low	1,355,174,827	23.34	6.36	4.59	18.92	657	2.71	97.0
Purchase	Second home	Low	224,882,778	22.26	5.41	4.70	17.68	700	0.24	99.3
Refi	Owner	Low	157,367,146	20.16	6.02	5.08	15.25	663	1.42	97.3
Purchase	Owner	Full	5,224,972,430	16.32	5.36	3.54	12.88	637	18.60	99.7
Cash-out	Owner	Full	1,651,981,480	14.48	4.87	3.35	11.28	635	14.66	96.7
Refi	Owner	Full	287,077,362	11.52	4.24	2.69	8.97	637	17.24	97.3

Source: LoanPerformance.

similar to those in the traditional subprime sector—risk layering, including more low docs, more purchase loans, and more high CLTVs (via more silent seconds)—created a perfect credit storm for second liens, just as they did for traditional subprime first liens. Since seconds do not go into foreclosure, losses have risen faster in seconds than they did in firsts. That also means losses will level off faster than in firsts. However, for seconds in traditional subprime deals as well as in standalone deals, the sharp trajectory of 60-day delinquencies and losses in the first year point to unusually high losses on 2005 and 2006 vintages.

Mortgage Securitizations

Features of Excess Spread/ Overcollateralization: The Principle Subprime Structure

As discussed in earlier chapters, credit and prepayments are the two principal risks inherent in agency and nonagency *mortgage-backed securities* (MBS). Agency MBS have minimal credit risk (although in certain stressful situations even Freddie Mac and Fannie Mae's credit can become an issue). Relative value for those securities, therefore, centers on prepayment risk. In the nonagency market prepayment risk is also present, but as you go down the credit spectrum from prime, to Alt-A, to subprime credit becomes the most important risk element.

In order to maximize the value of a securitized pool of nonagency loans, issuers need to address those credit concerns. They do this by separating the cash flow from a pool of loans into individual tranches (securities) with credit ratings that start at AAA and go down to B or unrated. One could structure a nonagency pool of loans as a security that looks like an agency pass-through, with a single tranche and a single rating. However, the greatest value for a given pool of nonagency loans is extracted when the deal is structured with a series of bonds with a range of credit ratings. This allows investors with a wide range of credit preferences to participate in the deal, from conservatively managed institutions that require AAA securities to hedge funds and private equity funds that are looking for high-yield returns.

In the nonagency market two principal structures have evolved that create a series of bonds with a range of credit ratings (which maximize the value of the deal). Most low *weighted average coupon* (WAC), low-risk *prime* deals have a "six-pack" structure (so named for the three mezzanine and three subordinate bonds serving as support). Most high WAC, high-risk *subprime* deals utilize an excess spread/overcollateralization (XS/OC) structure. Historically, most Alt-A deals used a six-pack structure, but as that sector evolved to include more low FICO, high WAC loans, some Alt-A deals were structured using an *excess spread/overcollateralizaton* (XS/OC) approach. In this chapter, we focus on the salient features of the XS/OC structure, since we are mainly interested in subprime MBS and their derivatives, but we will make frequent reference to the six-pack structure as point of comparison and clarification.

EXCESS SPREAD-BASED CREDIT ENHANCEMENT

One fundamental of all mortgage products is that loans with higher default risk carry higher interest rates. Prime and Alt-A loans carry higher loan rates than agency collateral, while subprime loans have higher rates than prime and Alt-A loans. Within the subprime market, higher-risk loans have higher interest rates. Before we explore the details of how an XS/OC structure works, we first show the degree to which loan rates cover losses in different credit categories within the subprime market.

As we discussed in earlier chapters, the rate on a mortgage is very strongly determined by that loan's characteristics. We know that credit grade, *loan-to-value* (LTV) and loan size were among the most important parameters across the entire credit spectrum of mortgages. It is natural to expect a very strong connection between *off-market spread* (OMS), the difference between a pool's WAC and the prevailing prime mortgage rate when the pool's loans were originated, and the credit performance on a pool, since loan characteristics that determine WAC also strongly affect collateral losses.

In Exhibit 4.1, we show subprime cumulative losses as a function of the pools' OMS. Note the apparent groupings of loss curves: from 200 to 400 basis points of OMS; 500 and above basis points; 100 and below basis points.

The OMS on a pool directly conditions its profitability; a higher OMS means more interest cash flows. At the same time, this higher OMS also indicates greater losses. We performed a simple calculation to determine which effect dominated—losses or extra interest. Exhibit 4.2 shows our results for each OMS bucket. Column 2 shows average cumulative losses after five years of seasoning. Column 3 is the interest multiple over five years, derived from the average prepayment experience on each OMS bucket (in other words, the sum of monthly factors over five years, divided by 12). Column 4 is the OMS times the multiple, that is, the accumulated amount of additional interest paid over five years compared to an at-the-money mortgage. The final column is the difference between Columns 4 and 2, and shows, as a percentage of original balance, how much accumulated OMS remains once losses are covered.

EXHIBIT 4.1   Impact of Off-Market Spread on Losses (fixed rate, subprime collateral)

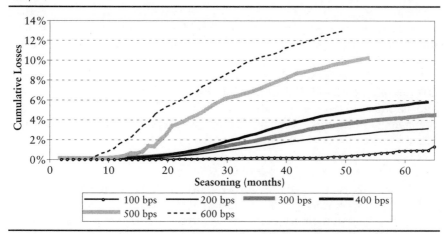

EXHIBIT 4.2   Profitability of HEL/Subprime Collateral, by Off-Market Spread

OMS (bps)	% Cum. Loss at Year 5	OMS Multiple up to Year 5	% Cum. Excess Spd. at Year 5	% Pickup
100	1.0	2.8	2.8	1.8
200	3.0	3.1	6.2	3.2
300	4.0	3.0	9.0	5.0
400	5.5	2.8	11.2	5.7
500	11.0	2.8	14.0	3.0
600	14.0	2.8	16.8	2.8

The analysis in Exhibit 4.2 tells us that all the OMS buckets are profitable, with the most profitable being in the 300 to 400 basis point OMS range. The low OMS bucket does not generate large pickups, because it is relatively close to the agency world (which is the basis of reference in our calculations). Nor does the high OMS bucket generate a large pickup, because it has significant losses associated with a relatively fast prepayment seasoning curve.

Excess Interest For Credit Enhancement

How can we turn the higher-than-average coupon on subprime mortgages into a credit enhancement? First, let's identify "excess interest." The excess interest is the difference between a deal's cost of funding (the coupon payments due on the bonds issued) and that deal's asset yield (the coupon paid by the collateral, less fees and expenses). In typical jumbo or Alt-A deals, using a "six-pack" structure available excess interest is typically monetized through an interest-only bond class. (We will discuss this in more detail later on.) In subprime deals, available excess interest is generally used as a first loss piece.

As we saw in Exhibit 4.2, cumulative off-market spread has, on average, compensated for cumulative losses. Exhibit 4.3A shows cumulative losses and cumulative excess spread for a typical subprime deal under several prepayment scenarios. Note that cumulative losses are lower than cumulative excess interest in all scenarios. As could be expected, fast prepayments decrease the amount of excess interest relative to the original balance, because they reduce the current balance.

However, what about current available interest versus current losses? Exhibit 4.3B shows the average evolution of monthly losses (relative to original balance) along with projected excess interest under the same prepayment scenarios. Implicitly, we assumed that losses would not be affected by prepayments—in other words, loans that will default are earmarked from the outset, and cannot prepay. In the fast prepayment scenario, the loss and excess interest curves intersect after about 2.5 years of seasoning, which means that from there on, current excess interest cannot compensate for losses.

Reserving Excess Spread For Future Losses

Now look at the available *excess spread*, which is equal to excess interest minus current losses because the result of that subtraction is what we can bank on to cover future losses. Exhibit 4.4 shows available excess spread (for several renditions of prepayments), and it is actually the difference between the three excess interest curves and heavy black current loss line in Exhibit 4.3. The shape of the curves in Exhibit 4.4 is fairly typical of available excess spread; it starts high (as excess interest is at its maximum then, thanks to a low cost of funding, a maximum pool balance and no current losses); then plummets quickly (as losses kick in and excess interest decreases). Note that a deal's cost of funding is likely to increase over time, as bonds paying the highest coupon are more likely to be paid last (because they are longer, or are subordinates). Also note that in the fast prepayment scenario, available excess spread actually becomes negative after 2.5 years.

Looking at this typical excess spread shape, the most obvious way to expand the protection provided by excess interest is to reserve some of it for those times when it is insufficient to cover losses. This protection can be provided either by building a cash reserve spread account or an overcollateralization account.

EXHIBIT 4.3   Typical Subprime Deal
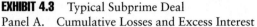

Panel A.   Cumulative Losses and Excess Interest

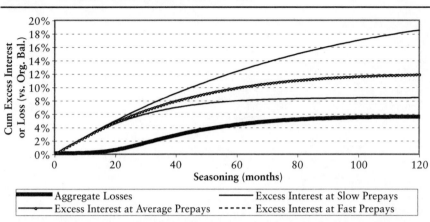

Panel B.   Current Losses and Excess Interest

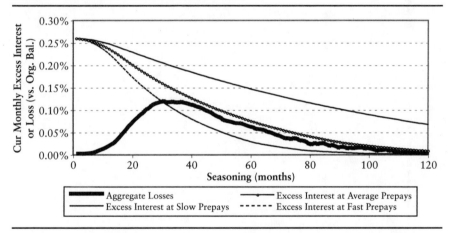

First, consider the case when the protection is a cash reserve account. Even though few recent subprime deals utilize a cash reserve account, historically it has been used frequently and we can use it to illustrate some key points in nonagency structures.

Exhibit 4.5 details the mechanism of reserving cash flows (to cover potential future losses) out of available excess spread. We show two cases: Case 1 has *fast* prepayment speeds, while Case 2 has *very fast* prepays (but both have the same loss levels). Early in the deal's life, all available excess spread is diverted to the reserve, until a certain target level is reached. In Case

EXHIBIT 4.4   Available Excess Spread

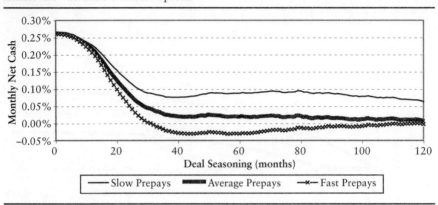

EXHIBIT 4.5   Reserving Cash Flows from Excess Spread against Future Losses

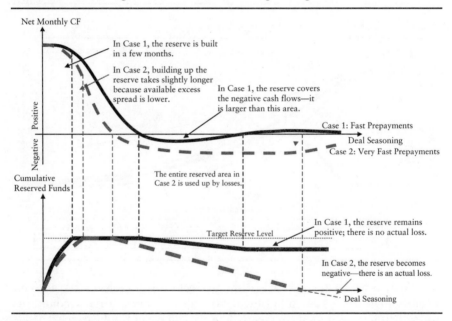

2, it takes a little longer than in Case 1 because the available excess spread declines faster. The bottom part of Exhibit 4.5 shows the amount stored in the reserve fund over time. After a while, available excess spread becomes negative because excess interest does not cover all current losses, but the reserve fund can be used to cover the residual loss. As shown in Exhibit 4.5, the reserve fund starts decreasing when available excess spread is negative.

In Case 1, available excess spread returns to being positive before all of the reserve fund is used up. In Case 2, available excess spread remains negative, and the entire reserve fund is depleted. Nevertheless, the reserve fund structure prevents losses from taking place early.

After excess interest has been used for credit enhancement, the remainder is typically distributed as a residual cash flow to the residual holder.

Triggers

Why not just reserve all available excess interest? Or why not push the target reserve level very high? The reason is simple: neither would be good for a deal's economics. High reserve levels reduce the value of residual cash flows, and raise the deal's cost of funding. Whether the remaining excess interest goes to an *interest-only* (IO) bond class or to the residual holder, it still represents a valuable stream of cash flows. So it does not make economic sense to pledge remaining excess interest entirely to credit enhancement. In general, target levels are determined with expected future losses in mind. Still, a situation such as that illustrated in Case 2 (Exhibit 4.5) should be avoided (that of a fair amount of excess spread being distributed to residuals, which could have been used later on to prevent losses).

In a deal structure, the difficult task of balancing cash flows between reserving too much or not having enough available excess spread is generally allocated to triggers. *Triggers* are thresholds for losses or delinquencies, and affect target reserve levels once they are hit. Triggers either increase the target reserve (step-ups), or prevent it from decreasing (step-downs). Triggers sometimes depend on the current credit support available in a deal, rather than on predetermined levels. That way they can better adjust actual credit enhancement, based on a deal's performance.

Deals often combine loss and delinquency triggers. As far as triggers are concerned, delinquencies are viewed as an early warning sign of future losses. For instance, go back to Case 2 in Exhibit 4.5. A step-up trigger based on current losses relative to the current balance could have been tripped by the pool factor dropping fast and the increasing current losses. The step-up would have raised the target reserve level, and available excess spread would have been diverted to the reserve fund, possibly in sufficient quantity to cover all future losses in Case 2.

Trigger mechanisms are designed to work in environments where losses evolve progressively. If losses increase more than had been anticipated at a deal's issuance, they are likely to be preceded by larger delinquencies. In that case, these triggers are hopefully able to divert sufficient excess spread toward the reserve, so that future losses will be covered.

EXHIBIT 4.6   Typical Evolution: OC Target and Actual OC

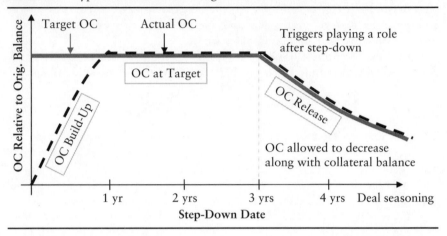

Note that triggers are often present in deals that do not use excess interest for credit enhancement. Instead, they affect the priority of principal payments across the bonds. For example, when a trigger is hit, bonds would be paid down in order of seniority, instead of pro rata.

In a typical deal using excess spread for credit enhancement (for example, through OC), triggers can only be activated after a specific point in time, called the step-down date. Exhibit 4.6 illustrates typical timing for the three phases in a deal with an XS/OC-based credit enhancement.

- The first phase is the build-up of the reserve (in this case, an OC build-up).
- In the second phase (after anywhere from a few months to one year, depending on the targeted reserve size relative to current excess spread), the OC target is reached.
- The third phase is OC release, conditional on various triggers not being hit (triggers generally have no impact on a deal before the step-down date).

In recent years many subprime deals used excess spread neither to build OC nor to build a reserve account, but rather to help provide cash flow to *net interest margin securities* (NIMs). NIMs are securities backed by the cash flow that normally would go to the residual holder. In the past several years, issuers found a ready market for these high-yielding products and it allowed them to monetize a large part of the residual risk they used to keep on their own balance sheets. Typically, when a NIM is included in a deal, the OC account is fully funded at origination (i.e. it is large enough to meet the rating agencies enhancement requirements). In that case, the dotted OC line in Exhibit 4.6, which shows a build up in OC, would start at the target OC level.

OC IN ALT-A-LAND

In the jumbo and Alt-A worlds, deals have traditionally been structured without excess spread because the strip of excess spread was generally too small to provide significant enhancement. With the broadening of the scope of the Alt-A market and the more frequent inclusion of loans with a relatively high off-market spread in Alt-A collateral, using excess spread for credit enhancement has started to make sense. A few recent deals were structured in this manner. Now see how the [Excess spread + OC] structure differs from a traditional senior-subordinated structure. A discussion of how an Alt-A XS/OC structure differs from an Alt-A "six-pack" structure can shed further light on low subprime XS/OC structures work.

Exhibit 4.7 shows a stylized view of classic nonagency senior-subordinated structure versus an excess spread-based structure. To the left of those two columns in Exhibit 4.7, we show principal and interest payments from the deal's collateral. In a traditional prime or Alt-A senior-subordinated structure, the principal is allocated amongst the senior tranches and the typical "six-pack" of mezzanine and subordinated bonds (ranging from AA all the way down to nonrated, with the nonrated tranche being the first loss position in the deal). Interest payments are distributed to the bonds, with the remainder often stripped as a WAC IO. The first loss piece is not rated because it is "guaranteed" to get hit by losses.

To understand the differences between these two structures, we need to ask, and answer, a few questions.

Out of the Same Collateral, How is an Excess Spread-OC Structure Built?

The main difference is that the IO portion in the traditional nonagency structures is, in fact, converted to a combination of [OC + Residuals]. Once interest on the bonds has been paid, then excess interest is allocated to build up OC, to cover losses, or it is paid out to the residual holders. Because the first loss piece is the residual (supported only by interest payments), all of the collateral's principal payments benefit from credit enhancement. The lowest-ranking bond therefore benefits from a rating (typically, a BBB). Note that relative sizing of the bonds in our chart is not realistic—more AAAs can be created in an excess spread OC structure, but not as many as the graph would suggest.

EXHIBIT 4.7   Senior-Subordinated Six-Pack versus Excess Spread/OC

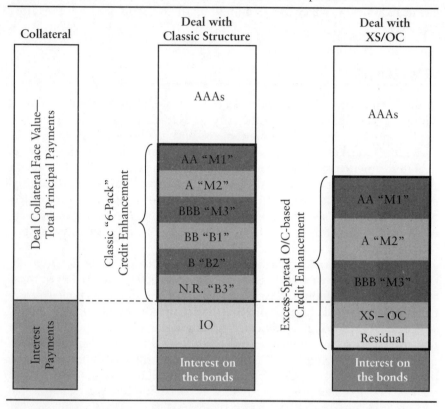

How Do the Cash Flows on the Bonds Differ Between the Traditional and OC-Based Credit Enhancements?

Exhibit 4.8 shows cash flows on two examples of Alt-A deals—(a) and (b) have OC, while (c) and (d) are traditional structure—and under two loss scenarios—(a) and (c) are baseline losses while (b) and (d) show increased losses. Start by comparing Exhibits 4.8A and 4.8C. In those baseline loss scenarios, the subordinated bonds are paid out mostly pro rata to more senior bonds. On the deal with OC, the step-down date is fixed at three years. At that step-down date, some principal payments are diverted to the subordinated bonds to maintain credit enhancement levels at their target levels, after which the bonds are paid pro rata (until the deal deleverages enough that the most junior bonds can be paid out). On the deal with a classic structure, the shifting interest locks out the mezzanine and subordinates from prepayments for five years, after which the bonds are paid pro rata according to the shifting interest schedule.

What if a Trigger Is Tripped?

Exhibits 4.8B and 4.8D show the cash flows when losses are increased such that a trigger is activated. On the deal with OC, the senior bonds are paid off entirely before the junior tranches get paid sequentially.

EXHIBIT 4.8 Cash Flows on Alt-A Deal Examples

Panel A. Residual and Principal Cash Flows on Alt-A Deal with OC: Baseline Losses

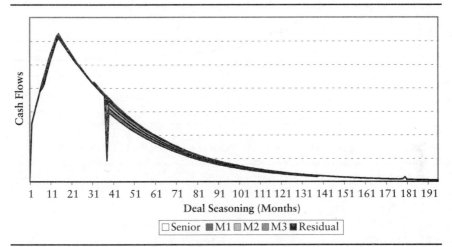

Panel B. Residual and Principal Cash Flows on Alt-A Deal with OC: Increased Losses

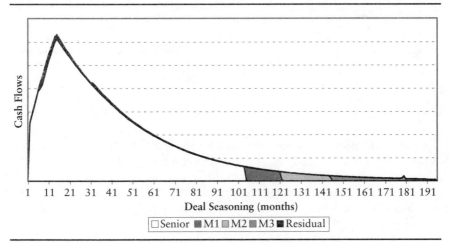

EXHIBIT 4.8 (Continued)

Panel C. Principal Cash Flows on Alt-A Deal with Six-Pack: Baseline Losses

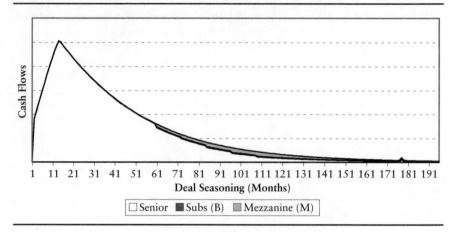

Panel D. Principal Cash Flows on Alt-A Deal with Six-Pack: Increased Losses

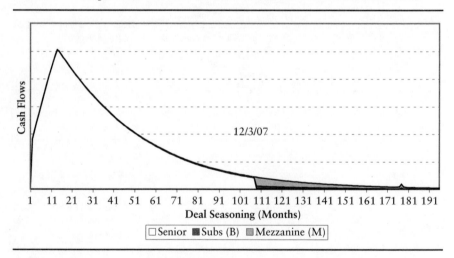

   The deal with a traditional structure also pays off the senior tranches almost entirely before paying the more junior bonds. (In our example, the very small strip of principal going to the senior bonds after the junior ones start getting paid is just a small *principal-only* (PO) tranche.) However, the six subordinated bonds are paid pro rata to each other, quite unlike the sequential tail in the case of the deal with OC.

EXHIBIT 4.9 Alt-A Collateral: Classic versus OC Structures

Tranche	WAL	Orig. Support	Max. Loss	Protection Increase
Deal with Classic Structure				
A1	0.2	8.0%	Large	Large
A2	6.0	8.0%	8.0%	0.0%
A3	9.0	8.0%	8.0%	0.0%
A4	1.2	8.0%	26.6%	18.6%
A5	1.2	8.0%	Large	Large
A6	3.5	8.0%	10.1%	2.1%
A7	1.2	8.0%	25.1%	17.1%
M1	9.4	5.5%	5.5%	0.0%
M2	9.4	3.5%	3.5%	0.0%
M3	9.4	2.1%	2.1%	0.0%
B1	9.4	1.5%	1.5%	0.0%
B2	9.4	1.1%	1.1%	0.0%
B3	4.7	0.0%	0.0%	0.0%
Deal with OC Structure				
A1	0.8	7.0%	Large	Large
A2	1.6	7.0%	59.5%	52.5%
A3	3.4	7.0%	21.0%	14.0%
A4	6.6	7.0%	9.0%	2.0%
M1	5.6	4.3%	6.6%	2.3%
M2	5.5	2.0%	4.5%	2.5%
M3	4.9	0.0%	2.6%	2.6%

Note: On the deal with OC, OC target is 0.75% of original bonds balance.

What Losses Can Both Structures Withstand?

Exhibit 4.9 shows for both deals we exampled in Exhibit 4.7, each tranche's average life, original support, and maximum collateral cumulative loss that the tranche can withstand. Let's focus on the *classic structure* deal first. In several instances, the maximum cumulative collateral loss the bond can withstand is larger than the original support. This happens when the bond is outstanding only for a relatively short period of time. The bond is paid out before the cumulative loss curve reaches its maximum. In the case of the deal with OC, the longest senior tranche (A4) can withstand 9% cumulative losses. Although the original senior support in the case of the classic structure is 8% (versus 7% for the OC structure), the deal with OC provides more protection (under our loss curve assumption). This pattern also applies to the *mezzanine bonds*. In the deal with OC, the mezzanine bonds have 0.5% to 1.0% greater effective protection compared to the corresponding tranches in the classic structure deal. Remember, that the measure of actual protection is dependent on the shape of the loss curve. In the very unlikely situation of losses jumping very high, very early on in the life of the deal, the OC structure would provide less protection than the traditional structure.

What About the Sensitivity to Prepayments on These Structures?

As illustrated earlier, prepayments significantly affect the amount of available excess spread in the deal if we keep losses fixed. Naturally, the [Excess spread + OC] structure suffers from faster-than-anticipated prepayments in that case. Exhibit 4.10 shows the maximum collateral loss until various bonds in our Alt-A deal with OC example incur a principal write-down, under three prepayment scenarios. *Fast prepays* clearly reduce the maximum collateral loss these tranches can withstand. At 150% of the baseline prepayment assumption, the actual support provided by the structure is still significantly higher than the original subordination ratios. However, fast prepayments drop this actual support down, approaching the original support on the sample deal without OC. In relative terms—credit enhancement on the most subordinated tranches is the most directional with respect to prepayments. Across the range of prepayment scenarios, we tested in Exhibit 4.10, Tranche A4's actual support ranges between 8% and 11%, versus a range of 1.5% to 4% for Tranche M3. Note that in Exhibit 4.10 we only show tranches with the longest payment windows.

The traditional senior/subordinated structure has a different exposure to prepayments. In terms of credit support, the reduction of excess interest due to fast prepays will not play any significant role. However, the shortening of all

EXHIBIT 4.10   Effect of Prepay Assumptions on Maximum Collateral Loss Until Principal Write-Down (deal with OC structure)

Tranche	Original Support	Prepayment Scenario		
		50%	100%	150%
A4	7.0%	10.8%	8.9%	8.2%
M1	4.3%	8.4%	6.4%	5.6%
M2	2.0%	6.3%	4.3%	3.4%
M3	0.0%	3.9%	2.1%	1.5%

Note: Loss curve assumption is relative to original balance.

collateral cash flows means that even the longest tranches might pay off a bit earlier and therefore be exposed to lower losses overall. The impact of prepayments on a traditional structure is more limited in magnitude and is actually in the reverse direction of the impact of prepayments on a structure with OC.

What Does OC Typically Change for Investors in Alt-A Securities?

- Mezzanine bonds are likely to have a shorter average life in an OC-based structure because of an earlier step-down. Also, the lowest-rated mezzanine bonds should be shorter than those with a higher rating if the deal deleverages fast enough (versus in a typical structure, mezzanine bonds are paid pro rata to each other).
- All else being equal, bonds in the OC structure are more likely to withstand higher collateral losses—assuming a reasonably shaped loss curve.
- Actual credit enhancement in the OC-based deal becomes more dependent on prepayments (which affect excess interest) and on the shape of the evolution of delinquencies and losses.

OC INTERNAL WORKINGS

In the previous section, we have focused on the use of excess interest as a tool for credit enhancement. In particular, we took a close look at structures based on excess spread and overcollateralization in the Alt-A market, since it allows a ready comparison to the traditional six-pack structure. In this final section we deal with the details of OC mechanisms, and analyze the conditions under which these mechanisms improve credit enhancement.

So far we have simplified our understanding of OC to something similar to a cash account. However, OC is naturally a bit more complicated than that. To understand how OC differs from an account with cash, look at Exhibit 4.11.

In the case of a spread account/reserve fund, the deal's collateral face value corresponds to the bonds' face value. Every dollar of principal received from the collateral is used to pay principal due on the bonds. Shortfalls (i.e., losses) are covered by excess spread, then by reserves, and finally by write-downs on the bonds. Cash flows from excess interest are used to build the reserve fund, which corresponds to credit enhancement. The reserve fund will help absorb future losses. If there are more current losses than excess interest, then uncovered losses will be paid with reserve fund monies.

In the case of a deal with OC, the deal's collateral face value is larger than the bonds' face value. The difference is overcollateralization. Excess

EXHIBIT 4.11   Overcollateralization versus Reserve Fund

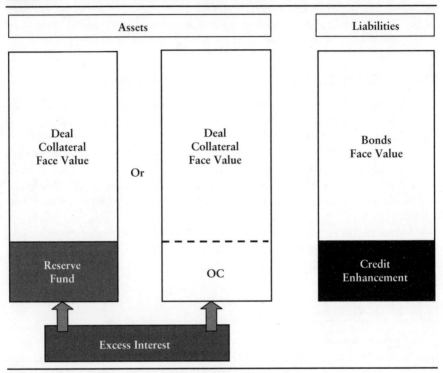

interest cannot be contributed to OC directly because OC is not a cash account. Nor can the deal collateral be changed over time. Instead, OC is increased by paying off the bonds' principal. When OC is being built up early in the life of a deal, the available excess spread is "converted" into principal, and used to accelerate payment of the bonds (following the principal waterfall at that time). Note that early in a typical deal's life, only the senior tranches receive significant amounts of principal. After the step-down date, OC is released by diverting principal payments from the bonds to the residuals. At any point in time, if excess interest drops below current losses, then OC is reduced (because the collateral balance decreases faster than the bonds' balance) and the loss amount is written down from the OC. In effect, OC decreases when the face value of the bonds is not allowed to, or cannot, drop in tandem with the collateral's face value.

Note that current losses are covered, up to [Current excess interest + Current amount of OC]. If losses prove larger than that, they would not be entirely covered, and the lowest bonds in the principal waterfall would advance the amount of the loss (as a write-down that could potentially be recovered). OC therefore differs from a straight cash account in that it affects principal distribution to the bonds. In an OC structure, excess interest is used to advance principal payments to the bonds. And when that excess interest has to be paid back during the OC release, then principal payments to the bonds are delayed.

One might wonder if it is worth setting up a complex structure, when a reserve fund or spread account is much simpler? Indeed, overcollateralization largely dominates other ways of using excess spread for credit enhancement. An OC structure is similar to investing the reserve fund into the deal's collateral, which means that it generates more cash flows for the residuals, all else being equal. When excess interest is diverted to a cash account, it has to be kept very safe, and cannot be invested in high-yielding securities. In the case of the OC structure, paying principal to the bonds reduces the deal's cost of funding (less coupons to pay to the bonds) and makes more excess interest available for residual holders. In other words, a reserve is reinvested in low interest rates securities, while OC is invested at the collateral rate.

OC and Principal Waterfall

When OC is initially building up, principal cash flows are typically channeled to senior tranches (as mentioned earlier). When the deal's performance is good and no triggers are tripped, OC starts being released after the step-down date. Releasing OC means that a portion of collateral principal payments that would otherwise go to the bonds instead goes to residual holders.

Simultaneously, the principal waterfall on the deal is also usually affected by the triggers. In a typical subprime deal, once the step-down date has been reached (and if no trigger has been tripped), then fast prepayments can accelerate payments to the most junior tranches. Indeed, if a deal deleverages very fast, then principal payments might be allocated to OC and to the most junior tranches to realign their current balances with the deal's post-step-down target support levels.

The way principal payment is impacted in a subprime deal after step-down is different from the so-called "shifting interest" structure used in typical jumbo or Alt-A senior/subordinated structures. Under those structures, subordinated bonds are locked out from principal payments (or sometimes from nonscheduled payments, which constitute most of principal payments), until the share of principal they can get is increased progressively (from a small percentage up to the full pro rata). *Shifting interest* refers to this share that changes over time. There are triggers in these traditional, nonagency deals preventing principal from being distributed to the subordinated bonds when losses or delinquencies are above a certain level. However, the subordinated bonds in a typical jumbo or Alt-A deal are locked out for 5 to 10 years, versus three years for typical subprime deals. Besides, the credit support levels are not typically decreased, even if they have increased significantly because of fast prepayments.

To illustrate how the principal waterfall evolves in parallel with OC, we looked at a typical subprime deal. We focused on the floating rate part of the deal, whose principal cash flows are shown in Exhibit 4.12 under three scenarios: baseline prepayments and losses; increased losses; and slow prepayments/low losses.

In the base scenario shown in Exhibit 4.12A, we can see that residual cash flows briefly stop after a few months of seasoning. Indeed, they are all allocated to the senior tranches as OC is being built up. In fact, this deal has an "OC holiday"; excess spread partially flows to the residuals for a few months before being diverted to build up OC. Since losses are very unlikely to occur so early in a deal's life, delaying OC build-up does not impact credit enhancement significantly. However, it allows residual holders to get cash flows very early on, which improves the typical negative cash flow situation of issuers. OC holidays, or prefunding OC, are essential tools in allowing the creation of NIMs. At the step-down date, after three years of seasoning, OC starts getting released, which slightly slows down principal payments to the bonds. We also see that principal stops flowing to the senior tranches for a few months, while principal priority is reversed on the subordinates. As the deal is performing well and no trigger has been hit, the current support level is allowed to decrease down to its post step-down target, where it hence remains. This is achieved by allocating just enough principal to the most senior tranches to maintain credit enhancement targets. Right at the step-down date, fast prepayments have deleveraged the deal so fast—that all the mezzanine bonds need to be paid some additional principal. The most junior one (M3) first receives all the principal; then M2; and then finally M1.

What happens if losses are much stronger than expected? In this case, Exhibit 4.12B shows us that the strip of residual cash flows stops early in the life of the deal. It is all used up to cover losses or to refill the overcollateralization used to cover the losses. Note that in our example, the most junior mezzanine bond is briefly paid some principal at the step-down date. Indeed, the deal is overenhanced at that point; however a trigger is tripped right after the step-down date. As soon as the trigger is in place, OC cannot be released. Besides, the bonds are paid sequentially by seniority.

In the third case, shown in Exhibit 4.12C, prepayments are very slow and losses are low. Residual cash flows are naturally large, but credit support in the deal does not increase very strongly due to the slow prepayments. Consequently, we do not observe large payments to the mezzanine bonds right after the step-down date. Instead, all bonds are paid pro rata directly afterwards.

EXHIBIT 4.12 Residual and Principal Cash Flows on Floater Tranches
Panel A. Baseline Prepay and Losses

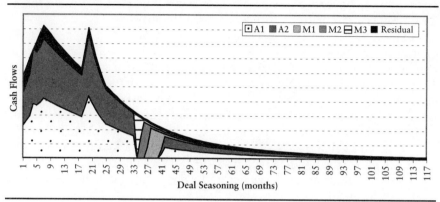

Panel B. Increased Losses

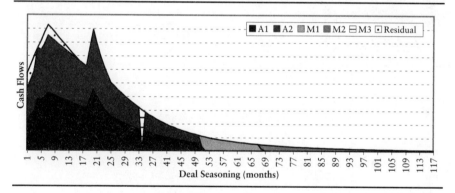

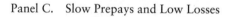

Panel C. Slow Prepays and Low Losses

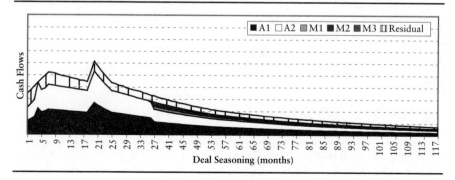

How Much Does OC Improve Credit Enhancement?

To find out by how much credit enhancement is improved by OC on top of the original subordination ratio, we stressed the structure.

Exhibit 4.13 shows the calculation for two groups in a subprime deal; a fixed and a floater (the floating rate group is the same as that shown in Exhibit 4.12). Column 3 in the exhibit shows the original supports. Column 4 is the maximum total collateral cumulative loss until the tranche suffers a loss (reached by progressively increasing a baseline loss curve, and assuming a fixed prepayment speed). Finally, Column 5 is the protection increase due in part to OC. Let's focus first on the subordinate bonds (M1, M2, M3). The maximum collateral loss before the bonds take a loss is between 6% and 8.5% above the bonds' original support, which illustrates that OC provides a very significant improvement to the deal's credit enhancement (even though the original OC target is only 0.50%).

EXHIBIT 4.13 Effect of Tranche Payment Window on Maximum Loss Until Principal Write-Down

Tranche	WAL	Orig. Support	Max. Loss	Protection Increase
Fixed				
A1	1.0	10.5%	37.8%	27.3%
A2	2.0	10.5%	31.2%	20.7%
A3	2.6	10.5%	25.5%	15.0%
A4	4.0	10.5%	19.7%	9.2%
A5	6.1	10.5%	15.9%	5.4%
A6	5.6	10.5%	15.8%	5.3%
M1	6.5	6.0%	12.1%	6.1%
M2	7.5	2.5%	9.6%	7.1%
M3	8.0	0.0%	8.5%	8.5%
Floating				
A1	2.1	10.5%	13.6%	3.1%
A2	2.1	10.5%	13.6%	3.1%
M1	4.1	6.0%	12.9%	6.9%
M2	3.9	2.5%	9.4%	6.9%
M3	3.4	0.0%	6.5%	6.5%

Note: Subprime deal with excess-spread OC structure. OC target is 0.5% of original bonds balance.

EXHIBIT 4.14 Effect of Loss Curve on Maximum Loss Until Principal Write-Down[a]

Tranche	Orig. Support	Max. Loss	Max. Loss, Steeper Curve
A	11.19%	15.94%	16.55%
M1	6.97%	11.97%	12.70%
M2	3.41%	8.35%	9.20%
M3	0.76%	5.32%	6.25%

[a] Subprime deal with excess spread OC structure and reserve fund.
Note: OC target is 0.75% of original bonds balance.

If we now look at the senior tranches, we see that on the floating rate side, OC improves credit enhancement by about 3%. On the fixed rate side, some tranches can withstand very large amounts of collateral losses before getting hit. In fact, these very high actual credit enhancement levels are misleading because they depend on the shape of the loss curve assumption. Indeed, short tranches having a small payment window are exposed to only a fraction of all the cumulated losses that will hit the collateral (depending on how losses ramp up). When keeping constant the cumulative losses on collateral, then longer tranches are likely to suffer a loss. On the fixed rate side in our example, the longest tranches (A5 and A6, with credit enhancement increases of about 5.4%) represent most accurately the amount of protection provided by OC.

The effect of the loss curve's shape on the measure of protection provided by OC can be counter intuitive, due to triggers. To illustrate this, we took another subprime deal, and followed the same approach as in Exhibit 4.9, with our results shown in Exhibit 4.14. Column 2 is the original support, while Column 3 shows actual supports calculated by stressing the loss curve. The pickups in protection (not shown in the table) range from 3% to 5%. Column 4 shows the actual support calculated by stressing a different baseline loss curve. The amount of protection in this case is actually larger than that of our original loss curve by about 1%.

However, the new curve is steeper than the original, and hits maximum current losses a little over a year earlier—so how do the bonds turn out to be better protected? The answer lies in the triggers. As current (and cumulative) losses rose earlier, they set off a loss trigger which prevented OC from being released, and therefore increased credit enhancement. Besides, even though these losses were steeper than before, they still were not larger than current available excess spread before the step-down date. Note that if we pushed the loss curve to the extreme, and jumped to its maximum level from the outset, then OC would not have sufficient time to build up and losses would hit the bonds early.

SUMMARY

In this chapter we have examined the salient features of the XS/OC structure used on most subprime securities since 1998. As the discussion in this chapter illustrates the cash flow for a bond from a deal using XS/OC is not straightforward. It is significantly more complex than the traditional "six-pack" structure. Even a small change in the prepayment or default rate can cause a major shift in cash flows which in turn can have a major impact on valuations. For example a slight change in a deal's delinquency rate could trip a trigger thereby altering the cash flow for all of the bonds in the deal. In the next chapter we will discuss triggers in detail and the large role they play in XS/OC deals.

The complexity of an XS/OC structure was exposed by the meltdown of the subprime industry. These structures accomplish the objective of shifting cash flow to more senior tranches if a deal is not performing well, but these features and their impacts on bond values are not intuitive and often confusing. This has made it difficult for institutions holding these securities to value them properly and this has contributed to the freezing up of the credit markets. The rating agencies have proposed several modifications to the XS/OC structure, but until the subprime market recovers it seems unlikely that any of these will be adopted by the industry. In the meantime, analysts and investors concerned about how the $700 billion of outstanding subprime securities should be valued will have to master the concepts described in this chapter.

CHAPTER 5

Subprime Triggers and Step-Downs

In this chapter, we review the basics of subprime triggers and step-downs, two distinguishing features of the *excess spread/overcollateralization* (XS/OC) structure. We also review the last few vintages of subprime deals that passed their step-down dates, and summarize the effect of the step-down and associated triggers on those deals.

THE STEP-DOWN AND THE TRIGGER

Almost all subprime deals contain a step-down provision. *Step-down* refers to conversion of deal structure from sequential pay to pro rata pay. There are three direct implications of the step-down:

1. End of principal lockout for all bonds below AAA (the mezzanine, subordinated, and OC tranches).
2. Reduction of subordination to poststep-down target levels.
3. Release of principal to all mezzanine, subordinated, and OC tranches (OC release).

While the terms *subordinated* (sub) and *mezzanine* (mezz) have no standard definition, in this chapter we refer to all investment grade support bonds below AAA as mezzanine bonds and all noninvestment grade support bonds below AAA as subordinated bonds.

In the first 36 months (the "lockout period"), all tranches other than the seniors are locked out and do not receive principal payments (unless the seniors have paid down completely, which we discuss here). By the step-down date (almost universally set 37 months from the deal's closing date), the deal collateral is sufficiently seasoned that its performance may be tested. If the aggregate collateral performance is satisfactory (the loans exhibiting a low percentage of cumulative losses and serious delinquencies) the deal is permitted to step-down.

The trigger defines the collateral tests. Typically there are two triggers in the subprime deal, one testing the deal's cumulative losses against an upward-sloping loss schedule, a second testing 60+-day delinquencies. The delinquency trigger comes in one of two flavors: a *hard/static* trigger comparing delinquencies against a static threshold, and a *soft/dynamic* trigger for delinquencies against a threshold computed based on the percent of senior subordination.

The deal steps down only if all triggers pass. As a matter of terminology, a trigger "failing" is equivalent to it being "in effect" or "tripped." Triggers are tested monthly, and may switch back and forth between pass and fail.

What is the purpose of the step-down? The step-down improves the economics of the deal by making the mezzanine/subordinated bonds more attractive. The step-down brings the beginning of the payment window of the mezzanine/subordinated bonds in from several years to 37 months, and can halve the average life of a BBB– compared to a sequential pay structure. All of this can help reduce the needed margins or coupons of the mezzanine/subordinated bonds, which reduces the cost of funding for the deal.

What is the purpose of the trigger? The trigger allows the deal structure to behave like two structures; a "Dr. Jekyll" mode for well-performing collateral, and a "Mr. Hyde" mode for poorly performing collateral. At any given period after step-down, the triggers determine which mode is in effect.

In Exhibit 5.1, we ran a sample subprime deal with pricing speeds and our historical loss assumption curve.[1] The exhibit shows the tranche current balances as a percentage of deal current balances from deal origination to month 120. The tranches are ordered on the diagram by seniority, with most senior bonds on top, so the amount of subordination at any period can be visualized as the distance to the floor (horizontal axis). The AAA bonds (tranches beginning with "A" in Exhibit 5.1) have equal seniority, and from a credit perspective should be regarded as a single tranche even though they pay sequentially. At any given period, only the tranche at the very bottom is exposed to write-downs. In the example shown in Exhibit 5.1, only the OC tranche (called SB) takes write-downs.

The 100% level of the graph denotes the entire current loan balance, which amortizes over time. Bonds not paying principal (such as mezzanine and subordinated bonds prior to month 37) will have a constant dollar versus a declining balance, and therefore grow in thickness over time. Bonds paying pro rata will exhibit a constant thickness (M1 through M9 from months 51 through 76.) Bonds paying sequentially will narrow over time (during the lockout period AII, or the sequential AAA group: AI1, AI2, AI3, and then AI4).

---

[1] Deal is RASC 2006-KS3 (included in ABX.HE 06-2), running as of pricing 3/29/2006, with pricing speeds (100 PPC ARM, 23 HEP FRM) and 130% of UBS Historical Estimate Loss Curve (described in "Subprime Break Points—It's *ALL* in The Assumptions," *UBS Mortgaqe Strategist,* October 31, 2007).

EXHIBIT 5.1 Tranche Balances/Credit Support in Step-Down

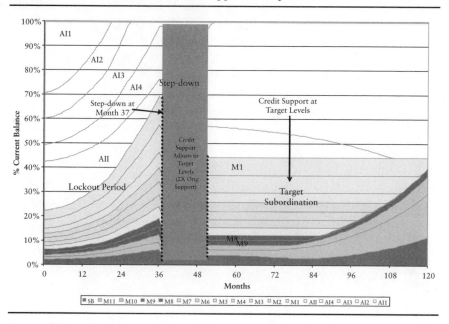

Source: UBS and Intex.

During the lockout period, subordination increases dramatically; bonds move farther from the floor. At step-down, subordination is reduced, and tranches move closer to the floor. In Exhibit 5.1, the deal steps down in month 37.

When the deal steps down, it reduces excess subordination levels by releasing OC (which we discuss). Once the poststep-down target subordination levels have been reached, the deal pays principal to all tranches (senior, mezzanine, subordinated, and OC) pro rata. The pro rata payment and target subordination levels are evident by the plateaus in Exhibit 5.1 after the step-down.

If the deal fails to step-down, the deal becomes a sequential pay structure, and principal continues to be directed to the seniors. Exhibit 5.2 shows the deal run with the same assumptions as in Exhibit 5.1, except step-down does *not* occur. In this case, we see subordination consistently increase for all tranches. This mode provides the greatest credit protection to the senior interests, and is appropriate for adverse credit.

Credit Support

The "Titanic model" of credit structure compares the level of credit support in a deal with the decks of an ocean liner. Support on the Titanic followed

EXHIBIT 5.2 Tranche Balances/Credit Support without Step-Down

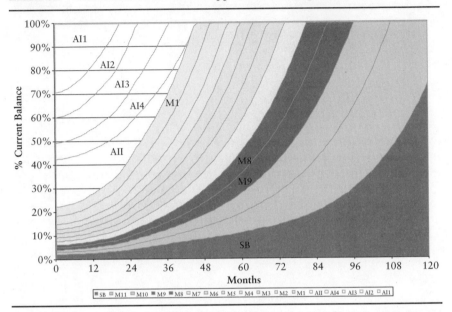

Source: UBS and Intex.

seniority: First-class suites occupied A–D decks (the top four decks); second-class staterooms occupied E deck; third-class berths filled the F and lower decks. A passenger on E deck would expect to stay dry until the F deck below was completely under water. In such a model, one would expect a tranche to be susceptible to a write-down if and only if every tranche below it in subordination were completely written down. In a sequential pay deal, this is in fact quite true. Losses flood the structure from the bottom, and principal is paid out through the top of the structure (with first-class passengers grabbing the lifeboats first).

How is the amount of credit support set? Using collateral characteristics and deal features, the rating agencies determine the amount of original credit support needed for every rated tranche in a deal. Credit support for a tranche M is measured as the balance of all tranches below M as a percentage of the deal's balance. As an example, a BBB– bond might have 4.10% of original credit support (the aggregate balance of all tranches below the BBB– make up 4.10% of the deal), while an AAA tranche might have 22.25% original credit support. (See Exhibit 5.3, where the AII class represents the AAA tranche and the M9 class represents the BBB– bond.) The 4.10% of credit support means that losses would need to eat through 4.10% of the deal's balance before the BBB– bond began to suffer write-downs. Credit support at deal issuance is called the *original support*, and support at any given period based on current balances is referred to as the *current support*.

Current support is a percent of the current deal balance; as the deal amortizes, the dollar amount will shrink over time. Contrast this with cum loss that is a percent of original balance. Can we say that an 8.20% cumulative loss will likely write-down a tranche with 8.20% current support? Not really. 8.20% of our sample deal's original balance is $94 million. The tranche started off with 4.10% of original support, or $47 million. Using our pricing assumptions, we generate cash flows and find the deal's excess interest totals $86 million. Furthermore, by period 31, losses exceed the 2.250% trigger threshold and the cum loss trigger fails, preventing the deal from stepping down. Therefore, $47 + $86 = $133 million is available as subordination to the BBB–, against $94 million in projected losses. The losses absorb all excess interest, all of the OC and BB tranches, and partially write-down the BB+ tranche. The BBB– is unscathed in this case. However, changes in prepayment assumptions, or the shape of the default curve, could have changed the outcome. Suffice it to say that 8.20% cumulative loss and 8.20% current subordination are not directly comparable.

EXHIBIT 5.3   Target Credit Support

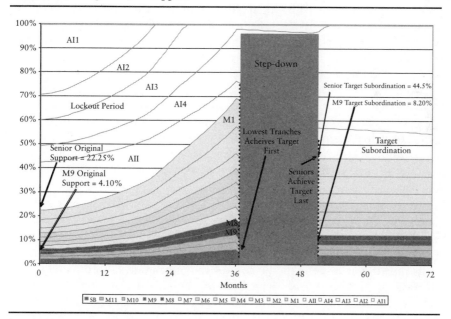

Source: UBS and Intex.

The other observation we can make regarding credit support measures is that the current support percentage includes subordination and over collateralization, but does not take excess spread into account.

At step-down, credit support across the entire capital structure is higher than at deal issuance, and often many times higher. This is due partially to the principal pay-down of seniors (factors for seniors prior to step-down average 3% to 4% for 2002 and 2003, and half of the seniors are completely paid down by step-down). In addition, subprime deals utilize excess spread (excess interest net of losses) to pay down principal, thus speeding up senior pay downs. Poststep-down, a target level of subordination is prescribed for all tranches, which is typically double their original subordination. For our BBB– example, the poststep-down credit support will be 8.20% (2× the 4.10% original support). This is typically much less than the current subordination in the deal immediately prior to step-down, which averaged 16% for BBB/BBB– bonds.

The process of transforming the deal from being overly credit-enhanced to the target (2× original) level of support is referred to as *releasing* OC. The process of releasing OC progresses from the bottom of the capital structure and works upwards. At each tranche level, the reduction of current balance is effected by making a principal payment to the bondholder. For example, if the BBB– in our example were supported by a single OC tranche providing 16% of support to the BBB–, then half of that balance would be paid out as principal to the holder of the OC piece, thus reducing the balance (and support) to 8% (the target amount). The BBB– would then reduce its balance to provide the ideal level of support to the BBB bond it supports, and so on. OC release typically takes several payment periods, as balances may be drawn down as principal only as fast as collateral cash flow comes into the deal. The OC release and support adjustment is a bit unusual, as payments are made in reverse priority relative to seniority. In fact, during OC release, senior principal payments are completely suspended.

Exhibit 5.4 shows our sample deal releasing OC. The exhibit is normalized so that each cash flow is shown as a percent of original tranche balance.

BBB STACK (ON THE KNIFE'S EDGE)

The BBB stack (BBB+, BBB, BBB–) is structurally significant, mainly because of its position at or near the bottom of the mezzanine/subordinated stack. Historically, subprime losses have been low enough that mostly OC tranches have experienced write-downs. However, as losses rise and approach the threshold of hitting the BBB stack, the trigger will have an important effect on the BBB/BBB– bondholders. Potential mezzanine/subordinated write-

EXHIBIT 5.4   Releasing OC: Mezzanine Bonds and OC Release Principal at Step-Down

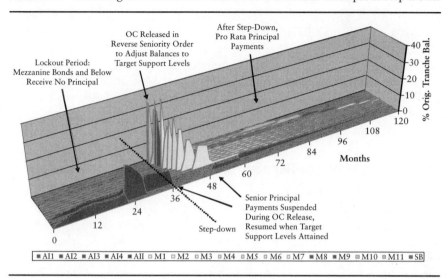

Source: UBS and Intex.

downs would happen years after the step-down test, thus the trigger's duty is to make a decision at the step-down date about reserving subordination today against future losses.

Given the challenging HPA environment, losses are expected to reach levels where many BBB+/BBB/BBB– bonds and even bonds higher in the capital structure will likely be written down. As the *loss waterline* rises, its effect on a particular tranche changes as the tranche becomes further "under water." In the following section, we discuss how this effect impacts the BBB and BBB– bonds in our sample deal.

EFFECT OF TRIGGERS AND THE LOSS WATERLINE

BBB/BBB– Below the Waterline

If losses are sufficiently high that the BBB has an expected loss of 100%, its interests become allied with the OC piece. When the BBB is deeply under water, a step-down is always desirable. In the most extreme example of this case, half (based on 2000–2004 historical experience) the BBB principal is paid at step-down and the remainder soon written down by high losses. The wrinkle is that losses of that magnitude are likely to trip the cumulative loss trigger and prevent the deal from stepping down.

BBB/BBB– Is "High and Dry" above the Waterline

In a low-loss scenario, a step-down is also desirable because of the early principal payment, and since the reduction of credit support does not materially increase the probability of write-down. The BBB's payment window and average life are significantly shorter when a deal steps down. In this case, the BBB's interests lay with the senior-most Mezzanine tranches. (The BBB can never properly be thought of as aligned with the AAA, since structurally the AAA enjoys special treatment, such as exclusive principal payment during the lockout period.)

BBB/BBB– Is at or near the Waterline

In a moderately high-loss scenario, a step-down may not be desirable because although the bond will receive principal at the step-down, so will the subordinate piece, therefore lowering the credit subordination of the remaining balance and increasing the probability of default. Another way of looking at this scenario is that principal is paid off to the OC holder, which can never be reclaimed for use as protection against future losses. In the nonstepped-down case, principal is only paid to bonds above the BBB stack, preserving its cash subordination. Even if a write-down never happens, a step-down in combination with realized losses could erode current support to the point of a ratings downgrade.

SAMPLING THE SUBPRIME UNIVERSE

To examine the effects of triggers and step-downs, we selected recent vintage deals which have stepped down and which meet the characteristics of the "plain-Jane" nonwrapped subprime deal. Using complete vintages past their step-down dates means restricting ourselves to 2003 and prior deals. We want deals with BBB or BBB– mezzanine bonds and those with step-down triggers. We would also like to exclude bonds that are reverse turbo, or do not pay in accordance with the rest of the mezzanine structure; restricting ourselves to the Intex "MEZ" bond type approximates this latter requirement. In the end, we are left with 250 subprime deals meeting our criteria, with either a BBB or BBB– mezzanine bond.

2000–2003 DEAL STEP-DOWN SUMMARY

The first order of business is to determine how often triggers pass, at what month they pass if they do, and deal condition at step-down. Exhibit 5.5

EXHIBIT 5.5   2000–2003 Deal Step-Downs

Vintage	Deals	% Deals Stepped Down	Avg. Step-Down Months	Deal Factor	AAA Factor	Seniors Paid Down by Step-Down
2000	8	75%	38.8	0.2338	0.1374	0%
2001	14	71%	35.5	0.2691	0.0857	50%
2002	68	85%	36.2	0.1690	0.0267	53%
2003	160	90%	35.5	0.1852	0.0374	53%
	250	87%	35.8	0.1871	0.0404	51%

Source: UBS and Intex.

shows aggregate step-down statistics. Deal structures containing BBB/BBB– mezzanine bonds have become far more popular post-2001, reflecting a move away from monoline wrap deals (no mezzanine/subordinated bonds) in favor of senior/subordinated structures.

Historically, deals are much more likely to step-down than never to step-down. In 2001 (worst vintage of our sample), two thirds of the deals stepped down, and overall, more than 80% of deals in our sample passed their triggers. Of the deals that stepped down, the average months to step-down has been dropping, averaging more than 36 months.[2]

The second notable statistic is that 50% of the deals completely paid off the seniors prior to stepping down. In many (but not all) structures, a step-down may take place immediately upon the retirement of the senior tranches. Note that not only will the lockout period contribute to the early retirement of the seniors, but excess spread also accelerates AAA paydowns.

Exhibit 5.6 Panels A–D show that while 37-month step-downs dominate, there's greater frequency of early step-downs in later vintages. In 2000–2001 only a handful stepped down prior to the step-down date. In 2002 and 2003 deals, a good number of deals stepped down in the 29- to 36-month range. That's due to fast prepays; paid-down seniors is the only way to step-down prior to month 37.

STEP-DOWN AND CREDIT EFFECTS

The step-down reduces both principal balance of the BBB/BBB– tranche and the subordination it enjoys. Exhibit 5.7 shows for each vintage the percent

---

[2] Note that 87% of step-down triggers passing does not equal to 13% failing. Many deals pass at step-down, but fail subsequently. A deal may even pass again at a later point. The first step-down is the most critical; it's the point at which the most extra subordination has been built up, and will be released as principal.

EXHIBIT 5.6   Step-Downs
Panel A.   2000 Step-Downs

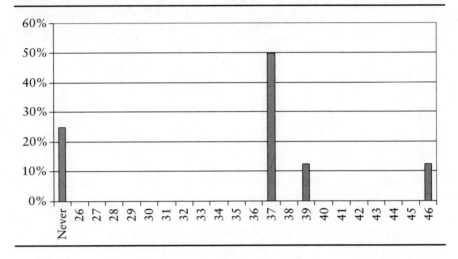

Panel B.   2001 Step-Downs

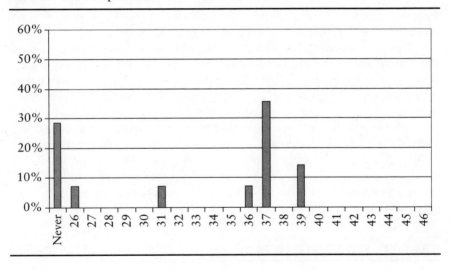

EXHIBIT 5.6 (Continued)
Panel C.   2002 Step-Downs

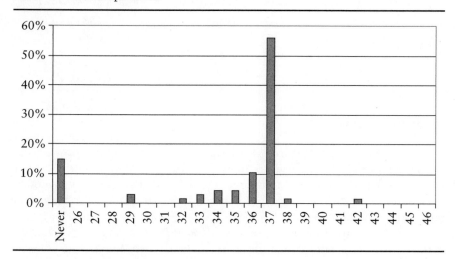

Panel D.   2003 Step-Downs

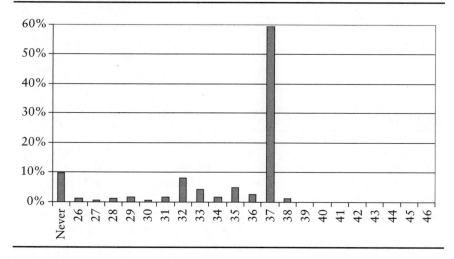

Source: UBS and Intex.

EXHIBIT 5.7   Step-Down Effects: Balance and Credit Support

Vintage	Loss of Subordination	Principal Pay-Down
2000	0.2136	0.5345
2001	0.0448	0.2761
2002	0.3871	0.6936
2003	0.2855	0.5247
	0.2974	0.5570

Source: UBS and Intex.

of current balance paid to the BBB bondholder as principal following the step-down (6 months is given, to allow OC release to trickle up the capital structure). This is compared to the reduction in credit support. On average, the amount of credit support lost is much less than principal returned in most years (the ratio is 1:2).

To the investor long the cash bond, the step-down statistics are reassuring. There is a high probability the deal will step-down, and when it does, a large amount of principal is released to the BBB/BBB– holder, with a relatively smaller reduction in credit support. This caps the amount of write-downs to the balance left after OC release.

But to the investor using the synthetic as a pure play to short the housing market, the step-down is problematic. It reduces the notional amount to half (based on historical averages), so even if the reference security experiences a write-down, the relative return will be proportionally diminished.

SUMMARY

We have summarized the rationale and mechanics of triggers and step-downs, and their effect on credit subordination principal cash flows. We've also looked at recent available vintages, and determined that 85% of these deals stepped down (most on the step-down date), and half had paid down the AAAs by step-down. When the deals did step-down, they released, on average, half of their principal and gave up 30% of their current subordination to reach target levels. This is good news to the BBB investor if his deal does in fact step-down. However, with delinquencies and losses expected to run well above historical norms, most subprime deals from 2006 and 2007 are likely to fail their triggers.

PART Three

Credit Default Swaps on Mortgage Securities

CHAPTER 6

Introduction to Credit Default Swap on ABS CDS

Credit default swaps (CDS) on ABS have been around since at least 1998. The motivation back then was to provide synthetic assets to ABS CDOs; instead of buying cash bonds, the CDO took on the risk of referenced ABS assets by selling credit protection via credit default swaps. Documentation at that time was nonstandard, one-off, and closely based on corporate CDS templates. As subprime securitization production increased, dealers wanted a means to hedge their warehouse risk while subprime mortgages were being aggregated for securitization. At the same time, hedge funds became interested in shorting subprime mortgage risk. The *dealer template* for transacting credit default swaps on ABS was first published in June 2005 and the *user* or *monoline* template followed soon after. A comparison of these ABS CDS forms, and their differences to corporate CDS, provides insight into the credit issues underlying ABS CDS. We discuss the evolution of ABS CDS in this chapter and show how it allowed the ABS CDO market to grow so big so fast in 2006. We begin by giving enough of an overview of the terms, structure, and advantages of corporate CDS to help clarify issues in ABS CDS.

CORPORATE CDS FUNDAMENTALS AND TERMINOLOGY

The dramatis personae of a corporate CDS are: a *credit protection buyer*, a *credit protection seller*, a *reference obligor,* and *reference obligations.* These parties are tied together by *notional amount, credit events, physical settlement,* and *cash settlement.*

The protection buyer buys credit protection from the protection seller in a dollar-amount size called the "notional amount." The protection buyer pays the protection seller a fee, which is based on a number of basis points a year times the notional amount. This fee, or premium, is paid by the protection buyer quarterly for the life of the CDS. The most liquid CDS maturity is five years.

EXHIBIT 6.1 Credit Default Swap Payment Flows

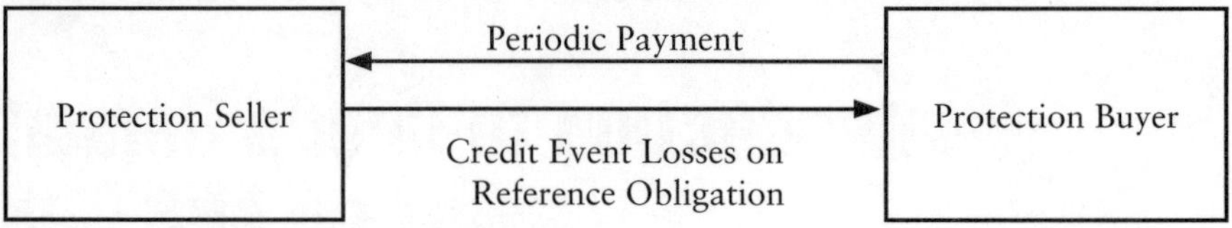

A reference obligor *credit event*, should it occur, triggers a payment from the protection seller to the protection buyer. Basically, a credit event is a bad thing that happens to the reference obligor, such as the reference obligor filing for bankruptcy. The payment from the protection seller to the protection buyer is effected in one of two ways:

1. In *physical delivery*, the protection buyer selects a reference obligation of the reference obligor and delivers it to the protection seller. The protection buyer can deliver a par amount of a reference obligation equal to the notional amount of the CDS. The protection seller must then pay the protection buyer par for the reference obligation.
2. In *cash settlement*, dealer polling determines the market value of the reference obligation. The protection seller pays the difference between the reference obligation's par and its market value in cash to the protection buyer. This arrangement is illustrated in Exhibit 6.1.

CDS can be customized in any manner to which both parties agree. One of the most hotly debated issues is what situations should be included in the definition of a credit event. After all, these are what trigger a payment from the protection seller to the protection buyer. To put a framework around these debates, the International Swaps and Derivatives Association (ISDA) created CDS definitions so that market participants would have a common language in which to negotiate.[1] For example, ISDA defines six different corporate credit events.

The three most important credit events are *bankruptcy*, *failure to pay*, and *restructuring*. Bankruptcy is voluntary or involuntary filing of bankruptcy. Failure to pay is the failure of the reference obligor to make principal or interest payments on one or more of its obligations. Restructuring is the diminishment of the financial terms of one or more of the reference obligor's obligations. This could be the reduction of the obligation's principal or cou-

---

[1] ISDA's web site, www.isda.org, has useful information about credit derivatives and their documentation.

pon. Each of these terms has a precise definition in the ISDA rubric and market participants refer to ISDA's definitions as they negotiate CDS terms.

The protection seller under a CDS is said to be the *seller* of the CDS, but he is also *long* the CDS and long the underlying credit. The logic behind selling protection and being long the CDS is that the protection seller is in the same credit position as someone who owns, or is long, a bond. Both investors root against default. Of course, there is a major difference between being long a bond and long a CDS. To be long a bond, one must buy it at its market price. To be long a CDS, one must simply promise to pay future credit event losses.[2]

CDS divorce the assumption of credit risk from the requirement to fund a purchase. One result is that CDS democratize the assumption of credit risk. A leveraged investor with a relatively high cost of funds (e.g., LIBOR + 200) could never profitably purchase a bond with a relatively low coupon (e.g., LIBOR + 100). However, as a credit protection seller, the high cost funder could profitably assume that same credit risk for the payment of, say, 80 basis points a year. The credit protection seller's position is also more purely a credit position than if it actually owned a bond, as a bond's market value or cash flows are much more affected by interest rate movements than is a CDS.

Conversely, the protection buyer under a CDS is said to be the buyer of the CDS, but *short* the CDS and *short* the underlying credit. A CDS allows the protection buyer to short a credit without the operational and practical difficulties of shorting a cash bond. The separation of credit risk and funding that a CDS achieves also allows low cost funders to fund a bond without taking on the bond's credit risk. A party with a low cost of funds (e.g., LIBOR + 5) could profitably purchase a bond with a relatively high coupon (e.g., LIBOR + 100). The low-cost funder could then insulate itself from credit risk by buying protection for 80 basis points a year and achieve a spread of 15 basis points (LIBOR + 100 minus LIBOR + 5 minus 80 basis points).[3] This is the analog to a high cost funder assuming credit risk without funding a bond.

CDS documentation evolved from interest rate swap documentation and some strange vestigial terminology remains from its origin. For example, interest rate swaps have fixed rate payers and floating rate payers for very obvious reasons. More opaquely, the protection buyer in a CDS is referred to as the fixed rate payer and the protection seller the floating rate payer. We show the various terms for protection buyer and protection seller in Exhibit 6.2.

---

[2] Moreover, this party must sometimes back up that promise with collateralization.

[3] This is an example of a negative basis trade. The basis is negative because the "basis," CDS premium (80 bps) minus the cash bond spread above LIBOR (100 bps), is negative (−20 bps).

EXHIBIT 6.2 CDS Terminology for Buyers and Sellers

Credit protection buyer	Credit protection seller
CDS buyer	CDS seller
Short credit risk	Long credit risk
Fixed rate payer	Floating rate payer

DIFFERENCES BETWEEN CORPORATE CDS AND ABS CDS

With that quick introduction to corporate CDS, we can now discuss the difference between corporate CDS and ABS CDS. Two differences between corporate credit and ABS credit drive the structure of their respective credit default swaps. The two major differences are with respect to:

- Generality versus specificity
- Clarity versus ambiguity

Unfortunately, these differences generally work against ABS CDS. We'll explain these differences below and the hurdles they present to the ABS CDS market. Later we describe the various attempts made in the ABS CDS market to overcome these obstacles.

Generality versus Specificity

The first difference is the *generality* of corporate credit risk versus the *specificity* of ABS credit risk. In the corporate market, the focus is on the corporate entity (e.g., General Motors) with less emphasis placed on the credit's individual obligations (e.g., the 4⅜% of 2008). In the ABS market, the focus is very specific: a particular tranche from a particular securitization of a particular originator (the Class M7 of Home Equity Loan Trust 2005-AB4 originated by Countrywide).

In corporate CDS, the usual practice is for all obligations of a particular seniority to be reference obligations (usually senior unsecured obligations; sometimes subordinate obligations). So corporate obligations may be retired and new ones created, but the corporate CDS overarches them all and has its own maturity. The corporate CDS market runs on the assumption that it doesn't much matter which senior unsecured obligation is tendered for physical settlement or marked to market for cash settlement. The model here is bankruptcy, where all senior unsecured debts are supposed to be treated the same in that their eventual recovery (in cash or new securities) is the same regardless of maturity or coupon. Credit events that allow for differences in the value of reference obligations, such as restructuring, are the source of concern, controversy, and remediation.[4]

Things could not be more different with ABS CDS. This is because each tranche in an ABS securitization intentionally has its own distinct credit quality from that of other tranches. This is reflected in the different ratings on tranches. For example, it is not uncommon for a subprime mortgage securitization to issue tranches in every investment-grade rating category from AAA down to BBB–. And of course, each securitization is backed by its own unique pool of assets. ABS CDS follow credit reality and focus on the specific tranche. ABS CDS maturity and amortization follow the maturity and amortization of the reference obligation.

Clarity versus Ambiguity

The second difference between corporate credit and structured finance is the *clarity* of a corporate credit problem versus the *ambiguity* of an ABS credit problem. The model in the corporate market is that a corporate fails to pay interest or principal on an obligation, cross default with its other obligations occurs, and pretty soon the corporate is filed into bankruptcy. That is, if the corporate does not file for bankruptcy first. These events are dramatic, easily discernable, and severe.

In contrast, a credit problem at an ABS securitization can be subtle. For example, an ABS securitization should never go into bankruptcy. In essence, the expense, delay, and uncertainty of bankruptcy are unnecessary evils as securitization documentation already encompasses the possibility that cash flows from collateral may not be enough to pay liabilities. In essence, an ABS securitization comes with a prepackaged insolvency plan that eliminates the need for judicial interference.

Furthermore, the flexibility of an ABS tranche's cash flows is such that the existence or extent of a credit problem is ambiguous. Problems may be minor, they may resolve themselves, or they may not rise to the same level of distress as a defined credit event in a corporate CDS. For example:

---

[4] The definition of a restructuring credit event has been modified twice and it is often eliminated altogether as a credit event in the U.S. market. The problem is that restructuring creates a *cheapest-to-deliver option*. What is a cheapest-to-deliver option? If, after a restructuring credit event, the reference obligor's bonds trade at different levels, it behooves the protection buyer to deliver the reference obligation with the lowest market value. The existence of a cheapest-to-deliver option argues against the case we have made that corporate CDS are obligor rather than obligation focused. But the efforts to eliminate the cheapest-to-deliver option argue that the market sees this as a problem. Indeed, the cheapest-to-deliver option impeded the corporate CDS market's growth.

- Many ABS tranches are structured to defer interest payments if collateral cash flow is insufficient due to delinquencies and defaults. Later, if collateral cash flow recovers, deferred interest is made up.
- Many ABS tranches are structured to defer interest payments if collateral cash flow is insufficient due to interest rate caps on underlying collateral. Many mortgages have restrictions on how fast homeowner payments can rise. These restrictions might cause an interest rate mismatch with the securitization's tranches. If so, the *available funds cap* causes tranches to defer interest, as they would if the shortfall in collateral cash flow had been caused by defaults. Later, if collateral cash flow recovers, deferred interest is made up.
- Many ABS securitizations call for the write-down of tranche principal in the case of collateral losses. From that point forward, interest and principal payments are based on the lower written down amount. However, some of these write-downs are reversible and in practice are reversed as collateral performance stabilizes or improves. Moody's calculates that 19% of such ABS impairments have been cured.[5]
- Some ABS securitizations don't use the write-down process. Tranche principal is not considered defaulted until some far off legal final maturity. So there is no official early acknowledgment of a principal default.
- Each ABS tranche has an expected maturity based on underlying collateral maturities and prepayments. However, this expected maturity could be violated due to either slower than expected collateral prepayments or higher than expected collateral losses.

We summarize the differences between corporate credit and structured finance credit in Exhibit 6.3. The *specificity* of ABS credit risk (as opposed to the *generality* of corporate credit risk) and the *ambiguity* of an ABS credit problem (versus the *clarity* of a corporate credit problem) hampers ABS CDS, as we shall discuss next.

EXHIBIT 6.3 Differences Between Corporate Credit and ABS Credit

	Corporate Credit	ABS Credit
Generality	All of a corporation's senior unsecured debt is affected in the same way by the corporation's bankruptcy.	Each tranche of a securitization has its own individual credit quality.
Clarity	A corporation's inability to make an interest payment is a significant event.	Missed payments might be small and might reverse.

[5] Jian Hu et al, *Default and Loss Rates of Structured Finance Securities: 1993–2004*, Moody's Investors Service, July 2005, Figure 6, p. 9.

DIFFICULTIES IN ABS CDS

The differences between corporate and ABS credit generally work against the creation of ABS CDS. Or more accurately, the differences work against creating ABS CDS in the image of corporate CDS.

Two consensuses drive the corporate CDS market:

- A credit event triggering a payment from the protection seller to the protection buyer should be the result of a significant credit problem.
- The settlement process should represent credit losses rather than market value risks such as the difficulty of valuing a defaulted obligation.

The ideal corporate CDS combination is therefore a bankruptcy credit event and a physical settlement. Bankruptcy is ideal because it indicates a severe credit problem. Physical settlement is ideal because if the credit problem is minor, the value of the reference obligation delivered should be high. Furthermore, the protection seller can decide to hold the reference obligation or sell it when the seller sees fit. Therefore, the protection payment is not subjected to noncredit risks associated with the market value polling process.

ABS credits lack anything as clear-cut as bankruptcy. Interruptions in interest payments are incremental and reversible. So are principal write-downs and some ABS securitizations do not even have principal write-downs. It violates CDS market consensus to trigger a credit event because of an interest deferral or principal write-down that is small and could very well be reversed later. On the other hand, it seems unfair to force a protection buyer to wait for a far-off legal final maturity before calling a credit event.

The small size of underlying ABS tranches presents settlement problems. Typically, ABS CDS are written on tranches in the BBB– to A+ range of the securitization. For a subprime mortgage securitization, these six tranches in aggregate make up only 5% to 10% of the deal's total capital structure. In a $1.6 billion securitization, these tranches are in the range of $5 to $25 million each. These small sizes would make it very difficult for a protection buyer (other than someone who already owned the tranche) to make physical settlement. Contrast this to the corporate CDS market where any unsecured debt of the reference obligor is deliverable.[6] The small sizes of ABS tranches (not to mention the difficulty of analyzing ABS credit) would also make dealer polling especially arbitrary.

---

[6] Not that it is always easy to find a corporate reference obligation to deliver. The notional of CDS on a corporate name might be a multiple of its outstanding debt. There have been reports of "squeezes" where protection buyers have had to overpay to get deliverable reference obligations. But the situation is better than in the ABS market.

So now we will look at three attempts to create ABS CDS documentation to overcome these problems:

1. Traditional ABS CDS circa 1998–2004 based on corporate CDS.
2. The dealer mixed pay-as-you-go and physical settlement template.
3. The end user pure pay-as-you-go template.

Note that in the discussion that follows, capitalized terms are ISDA (International Swaps and Derivatives Association)-defined terms that one will find in ABS CDS documentation. Lower-case terms are widely understood colloquialisms not found in the documentation.

Traditional ABS CDS and "Hard" Credit Events

The circuitous route of ABS CDS documentation begs the question as to whether we have gotten where we are today via random mutation or intelligent design. We stay away from that controversy. Suffice it to say that ABS CDS has been around, as the basis for the first synthetic ABS CDOs, since 1998. Underlying reference obligations in these CDOs were usually in the AAA and AA rating categories. These early synthetic ABS CDOs were often done for balance sheet purposes, in that the party buying protection from the CDO owned the underlying ABS tranches and achieved a reduction in required capital by sponsoring the CDO. Other ABS CDS of this era were driven by low cost funders buying individual ABS tranches and laying off their credit risk via single-name ABS CDS. The reference obligations of these trades were also usually highly rated.[7]

ISDA published corporate CDS definitions in 1999, produced three supplements in 2001, and published new corporate CDS definitions in 2003. As corporate CDS definitions became more known and accepted, early ABS CDS participants began to use the corporate CDS template with modifications to accommodate ABS credit. Over time, certain versions of these ABS modifications became, if not standard, at least well known and understood in the market. These ABS CDS followed corporate CDS credit events, with significant modifications, and corporate CDS settlement, without modification. Typical credit events for a synthetic ABS CDO were:

---

[7] Both the ABS CDO and the single underlying ABS CDS were made possible by a *negative basis*. A bond's basis is its CDS premium minus its spread above LIBOR. If this is a negative number, it means that an investor can purchase the bond, buy credit protection via a CDS, and enjoy a LIBOR plus net coupon. This would appeal to any investor with a cost of funds close to LIBOR. The negative basis trade investor is being paid to fund the bond without taking its credit risk.

- A version of the corporate CDS Failure to Pay
- ABS Failure to Pay Principal
- ABS Failure to Pay Interest
- Distressed Downgrade

The corporate CDS definition of *Failure to Pay* includes the situation in which an ABS tranche had not paid its principal by its legal final maturity. It would also include the situation where an ABS tranche, which is not allowed by its terms to defer interest, has in fact missed an interest payment.

ABS Failure to Pay Principal would encompass a principal write-down, so long as at least one other condition was met:

- The terms of the ABS tranche not allow written down principal to ever be written back up.
- The terms of the ABS tranche not allow interest to be paid on the written down principal, even if principal is written back up.
- The ABS tranche is downgraded to some rating, such as Ca or below by Moody's or CCC– and below by S&P.

ABS *Failure to Pay Interest* would encompass a missed interest payment, so long as at least one other condition was met:

- The terms of the ABS tranche not allow for unpaid interest to be paid at a later date.
- The terms of the ABS tranche not allow interest to be paid on deferred interest.
- The ABS tranche is downgraded to some rating, such as Ca or below by Moody's or CCC– and below by S&P.

A *Distressed Downgrade* would be a downgrade to C by Moody's and/or D by S&P. Note that the discrepancy in rating between the two agencies is because Moody's does not have a D rating (C is Moody's lowest rating.)

Other credit events were occasionally used. *Bankruptcy* was sometimes included as a credit event, even though the chance of an ABS securitization becoming bankrupt was next to nil. *Mathematical Impossibility, Under Collateralization*, or *Implied Write-down* was based on the impossibility of collateral cash flow being sufficient to pay principal and interest on an ABS tranche. This might be determined by taking the par amount of collateral, deducting the par of tranches senior to the referenced tranche, and then comparing the remainder to the par of the referenced tranche. Normally, a threshold level of undercollateralization was required to trigger a credit event. More sophisticated cash flow modeling approaches were also employed to test for under collateralization.

Rating Agency Concerns

Within the list of acceptable credit events, one notes the caution exercised in determining an allowable credit event. For an ABS tranche whose terms allow principal write-ups and interest to be paid on deferred interest, it normally took a rating agency downgrade to trigger a credit event. These terms were driven by two parties: the rating agencies, who rated ABS CDOs; and the monoline bond insurers, who were often the protection seller on AAA synthetic ABS CDO tranches and single-name ABS CDS trades.

One concern rating agencies had was with the applicability of their ratings on the ABS CDO's collateral. If an ABS security allows reversible write-downs and catch-ups of deferred interest, the rating of the security would not address the probability of those events. In rating an ABS security with those terms, the rating agency would focus solely on the security's ability to provide *eventual* payment of principal and interest. As eventual payment is easier for the security to achieve than timely payment, a security rated for eventual payment would achieve a higher rating than the same security rated for timely payment.

If a failure to make timely payment is a credit event in an ABS CDO, and the rating of the security only addresses eventual payment, the rating does not address the probability of a credit event.[8] The same goes with the triggering of an available funds cap. Because the rating agencies did not feel they could assess the interest rate risk (or because deal structurers did not want them to) of some structures, they neatly removed that risk from their analysis. So again, if the triggering of the available funds cap is a credit event, the security's rating does not address the probability of such a credit event. As the rating agencies base their CDO ratings in part on ratings of the CDO's underlying collateral, their analysis falls apart if their collateral ratings do not address the risk of credit events.

The rating agencies also felt that their ratings could not address the risks inherent in the cash settlement process. For example, Moody's noted "performing tranches of structured finance transactions are generally illiquid, while distressed tranches are even more illiquid."[9] The rating agencies were not confident that their recovery assumptions would prove valid in a dealer polling process.

---

[8] This is akin to a gymnastic judge's score being multiplied by the wrong difficulty factor. Not helpful? Then just read the sentence again.

[9] See, for example, Yuri Yoshizawa, *Moody's Approach to Rating Synthetic Resecuritizations*, Moody's Investors Service, October 29, 2003, which lays out rating agency concerns very well. Proving that nothing financial is truly new under the sun, Yoshizawa suggested "partial settlement," or pay-as-you-go settlement, as a positive solution to the ambiguity of credit events in an ABS CDS.

Meanwhile, monoline insurance companies are bound by statute to only guarantee the scheduled interest and principal amortization of the bonds they guarantee. Although they usually reserve the right to accelerate payment, they cannot legally bind themselves to immediate payout. The reason is the inherent liquidity strain such a requirement would impose upon the insurer. In essence, monoline insurance payments are "pay as you go," with an acceleration option owned by the insurance company.

It is understandable that protection sellers only want significant problems to count as credit events. It is also understandable that protection sellers do not want the uncertainty of dealer polling. Yet it also seems unfair for protection buyers to have to wait for the legal final maturity of an ABS security or be dependent upon rating agency downgrades before they collect protection payments on obviously impaired securities. Out of such concerns, the idea arose to supplement hard credit events and hard settlement with milder forms of both.

Pay as You Go, the Dealer Template

The innovation of *Pay as You Go* or *PayGo CDS* is softer and reversible credit events and partial, reversing settlements. Also, the CDS template eliminates Cash Settlement and the risks of dealer polling.

Under PayGo, if an ABS security experiences an Interest Shortfall, the protection seller pays the protection buyer the amount of the shortfall. The payment is made even if the interest on the ABS security is by its terms deferrable. But if the ABS security later catches up on interest payments, the protection buyer returns the payment to the protection seller. An ABS security can, of course, suffer multiple Interest Shortfalls and therefore a PayGo ABS CDS could suffer multiple Interest Shortfalls.

Interest Shortfall, as a Floating Amount Event, is more easily triggered than the equivalent problem as a Credit Event in traditional ABS CDS. A traditional ABS CDS would ignore the nonpayment of deferrable interest (i.e., an ABS security with a PIK [payment in kind] feature) unless the missed coupon was accompanied by a severe downgrade. But the payment of only the ABS security's missed coupon is a mild settlement event in contrast to physical or cash settlement of the entire notional amount that would occur in a traditional ABS CDS. Moreover, the PayGo settlement is reversible should the ABS security catch up on deferred interest. (There's more to say about Interest Shortfall, but we will defer that discussion for now.)

In PayGo terminology, the kinder, gentler events are *Floating Amount Events* and the payments from the protection seller to the protection buyer are *Floating Amounts*. Reversing payments from the protection buyer to the protection seller are *Additional Fixed Amounts*. They are "additional" to the premium payments the protection buyer already pays the protection seller.

One can guess how the PayGo concept is applied to principal write-downs. The protection seller pays the protection buyer the amount of principal write-down. The ABS CDS continues on with a smaller notional amount reflecting the partial settlement of the CDS. If the write-down is later reversed, the protection buyer returns the written down amount to the protection seller.

Again, the PayGo event is more easily triggered than a credit event in a traditional ABS CDS. A traditional ABS CDS would ignore a principal write-down that was reversible unless it was accompanied by a severe downgrade. But, again, the partial settlement of just the ABS security's written down amount is a mild settlement event and it is reversible should the principal be written back up. An ABS security can, of course, suffer multiple Write-downs and, therefore, a PayGo ABS CDS could suffer multiple Write-downs. Premiums from the protection buyer to the protection seller would be based on the written down amount of the ABS CDS.

The partial and fluid nature of the settlements is in contrast to the binary and severe nature of hard credit events and hard settlement and appropriate for minor credit problems. However, and this is a big however, the PayGo template allows the protection buyer to force a Physical Settlement of the CDS' entire notional amount upon a Write-down. And unlike traditional ABS CDS, this does not require that a ratings downgrade accompany the Write-down.

The PayGo treatments of Interest Shortfall and Write-down are at odds with each other. For Interest Shortfall, the innovation is a more sensitive trigger (because of the removal of the rating downgrade requirement) but a less severe settlement (because of the partial and reversible nature of the Pay-As-You-Go Settlement). For Write-down, the same applies, but only if the protection buyer chooses to call a Write-down a Floating Amount Event. If the Protection Buyer chooses to call a Write-down a Credit Event, it triggers Physical Settlement of the entire notional amount of the CDS. In Exhibit 6.4, we show the ways Interest Shortfall and Write-down can be classified and settled.

EXHIBIT 6.4   Different Treatments of Interest Shortfall and Write-Down

Event	Classification	Settlement
Interest shortfall	Floating amount event	Pay as you go
Write-down	Floating amount event or credit event	Pay-as-you-go or physical settlement

EXHIBIT 6.5   Floating Amount Events, Credit Events, and Buyer's Choice

Floating Amount Event and Pay-As-You-Go Settlement	Protection Buyer's Choice: Pay-As-You-Go Settlement or Physical Settlement	Credit Events and Physical Settlement
Interest shortfall	Write-down	Distress ratings downgrade
	Failure to pay principal	Maturity extension

The PayGo template documents the protection buyer's option by defining Write-down as both a Floating Amount Event (with Pay-As-You-Go Settlement) and as a Credit Event (with Physical Settlement). We show the PayGo template scheme of Floating Amount Events and Credit Events in Exhibit 6.5. In the exhibit, Interest Shortfall is shown as a Floating Amount Event with Pay-As-You-Go settlement. Write-down is shown as being, at the option of the protection buyer, either a Floating Amount Event with Pay-As-You-Go Settlement or a Credit Event with Physical Settlement.

Failure to Pay Principal is both a Floating Amount Event and a Credit Event. For the vast majority of ABS securities, this event is going to come at the security's legal final maturity or at the exhaustion of the ABS securitization's collateral portfolio. Having Failure to Pay Principal be both a Floating Amount Event and a Credit Event allows the protection buyer to receive a settlement amount whether or not the protection buyer owns the ABS security.

Distress Ratings Downgrade and Maturity Extension are purely Credit Events in the PayGo template and are designated as optional events. Distressed Ratings Downgrade is a holdover from the traditional ABS CDS. Maturity Extension covers the rare situation in which the legal final maturity of an ABS tranche has been extended.

PayGo and Interest Shortfalls

In determining that an Interest Shortfall has occurred, there is no differentiation between Interest Shortfalls that are due to defaults and losses in the underlying ABS security's collateral portfolio or Interest Shortfalls that are due to the workings of the ABS security's available funds cap.

We mentioned the available funds cap in our discussion of the ambiguities of an ABS credit problem. Many subprime and prime mortgage tranches are structured to defer part of their interest payments if collateral cash flow is insufficient due to interest rate caps on underlying loan collateral. Collateral cash flow may become insufficient, even if the collateral portfolio is performing well, because many mortgages have restrictions on how fast homeowner payments can rise. The *available funds cap* (AFC) limits the amount of interest the ABS tranche is required to pay in cash and creates an interest deferral that is payable in future periods. Later, as underlying collateral resets to higher coupons, these deferred amounts may be paid.

Since deferral is part of the ABS security's structure, the rating agencies do not rate the timely payments of these amounts, only their eventual payment. In fact, it is the rating agency's difficulty in assessing interest rate mismatches between mortgage loans and mortgage bonds that causes the carve-out of timely interest. Yet investors expect uncapped interest rate payments and consider an interest deferral to be a significant credit problem. Protection buyers want this eventuality to be covered by ABS CDS.

PayGo ABS CDS documentation provides for three ways to size the protection seller's responsibility for Interest Shortfalls under Floating Payment or Pay-As-You-Go settlement. Two of them, Interest Shortfall Cap Not Applicable and Variable Cap, are similar, while Fixed Cap greatly limits the protection seller's obligation.

Interest Shortfall Cap Not Applicable

The protection seller pays the protection buyer the full amount of the reference obligation's Interest Shortfall. If no interest whatsoever is paid on the reference obligation, the protection seller would pay the obligation's LIBOR index plus coupon spread. But this payment, like all Interest Shortfall payments to the protection buyer, is netted against the CDS premium payment the protection buyer pays the protection seller. So the protection seller's maximum obligation to the protection buyer for an Interest Shortfall is

LIBOR + Reference obligation's coupon spread – CDS premium

Variable Cap

The protection seller's obligation depends on the relationship of the CDS premium to the reference obligation's coupon spread. If the CDS premium is *less* than the reference obligation's coupon spread, the protection seller's gross payment is limited to the reference obligation's LIBOR index plus the CDS premium. If the CDS premium is *greater* than the reference obligation's coupon, the protection seller's gross payment is limited to the reference obligation's LIBOR index and coupon spread. Again, Interest Shortfall payments to the protection buyer are netted against the CDS premium payment the protection buyer pays the protection seller. So the maximum obligation of the protection seller to the protection buyer for an Interest Shortfall is

LIBOR + (Lesser of the CDS premium or reference obligation's coupon spread) – CDS premium

Fixed Cap or "Premium Squeeze to Zero"

The protection seller's payment to the protection buyer is limited to the CDS premium; that is, the protection seller is not responsible for the LIBOR component of the reference obligation's coupon. The net payment amount, then, can never be a payment from the protection seller to the protection buyer. An Interest Shortfall amount only reduces the premium the protection buyer pays the protection seller. It never reverses the direction of the payment. Note that the withholding of the CDS premium fully extinguishes the protection seller's obligation in that period, which is to say that the amount of interest lost on the reference obligation but not covered by withholding the CDS premium is not carried forward into future interest periods.

Under any of the three interest cap options, if the ABS catches up on an Interest Shortfall, the protection buyer must repay the Interest Shortfall amount to the protection seller. Compounding this reimbursement at LIBOR plus the CDS premium is optional, decided by mutual agreement of the protection seller and buyer at the inception of the ABS CDS.

PayGo and Step-Up

Many ABS securitizations have an expected maturity many years previous to the legal final maturity. The expected maturity takes into account expected collateral prepayments and defaults as well as a potential cleanup sale of collateral when the portfolio gets small. The view of rating agencies and investors regarding an ABS security's cleanup call is analogous to their view of PIK risk and AFC risk. The rating agencies do not feel they can assess the future level of prepayments or a sale of remaining collateral years in the future. Therefore, their rating does not address payment of the ABS security by its expected maturity. Investors, on the other hand, expect the expected maturity and consider extension risk to be a significant credit problem. It is common for the terms of an ABS security to require an increase in coupon (a step-up) if the security should extend beyond its expected maturity.

The PayGo CDS template offers counterparties a chance to choose Optional Early Step-Up. If elected, the premium on the ABS CDS steps up when the reference obligation steps up. However, the protection buyer has five business days to cancel the ABS CDS. If Optional Early Step-up is not elected, the ABS CDS ignores the expected maturity of the ABS tranche.

Pay As You Go, the End User (a.k.a. Monoline) Template

The dealer template we have been discussing was the result of a schism within the ISDA committee that had been charged with developing an ABS

PayGo CDS template. The other half of the committee is comprised of end users, most notably monoline insurers, and they put forward their own proposal in September 2005.

The biggest difference between the dealer template and the end user template is the elimination of Credit Events and Physical Settlement in the end user document. The end user template is purely a Pay-As-You-Go settlement. This affects the Write-down event the most. Recall that under the dealer template, the protection buyer has the option to take the Write-down Amount, or force physical settlement of the entire notional amount of the ABS CDS. In the end user template, the protection buyer can only receive the Write-down Amount.

Obviously, the removal of the Physical Settlement option appeals to protection sellers and not to protection buyers. Protection sellers can't be faced with a sudden liquidity requirement to fund the purchase of the reference obligation at par. Protection buyers lose an option to opportunistically choose the settlement of their choice. But it does seem that the end user version better honors the pragmatism of creating sensitive floating payment events that trigger incremental and reversible settlements.

However, another end user change reduces the sensitivity of floating payment events. This is the end user abolishment of Implied Write-down for ABS securities that do not have a codified Write-down process within their structure. If the amount of collateral in a securitization is insufficient to pay a reference obligation in full, it seems inequitable to delay the recognition of the Event until the legal final maturity of the ABS security.

The end user template does not allow the Protection Buyer to cancel the CDS at the ABS tranche's expected maturity. It is a principal of financial guaranty insurance that the insured not be able to cancel its policy when it determines it is not needed. Furthermore, any step-up in cash coupon must be passed through to the protection seller.

The final significant change in the end user template is the elimination of Interest Shortfalls due to the actions of an available funds cap. The view here seems to be that this is an interest rate risk rather than a credit risk.

Just Like Buying a Cash ABS Bond?

Investors are concerned about the fidelity of ABS CDS to a cash position in the ABS reference obligation. From the protection seller's point of view, what set of floating amount events, credit events, and settlement mechanisms best replicate the economic experience of owning the underlying reference ABS obligation?

The too easy answer is an ABS CDS structure that triggers physical settlement at the first sign of trouble. Obviously, the protection seller will get the cash instrument's cash flows if it buys the cash instrument as it essentially does in physical settlement. What we are looking for is the economic equivalence of a cash bond in *synthetic* form. So any physical settlement, as envisioned in the dealer template, is automatically disqualified. One should use the strict Pay-As-You-Go settlement of the end user template to create a truly synthetic experience.

However, if an ABS security is irrevocably impaired, there is no point in delaying the recognition of that economic fact. Therefore, the prohibition against implied write-down in the end user document should be shunned in favor of the dealer template flexibility on this point.

Owning a cash bond means having its available funds cap risk. Therefore, the protection seller should choose the Variable Cap under the dealer template and shun the end user template, which eliminates protection payments for Interest Shortfalls due to an available funds cap.

Owning a cash bond also means receiving the coupon step-up if the ABS security is not repaid by its expected maturity. Therefore, the ABS CDS should follow the end user template and cause the coupon step-up to be passed through to the protection seller.

ABS CDS EFFECT ON ABS CDO MANAGEMENT

From 2002 to 2005, the ABS CDO market was hampered by a relative scarcity of CDO assets, particularly in mezzanine tranches (rated BBB to A), where new issue sizes are small. Simply put, the demand for CDO liabilities was greater than the supply of cash CDO assets. This was frustrating to ABS CDO managers, who would sometimes do a considerable amount of credit work on a bond and get an insultingly small allocation. It was not unheard of for managers to receive $1 million of a bond when they put in an order for $5 million. Good managers were unable to scale up the size and frequency of their CDO offerings solely because of small asset allocations.

ABS CDS opened up access to ABS credits by allowing CDO managers to sell credit protection to security firms, macrohedge funds, and mortgage hedge funds. ABS CDS multiplied the supply of credit risk to ABS CDOs by about four times as 75% of mezzanine ABS CDO assets were acquired synthetically through ABS CDS. At the time, this was thought to be advantageous for a number of reasons:

- ABS CDO managers could do credit work on new issues, perhaps get only a small allocation in the new issue cash market, but sell protection via ABS CDS in a size that was a multiple of their cash allocation.

- ABS CDO managers became less beholding to the new issue pipeline and could select credits from older vintages. Seasoned issues were much more readily accessed via CDS than in the secondary cash market. For cash flow reasons, ABS CDS was an advantageous way for an ABS CDO to access bonds from earlier vintages that might be trading at a premium.[10]
- Decoupling from the new issue cash market was thought to allow ABS CDO managers to be pickier about credits and focus more intently on and be more discriminating about collateral attributes, structural features, originators, and servicers.
- Finally, the ABS CDS market allowed CDO managers to short credits they did not like. Therefore, the analysis leading to a "no-buy" decision was not wasted. ABS CDS allowed them to express a negative view about a credit other than by simply not buying it.

While a liberating experience for ABS CDO managers in 2005, the single-name ABS CDS swap market magnified the size of the ABS CDO disaster in 2007. The volume of mezzanine ABS CDOs increased from $27 billion in 2005 to $50 billion in 2006 before falling to $33 billion in 2007. Two new ABS CDO structures helped allow the inclusion of synthetic ABS risk in CDOs.

TWO NEW TYPES OF ABS CDOs

Both new ABS CDO structures were driven by the efficiency of their unfunded super-senior tranche, which was generally equal to about 70% of their capital structure. ABS CDOs were able to buy credit protection in unfunded form at a savings of about 10 basis points to funded tranches. And while some super-senior protection providers raised their prices in the face of strong demand, the economics of unfunded issuance were still advantageous in 2006 and even into the first quarter of 2007.

---

[10] ABS CDS sometimes trade with an up-front exchange when the market value of the *Reference Obligation* is not trading at par. For example, if the Reference Obligation is trading at a premium, the protection seller would pay the protection buyer the difference between market value and par. Then, the protection premium paid by the protection buyer to the protection seller is closer to the coupon spread of the Reference Obligation. When CDOs sell protection via single-name ABS CDS, they generally choose not to make the upfront exchange and instead set the protection premium closer to the Reference Obligation's discount margin. When a lot of ABS collateral was trading at a premium, this meant that the CDO did not pay an up-front exchange and instead accepted a lower protection premium.

"Hybrid" ABS CDOs were backed by a mixture of 30% to 40% cash assets and 60% to 70% ABS CDS. These CDOs almost naturally evolved from cash transactions, as CDO managers discovered, they could buy a new issue cash ABS security and subsequently access more of the same risk via the ABS CDS market. In some of these CDO, the manager had the ability to call for additional cash funding from super-senior tranche holders. This allowed the manager to opportunistically shift into cash collateral if cash spreads become attractive. The manager could also pay off the funding if it wanted to shift back into ABS CDS.

The other new form of ABS CDO structure was 100% synthetic and sourced credit risk completely through ABS CDS. These CDOs were much different than older synthetic ABS CDOs that contained higher-rated assets in the AAA to AA range that were done for balance sheet motivations.

SUMMARY

In this chapter, we contrasted ABS credit with corporate credit in order to highlight the unique problems in developing ABS CDS. The specific nature of ABS credit, at a tranche-by-tranche level of detail, makes physical settlement difficult and cash settlement extremely problematic. The subtle and reversible nature of ABS credit problems calls for the flexibility provided by Pay-As-You-Go settlement. Dealers and end users have both offered their visions of ABS CDS. We picked and choose among their terms to get a set that best replicated the economics of owning a cash ABS security.

ABS CDS gave ABS CDO managers a new way to access credit risk and freed them from the tyranny of the new issue market. Hybrid and fully synthetic ABS CDOs proved popular with managers and investors in 2006 and increased issuance beyond the limits of cash subprime issuance. The willingness of ABS CDO managers to sell credit protection allowed a few hedge funds to reap billions in profits as the subprime market meltdown unfolded in 2007.

CHAPTER 7

The ABX and TABX Indices

Many market participants who have historically not been active in the U.S. mortgage markets have turned to the ABX indices as a way to express their views on mortgage credit. In this chapter, we take a careful look at the ABX indices, as well as the TABX indices: how they are constructed and their trading mechanics. In Chapter 11, we look at pricing.

BACKGROUND

Trading in the home equity asset-backed credit default benchmark indices, hereafter referred to as *ABX indices* or *ABX.HE indices*, commenced January 2006. The trading is offered by CDSIndexCo, a consortium of 16 credit derivative desks.[1] All members (except for HSBC) contribute to the ABX indices, which are managed by Markit Group. These two organizations also offer and manage trading of the Dow Jones CDX indices, which are the most actively traded corporate CDS indices.

The ABX.HE indices consist of five separate subindices, one for each of the rating categories: AAA, AA, A, BBB, and BBB–. Appropriately, the names of the five subindices are ABX.HE.AAA, ABX.HE.AA, ABX.HE.A, ABX.HE.BBB, and ABX.HE.BBB–. Each subindex consists of 20 tranches (of the same rating as the rating category for that particular subindex) from the 20 HEQ ABS deals, with each deal represented once in each subindex.

A new set of ABX.HE indices is launched every six months on January 19 and July 19, referred to as *roll dates*. As of November 2007, four sets of ABX indices are outstanding: ABX 06-1, ABX 06-2, ABX 07-1, and ABX 07-2.[2]

---

[1] Members of that group are Bank of America, Barclays Capital, Bear Stearns, BNP Paribus, Citibank, Credit Suisse, Deutsche Bank, Goldman Sachs, HSBC, JPMorgan, Lehman, Merrill Lynch, Morgan Stanley, RBS Greenwich Capital, UBS and Wachovia.

[2] Given the limited subprime issuance during the second half of 2007, ABX 08-1 was not released on the January 19, 2008 roll date.

Closing midmarket prices are published daily for each set of ABX indices. The administrator, Markit, employs a filtering process similar to that used by the British Banker's Association to calculate LIBOR. This entails taking the quotes received, discarding those in the top and bottom quartiles, then calculating an arithmetic mean of the remainder. To calculate the official fixing value for a particular subindex, the administrator must receive closing midmarket prices from the greater of (1) 50% of ABX.HE contributors or (2) five ABX.HE contributors. If, on any date, the administrator receives fewer closing prices for a subindex than the minimum fixing number, no fixing number is published for that date.

HOW A DEAL GETS INTO THE INDEX

To be eligible for inclusion in the semiannual ABX.HE indices, a deal must:

- Be greater $500 million.
- Have a weighted average FICO score less than or equal to 660 on its issuance date.
- Consist of 90% firs lien loans.
- Have tranches with ratings of AAA, AA, A, BBB, and BBB–.
- Have issued the five required tranches within the six months prior to the applicable semiannual roll date (e.g., all deals included in the 1/19/2007 launch issued their five required tranches between 7/20/2006 and 1/19/2007).
- Have an average life at issuance (based on deal pricing speeds) of that is not less than five years for the required AAA tranche, and for years for the other four required tranches.
- Have the 25th of each month as the scheduled interest payment date for all five required tranches.
- Have a floating rate interest based on one-month LIBOR for all five required tranches.
- Be listed on Bloomberg the identity and principal economic terms of each of the five required tranches.

Each set of semiannual ABX.HE indices consists of one deal from each of the "top 20" issuers. That group is selected based on total issuance volume for a six-month period just prior to the roll date for that set of indices. It is important to reemphasize that all the indices done at a particular time contain the same set of deals. That is why the inclusion criteria require the deal to have a tranche with each of the rating levels for which there are indices (AAA, AA, A, BBB, and BBB–). The deal included from each issuer is (1) based on a poll of the 15 consortium deals[3] and (2) selected from each issuer's two largest deals.

Of deals eligible for inclusion in the ABX Index, if more than four have the same originator or more than six have the same servicer, then deals from the "top 20" will be replaced by deals from the next five top issuers (i.e., issuers ranked #21 to #25). Exhibit 7.1 shows the deals in each of the first four ABX indices.

EXHIBIT 7.1   Deals in ABX HE Indices

Index	Deals
ABX-HE 06-1	ACE Securities Corp. Home Equity Loan Trust, Series 2005-HE7 Asset Backed Pass-Through Certificates (ACE 05-HE7)
	Asset-Backed Pass-Through Certificates, Series 2005-R11 (AMSI 05-R11)
	Argent Securities Inc. 05-W2 (ARSI 05-W2)
	Bear Stearns Asset Backed Securities I Trust 2005-HE11 (BSABS 05-HE11)
	CWABS Asset-Backed Certificates Trust 2005-BC5 (CWL 05-BC5)
	First Franklin Mortgage Loan Trust, Series 2005-FF12 (FFML 05-FF12)
	GSAMP Trust 2005-HE4 (GSAMP 05-HE4)
	Home Equity Asset Trust 2005-8 (HEAT 05-8)
	J.P. Morgan Mortgage Acquisition Corp. 2005-OPT1 (JPMAC 05-OPT1)
	Long Beach Mortgage Loan Trust 2005-WL2 (LBMLT 05-WL2)
	MASTR Asset Backed Securities Trust 2005-NC2 (MABS 05-NC2)
	Merrill Lynch Mortgage Investors Trust, Series 2005-AR1 (MLMI 05-AR1)
	Morgan Stanley ABS Capital I Inc. Trust 2005-HE5 (MSAC 05-HE5)
	New Century Home Equity Loan Trust 2005-4 (NCHET 05-4)
	RASC 05-KS11 TR (RASC 05-KS11)
	RAMP 05-EFC4 TR (RAMP 05-EFC4)
	Securitized Asset-Backed Receivables LLC Trust 2005-HE1 (SABR 05-HE1)
	Soundview Home Loan Trust 2005-4 (SVHE 05-4)
	Structured Asset Securities Co Mortgage Loan Trust 05-WF4 (SASC 05-WF4)
	Structured Asset Investment Loan Trust 2005-HE3 (SAILT 05-HE3)
ABX-HE 06-2	Structured Asset Securities Corporation Mortgage Loan Trust 2006-WF2 (SASC 06-WF2)
	Merrill Lynch Mortgage Investors Trust Mortgage Loan Asset-Backed Certificates, Series 2006-HE1 (MLM 06-E1)
	RASC Series 2006 KS3 Trust (RASC 06-KS3)
	Long Beach Mortgage Loan Trust 2006 1 (LBMLT 06-1)
	CWABS Asset-Backed Certificates Trust 2006-8 (CWL 06-8)
	Morgan Stanley ABS Capital I Inc. Trust 2006-WMC2 (MSAC 06-WMC2)
	Argent Securities Trust 2006-W1 (ARSI 06-W1)
	FFMLT Trust 2006-FF4 (FFML 06-FF4)
	ACE Securities Corp. Home Equity Loan Trust, Series 2006-NC1 (ACE 06-NC1)
	Soundview Home Loan Trust 2006-OPT5 (SVHE 06-OPT5)
	Structured Asset Investment Loan Trust 2006-4 (SAIL 06-4)
	GSAMP Trust 2006-HE3 (GSAMP 06-HE3)

---

[3] The consortium includes the 16 credit derivative desks comprising CDSIndexCo, which trade the ABX indices, excepting HSBC.

EXHIBIT 7.1   (Continued)

Index	Deals
ABX-HE 06-2	J.P. Morgan Mortgage Acquisition Corp. 2006-FRE1 (JPMAC 06-FRE1)
	Ramp Series 2006-NC2 Trust (RAMP 06-NC2)
	Home Equity Asset Trust 2006-4 (HEAT 06-4)
	Bear Stearns Asset-Backed Securities I Trust 2006-HE3 (BSABS 06-HE3)
	MASTR Asset-Backed Securities Trust 2006-NC1 (MABS 06-NC1)
	Carrington Mortgage Loan Trust, Series 2006-NC1 (CARR 06-NC1)
	Securitized Asset-Backed Receivables LLC Trust 2006-OP1 (SABR 06-OP1)
	Morgan Stanley Capital I Inc. Trust 2006-HE2 (MSCT 06-HE2)
ABX-HE 07-1	Fremont Home Loan Trust 2006-3 (FHLT 06-3)
	Home Equity Asset Trust 2006-7 (HEAT 06-7)
	Long Beach Mortgage Loan Trust 2006-6 (LBMLT 06-6)
	CWABS Asset-Backed Certificates Trust 2006-18 (CWABT 06-18)
	Morgan Stanley ABS Capital I Inc. Trust 2006-HE6 (MSAC 06-HE6)
	RASC Series 2006-KS9 Trust (RASC 06-KS9)
	Structured Asset Securities Corporation Mortgage Loan Trust 2006-BC4 (SASC 06-BC4)
	C-BASS 2006-CB6 Trust (CBASS 06-CB6)
	J.P. Morgan Mortgage Acquisition Trust 2006-CH2 (JPMMA 06-CH2)
	MASTR Asset-Backed Securities Trust 2006-NC3 (MABST 06-NC3)
	Merrill Lynch Mortgage Investors Trust, Series 2006-HE5 (MLMIT 06-HE5)
	Securitized Asset-Backed Receivables LLC Trust 2006-HE2 (SABRT 06-HE2)
	Soundview Home Loan Trust 2006-EQ1 (SVHLT 06-EQ1)
	FFMLT Trust 2006-FF13 (FFMLT 06-FF13)
	GSAMP Trust 2006-HE5 (GSAMPT 06-HE5)
	ABFC 2006-OPT2 Trust (ABFCAB 06-OPT2)
	ACE Securities Corp. Home Equity Loan Trust, Series 2006-NC3 (ACE-HELT 06-NC3)
	Bear Stearns Asset-Backed Securities I Trust 2006-HE10 (BSABST 06-HE10)
	Carrington Mortgage Loan Trust, Series 2006-NC4 (CARRMLT 06-NC4)
	Citigroup Mortgage Loan Trust 2006-WFHE3 (CITIMLT 06-WFHE3)
ABX-HE 07-2	ACE Securities Corp. Home Equity Loan Trust, Series 2007-HE4 (ACE-HELT 07-HE4)
	Bear Stearns Asset-Backed Securities I Trust 2007-HE3 (BSABST 07-HE3)
	Citigroup Mortgage Loan Trust 2007-AMC2 (CITIMLT 07-AMC2)
	CWABS Asset-Backed Certificates Trust 2007-1 (CWABT 07-1)
	First Franklin Mortgage Loan Trust, Series 2007-FF1 (FFMLT 07-FF1)
	GSAMP Trust 2007-NC1 (GSAMPT 07-NC1)
	Home Equity Asset Trust 2007-2 (HEAT 07-2)
	HSI Asset Securitization Corporation Trust 2007-NC1 (HISAST 07-NC1)
	J.P. Morgan Mortgage Acquisition Trust 2007-CH3 (JPMMA 07-CH3)
	Merrill Lynch First Franklin Mortgage Loan Trust, Series 2007-2 (MLFFMLT 07-2)
	Merrill Lynch Mortgage Investors Trust, Series 2007-MLN1 (MLMIT 07-MLN1)
	Morgan Stanley ABS Capital I Inc. Trust 2007-NC3 (MSAC 07-NC3)
	Nomura Home Equity Loan, Inc., Home Equity Loan Trust Series 2007-2 (NHELI 07-2)
	NovaStar Mortgage Funding Trust, Series 2007-2 (NSMFT 07-2)

EXHIBIT 7.1　(Continued)

Index	Deals
ABX-HE 07-2	Option One Mortgage Loan Trust 2007-5 (OOMLT 07-5)
	RASC Series 2007-KS2 Trust (RASC 07-KS2)
	Securitized Asset-Backed Receivables LLC Trust 2007-BR4 (SABRT 07-BR4)
	Structured Asset Securities Corporation Mortgage Loan Trust 2007-BC1 (SASC 07-BC1)
	Soundview Home Loan Trust 2007-OPT1 (SVHLT 07-OPT1)
	WaMu Asset-Backed Certificates WaMu Series 2007-HE2 (WMHE 07-HE2)

Source: Markit.

In practice, deals selected for the index tend to closely mirror production over the period in terms of characteristics and credit performance. Note that deal issuance in the first half of 2006 (which comprises ABX 06-2) is actually made up of loans originated three months earlier (Q4 2005–Q1 2006). In Exhibit 7.2, we show characteristics of the 06-1, 06-2, 07-1, and 07-2 indices versus those of loans originated during the same period. They are consistently very close: the *combined loan-to-value ratio* (CLTV), silent seconds, purchase percentage, FICO scored, *interest-only loans* (IO), and 40-year mortgages. The only factors on which they significantly differ are the percentage of second lien mortgages and the percentage of *adjustable rate mortgages* (ARMs)—the index has less of both than were originated (as there are separate pools that consist only of second- lien mortgages or only of fixed rate mortgages). For example, ABX 06-2 had 4% second lien mortgages, while 8% of mortgages originated during that time had second lien mortgages. Similarly, ABX 06-2 had 84% ARMs, versus 79% for the collateral originated at the same time. It is important to emphasize that 15% to 20% of the collateral backing floating rate subprime deals are actually fixed rate mortgages. However, the origination share of subprime fixed rate mortgages are larger than what can be accommodated within these deals. Thus, fixed rate mortgages not used in floating rate subprime pools are securitized in separate fixed rate deals.

Exhibit 7.3 shows delinquency behavior of each of the indices versus that of loans originated at the same time. The data reported in this exhibit reinforces the point that the ABX indices tend to mirror the underlying production.

INDEX MECHANICS

For the purpose of index pricing, each of the 20 tranches within each sub-index will be assigned an initial weight of 5%, regardless of tranche or

EXHIBIT 7.2 Collateral Characteristics: ABX vs. Specified Subprime Origination Period

ABX Index	2006-1	05Q2-05Q3	2006-2	05Q4-06Q1	2007-1	06Q2-06Q3	2007-2	06Q4-07Q1
CLTV	86	86	86	86	86	88	87	87
CLTV ≥ 90	50%	51%	48%	51%	51%	57%	55%	54%
CLTV > 80	64%	63%	60%	63%	64%	68%	69%	67%
Silent seconds	26%	25%	25%	26%	27%	28%	26%	22%
Full doc	57%	57%	56%	54%	58%	55%	57%	56%
Purchase	42%	45%	45%	44%	42%	45%	38%	37%
Seconds	3%	6%	4%	8%	4%	10%	3%	10%
FICO	630	632	625	627	626	631	625	631
FICO < 600	30%	30%	32%	31%	31%	29%	31%	29%
ARM	84%	79%	82%	78%	78%	72%	77%	69%
IO	30%	30%	22%	20%	15%	16%	17%	17%
Investor	5%	5%	5%	6%	5%	5%	5%	5%
40 year	5%	5%	20%	20%	32%	31%	25%	33%
Single family	75%	73%	74%	74%	75%	74%	73%	74%
Margin	5.71	5.72	5.98	5.95	5.93	6.00	5.89	5.84
DTI (back-end)	41	41	42	42	42	42	42	42
Original note rate	7.22	7.33	7.98	8.16	8.35	8.50	8.19	8.30
2-year hybrid	69%	64%	71%	65%	63%	59%	61%	53%
3-year hybrid	13%	13%	9%	10%	12%	10%	12%	12%

Source: CPR & CDR Technologies, Inc.

EXHIBIT 7.3　Delinquency Behavior: ABX versus Specified Subprime Origination Period

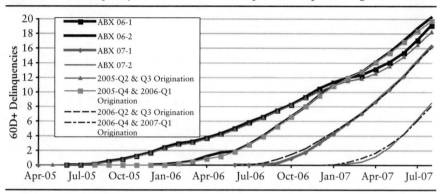

Source: LoanPerformance.

EXHIBIT 7.4　ABX Indices Tranche Margin

	Tranche Margin				
Index	AAA	AA	A	BBB	BBB–
ABX 06-1	18	32	54	154	267
ABX 06-2	11	17	44	133	242
ABX 07-1	9	15	64	224	389
ABX 07-2	76	192	369	500	500

Source: Markit.

deal size. The fixed rate (equivalent to a credit default swap premium for a single-name ABCDS) for each subindex is set the evening before trading in that subindex starts (based on each subindex' dealer consensus discount margin), and remains constant throughout the life of each subindex. For example, if a subindex starts trading with a fixed rate of 300 bps on its launch date, it will always trade with a fixed rate of 300 bps. Exhibit 7.4 shows the margin for each tranche in each of the indices. Each subindex's maturity date will be the longest legal final maturity date across the 20 tranches that comprise the subindex.

A position in an ABX.HE subindex is equivalent to a position in each of the 20 tranches. Once trading in a set of ABX.HE indices starts, the underlying principal for each subindex will amortize at the same rate as the individual tranches within each subindex. Thus, to the extent a tranche amortizes more quickly (slowly) than average, its price weighting will be less (more) important to its subindex.

For example, assume a $20 million notional trade in an ABX subindex. After one year, if one tranche amortizes 25%, another amortizes 50%, and the remaining 18 experience no amortization, then the initial $20 million position would have an exposure of $750,000 to the 25% amortizer, $500,000 to the 50% amortizer, and $1,000,000 to each of the other 18 tranches.

Pricing on the ABX indices is relative to 100, and is similar to calculating the mark-to-market value of an interest rate swap. Initially, the indices were quoted on spread. As spreads widened relative to the fixed rate, then the price of the ABX index would decrease (and vice versa if spreads tightened). However, as the subprime crises of the summer of 2007 deepened, the indices started to trade on price.

Cash flows are exchanged both upfront and monthly. At the inception of a trade, if the price on an ABX index differs from 100, there is an *upfront* payment. More specifically:

■ If the price is below 100, the protection buyer pays the seller. Thus, for a price of 75, the buyer pays the seller

$$(100 - \text{The index } 75)\% \times (\text{Notional}) \times (\text{Factor})$$

The upfront payment therefore is

$$25\% \times \text{Notional} \times \text{Factor}$$

■ The seller pays the buyer-accrued premium from the end of the last accrual period until the trade effective date.

On a *monthly* basis, the protection buyer pays the coupon to the counterparty on the notional amount. This will decline over time, based on the amorizaton of the reference obligations. The protection buyer receives payments in the event of interest shortfall, principal shortfall, or write-downs. If these are "made up," the protection buyer reimburses the protection seller.

INDEX PRICING OVER TIME

Exhibit 7.5 shows the historical price history on each ABX index as of the close on Friday, November 9, 2007. We note the following points:

■ All indices have performed very poorly, at every rating level.
■ At every rating level, the ABX 06-1 price is higher than the same coupon on each of the other indices, as the subprime deals issued in the

second half of 2005 (loans originated Q2 2005–Q3 2005) are considerably better than later issuance.

■ On early indices (06-1, 06-2, 07-1), all tranches carried coupons to be priced near par. However, note that on ABX 07-2 BBB–, the coupon carried the maximum value of 500 bps and the bonds initially traded well below par.

Exhibit 7.6A displays the data on ABX 07-1 AA, A, BBB, BBB–. Note that in February 2007 and again in May and most of June, the BBB and BBB– declined sharply in value, while the A and AA held their values. And, in fact, most of the volume was in the BBB and BBB– securities.

EXHIBIT 7.5   ABX Indices: Price Levels
Panel A.   BBB–

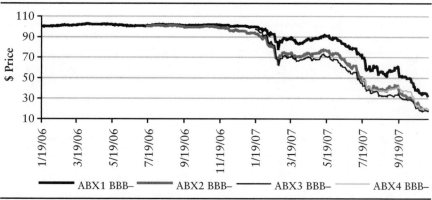

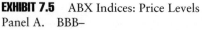

Panel B.   BBB

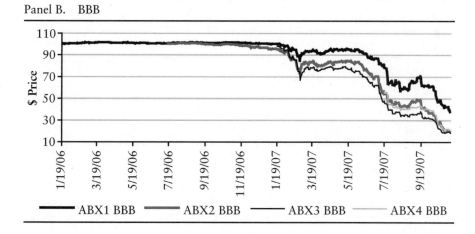

EXHIBIT 7.5 (Continued)

Panel C.   A

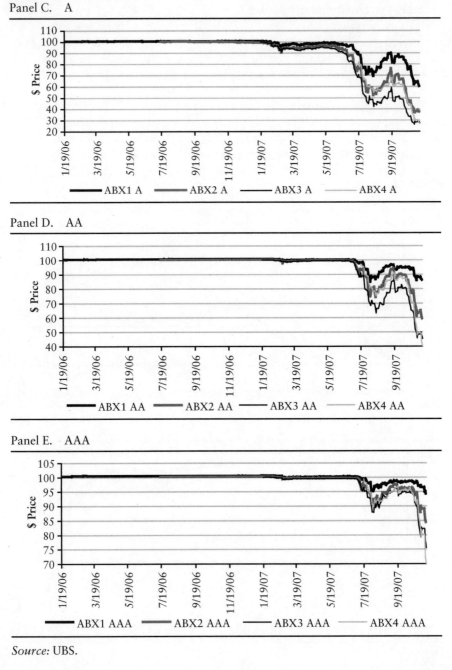

Panel D.   AA

Panel E.   AAA

Source: UBS.

EXHIBIT 7.6 ABX3 Prices

Panel A. ABX3 Price Levels: A, AA, BBB, and BBB–

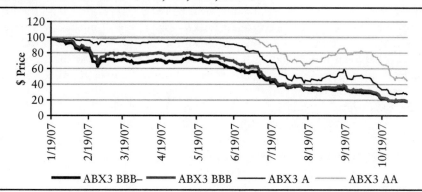

Panel B. Price Spread: ABX3 A – ABX3 BBB swap

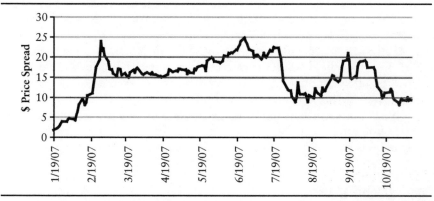

Panel C. Price Spread: ABX3 AA – ABX3 A swap

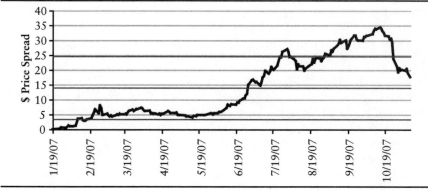

Source: UBS.

However, in late June 2007, the market reevaluated its loss expectations on 2006-issued ABS securities. It was clear that (1) losses were high enough to hit the A rated securities on some of the deals; and (2) prices on the BBB and BBB– descended to the level at which upside and downside were more balanced (while the A had only downside). Exhibit 7.6B shows that the spread between the A and BBB index reached 25 points. At that juncture, hedgers started to short the A, and it gained liquidity. In September 2007, as loss expectations deepened further and it became very difficult to take out a new subprime mortgage, two thing became clear. First, the AA securities would suffer some losses on some of the deals. Second, the 34 point spread between the AA and A was too wide. This is shown in Exhibit 7.6C. The AAs and eventually the AAAs began to decline in price.

It is important to realize that the ABX is the only direct, relatively liquid way for an investor to take a short position in mortgage credit. In late 2006 and early 2007, short positions in the ABX were primarily macroeconomic hedge funds looking for a way to short mortgage credit. By April 2007, it was clear to the dealer community that the subprime crisis was deepening. Dealers had a considerable amount of mortgage risk and looked to short the ABX to hedge the risk. In fact, to hedge their risk, most dealers were short the ABX, short whatever they could accumulate in the illiquid single-name default swap market, as well as short the CDS and equities of mortgage-related corporate entities. The bottom line is that in late 2007, there were many natural sellers of mortgage credit (including hedge funds and the dealer community), but few natural buyers. Thus, it is not surprising that most models had ABX prices considerably above their actual levels.

ABX TRANCHE TRADING

ABX tranches (TABX), the benchmark index tranche product in CDS of ABS, began trading on February 2007. It was designed to promote standardization, liquidity, and transparency.

The TABX tranches references a portfolio of 40 names, which are the most recent (as of the formation date for that TABX tranche): two sets (of 20 each) reference obligations for the ABX.HE series of a similar rating. The first set of reference obligations to be tranched were the 40 names in the ABX 06-2 and ABX 07-1 indices. That was followed by the 40 names in the ABS 07-1 and ABX 07-2 indices. Two tranche baskets for each set of indices are used: BBB and BBB–, each with distinct attachment and detachment points, as shown in Exhibit 7.7.

Thus, the TABX.HE.07-1.06-2.BBB3-7 refers to the TABX that combines the reference entities of 07-1 and 06-2 at the BBB level. The "3-7"

EXHIBIT 7.7   Attachment/Exhaustion Points: ABX Tranche Trading

Equivalent Rating	BBB Index	BBB– Index
AAA Super Senior	35–100	40–100
AAA Mezzanine	20–35	25–40
AA	12–20	15–25
A	7–12	10–15
BBB	3–7	5–10
Equity	0–3	0–5

Source: UBS.

refers to the attachment and detachment points; that is, the points of expo-sure to the capital structure. Thus, 3-7 means that the bond attaches if losses on the 40 underlying BBB credits exceed 3%, it detaches if losses on the 40 underlying BBB credits exceed 7%. Similarly, the TABX.HE.07-1.06-2BBB-5-10 refers to the TABX that combines the reference entities of 07-1 and 06-2 and the BBB– level, with "5-10" referring to attachment/detachment points. Thus, if losses on the underlying BBB– bonds exceed 5%, the TABX 5-10 index will experience losses; if losses exceed 10%, it will experience a total loss of principal.

Pricing for the indices as of November 9, 2007, along with their cou-pon, is shown in Exhibit 7.8. Note that this index trades on a price basis. The coupon for each tranche is determined by a dealer poll, such that the initial price will be 100. The exception is that the coupon for each tranche is capped at +500; thus in distressed markets, we would expect the indices to begin trading at a discount.[4]

TABX PRICING

Theoretically, the weighted average price of the TABX BBB subindex should be approximately equal to the average price of the underlying ABX subindi-ces, corrected for any coupon differential.[5] That is, since the same bonds are contained in both indices, the arbitrage should hold.

---

[4] In fact, that's exactly what happened. Exhibit 7.8 shows that on TABX 07-2.07-1, four of the six BBBs had a coupon equal to the maximum, hence sold at a discount at origination.

[5] There are no interest shortfalls on the TABX. It will always pay the full stated coupon on the reference bonds, regardless of possible interest shortfalls on the underlying ABS names, whereas the ABX index passes through shortfalls up to the spread premium.

EXHIBIT 7.8 TABX Coupon and Prices

	11/9/07	
Index	Coupon	Price
TABX-HE 07-1 06-2 BBB 0–3	500	15.45
TABX-HE 07-1 06-2 BBB 3–7	500	17.59
TABX-HE 07-1 06-2 BBB 7–12	500	19.62
TABX-HE 07-1 06-2 BBB 12–20	467	21.05
TABX-HE 07-1 06-2 BBB 20–35	200	21.46
TABX-HE 07-1 06-2 BBB 35–100	51	25.97
TABX weighted average:	161	23.93
Average on ABX BBB 07-1 06-2	179	19.04
TABX-HE 07-1 06-2 BBB– 0–5	500	11.91
TABX-HE 07-1 06-2 BBB– 5–10	500	13.68
TABX-HE 07-1 06-2 BBB– 10–15	500	14.18
TABX-HE 07-1 06-2 BBB– 15–25	500	15.00
TABX-HE 07-1 06-2 BBB– 25–40	267	14.65
TABX-HE 07-1 06-2 BBB– 40–100	72	15.27
TABX weighted average:	208	14.85
Average on ABX BBB- 07-1 06-2	316	17.93
TABX-HE 07-2 07-1 BBB 0–3	500	18.00
TABX-HE 07-2 07-1 BBB 3–7	500	19.00
TABX-HE 07-2 07-1 BBB 7–12	500	20.18
TABX-HE 07-2 07-1 BBB 12–20	500	22.20
TABX-HE 07-2 07-1 BBB 20–35	500	24.01
TABX-HE 07-2 07-1 BBB 35–100	410	36.84
TABX weighted average:	442	31.63
Average on ABX BBB 07-2 07-1	362	19.65
TABX-HE 07-2 07-1 BBB– 0–5	500	16.03
TABX-HE 07-2 07-1 BBB– 5–10	500	17.81
TABX-HE 07-2 07-1 BBB– 10–15	500	19.19
TABX-HE 07-2 07-1 BBB– 15–25	500	20.44
TABX-HE 07-2 07-1 BBB– 25–40	500	21.44
TABX-HE 07-2 07-1 BBB– 40–100	410	28.05
TABX weighted average:	446	24.74
Average on ABX BBB– 07-2 07-1	445	18.52

Source: Markit.

In Exhibit 7.8, using 11/9/2007 closes, we show that there can be sizeable discrepancies between TABX pricing and the underlying ABX tranches. Note that for TABX07-1.06-2, the weighted average price (each price weighted by the width of the slice) of the BBB tranches is 23.93. The BBBs on ABX 06-2 were selling at 19.57, and the BBBs on ABX 07-2 were at 18.5, for an average of 19.04 and a differential of 4.89. The coupon on the ABX BBB indices was 179 bps, while the average coupon of the TABX was 161 bps. Even if we expect this 16 bps differential to be received for four years, that only explains part of the 4.89 price differential. Exhibit 7.8 shows that price differentials between the TABX 07-2.07-1 and the underlying ABX indices exceeded the price differentials between TABX 07-1.06-2 and the underlying ABX indices. For example, with almost no coupon differential, the TABX 07-2.07-1 was $6.22 higher than the underlying ABX indices.

As a practical matter, the differences cannot be simply arbitraged out. Liquidity and bid-ask spreads keep the indices from pricing on top of one another. In fact, the differentials were larger on the TABX 07-2.07-1 relative to the ABX than on TABX 07-1.06-2 relative to the ABX, reflecting the fact that the newer TABX was traded less frequently than the older TABX. It is important to realize that the ABX is a more liquid market than the TABX, so the former is the market used to hedge positions. With the large numbers of natural shorts, and relatively few natural longs, it is no surprise than the ABX is the more depressed of the two alternatives.

TABX VERSUS CDOs

A number of investors have attempted to value the less liquid CDO market by importing valuations from the more transparent TABX market. That approach is misguided.

While *attachment points* may be vaguely similar, the *bonds* may be very different, so any type of valuation imported from the TABX market will be suspect. And, as we will show in Chapter 11, collateral from the 2005 vintage was expected to experience significantly lower losses than that from the 2006 vintage. Let's take an early-2007 CDO deal (which was probably 10% cash collateral and 90% synthetic collateral). The 10% cash collateral was most likely similar to that backing 07-1, as the CDO manager was tied to new deal activity. However, the 90% synthetic component could vary tremendously in quality. At one extreme, it could look just like the cash securities, which given their vintage were most likely poor quality. At the other extreme, it could consist of very good quality collateral from earlier vintages. Until an investor looks at a CDO's holdings, there is no way of determining collateral quality and value. Thus, there is no way to use TABX pricing as the benchmark for CDO pricing.

SUMMARY

In this chapter, we looked at ABX and TABX indices, and discussed index composition and trading relationships between the two. We showed that the characteristics of deals underlying the ABX indices reflect very closely the characteristics of the loans produced at the same time, with similar delinquency experience. We also have shown that the ABX is one of the few ways to sell housing credit. Given the number of participants who need or want to go short, it is easy to see that ABX can trade for a lower value than would be indicated by model values or by TABX levels.

CHAPTER 8

Relationship among Cash, ABCDS, and the ABX

Market participants can take on subprime mortgage risk in three different forms:

1. Traditional cash tranches of subprime mortgage deals
2. Single-name credit default swaps referencing cash tranches
3. Indices of credit default swaps

Prior to 2005, the only way to take subprime exposure was in the form of cash bonds. The single-name ABCDS market grew rapidly after the International Swaps and Derivatives Association (ISDA) released (June 2005) a standard pay-as-you-go (PAUG) template. The ABX index (an index of 20 credit default swaps) debuted in January 2006. Trading of standardized tranches off the index (TABX) began in January 2007, although there had already been considerable activity in customized tranches. The introduction of these derivative instruments completely altered the nature of the subprime landscape, and enabled the rapid growth of the ABS CDO business. Synthetics simply allow risk transfer, which ultimately enables subprime credit risk to be distributed more broadly than it would otherwise have been absent the synthetic market.

In this chapter, we look at how the three different forms of subprime mortgage risk listed above differ, and what drives their relative spreads. We explain spread differences from two perspectives: (1) given their credit and cash flow characteristics, how the forms of subprime risk *should* trade relative to each other, and (2) given *supply and demand technicals*, how they *actually* traded relative to each other.

FUNDAMENTAL CONTRACTUAL DIFFERENCES: SINGLE-NAME ABCDS/ABX INDEX/CASH

There are notable differences between single-name ABCDS and the ABX. First, the ABX index PAUG contract does not include "distressed ratings downgrade" as a condition of default. Second, the ABX PAUG contract does not allow physical settlement; all settlement is PAUG. Finally, the ABX PAUG contract stipulates initial payment, fixed cap applicable, and coupon step-up not applicable. This contrasts to the bulk of the single-name ABCDS trades, which have stipulated no initial payment, fixed cap applicable, and coupon step-up applicable.

In examining how the cash, single-name ABCDS, and the ABX should trade vis-à-vis each other, we first look at how the following contractual differences affect relative spreads:

- Funding—cash bonds require funding; single-name ABCDS and the ABX do not.
- ABCDS has a termination option; ABX has no step-up provisions.
- Different caps on interest shortfalls.
- Differences in up-front payment arrangements.
- Distressed ratings downgrade on ABCDS.

Some of these effects should make cash tighter than ABCDS and the ABX index; others work in the opposite direction. Our results are summarized in Exhibit 8.1. After discussing each factor, we review the supply/demand considerations that came to dominate these markets and caused spread relationships to be what they are.

EXHIBIT 8.1   Differences for Cash/ABX/CDS Basics: Summary

	Effect		
Feature	Pushes ABX Wider/Tighter vs. Cash	Pushes ABCDS Wider/Tighter vs. Cash	Pushes ABCDS Wider/Tighter vs. ABX
Funding	Tighter	Tighter	0
Coupon step-up	Wider	Wider	Wider
Cap treatment	Tighter	Tighter	0
Intial cash flow exchange	0	0	0
Distressed rating downgrade	0	Wider (minor)	Wider (minor)

Source: UBS CDO Research.

Funding

The most important differential is that the cash bonds require funding, but single-name ABCDS and the ABX do not. This feature, taken in isolation, suggests that the synthetic should trade tighter than the cash. How do we value this? A few possibilities are detailed in Exhibit 8.2.

If the marginal buyer is a real money account, with the choice of (1) buying the cash bond or (2) buying the synthetic and investing the money at LIBOR, then there is no reason for any spread differential. However, marginal buyers are more often hedge funds, basing their analysis on a risk-adjusted return on equity. Many analysts look at the value of the funding by equating the return on equity for a cash and synthetic position. In Exhibit 8.2, we show cash spread, repo rate, and haircut for a financed cash position, and the margin applicable on synthetic trades. We assume that the haircut for financing a cash position rated A is 25%, and the margin applicable to synthetic trades is 10%. As shown in Exhibit 8.2, A rated cash trades at [LIBOR + 900]. Investors can finance up to 75% of the position (25% haircut) at [LIBOR + 40], so the return on the 20% equity investment on this position is equal to 39.58%. Intuitively,

> Investors earn [LIBOR + 900] spread on the entire A position, and pay [LIBOR + 40] on 75% of the A position.

With LIBOR = 4.78, we have for the *return on equity* (ROE):

$$ROE = [((L + 9.00) - ((1 - hc) \times (L + 0.40)))/hc)] = 39.58\%$$

Referring again to Exhibit 8.2, to earn the same return on equity on a 10% synthetic margin, the spread on the synthetic need only be 348 bps ("Return on Equity, Breakeven CDS Premium" column and the A rating row). The difference between the +900 cash spread and the +348 breakeven synthetic spread is 552 bps (Return on Equity, FV (Cash – CDS) column and the A rating row). The problem with this analysis is that risk on the two positions is not nearly equivalent: the cash position has 25% equity, the synthetic 10% equity. This suggests that investors are willing to use a very aggressive 10× leverage on the CDS position.

The more rational way to look at this is via a risk-adjusted position. We formulate that by asking the following question: If you were required to hold the same equity for a synthetic position as for a cash position, what is the required synthetic spread? For the As, the answer is 900 bps cash spread minus the 30 bps differential to cash (Risk-Adjusted Measure, FV (Cash – CDS) column, A row) for a value of 870 bps (Risk-Adjusted Measure, Breakeven CDS premium column, A row). Intuitively, the differential

EXHIBIT 8.2 Funded *vs.* Synthetic Positions: Value (as of 10/19/2007)

Rating Level	Cash Spread	Repo Rate	Haircut	Synthetic Margins	Return on Equity		Risk-Adjusted Measure		Unfunded SS
					Breakeven CDS Premium (ROE Method)	F(Cash – CDS) ROE Method	Breakeven CDS Premium RA Method	FV(Cash – CDS) RA Method	Applicable in 2006: FV(Cash – CDS) w/Unfunded Super Senior
AAA	140	20	10	3	36.6	103.4	122.0	18.0	12.0
AA	400	35	20	5	93.0	307.0	372.0	28.0	12.0
A	900	40	25	10	348.0	552.0	870.0	30.0	12.0
BBB	2,000	50	35	20	1124.3	875.7	1967.5	32.5	12.0
BBB-	2,500	60	40	20	1232.0	1268.0	2464.0	36.0	12.0

arises because a cash investor bears the financing penalty, which is the [Repo spread × The maximum amount you can finance]; thus 30 bps financing penalty = 40 bps on the 75% of the position that can be financed. We see this risk-adjusted return comparison as a far better way than ROE to look at the value of funded versus unfunded positions.

In 2006, the marginal buyer of the BBB, BBB–, and many of the A rated securities were CDOs. Thus the synthetic portion could be sold as an unfunded super senior. The unfunded super-senior traded at a spread of 18 bps, approximately 12 bps tighter than spreads on the funded bond. Using synthetic collateral for part of the deal allowed 12 bps better funding (shown in the last column of Exhibit 8.2).

Regardless of the method chosen, the fact that the synthetics do not have to be funded but the cash does suggests that the cash should sell wider than the synthetics, as reflected in Exhibit 8.1. It is important to realize that Exhibit 8.2 implicitly assumed all securities were trading close to par. To the extent cash securities are trading at a discount to par, the spread differential between cash and synthetic should be lower, as the market value of the cash to be financed is less.

Treatment at the Call

As mentioned earlier, there are two ways to treat the coupon step-up: applicable and nonapplicable. Single-name ABCDS contracts usually contain a *coupon step-up applicable clause*. This gives the ABCDS protection buyer a one-time right to terminate the contract within five days of the contract hitting its coupon step-up trigger. If exercised, there is no termination payment in either direction. If the protection buyer does not terminate the contract within five days, then the contract continues, but with the protection buyer paying a stepped-up CDS premium for the rest of the contract's life.

Let's briefly consider this option. If the deal is performing well, it is likely to get called. If the deal is performing poorly, the buyer of protection will want to remain in the ABCDS, as write-downs will likely be much higher than the step-up coupon. There are some "in between" cases where the protection buyer may opt to terminate (i.e., the deal is not called, but losses are low enough that continued protection payments will be higher than expected write-downs). This option has some value to the protection buyer, therefore single-name CDS should trade wider than cash or the ABX.

Partially offsetting this, the ABX index stipulates that the coupon step-up is "not applicable." This means the protection buyer of the ABX index does not have to pay the step-up coupon after the call date if the deal is not called; the protection buyer continues to pay the original premium. Again, if the deal is performing well, it is likely to be called; if performing poorly, the bond could be completely written down by the call date. However, there will be scenarios in which collateral losses are high enough that the deal is not called, but low enough that the bond has not been written completely down. In such cases, the buyer of BBB protection does not have to pay the step-up coupon. All else being equal, this suggests that the ABX trades wider than the cash.

This feature, taken in isolation, suggests that both single-name ABCDS and the ABX should be wider than the cash (which is reflected in Exhibit 8.1). Moreover, the termination option in a single-name ABCDS should be worth slightly more than ABX, which does not have the termination feature, thus pushing the ABCDS wider to the ABX.

Cap Treatment

There are also minor basis differences caused by the differential cap treatment. Both single-name ABCDS and the ABX specify a "fixed cap" arrangement. This means that if there is an interest shortfall, the protection seller's payment to the protection buyer is limited to the CDS premium. The net payment amount, then, can never be a payment from the protection seller to the protection buyer. An interest shortfall simply reduces the premium the protection buyer pays the production seller. In a cash bond, if there is an interest shortfall, the investor (protection seller) bears the full cost of both the premium above LIBOR as well as the LIBOR component of the coupon. In CDS documentation, the "interest shortfall cap not applicable" would have the same economic consequences as owning the bond directly (i.e., the protection seller pays the protection buyer the full amount of the cash interest shortfall). Consequently, sellers of CDS protection do a bit better in the fixed cap arrangement. This suggests that CDS protection sellers should collect less of a premium than cash spreads, hence, as reflected in Exhibit 8.1, ABCDS and the ABX should trade tighter than cash.

Initial Cash Exchange

The cash flow features are very different for each instrument. Both the ABX Indices and cash securities have coupons set at inception, and prices on these instruments will fluctuate. However, if the ABX index is selling below par, the protection seller receives an upfront payment equal to the difference between par and the index value. Thus, if the index is selling at $90, the protection seller receives $10 upfront ($100 par minus $90 price of index). In the single-name ABCDS market, market conventions have changed through time. In 2005, 2006, and early 2007, there was no initial cash flow exchange. The coupon was set to the then-current market conditions. Single-name ABCDS were much easier to use in a CDO deal than either cash or the ABX indices, as there is no markup or markdown from par. In late 2005 and all 2006, CDOs were the primarily sellers of single-name protection; these provisions, at the margin, drove spreads marginally tighter in the single-name ABCDS versus cash and the ABX.

In 2007, with the price of subprime cash securities and the ABX trading well below par, the required protection payments on the single-name CDS became extremely large, as would be required to compensate for the price discount on the cash and ABX. As a result, in mid-2007 the market moved to trading with an initial cash exchange, similar to the ABX. To see why, let's consider the ABX 06-2 BBB-trading at $20. The coupon is 242 bps per year. What would the coupon have to be on a hypothetical single-name CDS to give the same return to the protection seller? We calculate:

- Seller of protection earns 242 bps.
- Seller of protection receives $80 upfront ($100 par minus $20 dollar price). We assume these funds are invested at one-month LIBOR (4.78% as of this writing).Thus, the interest received on this $80; totals $3.82 (4.78% × $80).

Adding the two components, the protection seller earns $6.24 ($2.42 + $3.82) on the $20 exposure. To get the same return on a single-name CDS, the protection payment would have to be 31.20% per year, or 3,120 bps. This is an unrealistically large up-front payment.

For the purposes of Exhibit 8.1, the initial cash exchange does not change the economics of how the instruments should trade. However, when calculating the return on the ABX or a single-name CDS, it is important to include interest received on the cash received up-front.

Distressed Rating Downgrade

Distressed ratings downgrade is a credit event allowing physical settlement in the single-name ABCDS market, but not in the ABX market. A distressed ratings downgrade occurs if any rating agency downgrades the ABS tranche to CCC/Caa2 or below, or withdraws its rating. This credit event gives the buyer of protection the option of delivering the security, and getting paid out at par on the ABCDS. The existence of this additional option suggests that the single-name ABCDS should sell wider than cash or ABX. This is a relatively minor benefit, as it is primarily a timing issue. Moreover, ABCDS volumes are multiples of the cash market, making physical settlement less likely. If the bond has performed poorly enough to experience a downgrade to a distressed level (CCC), write-downs are likely and just a matter of time. The net result will be very similar if the exposure is held in CDS or in physical form. Again, physical delivery of the bond is an option for the protection buyer, not an obligation. If the bond is not delivered, write-downs occur in the normal course of events. We see Distressed Ratings Downgrade as a minor benefit to protection buyers, and thus in Exhibit 8.1 only peg it as a minor spread widening factor for single-name ABCDS and ABX.

Summary of the Impact of Contractual Differences

We have shown a number of *contractual differences* between cash, single-name ABCDS, and ABX, which cause mixed results as to where these three instruments should trade vis-à-vis each other. The fact that the cash needs to be financed suggests that it should be wider than either the ABX or single-name ABCDS. Howeve, both the ABX and single-name ABCDS grant advantages to the seller (buyer of protection) to either terminate the contract or avoid paying the step-up amount, which should make the cash tighter than the synthetic. Other differences (in cap treatment, initial payment, distressed rating downgrade) are minor.

SUPPLY/DEMAND TECHNICALS

The contractual differences mentioned above are relatively modest, and should result in a very stable spread relationship between cash, the single-name ABCDS market, and the ABX index. However, relative spreads have varied tremendously. We now focus on *supply-and-demand technicals* that can overwhelm the contractual differences. We show that in October 2007 the dislocation (i.e., ABX much cheaper than either single-name or cash) was caused by the ABX having become the hedging vehicle of choice. Many mortgage market participants, including the dealer community, were long mortgage credit. The only way to short mortgage credit was in synthetic form. And with single-name CDS trading in an illiquid manner at this point in time, the ABX is the only market in which market participants could get execution and some degree of price transparency. Thus, the ABX was now trading cheaper than the other vehicles.

Exhibit 8.3 shows the relationship between BBB– cash, ABCDS, and ABX spreads at three dates: 11/28/2006, 7/6/2007, and 10/19/2007. Note that representative cash and ABCDS spreads capture the "average" credit at each rating level, whereas those relationships actually varied widely over time, reflecting supply/demand dynamics.

Look Back at 11/28/2006

The major reason the ABX.HE.06-2 BBB– traded wider than the cash and ABCDS markets (299 on the ABX.HE 06-2 BBB– versus 240 on the cash

EXHIBIT 8.3   ABX Market: Basis Relationship

	ABX 06-1	ABX 06-2	ABX 07-1	ABX 07-2	Single-Name CDS (on-the-run spreads)	Cash
11/28/2006						
AAA	12	9	n/a	n/a	n/a	16
AA	14	14	n/a	n/a	n/a	30
A	46	54	n/a	n/a	40	42
BBB	130	188	n/a	n/a	125	130
BBB–	241	299	n/a	n/a	250	240
7/6/2007						
AAA	18	22	21	n/a	n/a	20
AA	36	57	54	n/a	n/a	30
A	183	460	570	n/a	175	175
BBB	684	1217	1477	n/a	550	500
BBB–	1166	1774	2014	n/a	700	650
10/19/2007						
AAA	72	132	182	234	n/a	140
AA	229	736	954	970	n/a	400
A	971	1826	1992	2005	900	900
BBB	2234	2798	2791	2751	2000	2000
BBB–	2836	3241	3272	2828	2500	2500

Source: UBS.

and 250 on the single-name CDS) was that ABX clientele at the time consisted primarily of macrohedge funds. These funds were looking to sell the ABX index (buy protection) as a way of playing a housing slowdown. In fact, for a macrohedge fund, there are only a limited number of ways to bet on a fall in home prices. They could short equities of subprime mortgage originators, home builders, or REITs; or buy protection on subordinate tranches of subprime mortgage deals. It was better to buy protection on the subordinate tranches of subprime mortgage deals since the equities of subprime originators and homebuilders were considerably off their highs (so shorting already had some potential steam taken out of it), whereas spreads on Baa2 and Baa3 bonds were near historic tights. The macrohedge funds were less interested in the characteristics of the individual credits, thus it was more desirable to sell protection on the ABX than on individual deals. As a result, macrohedge fund participation in the ABX market was high in the second half of 2006. The way they saw it, economic data suggested a housing correction was under way. Studies had shown that in a flat *home price appreciation* (HPA) environment, losses on subprime deals were likely to be in the 8% to 9% range. With negative HPA, losses were expected to be 12% to 13%. Most subprime BBB– bonds begin to take losses in the 8% to 10% range. Thus, macrohedge funds viewed the BBB– ABX as a cheap option—they paid 290 bps per year for a potentially large upside. And even if the ABX BBB– index did not experience a write-down, spreads were expected to widen from then-current levels as the housing market contracted.

By contrast, late in 2006, the clientele for the cash and single-name ABCDS markets was primarily from CDOs. These investors are buyers of mortgage credit (i.e., sellers of protection). They do their homework on the characteristics of individual deals, then opt to buy (sell protection on) deals in which they are comfortable with the collateral, originator, and servicer. CDO managers do extensive stress testing on each deal, and select portfolios that will withstand housing market downturns. In their view, current spreads on these deals were sufficient to pay all CDO liabilities and generate an attractive equity yield. (In the appendix to this chapter, we discuss the evolution of ABX CDOs, highlighting the importance of single-name CDS.)

In late 2006, the basis at the BBB and BBB– level resulted primarily from a tug-of-war between macrohedge fund protection buyers of the ABX index and CDO protection sellers of cash and single-name ABCDS. When the basis got too wide, CDO managers began to use the ABX as a substitute for single-name assets, buying back protection on credits in the ABX that they don't want to position. Even so, at the BBB and BBB– level, the ABX traded wider than either single-name CDS or cash.

Exhibit 8.3 shows that in late 2006, at the AAA and AA ratings, cash was much wider than the ABX. For example, the ABX index had AAs at 14; the cash market was selling them at 30, which primarily reflected funding differences (discussed earlier in this chapter). Moreover, at that point, trading volume in the ABX's AAA and AA rated tranches was low (approximately 5% of total ABX volume). The A, BBB, and BBB– ABX tranches traded more actively (A tranches being approximately 15% of trading volume; BBB 30%; and BBB– 50% of total trading volume).

By July 6, 2007

The middle section of Exhibit 8.3 shows how the dynamics had shifted considerably. At the BBB level, the ABX was much wider than either the cash or the single-name CDS. This reflected the escalating subprime crises, and new CDOs not getting done. Thus CDO managers were not selling protection on the single-name CDS. The demand for cash securities at the BBB level was also very weak, and very little was trading. The small amount of trading was occurring at distressed pricing, and dealers decided to hold the positions they owned rather than sell at these distressed levels. Meanwhile, both the macrohedge funds and the dealer community were trying to buy protection—the macrohedge funds intending to profit from continued house price depreciation; the dealer community to hedge mortgage credit exposure. Thus most of the trading was centered on the ABX, with more protection buyers than protection sellers, which pushed prices down. Hence the ABX was trading very cheap to the cash and single-name CDS (BBB spreads were 500 on the cash securities, 550 on single-name CDS, 1,477 on ABX 07-1), although relatively little of either cash or single-name CDS was actually trading.

At the AAA level, spreads on cash were roughly equal those on single-name CDS. The funding advantage of the ABX vis-à-vis cash was offset by the demand to short (buy protection on) the AAA ABX.

By October 19, 2007

As can been seen in the bottom section of Exhibit 8.3, the ABX traded at wider levels than the cash or single-name CDS at every rating level. From July to October 2007, BBB securities slid to levels where any gain from being short the securities was relatively low. Thus, macrohedge funds and dealers shorted (bought protection on) the AA, the A, and to a lesser extent, the AAA indices. The heavy demand to sell (buy protection on) the ABX at every level more than offset any funding advantage of the ABX vis-à-vis the cash.

WHAT KEEPS THE ARBITRAGE FROM GOING AWAY?

Clearly, the primary reason the ABX was wider than the single-name ABCDS market or the cash market is that macrohedge funds and the dealer community are primarily sellers of the ABX, placing downward pressure on this index. But why is that differential not arbitraged away? There are four reasons.

First, not all credits in the ABX are actively traded. Exhibit 8.4 shows (as of July 6, 2007) individual midmarket CDS spreads at the BBB– level on credits that are actively traded, and UBS estimates for those less actively traded. It would be very difficult to replicate the index using single-name credits, as the least actively traded securities are those with the widest bid/offer spreads, with some not trading at all. Thus, the indicative spreads in Exhibit 8.3 are for the "better" credits that do trade.

EXHIBIT 8.4   ABX 06-2 BBB– Index (as of 7/6/2007)

	CUSIP	Spread
SAIL 2006-4 M8	86360WAN2	2,000
LBMLT 2006-1 M9	542514RW6	2,000
RAMP 2006-NC2 M9	75156TAM2	2,000
MSC 2006-HE2 B3	617451FE4	2,000
MSAC 2006-WMC2 B3	61749KAQ6	2,000
ARSI 2006-W1 M9	040104RR4	1,650
MABS 2006-NC1 M9	57643LNQ5	1,650
RASC 2006-KS3 M9	76113ABU4	1,550
BSABS 2006-HE3 M9	07387UJA0	1,550
FFML 2006-FF4 B1	362334GJ7	1,650
CWL 2006-8 M9	045427AN1	1,550
HEAT 2006-4 B1	437084VZ6	1,050
JPMAC 2006-FRE1 M9	46626LFW5	1,050
GSAMP 2006-HE3 M9	36244KAP0	1,050
MLMI 2006-HE1 B3A	59020U3Q6	750
ACE 2006-NC1 M9	004421VC4	600
SVHE 2006-OPT5 M9	83612CAP4	750
SABR 2006-OP1 B3	81375WJP2	700
CARR 2006-NC1 M9	144531FG0	650
SASC 2006-WF2 M9	86360LAN6	450
Average		1,333

Source: UBS.

Second, the single-name CDS market is much less liquid than the ABX. In early July 2007, the synthetic tranches generally had a bid-ask spread of approximately 50 to 100 bps at the BBB– level, with the weaker credit having even wider bid-ask spreads. The ABX market has a bid-ask spread of 2–3 points at the BBB– level. The sizeable bid-ask spreads in the single-name market inhibits investors from trading back and forth.

Third, cash cannot be shorted; its market is very thin. Cash can remain rich to CDS for a long time, as there is no way to alleviate richness in cash other than through increased supply. In 2007, new subprime production ceased, leaving new supply limited.

Finally, pricing on the ABX indices is reasonably transparent, but that on cash and single-name CDS pricing is not. This problem became more acute in late 2007, as trading in both the cash and single-name CDS markets became very limited, leaving the market with less price transparency.

SUMMARY

In this chapter, we looked at how the three forms of subprime mortgage risk—cash, single-name ABCDS, and the ABX—differ and what drives their relative spreads. We looked at theoretical spread differentials as a result of differences between the contracts. We also looked at the differences between the instruments from a supply and demand perspective, arguing that for most of 2007, this resulted in making it more expensive to buy protection on the ABX than the alternatives. (Stated differently, the ABX is cheaper than alternatives.) In particular, with both the macrohedge funds and the dealer community primarily heavy sellers of the ABX, downward pressure on these indices was quite strong. Moreover, "arbitrage" between the sectors is much less than perfect. It is impossible to short cash; single-name ABCDS trading volumes for the bottom bonds in the ABX are limited; bid-ask spreads in single-name ABCDS are very wide; and price discovery in the cash and single-name ABCDS market is poor.

APPENDIX: IMPORTANCE OF ABCDS TO CDO MANAGERS

ABCDS were very important to mezzanine ABS CDOs. Prior to the release of the PAUG template in June 2005, mezzanine ABS CDOs averaged $300 to $400 million in deal size, and took an average of 8 to 9 months to ramp. However, the demand to buy protection in the single-name ABCDS market enabled CDO managers to ramp mezzanine ABS CDO deals in 2 to 5 weeks, with sizes as much as three times that of pre-June 2005 deals. In other words, CDO managers were able to ramp deals by assembling a portfolio of single-name ABCDS, on which they had sold protection, instead of accumulating a portfolio of subprime cash bonds.

Besides reducing ramping time, ABCDS enabled greater mezzanine ABS CDO issuance, as dealers were no longer constrained by the amount of available cash collateral. During 2006, $50 billion of mezzanine ABS CDOs were issued (almost doubling 2005's $28 billion). This deal volume could not have occurred in the absence of the ABCDS market.

Let's do some math. During 2006, subprime origination totaled $477 billion. Exhibit 8.5 demonstrates that only 2.9% of that was rated BBB+,

EXHIBIT 8.5   2006 Home Equity Issuance, by Ratings (12/31/2006)

Rating	Amount Offered	Percent
AAA	$358,063,183,012	75.1%
AA+	20,385,950,003	4.3%
AA	19,146,227,010	4.0%
AA−	7,451,985,011	1.6%
A+	7,450,556,031	1.6%
A	7,809,954,077	1.6%
A−	5,598,413,045	1.2%
BBB+	5,638,973,064	1.2%
BBB	4,196,207,062	0.9%
BBB−	3,811,321,092	0.8%
BB+	2,569,736,435	0.5%
BB	956,681,018	0.2%
BB−	61,610,001	0.0%
B+	18,966,000	0.0%
B	34,576,002	0.0%
B−	26,861,003	0.0%
N.A.	32,250,078,009	6.8%
NR	1,190,132,003	0.2%
Total	$476,661,409,878	100.0%

Source: MCM and UBS CDO calculations.

BBB, and BBB−, and only 1.7% was BBB and BBB− (the two ratings most desired by mezzanine ABS CDO managers). That is, of the 2.9% in the BBB range, 1.2% was BBB+, 0.9% was BBB, and 0.8% was BBB−. In fact, if every BBB and BBB− produced in 2006 ($8.0 billion) went into mezzanine ABS CDOs, and this segment of the market comprised only 65% of their collateral, mezzanine ABS CDO capacity would only have been $12.3 billion ($8.0 billion/0.65). Adding all $5.6 billion of BBB+ collateral would only have produced $20.9 billion ($13.6 billion/0.65) in total CDO volume.

In fact, of the $50 billion in mezzanine ABS CDO deal volume during 2006, ABCDS underlyings constituted approximately $40 billion. This allowed for two changes in the composition of mezzanine ABS CDO deals (as illustrated in Exhibit 8.6):

1. *An increase in the residential B and C collateral in mezzanine ABS CDOs.* Residential B and C and subprime/high LTV collateral in mezzanine ABS CDOs had historically ranged from 65% to 70%. Obtaining this collateral was so much of an issue that equivalently rated collateral from other asset classes was also used extensively. With the use of ABCDS, mezzanine ABS CDOs were commonly 85% residential B and C.
2. *The ratings distribution of collateral used in mezzanine ABS CDOs was more concentrated in BBB and BBB–.* This is very different from the historical case, as cash bonds were simply unavailable. In early 2005, approximately 25% to 30% of CDO collateral was rated A; 65% to 70% were BBB; and 5% to 10% were rated BB. In a sample of late 2006 deals, we found 2% of the collateral rated A, 3% rated BB, 5% rated BBB+, and 90% rated BBB or BBB–.

Not only did the ABCDS market provide the raw material for greater deal volume, it also improved the CDO arbitrage. Exhibit 8.7 shows a hypothetical late 2006 hybrid deal (cash + ABCDS) and a hypothetical cash deal from the same period. In both cases, the rating splits are identical: 65% senior AAA, 12% junior AAA, 9% AA, 7% A, 1% BBB, 2% BBB, 1% BBB–, and 4% equity. In the hybrid deal, using ABCDS allowed the use of an unfunded super-senior tranche. Consistent with then prevailing market conditions, we assumed the unfunded super-senior tranche would have traded 12 bps tighter than cash. We also assumed that the bonds purchased in the single-name ABCDS market are about 23 (1.88 − 1.65) bps wider than the cash.

The result of these changes is very dramatic for the CDO arbitrage. Note that the equity on the hybrid CDO is able to achieve an attractive 21% internal rate of return. By contrast, the cash deal is only able to achieve a 13% internal rate of return.

Finally, the ABCDS market allowed the CDO managers a good deal of increased flexibility. New issuance was very light at certain times, and a CDO manager may not necessarily be able to find issuer names that he

EXHIBIT 8.6 Residential B and C: Percentage and Rating Distribution

	Residential B & C and	Rating Distribution				
Deal	Suprime/High LTV	A	BBB+	BBB	BBB–	BB
Early 2005	65–70%	30	22	22	21	5
Early 2006	85%	2	5	52	38	3

Source: UBS CDO Research.

EXHIBIT 8.7   Hybrids and Cash Mezzanine ABS CDO Aribtrage (late 2006)

	Percent	Hybrid Spread	Cash Spread
Senior AAA	65%	0.18%	0.30%
Junior AAA	12%	0.44%	0.44%
AA	9%	0.53%	0.53%
A	7%	1.40%	1.40%
BBB+	1%	2.65%	2.65%
BBB	2%	3.30%	3.30%
BBB–	1%	3.70%	3.70%
Equity	4%		
Total	100%		
Average debt spread		0.46%	0.54%
Upfront and running fees		0.78%	0.78%
Total debt and fee spread		1.24%	1.32%
Average asset spread		1.88%	1.65%
Excess spread		0.64%	0.33%
Times 25 leverage		16.06%	8.28%
Plus swap rate		5.00%	5.00%
Targeted equity return		21.06%	13.28%

Source: UBS CDO Research.

liked. The ABCDS market allowed ABS CDO managers to sell protection on subprime mortgage tranches of their choosing (as long as they found willing buyers of protection).

The rise of the synthetic market also provided for a considerable amount of performance variation in 2006 and early 2007 mezzanine ABS CDO deals. Some managers that had sold protection in single-name CDS form opted to do so on 2005 and earlier origination at tighter spreads; others sold protection on 2006 deals at wider spreads. CDOs that have a larger amount of 2005 and earlier collateral have experienced relatively better performance.

CHAPTER 9

Credit Default Swaps on CDOs

In June 2006, the International Swap and Derivatives Association (ISDA) released a template that sellers and buyers of credit protection can use to negotiate the terms of *credit default swaps* (CDS) on *collateralized debt obligations* (CDOs). Standardized documentation improved the liquidity of CDO CDS, which was important to CDO investors for four reasons.

First, selling protection on a CDO CDS provided a new way to access CDO risk, and opened up investment opportunities to a broader range of CDOs than those available in the cash market. Second, CDO CDS allowed one to efficiently short CDOs for the first time. Applications ranged from simply providing another way to get out of long cash CDO positions to the execution of various long-short strategies. These long-short strategies could involve tranches within the same CDO, tranches from different CDOs, or CDO tranches and underlying CDO assets. Third, supply and demand technicals across cash and synthetic CDO markets almost guaranteed price misalignments and, therefore, profitable trading opportunities. Finally, trading levels of CDO CDS enlightened one's view of the cash CDO market. Price distinctions among vintages and managers are often more apparent, or apparent sooner, in the synthetic market than in the cash market. Even if CDO CDS levels do not affect one's view of the quality and value of cash CDOs, CDS levels will impact the views of other cash market participants. One needs to understand what others are thinking to trade optimally.

In this chapter, we explain the documentation for trades of CDS on CDOs. In a simple, straightforward way, we explain the CDO credit problems the documentation recognizes, the consequences for which CDO CDS documentation provides, and the choices of interest rate cap. We also address miscellaneous CDO CDS terms, the differences between selling protection on a CDS and owning a cash CDO, how one exits a CDO CDS, and rating agency concerns when a CDO enters into a CDO CDS.

Note that in this chapter, capitalized terms are ISDA-defined terms that one will find in CDO CDS documentation. Lowercase terms are widely-understood colloquialisms not found in CDO CDS documents.

CDO CDS NOMENCLATURE

It takes two parties to make a CDO CDS: a *credit protection buyer* and a *credit protection seller*. Naturally, it also takes a CDO tranche to be the subject of the CDO CDS between the two parties. Formally, the CDO tranche is the *reference obligation* and the CDO it is part of is the *reference entity*. The protection buyer buys credit protection from the protection seller on a specific CDO tranche in a dollar-amount size called the *notional amount*. As shown in Exhibit 9.1, the protection buyer pays the protection seller a fee based on a number of basis points per annum times the notional amount times the appropriate day-count fraction of a year. These payments are paid quarterly by the protection buyer for the life of the CDO CDS, assuming certain CDO credit problems (defined next) do not occur.

As shown in Exhibit 9.2, the protection buyer is known as the *Fixed Rate Payer,* while the protection seller is known as the *Floating Rate Payer*, in ISDA swap documentation. This is holdover from ISDA interest rate swap terminology in which one party pays a fixed interest rate and the other party pays a floating interest rate. The buyer of protection is said to be long the CDS, but since this party to the trade has a similar risk to someone who has shorted the referenced CDO tranche (the short benefits from defaults), this party is said to be short the CDO. The seller of protection is short the CDS, but since this party has a similar risk to someone who owns the referenced CDO tranche (the owner is hurt by defaults), this party is long the CDO.

In a CDO CDS, the notional amount of the CDS amortizes in step with the CDO tranche. For example, if 50% of the CDO tranche amortizes, 50% of the CDS notional is considered to have amortized. Therefore, the life span of a CDO CDS mirrors the life span of the CDO tranche. The amor-

EXHIBIT 9.1   Initial Cash Flows of a Credit Default Swap

Credit Protection Buyer	Periodic Payments → Basis points × Notional amount	Credit Protection Seller

EXHIBIT 9.2   Equivalent Buyer and Seller Designations

Credit Protection Buyer Fixed rate payer is long the CDS and short the underlying CDO.	Periodic Payments → Basis points × Notional amount	**Credit Protection Seller** Floating rate payer is short the CDS and long the underlying CDO.

tization of CDO CDS is in contrast to corporate CDS. While a corporate CDS has a *single* Reference Entity (e.g., IBM), it usually encompasses a class of Reference Obligations (e.g., all senior unsecured debt of IBM). The *term* of the corporate CDS overarches specific Reference Obligations. In other words, Reference Obligations may be issued or retired over the life of the corporate CDS, but as long as some issue of the Reference Entity fits the Reference Obligation definition, the corporate CDS can continue. In contrast, the specificity of CDO CDS to a particular CDO tranche drives CDO CDS amortization and restricts CDO CDS tenor.

CDO CREDIT PROBLEMS AND THEIR CONSEQUENCES

As we all know, a CDO can experience credit problems. ISDA CDO CDS documentation specifically defines five CDO credit problems with respect to a CDO tranche. As shown in the left column of Exhibit 9.3, these are: *Interest Shortfall, Failure to Pay Interest, Write-down and Implied Write-down, Failure to Pay Principal,* and *Distressed Ratings Downgrade.*

Now note that shown across the top of Exhibit 9.2 are two consequences of a CDO credit problem: *Floating Amount Events* and *Credit Events*. As shown in the exhibit, Floating Amount Events are subject to Floating Payments, which is known colloquially as *pay-as-you-go settlement*. Credit Events are subject to *Physical Settlement*. ISDA documentation also has specific definitions of these terms.

Different CDO credit problems have different consequences. For now, just note that Exhibit 9.3 shows that the consequence of some CDO credit problems is a Floating Amount Event, the consequence of other CDO credit

EXHIBIT 9.3   CDO Credit Problems and Their Consequences

	Two Consequences	
	Floating Amount Events	Credit Events
Five CDO credit problems	Subject to floating payments (pay-as-you-go settlement)	Subject to physical settlement
Interest shortfall	X	
Failure to pay interest		X
Write-down and implied write-down	X	X
Failure to pay principal	X	X
Distressed ratings downgrade		X

problems is a Credit Event, and some CDO credit problems can have either a Floating Amount Event or a Credit Event consequence.

In the next section, we discuss the five CDO credit problems that ISDA CDO CDS documentation recognizes and defines. Then we will discuss the two consequences for which the documentation provides. Afterwards, the CDO CDS system of CDO credit problems and consequences will gel.

CDO Credit Problems

Interest Shortfall is the failure of the CDO to pay all interest due on the Reference Obligation. Note that interest due includes interest that is PIKable[1] under the terms of the CDO tranche.

Failure to Pay Interest has a more stringent definition than Interest Shortfall. Skipping a PIKable interest coupon does not trigger Failure to Pay Interest unless the CDO has been PIKing for one year. Furthermore, for both non-PIK and PIKable CDO tranches, the amount of unpaid interest involved must be at least $10,000. The more stringent requirement of Failure to Pay Interest over Interest Shortfall has to do with their differing consequences. Interest Shortfall is Floating Amount Event subject to a Floating Payment (pay-as-you-go settlement) while the Failure to Pay Interest is a Credit Event subject to Physical Settlement.[2]

CDOs rarely have mechanisms that formally realize principal losses due to credit losses in the underlying collateral portfolio. But if a CDO did have this feature, those events would be captured by the *Write-down* definition. In the absence of a Write-down mechanism in the CDO, the parties to a CDO CDS can elect to use *Implied Write-down*. Simplified, a CDO tranche is implicitly written down if its par overcollateralization ratio falls below 100%. For purposes of Implied Write-down, overcollateralization is calculated by the terms of the indenture, including its treatment of par haircuts for downgraded or defaulted collateral.[3]

Failure to Pay Principal is the failure of the reference CDO to pay the reference tranche's principal by the *effective* maturity of the CDO, which is the earlier of (1) the time the CDO's assets have all been amortized or liquidated or by (2) the legal final maturity of the Reference Obligation.

Distressed Ratings Downgrade occurs if any rating agency downgrades the CDO tranche to CCC/Caa2 or below or withdraws its rating.

---

[1] A *pay-in-kind* (PIK) bond or *PIK* feature is one where instead of paying current coupon, the par value of bond is increased by the appropriate amount.

[2] For those interested in the differences between CDO CDS and ABS CDS standard documentation, Failure to Pay Interest is not a Credit Event in ABS CDS.

[3] Regarding the differences between CDO CDS and ABS CDS standard documentation, Implied Write-down is mandatory for ABS CDS, but optional for CDO CDS.

Consequences

As we said, ISDA documentation also defines two "consequences" of a "CDO credit problem": Floating Payments (pay-as-you-go settlement) or Physical Settlement. Note again that Implied Write-down and Failure to Pay Principal can be either a Floating Amount Event or a Credit Event. The choice is up to the protection buyer.

Floating Amount Events cause Floating Payments, or pay-as-you-go settlement. Interest Shortfall, Implied Write-down, and Failure to Pay Principal are Floating Amount Events. The protection seller must pay the amount of the Interest Shortfall or Implied Write-down to the protection buyer. Note that the amounts involved in an Interest Shortfall or an Implied Write-down might be small relative to the notional amount of the swap. Any payment period's Interest Shortfall can be no more than the amount of interest due in that payment period. The amount of an Implied Write-down could be a small fraction of CDS notional.

A unique aspect of Interest Shortfall and Implied Write-down is that they are reversible. If a CDO pays previously PIKed interest on the reference tranche, or if a CDO tranche's par overcollateralization ratio climbs back above its trigger amount, the credit protection buyer must make a reversing payment to the protection seller called an *Additional Fixed Payment*. These reversing payments can take place up to one year and five days after the effective maturity of the CDO.

Because unpaid PIKable interest is included in Interest Shortfall, and paid by the Protection Seller at the time of the shortfall, interest on capitalized PIK interest is *excluded* from future calculations of Interest Shortfall. This is only fair: The protection buyer has received the interest payment from the protection seller and should not be entitled to interest on interest.

Failure to Pay Principal is a Floating Amount Event so that at the end of the CDO, the protection buyer can receive a payment even if he does not own the CDO. In this case, the protection seller pays the remaining notional amount of the CDO CDS to the protection buyer. Note that the protection buyer does not get to double count Implied Write-downs and Failure to Pay Principal. When an Implied Write-down amount is paid, the notional amount of the CDO CDS is reduced. That is, to the extent that Implied Write-downs have been taken, CDO CDS notional is reduced. The protection buyer can't subsequently claim the written down amount again as a Failure to Pay Principal.

Credit Events cause Physical Settlement. At the protection buyer's option, the protection buyer delivers the CDO tranche and the protection seller pays par. Failure to Pay Principal, Implied Write-down, Failure to Pay Interest, and Distressed Ratings Downgrade are Credit Events causing

Physical Settlement. Once done, Physical Settlement cannot be reversed. The protection buyer can deliver less than the full notional amount of the CDS and the remainder of the CDS notional will continue in force.

Note that there is no cash flow effect to the CDO from a ratings downgrade and no dollar amount of impairment can be specified. Therefore, Distressed Ratings Downgrade is only a Credit Event causing Physical Settlement and can not be a Floating Payment Event causing pay-as-you-go settlement.

An advantage of Floating Payments over Physical Settlement is that the protection buyer does not have to own the CDO tranche to collect a protection payment. Both Floating Payment and Physical Settlement have an advantage over Cash Settlement in that they eliminate the need to poll dealers for the market price of what may be an extremely illiquid instrument by the time it is in severe distress. Cash Settlement is not a standard choice under CDO CDS documentation, as it is in corporate CDS because of the difficulty of determining a market price for a failing CDO tranche. Pay-as-you-go settlement was, in fact, developed to provide a practical alternative to cash settlement.

ALTERNATIVE INTEREST CAP OPTIONS

Standard CDO CDS documentation provides for three ways to size the protection seller's responsibility for Interest Shortfalls under Floating Payment or pay-as-you-go settlement. Two of them, *Interest Shortfall Cap Not Applicable* and *Variable Cap*, are similar, while Fixed Cap greatly limits the protection seller's obligation.[4]

Interest Shortfall Cap Not Applicable

The protection seller pays the protection buyer the full amount of the cash CDO's Interest Shortfall. If no interest whatsoever is paid on the reference obligation, the protection seller would pay the obligation's LIBOR index plus coupon spread. But this payment, like all Interest Shortfall payments to the protection buyer, is netted against the CDS premium payment the protection buyer pays the protection seller. So the protection seller's maximum obligation to the protection buyer for an Interest Shortfall is

$$\text{LIBOR} + \text{Cash CDO coupon spread} - \text{CDS premium}$$

---

[4] For those interested in the differences between CDO CDS and ABS CDS standard documentation, note that these interest cap options are the same as those for ABS CDS.

Variable Cap

The protection seller's obligation depends on the relationship of the CDS premium to the cash CDO coupon spread. If the CDS premium is *less* than the cash CDO coupon spread, the protection seller's gross payment is limited to the reference obligation's LIBOR index plus the CDS premium. If the CDS premium is *greater* than the cash CDO's coupon, the protection seller's gross payment is limited to the reference obligation's LIBOR index and coupon spread. Again, Interest Shortfall payments to the protection buyer are netted against the CDS premium payment the protection buyer pays the protection seller. So the maximum obligation of the protection seller to the protection buyer for an Interest Shortfall is

LIBOR + (Lesser of the CDS premium or cash CDO coupon spread) – CDS premium

Fixed Cap or "Premium Squeeze to Zero"

The protection seller's payment to the protection buyer is limited to the CDS premium, that is, the protection seller is not responsible for the LIBOR component of the cash CDO coupon. The net payment amount, then, can never be a payment from the protection seller to the protection buyer. An Interest Shortfall amount only reduces the premium the protection buyer pays the protection seller. It never reverses the direction of the payment. Note that the withholding of the CDS premium fully extinguishes the protection seller's obligation in that period, which is to say that the amount of interest lost on the cash CDO but not covered by withholding the CDS premium is not carried forward into future interest periods.

Under any of the three interest cap options, if the CDO tranche catches up on an Interest Shortfall, the protection buyer must repay the Interest Shortfall amount to the protection seller. Compounding this reimbursement at LIBOR plus the CDS premium is optional, decided by mutual agreement of the protection seller and buyer at the inception of the CDO CDS.

Exhibit 9.4 illustrates these interest cap options using the example of a cash CDO tranche with a coupon of LIBOR + 300 bps, a CDO CDS with a premium of 280 bps, and where LIBOR equals 4%. In the exhibit, the maximum the protection seller can pay under No Cap Applicable is the coupon on the CDO (LIBOR + 300 bps) netted against the CDO CDS premium (280 bps) or LIBOR + 20 bps. Assuming LIBOR equals 4%, this comes to 420 bps. The maximum the protection seller can pay under Variable Cap is LIBOR plus the CDO CDS premium (LIBOR + 280 bps) netted against the CDO CDS premium (280 bps) or LIBOR flat. As we assume LIBOR equal

EXHIBIT 9.4 Example of CDO CDS Interest Rate Caps

Assumptions

CDO Coupon = LIBOR + 300 bps
CDO CDS Premium = 280 bps
LIBOR = 4%

Cash Bond Pays LIBOR + 300	Protection Seller's Gross Payment	Protection Seller's Net Receipt/(Payment)
Cap not applicable	0 bps	280 bps
Variable cap	0 bps	280 bps
Fixed cap	0 bps	280 bps

Cash Bond Pays LIBOR + 280	Protection Seller's Gross Payment	Protection Seller's Net Receipt/(Payment)
Cap not applicable	20 bps	260 bps
Variable cap	20 bps	260 bps
Fixed cap	20 bps	260 bps

Cash Bond Pays LIBOR + 100	Protection Seller's Gross Payment	Protection Seller's Net Receipt/(Payment)
Cap not applicable	200 bps	80 bps
Variable cap	200 bps	80 bps
Fixed cap	200 bps	80 bps

Cash Bond Pays LIBOR + 0	Protection Seller's Gross Payment	Protection Seller's Net Receipt/(Payment)
Cap not applicable	300 bps	(20 bps)
Variable cap	300 bps	(20 bps)
Fixed cap	280 bps	0 bps

Cash Bond Pays LIBOR – 200	Protection Seller's Gross Payment	Protection Seller's Net Receipt/(Payment)
Cap not applicable	500 bps	(220 bps)
Variable cap	500 bps	(220 bps)
Fixed cap	280 bps	0 bps

Cash Bond Pays LIBOR – 400	Protection Seller's Gross Payment	Protection Seller's Net Receipt/(Payment)
Cap not applicable	700 bps	(420 bps)
Variable cap	680 bps	(400 bps)
Fixed cap	280 bps	0 bps

EXHIBIT 9.5 Protection Seller Receipt: Payment

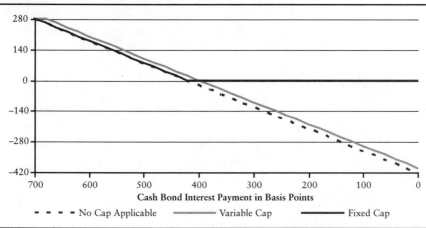

4%, this comes to 400 bps. Finally, the maximum the protection seller has to pay under Fixed Cap is the premium on the CDO CDS (280 bps) netted against the CDO CDS premium (280 bps) or 0 bps. We graph these results in Exhibit 9.5.

Exhibits 9.4 and 9.5 make clear which interest cap terms a protection seller or protection buyer would like to have. All other things equal, including CDO CDS premium, a protection buyer wants No Cap or Variable Cap; a protection seller wants Fixed Cap.

MISCELLANEOUS TERMS

There are a few other points to make about the standard CDO CDS contract.

CDO Tranche Events of Default

Some circumstances constituting Events of Default on the underlying cash CDO tranche may not be Floating Payment Events or Credit Events under the CDO CDS. These cash CDO Events of Default have no effect on the CDO CDS. Examples include: low overcollateralization results, manager bankruptcy or fraud, and the CDO being required to register as an investment company. The effects of these problems may, of course, result in a Floating Payment Event or a Credit Event.

Voting Right and Control

A cash CDO debt tranche might gain control of the CDO as classes below it are wiped out. A protection seller doesn't gain voting rights or control unless delivered the cash bond via Physical Settlement.

Upfront Exchange

Instead of adjusting the CDS premium to reflect current market spreads, an upfront exchange can be made. For example, suppose a CDO with a coupon of LIBOR + 200 bps trades at 102% of par, providing a discount margin of LIBOR + 150 bps, given expected amortization. Instead of setting the CDS premium equal to the discount margin of 150 bps, the CDS premium can be set at 200 bps and the protection seller can pay the protection buyer $2 upfront.

Documents and Calculations

The protection buyer is responsible for providing trustee reports to the protection seller. In trades between two dealers, the protection seller is the Calculation Agent. In trades between a dealer and an end user, the dealer is the Calculation Agent.

CASH CDO VERSUS CDO CDS

Some investors are concerned about the fidelity of CDO CDS to a cash position in the referenced CDO. From the protection seller's point of view, how well do the Floating Amount Events and Credit Events replicate the economic experience of owning the underlying reference CDO?

The too easy answer is that Credit Events and Physical Settlement provide the closest fit to owning a cash CDO. Obviously, the protection seller will get the cash instrument's cash flows if he buys the cash instrument, as one essentially does in Physical Settlement. But if that's what the protection seller really wants, he should buy the cash CDO to begin with. What one is probably looking for in a CDO CDS is the economic equivalence of a cash CDO in *synthetic* form. Without the uncertainties of the mark-to-market process in a total return swap, the protection seller wants to monetize the pluses and minuses, due to credit experience, of owning the cash CDO.

By this logic, Credit Events and Physical Settlement, except for Failure to Pay Principal which occurs at the end of the CDO's life, do not do a good job of replicating the credit pluses and minuses of owning the cash CDO. On the other hand, Implied Write-down attempts to quantify credit deterioration of the cash CDO as it occurs. No Cap Applicable and Variable Cap do the best job of capturing the effect of lost interest payments. The reversible nature of Floating Amount Events compensates the protection seller if the initial loss measurement is too sensitive.

Current documentation trends, however, tend to split the difference between the cash replication of Implied Write-down on one hand and the cash replication of No Cap or Variable Cap on the other. The two most popular combinations of CDO CDS are Variable Cap with no Implied Write-down and Fixed Cap with Implied Write-down. Obviously, the protection seller likes Fixed Cap, as the responsibility for Interest Shortfalls is limited to loss of the incoming CDS premium. Likewise, no Implied Write-down delays payment of CDS notional to the protection buyer. No Implied Write-down also maintains the CDS premium at a higher amount, as it is calculated off a higher notional amount. On the other hand, not writing down the CDO may mean that the protection seller has to protect the interest due on that unwritten-down amount.

EXITING A CDO CDS

Investors considering getting into a CDO CDS should also consider how they would get *out* of the trade. Naturally, the CDO CDS can be held to maturity, but there are three routes for exiting the trade before that time.

Termination

By mutual agreement, the two counterparties to the CDO CDS tear up the swap and it exists no more. This usually involves a termination payment from one party to another. The direction of the termination payment is determined by the relationship of the contracted premium protection and the current market price of protection on the referenced CDO tranche. For example, suppose the CDO CDS premium is 20 bps lower than the current cost of protection on the CDO tranche. The protection buyer will have to pay 20 bps more to enter into a replacement CDO CDS with a new counterparty. In this case, the protection seller needs to compensate the protection buyer to terminate (also known as *unwind*) the CDO CDS. The payment will be based on the present value of the 20 bps times the notional amount of the CDS over the expected amortization of the CDO tranche.

Assignment

The party wishing to exit the CDO CDS finds another to take its place in the transaction. The replacement must be agreeable to the party who wishes to continue in the CDO CDS. The exiting party pays (receives) an assignment fee to (from) the new party to the CDO CDS. Analogous to a termination fee, the assignment fee compensates the new counterparty for entering into an off-market transaction; that is, a CDO CDS done at a premium other than the current market premium.

Offsetting

The party wishing to exit the CDO CDS does an offsetting trade. A party reverses out of a CDO CDS it has sold protection on, for example, by buying protection on the same underlying CDO with a new counterparty at the going market rate. Now the party has two trades whose terms might not be completely identical and whose premiums might be different. To equalize cash flows as much as possible, the party should match their actions on the CDO CDS that they have bought protection on to those of the protection buyer of the CDO CDS they sold protection on. That is, they should call Floating Payment Events and Credit Events when the protection buyer does. Alternatively, if they feel the protection buyer has suboptimally called an Event, they can refrain from calling an Event on the offsetting position and take a position on the cash flow differences between the two CDO CDS. Offsetting is the most common way to exit ABS CDS; it may also become the most common exit for CDO CDS.

RATING AGENCY CONCERNS ON CDOs THAT SELL PROTECTION VIA CDO CDS

When a CDO^2 (*CDO squared*) or any CDO sells protection via CDO CDS, rating agencies are concerned that the CDO take on no more risk than it would if it purchased cash CDO tranches outright. Rating agencies rely on their default studies and sometimes have a hard time sizing risks not incorporated in those default studies or otherwise reflected in the modeling and stress testing they put CDO tranches through. One such concern is market value risks. For example, rating agencies do not want to see a CDO manager forced to sell cash collateral upon a default. Instead, they want the manager to time any liquidation optimally. When analyzing a CDO, the rating agencies do not want the manager to be forced to sell CDO tranches received via Physical Settlement. If the CDO structure requires the quick sale of such a CDO, the rating agencies will assume a lower recovery value than if the timing of the sale is up to the CDO manager.

A CDO selling protection via CDO CDS might also have to make payments under pay-as-you-go settlement. To the extent these reflect risks not incorporated in rating agency default studies, the CDO must have additional protections and liquidity. To limit this risk, CDOs usually choose to not include Implied Write-down as a Floating Amount Event or Credit Event.

SUMMARY

An understanding of ISDA CDO CDS documentation is important to all who want to go long and short this derivative or understand more about the market pricing of cash underlyings. We broke the document into its working parts and explained each. We think Exhibit 9.3 nicely sorts out the five credit problems the documentation recognizes can happen to a CDO and the two consequences for which the documentation provides. We also addressed the three choices of interest rate cap, miscellaneous CDO CDS terms, the differences between selling protection on a CDS and owning a cash CDO, how one exits a CDO CDS, and rating agency concerns when a CDO enters into a CDO CDS.

Loss Projection and Security Valuation

CHAPTER 10

Loss Projection for Subprime, Alt-A, and Second Lien Mortgages

In this chapter, we provide a detailed, completely transparent approach in projecting collateral cumulative losses. We outline and then expand on a simple loss projection model that is based on what we call *default pipeline* and *default timing curve*. We also provide an alternative specification of the simple model, which further allows users to take the effect of prepayment into account in loss projections. Finally, we elaborate on the slight differences between applying our methodology to subprime, Alt-A, and second lien collateral.

TWO WAYS OF PROJECTING LOSS

There are two ways of predicting collateral losses. The first way is through a full-blown econometric/statistical model. Typical inputs are *collateral characteristics*, namely, FICO, LTV, documentation type, loan purpose, loan size, and so on. *Macroeconomics factors*, the most common being *home price appreciation* (HPA) and interest rates, are also model inputs and need to be forecasted. There will also be *interactions* among various factors. For example, HPA may have a larger effect on high LTV loans than on low LTV loans. Some effects are *age-dependent* (e.g., FICO effect on default seems to dissipate over time). Many effects could also be *nonlinear*. Some models also include *performance history* (e.g., delinquency status) to forecast future performance.

An econometric model is estimated by running many regressions on historical data. There will be out-of-sample cross-validation; stress testing may also be conducted. Pricing will be accomplished using model projections. After many iterations of this process, a model will finally be in production.

The advantage of building an econometric model is that it gives users a full suite of outputs (namely, prepayment, default, severity, percentage of

60+ days delinquent), which jointly determines the magnitude and timing of cash flow. The disadvantage is that it has a lot of assumptions and interactions of various variables that are not overly transparent to users. Building such models also requires a great deal of human/technology resources.

Another main drawback of most econometric models is that they overly rely upon historical relationships between collateral characteristics, macroeconomic factors, and performance. Many of these relationships have broken down in the current environment (specifically on loans that were poorly underwritten), or are going through negative HPA and have little or no prospect of being refinanced. Most econometric models also tend to put too much emphasis on collateral characteristics at origination, and fail to put enough on up-to-date collateral performance. In statistical jargon, these models are nonBayesian (i.e., they are incapable of revising probabilities based on updated information).

In contrast, the second way to predict collateral losses and the one that we outline in this chapter is much more straightforward; it is completely transparent, with no hidden assumptions. One can easily replicate our results and apply the same methodology to subprime, Alt-A, and closed-end second deals. We like to refer to this way of predicting collateral losses as the "autopilot" model of loss projection; once a deal is formed, it is the performance to-date that will drive future performance. Origination collateral characteristics only matter to the extent they affected performance thus far. Put differently, if a deal performs badly even though it has good collateral characteristics (for example, high FICO, low LTV, and so on), this approach predicts continuing bad future performance.

DEFAULT TIMING

What is default? Unfortunately, there is no universally agreed upon definition of default. In our "autopilot" model, we define default as when a loan first hits foreclosure status or worse—*real-estate-owned* (REO) status and losses. For those who are technically savvy, loans can transition directly from 60 or 90+ days delinquent to loss liquidation without going through foreclosure process. This definition applies to subprime and Alt-A deals but not close-end seconds.

This is a very broadly defined concept of default, which produces relative high default but low loss severity rates (as many defaults produce no losses). Note also that our default definition does not require a liquidation event. In a high HPA environment, there could also be loans transitioning (or curing) out of the foreclosure process, although such curing is highly unlikely under low HPA.

Also note that our definition of default ensures we have enough actual and pipeline default (before liquidation) when the deal is relatively unseasoned, thus enabling us to extrapolate along the default timing curve.

Exhibit 10.1 shows default timing curves across various vintages. We only selected loans that have been through a low HPA environment (less than 5% annualized), as they are more representative of the current (early 2008) and future environment. Benchmarked against cumulative default at month 60, we reach 25% of total default at month 14, 50% at month 23, and 75% at month 35. It would have been ideal if there were data that capture the default timing curve under negative HPA. However, the sample size of such data is too small for us to draw any meaningful inference.

The choice of month 60 as the cutoff, again, is determined mostly by the availability of data. It would have been ideal if we could use a cutoff of 72 months or more. However, that would eliminate the 2002 vintage from our sample, and we were reluctant to do so since we did not have much data to begin with. The disadvantage of cutting data off at month 60 is that our model will not be able to predict defaults and losses after month 60.

STEPS IN PREDICTING COLLATAL LOSSES

The following six steps are involved in projecting collateral losses:

EXHIBIT 10.1   Default Timing Curve under Low HPA (< 5% annualized)

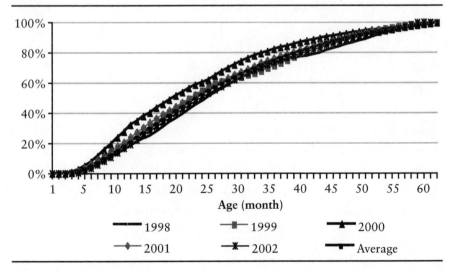

Source: LoanPerformance.

Step 1: Convert 60, 90+ days delinquent and bankruptcy loans to pipeline default.
Step 2: Calculate the default pipeline as percent of the current balance.
Step 3: Calculate the total default as a percent of the original balance.
Step 4: Project the Cumulative Default from Default Timing Curve and Total Default in Step 3.
Step 5: Project the Cumulative Loss.

We describe these five steps below. We will use the deal listed in Exhibit 10.2 to illustrate the calculations in the five steps. The deal is Ace Securities Corp., Home Equity Series 2006-Nc1 and is in ABX 06-2 All rows above "WALA" (weighted average loan age) in the exhibit are direct from Intex Solutions; rows above WALA are calculated fields, which we will describe in Exhibit 10.2.

EXHIBIT 10.2   Data and Calculated Values for Ace Securities Corp., Home Equity Series 2006-Nc1

Original balance	1,324.27
Collateral balance	733.73
30-day DQ	4.05
60-day DQ	4.26
90+ DQ	1.85
Foreclosure (FC)	11.26
REO	6.30
Bankruptcy	2.82
Cumulative loss percent	1.00
WALA	27
Default age factor	0.68
Default pipepline (percent of current balance)	23.81
Total default (percent of current balance)	15.42
Projected cumulative default (percent of current balance)	22.77
Projected cumulative default (percent of original balance)	10.25
Projected cumulative loss (percent of original balance)	9.32
Projected future cumulative default (percent of current balance)	37.08
Projected future cumulative loss (percent of current balance)	16.69

Note: All rows above "WALA" in the exhibit are direct from Intex Solutions; rows above WALA are calculated fields.

Default Age Factor references the default timing in Exhibit 10.1. For example, we expect that at month 23, a deal would have generated 50% of total defaults. So if a deal has 10% default generated by month 23, we expect life time cumulative default to be 20% (= 10%/0.5).

Convert 60, 90+ Days Delinquent and Bankruptcy Loans to Pipeline Default

We estimate that 70% of loans currently 60 and 90+ days delinquent (denoted by "60/90+DQ") will eventually migrate into defaults. Exhibit 10.3 shows historical transition probability of 60/90+DQ loans. We can see that as HPA rises, the 60/90+DQ to default transition probability decreases. That makes sense. As borrowers have more equity built up in their properties, they become less likely to default on mortgages because they can sell their properties and pay off the loans. We also see that the average transition time to default is four months.

EXHIBIT 10.3 Subprime 60 and 90+DQ to Default – Transition Probability

HPA	Age	Probability Transitioning to Default from 60DQ	Probability Transitioning to Default from 90+DQ	Time to Default from 60DQ	Time to Default from 90+DQ
< 5%	< 12	72%	71%	3.3	3.7
< 5%	12 to 24	66%	68%	4.0	4.4
< 5%	24 to 36	70%	72%	4.4	5.0
< 5%	36 to 48	67%	70%	4.9	5.1
5 to 10%	< 12	76%	74%	3.7	4.2
5 to 10%	12 to 24	64%	67%	3.7	4.1
5 to 10%	24 to 36	59%	61%	4.0	4.5
5 to 10%	36 to 48	58%	60%	4.8	5.0
10 to 15%	< 12	74%	69%	3.3	3.5
10 to 15%	12 to 24	62%	62%	3.1	3.4
10 to 15%	24 to 36	53%	53%	3.1	3.4
10 to 15%	36 to 48	50%	54%	3.5	3.8
≥ 15%	< 12	66%	63%	3.5	3.6
≥ 15%	12 to 24	57%	57%	3.2	3.6
≥ 15%	24 to 36	50%	47%	2.6	3.3
≥ 15%	36 to 48	42%	41%	2.7	2.9

Source: LoanPerformance.

EXHIBIT 10.4   Distribution – Delinquency Status of BK Loans (All < 5% HPA)

Year	Current	30DQ	60DQ	90+DQ	Foreclosure	REO
1998	34	6	6	54	0	0
1999	28	5	6	61	1	0
2000	23	5	5	66	1	0
2001	25	5	5	63	1	0
2002	27	6	6	60	1	0
2003	25	6	6	62	1	0
2004	25	6	6	62	0	0
2005	28	7	6	59	0	0
2006	25	6	6	62	0	0
Combined	26	6	6	61	1	0

Source: LoanPerformance.

Historically, 60% to 70% of subprime *bankruptcy* (BK) loans are in the 60DQ or 90+DQ category, while the rest are actually current (see Exhibit 10.4). As a result (also to keep our analyses simple), we treat all BK loans the same as 90+DQ loans. That is, 70% of BK loans will eventually transition to default.

One additional thing to note about BK loans is that in Intex Solutions, some deals include BK loans in different delinquency categories (they double count), while other deals do not. It is our understanding that all deals in the four ABX indices do not involve double counting. However, when applying our methodology on other deals in Intex Solutions, be aware of this peculiarity.

Step 2: Calculate the Default Pipeline as a Percent of the Current Balance

The default pipeline as a percent of the current balance is calculated as following

$$\text{Default pipeline} = 0.7(60DQ + 90{+}DQ + BK) + (FC + REO)$$

where

$60DQ$ = percent of current balance that is 60 days delinquent
$90{+}DQ$ = percent of current balance that is 90+ days delinquent
BK = percent of current balance that is bankruptcy loans

FC   = percent of current balance that is in foreclosure
REO   = percent of current balance that is real estate owned

Using the data shown in Exhibit 10.2 for ACE 2006-Nc1, the default pipeline as a percent of the current balance is

Default pipeline = 0.7(4.26 + 1.85 + 2.82) + (11.26 + 6.3) = 23.81

Step 3: Calculate the Total Default as a Percent of the Original Balance

The total default as a percent of the original balance is calculated as follows:

Total default
= Default pipeline × (Coll. bal./Orig. bal.) + (Cum. loss%/Severity)

where

Coll. bal.   = collateral balance
Orig. bal.   = original balance
Cum. Loss% = cumulative loss percent
Severity   = loss severity rate

The collateral balance divided by the original balance is called the *pool factor.*

Note the following about the total default equation. First, the default pipeline is expressed as a percent of the current balance and by multiplying it by the pool factor gives the default pipeline as a percent of the original balance. Second, by dividing the cumulative loss percent by the severity rate gives the defaults that have already gone through the liquidation process.

For ACE 2006-Nc1, the total default assuming a loss severity rate of 45% (which we will show how to we arrived at below) is

Total default = 23.81($733.73/$1324.27) + 1/0.45 = 15.42

Step 4: Project the Cumulative Default from Default Timing Curve and Total Default in Step 3

Now we are equipped with the default timing curve in Exhibit 10.1 and total default from Step 3, and ready to derive lifetime defaults. However, there's one minor detail we need to tackle before proceeding.

From Exhibit 10.3, we see that the average transition time from 60DQ and 90+DQ to default is four months. On the other hand, our default timing curve is based on the default being defined as first time hitting foreclosure or worse. This implies that our total default calculated from Step 3 should be mapped to the default timing curve four months forward.

For example, for ACE 2006-Nc1, a WALA of 27 is given in the June's remittance report. The corresponding default age factor should be the default timing curve at month 31 (four months forward from month 27), which is 0.68. Basically, we are adjusting the transition time between 60/90+DQ and default when we map total default onto the default timing curve. For ACE 2006-Nc1, the projected cumulative default is 15.42/0.68 = 22.77.

Step 5: Project the Cumulative Loss

To calculate the cumulative loss, we need the severity rate. Exhibit 10.5 shows the cumulative default, cumulative loss, and loss severity rate. Assuming a 45% loss severity rate gives a projected cumulative loss of 10.25 for ACE 2006-Nc1. The magnitude of the loss severity rate depends on the HPA. With the current housing market (as of early 2008), we expect HPA of at least –5% per year (or possibly lower) for the next two years. However, we only have had historical loss severity rates on loans experiencing 0% HPA, which is approximately 37%. A linear extrapolation of the last two rows in Exhibit 10.5 gives us a loss severity rate of 45%.

Note that our loss severity rate of 45% may seem low to many if we assume home prices will decline by more than 10% from the current level. But we are using a very broad definition of default (first time hitting foreclosure or worse). Since cumulative loss is fixed regardless of the choice of default definition, a broader definition of default naturally suggests a lower loss severity rate.

Step 5 also automatically gives us the projected future losses as a percent of the outstanding balance by subtracting the cumulative loss percent from the projected cumulative loss and then dividing by the pool factor. For ACE 2006-Nc1 it is 16.69%.

EXHIBIT 10.5   Subprime Cumulative Default, Loss, and Severity

HPA	Cum. Default %	Loss Severity %	Cum. Loss %
> 10%	15	10	1.5
7% to 10%	20	17.5	3.5
4% to 7%	22	30	6.6
1% to 4%	28	32.0	9
< 1%	35	37	12.9

Source: LoanPerformance.

PROS AND CONS OF THE DEFAULT TIMING CURVE

The fundamental assumption of our model, which is based on the concept of default timing curve, is that once deals become somewhat seasoned, the historical deal performance is a much more powerful predictor of future performance than origination collateral characteristics. In addition, this methodology assumes that future performance will follow the path of past performance. Put differently, what we have seen is what we will get. The advantage of the default timing curve model approach is that it explicitly takes the deal performance to date into consideration, and uses this updated information to project future performance. From this perspective, this approach is superior to any econometric models that rely heavily on origination characteristics and do not take into account updated deal performance information.

The proper working of our methodology requires the performance to be somewhat stable over the age of the deal since timing is everything (especially in a model based on the default timing curve). If performance changes significantly over time (for example, a lot of early defaults, but not many when the deal becomes seasoned) due to changes in the macroeconomic environment (such as HPA and interest rates) and servicer disruptions, then the model may produce poor predictions. However, such criticism applies to all models, including sophisticated econometric/statistical models.

Also, since there is no explicit HPA or interest rate assumption, we cannot readily shock the model, for example, if users want to know how the default timing curve looks (more front- or back-loaded, and by how many months) if, say, HPA is −10% not −5%. It is also difficult to say how much cumulative loss increases or how the default timing curve looks if prepayments slow 50%.

A more basic disadvantage of our model is that it only produces one singular output—cumulative loss. The model is incapable of producing time series of prepayments as measured by the *conditional prepayment rate* (CPR), *conditional default rate* (CDR), loss severity rate (our severity is a static number), and 60+DQ%. Since no cash flow is generated on a per month basis, then price/yield, write-down and other valuation exercises cannot be readily done using this methodology alone.

HISTORICAL MODEL FIT VERSUS ACTUAL

How good is our model? We estimated the model using 230+ subprime deals issued from 1998 to 2002 (see Exhibit 10.6). The actual cumulative

EXHIBIT 10.6 Model Error: Model Projected Cum Loss – Actual Cum Loss at WALA 60

Issue Year	WALA	Default Age Factor	Number of Deals	Mean	Standard Deviation
Combined	10	25%	210	1.9%	2.7%
Combined	19	50%	232	1.4%	1.7%
Combined	31	75%	238	0.9%	1.0%
1998	10	25%	29	1.0%	2.8%
1998	19	50%	38	0.5%	1.3%
1998	31	75%	38	0.6%	0.9%
1999	10	25%	45	1.2%	2.4%
1999	19	50%	51	0.8%	1.5%
1999	31	75%	53	0.5%	1.1%
2000	10	25%	44	2.3%	2.6%
2000	19	50%	44	1.6%	1.8%
2000	31	75%	47	0.9%	1.1%
2001	10	25%	40	3.0%	3.3%
2001	19	50%	44	2.5%	1.3%
2001	31	75%	44	1.5%	0.7%
2002	10	25%	52	1.8%	2.1%
2002	19	50%	55	1.5%	1.6%
2002	31	75%	56	1.0%	0.7%

Source: LoanPerformance.

loss is measured at WALA 60 for each deal.[1] We ran projections at WALA 10, 19, and 31, corresponding to default age factors (after shifting four months forward) of 25%, 50%, and 75%, respectively. Then we compared projected cumulative loss against the actual cumulative loss at WALA 60. We observed the following.

First, as WALA rises, model performance increases (i.e., the mean error gets smaller), as does the standard deviation of errors. That's expected, since more seasoned deals are more heavily driven by default pipeline.

Second, our model generally overpredicts. Again this is expected, due to the following facts. There will be additional losses after WALA 60, so over the deal's lifetime, actual loss will be higher than losses at WALA 60,

[1] We considered choosing a higher WALA, but decided against it since every additional 12 WALA reduce our sample size by 20%.

and the resulting errors will be smaller. The other factor is that 60/90+DQ loans are much more frontloaded among these vintages. As a result, we have many pipeline defaults early on. The significant rise in HPA in later stages of these loans bailed them out of foreclosure/REO processes, and many avoided defaults altogether. Therefore, our model, which is based on higher pipeline defaults when the deal was young, overpredicted. We see this as both a strength and a weakness of our "autopilot" model. In an environment where the HPA regime moves about (such as that from the late 1990s to the end of 2005), our approach may either over- or underpredict. On the other hand, if we believe HPA will remain low for a prolonged period of time (which we do as of this writing), then the model will do well, since it projects the future based on the recent environment and performance, which is associated with a depressed housing market.

DEFAULT TIMING IS NOT EQUAL TO LOSS TIMING

Remember that *default* timing is not the equivalent of *loss* timing. Default timing depends on default definition. A wider definition of default implies more front-loaded default, with the opposite true, as well. On the other hand, there are no different definitions of losses, and losses are much more back-loaded than defaults. This is because it takes time for loans to go through foreclosure/REO and liquidation processes. Exhibit 10.7 shows average loss timing of 1998–2002 vintage (loans under less than 5% HPA). 25%, 50%, and 75% loss timing are at months 32, 44, and 56, respectively (which are 18, 21, and 21 months beyond where they are on the default timing curve). The long lag between default and loss is due to our default definition (i.e., first time foreclosure or worse).

AN ALTERNATIVE SPECIFICATION

In this section, we will provide an alternate specification for our model, yet our original approach still applies (i.e., investors can do all the calculations with a paper and pencil, or on a spreadsheet).

Recall that our original specification of the model is based on the premise of a so-called "default timing curve." The concept of a default timing curve is such that life-time cumulative default accumulates smoothly over time and reaches certain percentages at certain ages. However, such smooth accumulation and the timing of such accumulation require relatively stable prepayment patterns over time. Note that prepayment *speeds* need not be constant month to month; it is the *pattern* that needs to be stable. For exam-

EXHIBIT 10.7   Loss and Default Timing (Average of 1998–2002 vintage, < 5% annual HPA)

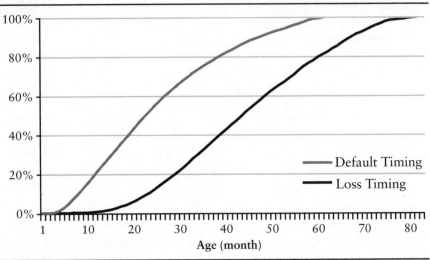

Source: LoanPerformance.

ple, prepayments can be 20 CPR at month (age) 23, then 60 CPR at month 24; as long as similar prepayments always take place at the same age, our default timing curve would function properly.

The reality is that prepayment patterns are not necessarily stable across deals over time. For example, a deal consisting mostly of fixed rate collateral will prepay more slowly than one with many ARMs. Intuitively, we would expect fixed rate mortgages and ARMs to have different default timing curves. Exhibit 10.8 confirms our intuition. Then how do we account for different prepayment patterns in our projections?

Under the alternative specification, we propose that instead of evaluating a default timing curve, we analyze a default factor curve, as shown in Exhibit 10.9, which graphs cumulative default against 100 minus the pool factor. (As pools pay down, going left to right in the exhibit, the default curve factor rises from 0 to 100.) Comparing Exhibit 10.9 to Exhibit 10.8, it seems that the relationship between cumulative defaults and pool factor is much stronger than that between cumulative defaults and age. Fixed rate mortgages and ARMs may have different default timing curves, but their respective default factor curves look quite similar.

We also observe that the relationship between cumulative defaults and pool factor is quite linear after a certain point. The initial slope is steep, and after the pools pay down somewhat, the slope is almost a constant. Put dif-

EXHIBIT 10.8   Default Timing (< 5% HPA, 1998–2002 vintage combined)

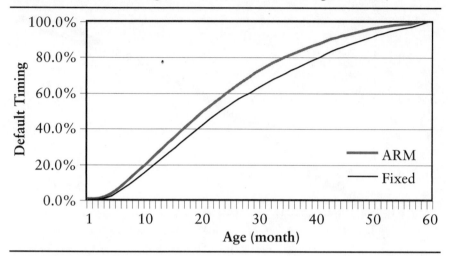

Source: LoanPerformance.

EXHIBIT 10.9   Cumulative Default versus Pool Factor (1998–2002 vintage combined, < 5% HPA)

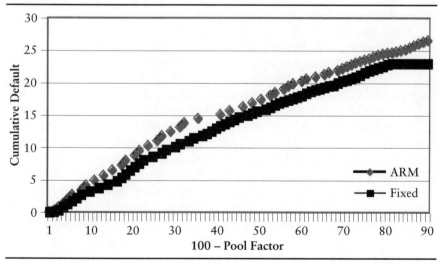

Source: LoanPerformance.

EXHIBIT 10.10   Default Factor Curve (1998–2002 vintage combined, < 5% HPA)

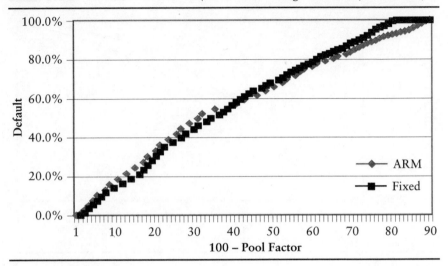

Source: LoanPerformance.

ferently, after the pool becomes somewhat seasoned, one unit of pool factor reduction generates a constant absolute amount of defaults. Exhibit 10.10 shows the default factor curve based on this alternative specification.

The application of the alternative specification is also straightforward. Steps 1, 2, and 3 will be the same as we outlined earlier. In Step 4, instead of mapping to a default timing curve, we project cumulative default using a default factor curve based on the pool factor. To account for the four-month lag between delinquency and default, we shift the default factor curve a few percentage points forward (similar to what we did in the previous section).

Numerically, the pool factor for ACE 2006-NC1 at the time of calculation is 55.4 (= $733.73/$1324.27). Therefore, 100 minus the pool factor is 44.6. Shifting the default factor curve forward five percentage points yields 49.6 (44.6 + 5); the corresponding default factor is 65%.

The projected cumulative default is then equal to 23.72 (= 15.42/0.65) where 15.42 is calculated from Step 3, which is less than 1% higher (22.77) than the projected cumulative default derived from our original model.

ALT-A AND CLOSED-END SECONDS

We use the same default definition and methodology in projecting cumulative losses on Alt-A deals. The differences between subprime and Alt-A are the following:

1. Subprime default timing is on average one to two months more front-loaded than Alt-A, as seen in Exhibit 10.11.
2. We estimate that 60% of Alt-A loans currently in 60DQ will eventually migrate to default versus 70% for subprime loans (see Exhibit 10.12).
3. The loss severity rate under a 0% HPA is 25% on Alt-A loans versus 37% on subprime. Under –5% HPA, based on linear extrapolation, we expect a loss severity rate on Alt-A to approach 40% versus 45% on subprime (see Exhibit 10.13).

For second lien loans, we change the definition of default from first time reaching foreclosure (or worse) to first time reaching 60+DQ status, since second lien loans rarely go to foreclosure. Recovery is minimal (if any) compared to the cost of foreclosure. Servicers generally write these loans off after a few months of lingering in serious delinquency. (Note, however, that liens still exist on the properties.)

Since we changed our default definition to first time 60+DQ status, no transition probability is needed (although one might argue we should take 30DQ loans into account, as 70% of 30DQ loans eventually transition to 60+DQ for 2006 and 2007 production).

Finally, given the current home price environment, we expect second lien loans reaching 60+DQ status to have a 100% loss severity.

Exhibit 10.14 shows the default timing curve of second lien loans originated 1998–2002. Why is the second lien loan default timing curve more

EXHIBIT 10.11 Alt-A and Subprime Default Timing Curve (2000 to 2002 vintage, < 5% HPA)

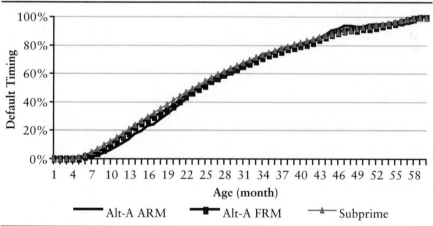

Source: LoanPerformance.

EXHIBIT 10.12   Alt-A 60 and 90+DQ to Default: Transition Probability

HPA	Age	Probability Transitioning to Default from 60DQ	Probability Transitioning to Default from 90+DQ	Time to Default from 60DQ	Time to Default from 90+DQ
< 5%	< 12	68%	68%	2.5	3.0
< 5%	12 to 24	63%	68%	2.9	4.1
< 5%	24 to 36	59%	66%	3.4	4.6
< 5%	36 to 48	51%	58%	3.8	4.6
5 to 10%	< 12	74%	71%	3.0	3.2
5 to 10%	12 to 24	63%	63%	2.6	3.6
5 to 10%	24 to 36	49%	51%	3.0	4.1
5 to 10%	36 to 48	44%	47%	4.2	4.6
10 to 15%	< 12	68%	58%	3.3	3.5
10 to 15%	12 to 24	62%	55%	2.9	3.7
10 to 15%	24 to 36	50%	46%	3.2	4.2
10 to 15%	36 to 48	43%	43%	4.1	4.1
≥ 15%	< 12	58%	57%	3.8	3.7
≥ 15%	12 to 24	58%	56%	3.4	4.2
≥ 15%	24 to 36	50%	46%	2.9	3.9
≥ 15%	36 to 48	43%	31%	2.4	3.8

Source: LoanPerformance.

EXHIBIT 10.13   Alt-A Cumulative Default, Loss, and Severity

HPA	Cum. Default %	Loss Severity %	Cum. Loss %
> 10%	4	7.5	0.3
7% to 10%	5	10	0.5
4% to 7%	7.5	16	1.2
1% to 4%	9	17.0	1.5
< 1%	10	25	2.5

Source: LoanPerformance.

EXHIBIT 10.14   First and Second Lien Default Timing Curve

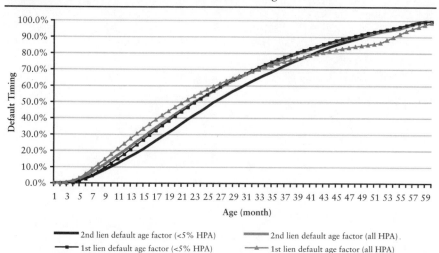

Source: LoanPerformance.

back loaded than its first lien counterpart? We believe it is because second lien loans originated five to eight years ago were mostly cash-out refinancing loans and had a very high percentage of full documentation loans, hence the back-loading of default timing. However, when it comes to loss timing, second lien loans are much more front-loaded than first liens, as second liens rarely go to foreclosure. On average, it takes 15 to 18 months for first liens to go through foreclosure and REO process; but 60+DQ second liens are written off in six months.

Using our default timing curve for second liens, mathematically

Projected cumulative loss
= Pool factor × (60+DQ%) + Realized cumulative loss)/Default age factor

SUMMARY

In this chapter, we presented a simple but powerful loss projection model that is based on the concept of a default timing curve. We went through a detailed numerical example on a subprime deal. We also provided an alternative specification and summarized some of the differences when applying this model on deals backed by Alt-A and second lien collateral.

CHAPTER 11

Valuing the ABX

In earlier chapters, we discussed the basic structures of ABS derivatives such as ABS CDS and the ABX. In this chapter we describe our approach to valuing the subindices of the ABX. Since there are four ABX series, each with five subindices (AAA, AA, A, BBB, and BBB–) and each subindex references 20 subprime MBS securities, this task involves estimating the expected write-downs on 400 securities. In this chapter, we have taken two fundamentally different approaches, one based on a full-blown econometric model and another based on the current delinquency pipeline (our simple model). The two approaches reflect the need for a model that incorporates historical data but one that is also robust and intuitive.

We also illustrate both of these approaches. Both have much to commend them. For our ongoing analysis of the ABX, we use most the simple approach as explained in the previous chapter. We also use the econometric approach for calibrating the simple model and for exploring other implications of changes in speed and default rates.

REVIEW OF BASIC VALUATION FOR ABX INDICES

Before we review the two approaches, it seems useful to briefly review the basic valuation equation for the ABX indices we are attempting to price. The price of an ABX CDS can be represented by the following equation:

$$\text{Price} = 100 + (\text{Expected present value of coupon cash flow} - \text{Expected present value of write-downs})$$

This equation says that if the expected present value of the coupons received for writing (i.e., selling) protection on the subindex is just equal to the expected present value of the write-downs, the price of an ABX CDS is equal to 100. When the ABX subindices were first established, a coupon was chosen for each subindex such that the present value of that coupon cash flow would just offset the present value of the expected write-downs and hence the original price of an ABX CDS were mostly 100. (For some of the later ABX subindices, the original price was less than par since the initial coupons were capped at 500 and the spreads on those subprime securities were trading wider than LIBOR + 500 when the subindices were launched.)

As can be see from this equation, if the market expects losses to increase (i.e., write-downs to increase), then the expected present value of the write-downs increases and the price of the CDS goes down. Likewise, if the timing of the write-downs is accelerated and the write-downs occur sooner (losses are more front-loaded), the expected present value of the write-downs increases and the price of the CDS goes down.

REVIEW OF VALUATION APPROACHES

The first approach we can use to value the ABX is a full blown econometric approach which entails forecasting the cash flows for each of the 20 underlying subprime securities for each subindex. This is accomplished by producing a set of *conditional prepayment rates* (CPR), CRD, loss severity, and 60+-day delinquency vectors for each subprime security, running those vectors through Intex Solutions, and using the resulting write-down timing and amount to calculate the present values of the coupon cash flows and write-downs.

While there are many positives to this approach, a major negative is that it requires a great deal of computing time and resources to construct and continuously update the econometric model that forecasts all of these variables. This approach has become especially burdensome and suspect in today's subprime environment given the virtual shutdown of the subprime and Alt-A markets. Also, since this approach involves a large number of highly complex equations, it is hard to develop an intuitive feel for how the change in a single input might affect the outcome of the model. Another drawback is that given the complex nature of the model it is difficult to compare its structure with other models that might be producing different results. For all of these reasons, we shift our emphasis to a simpler approach.

While we often refer to this second, simpler approach as our "simple" model, it still involves a fair number of steps and several critical assumptions. Nonetheless, the term *simple* does capture the essence of this approach in that it is not based on a large econometric model. There are the following four steps in our simple approach:

Step 1: Estimate cumulative losses for each referenced subprime MBS using the current delinquency pipeline. By using a historical default timing curve and historical roll rates (the percentage of one delinquency category that rolls into another), we project total cumulative losses for the life of the deal from the latest delinquency pipeline data.

Step 2: Estimate the level of cumulative losses needed to cause the first dollar loss on a particular referenced subprime MBS. We do this using the *prospectus prepayment curve* (PPC) prepayment speed on the deal and a standard default curve that we increase until the first dollar loss occurs.

Step 3: Compare the cumulative loss forecast with the cumulative loss needed to cause the first dollar of bond loss and determine whether or not the bond will be written down.

Step 4: Add up the number and timing of bonds written down out of the 20 referenced by a particular ABX subindex. From a standard "number and timing of write-downs = price" table we find the ABX price associated with that number and timing of write-downs.

This may seem like a convoluted approach, but each step is relatively simple and straightforward, can be easily replicated (if you have access to Intex Solutions), can be quickly adjusted to incorporate a changing environment, and is much more transparent than the a large econometric model.

Before we proceed, there is a shortcoming with both the full econometric and simple approaches that should be mentioned, namely neither incorporate loss volatility or correlation. We know that losses on subprime deals vary a great deal between issuers and within issuers. For any one of the 20 referenced bonds in an ABX index, it would be more realistic to use a range of expected losses rather than a point estimate. For the 20 as a group (i.e., for an ABX subindex), one needs to incorporate the degree of correlation between the 20 different securities.[1]

Finally, over time periods such as the course of 2007 as the subprime crisis deepened, it becomes necessary to continuously update the ABX valuations to keep pace with market conditions. No matter what approach one uses to calculate fair value for the ABX, one needs to account for any crisis that confronts the subprime market. A model built on historical data will neither produce a loss number consistent with current delinquency trends

---

[1] Several of the authors of this book are in the process of developing a model that will incorporate these factors, but that work will not be completed in time for inclusion in this book.

nor with current prices on the ABX. Consequently, analysts and investors will find it necessary to apply some subjective upward revision to their model outputs. This is perhaps the most compelling reason to use a simple approach. If in the final analysis an analyst or investor needs to make a large subjective adjustment to get model outputs to agree with market pricing, then a simple approach is probably the best place to start.

ECONOMETRIC APPROACH

This section which describes an econometric approach to valuing the ABX was done in March 2007. For this reason, the projected prices for the ABX are dramatically higher than prices at the beginning of 2008 as this book was being finalized to go to press. However, the approach used and the impact of various assumptions used are still operative and can help inform how changes in prepayments and defaults can impact ABX valuations.

Also, in the examples used in this section our model produced average collateral losses for ABX 06-2 of 9.06%. By early 2008, that loss estimate had risen to 16.0%. The earlier projected loss estimates were made before the subprime market shutdown in July–August of 2007. That shutdown, along with a steady deterioration in performance, caused us to sharply increase our loss estimates for subprime collateral.

In this discussion, we chose to focus on the 20 bonds that comprise ABX 06-2 mainly because the delinquency pipeline is well seasoned and unlike ABX 06-1 is referenced to the 2006 collateral that has caused much of the problem in the subprime space.

Here is a blueprint of the structure of the sections to follow:

Prepayment and default analysis. We begin by discussing our assumptions regarding prepayments, defaults and loss severities on the referenced bonds, and show how these make sense in the light of historical experience. From this historical experience we develop a base-case set of vectors for each of the 20 bonds in the index. We then increase/decrease those base vectors by ±25% (for a range of outcomes to account for uncertainties surrounding our assumptions).

Deal structure: Triggers, waterfall, and cash flow priorities. We next show the results of running our prepayment, default and loss severity vectors through Intex's cash flow model (producing a series of principal balances and write-downs for each of the 20 bonds based on each deal's structure, which includes triggers, step-down criteria and cash flow priorities).

Valuation model. Outputs from the Intex model are used as inputs into our "fair value" discounted cash flow model. We view the cash flows as being long the ABX, so premium payments are a positive cash flow. Monthly premium payments are determined by (1) monthly principal balances of the bond tranches from the Intex model, multiplied by (2) the ABX premium (for ABX 06-2 BBB– the ABX premium = 242 basis points). Bond write-downs (due to collateral losses) are negative inputs to our cash flow model.

The final step is to select an appropriate rate for discounting premium payments and write-downs. This area is controversial, since there is no consensus on how to discount these cash flows. We discuss several possible discount factors, and the rationale for each.

Using this approach, we arrive at the following fair values for ABX 06-2 BBB–:

- Optimistic scenario (75% base defaults, 125% base prepayments) = 101
- Base-case scenario (100% base defaults, 100% base prepayments) = 79
- Pessimistic scenario (125% base defaults, 75% base prepayments) = 50

Models and Reality: Prepayments, Defaults, Loss Severities, and Delinquencies

We now discuss how we arrived at our prepayment, default, severity, and delinquency (percent of 60+) assumptions. The first three jointly determine the magnitude and timing of losses; delinquency and losses impact the pass/fail triggers and the cash flow waterfall.

Model Construction

The objectives of our model are to predict prepayment, default, severity, and delinquency. Typical inputs are collateral characteristics, namely, FICO, LTV, documentation type, loan purpose, loan size, and so on. Macroeconomics factors (the most common are HPA and interest rates) are also model inputs and need be forecasted. There will also be *interactions* among various factors. For example, HPA may have a larger effect on high LTV loans than on low LTV loans. Some effects are *age-dependent* (e.g., FICO effect on default seems to dissipate over time). Many effects could also be *nonlinear*. Some models also include *performance* history (*e.g.*, delinquency status) to forecast future performance.

An econometric model is estimated by running many regressions on historical data. There will be out-of-sample cross-validation. Stress testing may also be conducted. Pricing will be done using model projections. After many iterations of this process, a model will finally be in production.

Hallmarks of a Good Model

In the prime world, model performance is evaluated monthly by comparing actual prepayments versus model forecast, and statements such as "2006 5.5s prepaid 1 CPR faster than our model projections" can be made. Unfortunately, in the subprime world, because of the short performance history and diverse and ever-changing collateral mix, the accuracy of models is unambiguously worse. Put differently, there is more model uncertainty in the subprime sector.

How do we evaluate outputs of a model before applying them to value securities such as the ABX? In our opinion, a good model has to produce the following:

1. *Average has to make sense.* For example, if a model predicts an *average* life time cumulative loss of 5% under an assumption of 0 HPA, we may suspect the model's usefulness, as that seems too low.
2. *Timing has to be right.* As we demonstrate in the next section, magnitude of loss is a one-dimensional measurement. However, loss timing also has important implications on the amount of write-downs and hence the valuation of subprime securities.
3. *Variations across deals.* This is where most models fail. Regressions by definition are centered around the mean. Reality delivers us significant performance variations.

Model Projections versus Historical Performance

Before evaluating our model projections, we briefly review historical performance under different HPA environments. We use MSA level HPA in calculating annualized cumulative HPA. Exhibits 11.1 to 11.4 show prepayment, default, severity, and delinquency curves under different levels of HPA. The message is very consistent: robust HPA implies high prepayment, low default, low severity and low delinquency.

How do our model projections stack up against historical performance? We evaluate the projections from our model based on the *average, timing, and variation* (ATV) criteria outlined earlier.

1. Does the *average* make sense? On average, for the 20 deals in ABX 06-2, model-projected cumulative loss (assuming 0% HPA for life) is 9.5%, consistent with historical observations in a less than 5% HPA environ-

EXHIBIT 11.1   Subprime Voluntary Prepayment by HPA

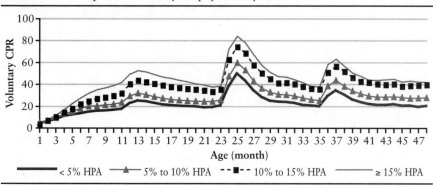

Source: LoanPerformance and UBS.

EXHIBIT 11.2   Subprime Default Rate by HPA

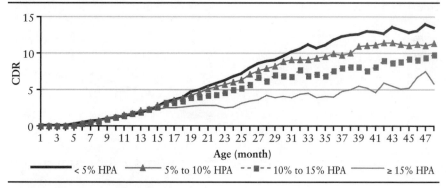

Source: LoanPerformance and UBS.

EXHIBIT 11.3   Subprime Severity by HPA

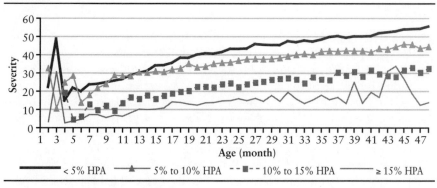

Source: LoanPerformance and UBS.

EXHIBIT 11.4   Subprime %60+ (by HPA)

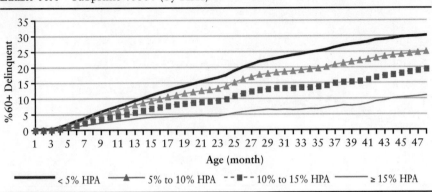

Source: LoanPerformance and UBS.

EXHIBIT 11.5   Cumulative Loss in < 5% HPA (by vintage)

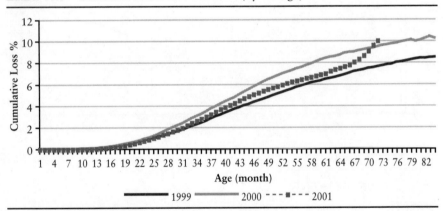

Source: LoanPerformance and UBS.

ment (Exhibit 11.5). We admit that most of our historical data with less than 5% HPA fall between 2.5% and 5%, since very few observations have 0% or negative HPA. We feel the 2000 vintage is probably more indicative of the cumulative losses we expect in a 0% HPA, as the national economy went through a recession in 2001, and the combined effect of a [Minor recession + Low HPA (< 5%)] is roughly comparable to 0% HPA. Exhibits 11.6 and 11.7 show average model severity and delinquency (%60+) versus the historical average. Both seem consistent with historical experience in a low HPA (< 5%) environment. Note that severity also has a seasoning curve. Finally, in Exhibit 11.8, we compare

EXHIBIT 11.6   Severity: Model versus Actual

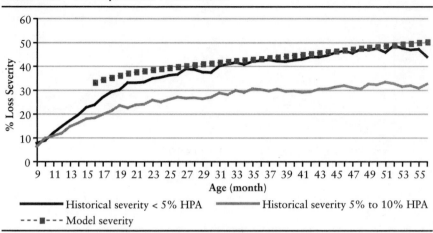

Source: LoanPerformance, CPR/CDR, and UBS.

EXHIBIT 11.7   %60+: Model versus Actual

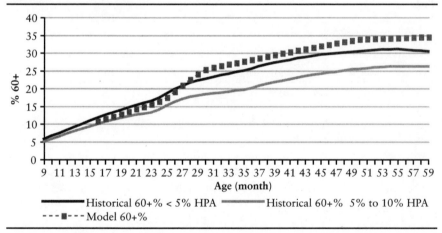

Source: LoanPerformance, CPR/CDR, and UBS.

the prepayment curve (CPR) to historical experiences. The flatter CPR curve is because the model projection in that figure at the deal level is a weighted average of loans at different ages.

2. Is the *timing* right? Exhibit 11.9 summarizes historical loss timing in a less than 5% HPA environment. Our model results reach 50% of life time cumulative loss between months (loan age) 42 and 46. The 0%

EXHIBIT 11.8   Voluntary Prepayment: Model versus Actual

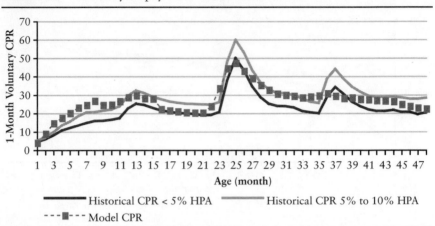

Source: LoanPerformance, CPR/CDR, and UBS.

EXHIBIT 11.9   Historical Loss Timing (< 5% annual HPA) by Vintage

	1999	2000	2001
Month to reach 25% of cumulative loss	33	32	32
Month to reach 50% of cumulative loss	46	43	42
Month to reach 75% of cumulative loss	58	56	59

Source: LoanPerformance and UBS.

HPA assumption in model projection has slightly front loaded the losses by six to nine months.

3. Does it capture the variations? Exhibit 11.10 shows historical variations of cumulative losses by vintage. Our model variation is approximately 30%, somewhat lower than historical which is in the 40% to 60% range. We suspect our running a 0% HPA for every single loan probably contributes to lower variations across deals.

Applying the Model

Using the guidelines discussed, we generated prepayment, default, severity, and delinquency projections for the 20 subprime deals in ABX.HE 06-2 indices.[2] We chose the 06-2 because (1) the deals were well seasoned giving us a large amount of history with which to estimate future performance, and

---

[2] We acknowledge CPR & CDR Technologies, Inc. for providing the tools and models to create the pricing curves.

EXHIBIT 11.10   Subprime Cumulative Losses by Vintage

Year	Avg. Loss	Std. Dev.	Std. Dev./Avg. Loss	Issuers	Deals
1994	3.149	1.582	50.23%	15	36
1995	4.700	1.908	40.58%	21	52
1996	4.302	2.510	58.34%	36	99
1997	5.138	2.482	48.30%	47	132
1998	5.448	2.355	43.24%	57	142
1999	5.188	2.600	50.12%	51	133
2000	4.680	2.637	56.34%	43	102
2001	3.819	2.585	67.68%	40	121
2002	2.084	1.507	72.29%	42	168
2003	0.952	0.627	65.84%	49	233
2004	0.489	0.402	82.20%	57	331
2005	0.174	0.191	109.95%	61	406
2006	0.041	0.052	128.43%	34	109

Source: UBS and Intex.

(2) the 06-2 collateral is from the 2006 vintage, the source of much of the subprime problems. Our curves are based on a combination of loan analysis and recent delinquency data.

Pricing curves directly drive collateral and bond cash flows when input into a cash flow generator such as Intex. The prepayment curves determine principal cash flows, the default and severity curves drive the timing and magnitude of losses, and the delinquency curve is used by the cash flow generator to evaluate delinquency triggers. The cash flow generator produces collateral cash flows, cumulative losses, bond cash flows, and write-downs.

Model-Generated Curves

Our strategy uses a literal interpretation of pricing curves generated by the model since each curve was generated specifically for the specific loans in each deal. We gave a basic assumption of [0 HPA + Flat yield curve] to project default and prepay curves customized for a particular deal. Utilizing these curves without adjustment, the cumulative losses will fall where they may and will demonstrate performance tiering between issues and issuers. Additionally, the curves will work together in a consistent manner, at least in the base-case. This is evident when we consider how defaults and severities work together. We will further consider how prepayments and defaults interact to produce losses. Exhibits 11.11 to 11.13 show the input curves generated by the model. Note that these curves contain values corresponding to specific dates rather than periods on a seasoning curve. As of the settle date of 2/28/2007, the deal age ranged 8 to 13 months (mean = 11 months), with a slightly older loan age.

Model Results

We ran each of the 20 deals using the input curves. We assumed 100% servicer advance and a recovery lag of 12 months. We run all bonds to maturity (i.e., no call is assumed) Cleanup calls give the master servicer or residual holder the option of purchasing the mortgage loans from the trust and redeeming the bond certificates.[3]

The model-projected cumulative losses and write-downs for the BBB–bonds are shown in Exhibits 11.15 and 11.16. We see a healthy dispersion of cumulative losses, ranging from 3% to 11% at the 10-month point. This diversity is one of the advantages to allowing the model to drive losses, rather than using iteration and a generic curve to solve for a common loss value as described previously.

EXHIBIT 11.11   Model-Projected Prepayments

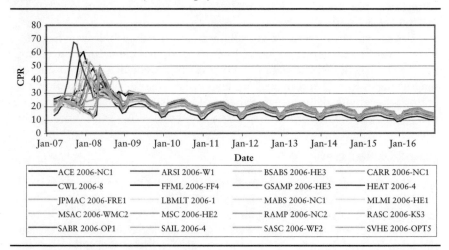

Source: UBS and CPR and CDR.

---

[3] Modeling the call is an interesting topic, as calls have historically not been exercised in an economically "ruthless" manner.

EXHIBIT 11.12 Model-Projected Defaults

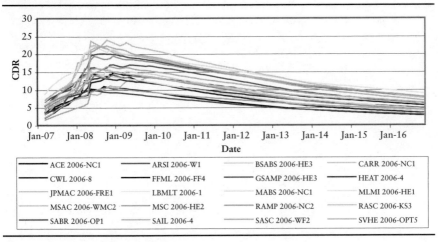

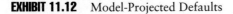

Source: UBS and CPR and CDR.

EXHIBIT 11.13 Model-Projected Severities

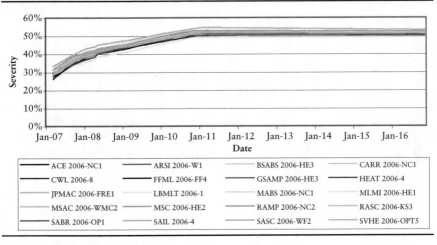

Source: UBS and CPR and CDR.

EXHIBIT 11.14 Model-Projected Delinquencies

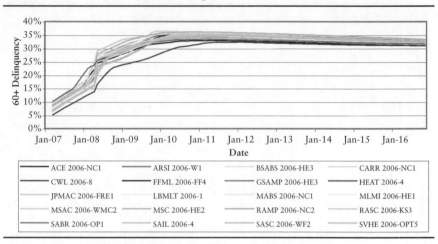

Source: UBS and CPR and CDR.

EXHIBIT 11.15 Cumulative Losses Using Model Curves

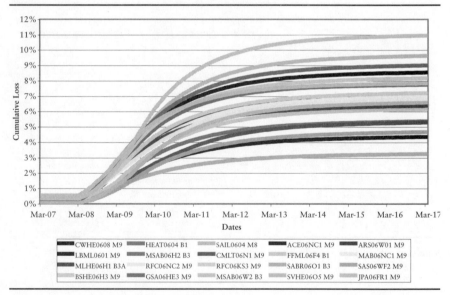

Source: UBS, Intex, and CPR and CDR.

EXHIBIT 11.16 BBB– Write-Downs Using Model Curves

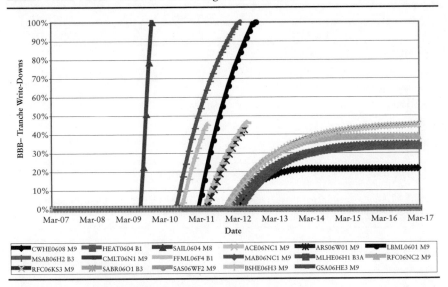

Source: UBS, Intex, and CPR and CDR.

Write-downs are levered with respect to losses, as we would expect from a subordinated 1% slice at approximately the 9% level within a deal's capital structure. We make further observations when we examine write-downs as a function of losses using the level of defaults and prepayments as factors.

Generating Scenarios

Because of the subprime ABS bonds' uncertain cash flows, we ideally like to run bonds using scenarios which stress defaults and prepayments. The sensitivity approach we used was to generate a reasonable baseline of parameters, stress key parameters, and observes how the bonds behave.

This approach allows us to concentrate on isolating the effects of subprime cash flow assumptions on the BBB– bonds. We use our base-case 0 HPA curves and independently vary prepayments and defaults by ±25%. This produces a cube of results, depicted in Exhibit 11.17. The combination of [low defaults + high prepayments] produces the lowest collateral losses; [high defaults + low prepayments] produces the highest collateral losses.

The relationship of prepayment and loss sensitivity is illustrated in Exhibit 11.18. In this exhibit, we show the progression of cumulative losses as we independently vary the default and prepay. Notice in Exhibit 11.18 that the effect of a 25% shift of the prepayment curve is even greater to a deal's ultimate cumulative losses than is a 25% shift of the default curve.

EXHIBIT 11.17 Scenario Cube

		Defaults		
		Low	**Base**	**High**
Prepays	**High**	Expectation: Low Losses Low Write-downs		
	Base		Base-case	
	Low			Expectation: High Losses High Write-downs

Source: UBS.

EXHIBIT 11.18 Cumulative Loss over Time with Prepayment and Default Scenarios

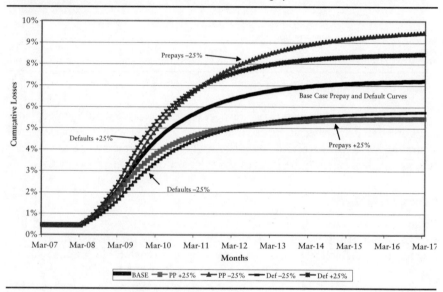

Source: UBS, Intex, and CPR and CDR.

Prepayments and defaults compete for every dollar of balance (i.e., dollars prepaid can never be lost through default). CPRs and CDRs are measures of prepayments, and defaults specified as annualized percentages of current balance, so as fast prepays reduce the balance more quickly, there is less absolute dollars for CDRs to liquidate. Note, too, that in terms of magnitude, CPRs are several times larger than CDRs, and the effect of the default is further tempered by the severity. That is why stressing the prepayment curve has such a large effect on losses.

EXHIBIT 11.19   Results for Model Scenarios

	Optimistic		Base-case		Severe Losses		Average 9 Scenarios	
	Cum. Loss	Write- Down	Cum. Loss	Write- Down	Cum. Loss	Write- Down	Cum. Loss	Write- Down
Mean	6.21%	17.22%	9.69%	40.31%	13.97%	70.00%	9.78%	42.40%
Std. Dev.	1.89%	35.44%	2.56%	43.99%	3.14%	47.02%	3.41%	45.21%
CV	30.39%	205.80%	26.44%	109.13%	22.47%	67.17%	34.83%	106.63%

Source: UBS, Intex, and CPR and CDR.

Model Results

We ran the nine scenarios on each of the 20 bonds, generating 180 sets of results, shown in Exhibit 11.19. Exhibit 11.20 summarizes the loss and write-down results: the base-case average projection is for 10% cumulative losses, and the best and worse scenarios average 6% to nearly 20%. Write-downs in the base-case averaged 40%, and ranged from 17% to 70% in the best to worst scenarios. We see a 25% coefficient of variation in cumulative losses, which passes one of the model smell tests. We see that variation of write-downs is much higher.

EXHIBIT 11.20   Summary of Model Cumulative Loss and Write-Down

		Default	Prepay	Wal.	Yield	Write- Down	Cum. Loss	Step- Down	1st Trig. Fail.
CWHE0608	M9	–25%	+25%	4.65	7.23	0%	6.87%	45	DLQ
CWHE0608	M9	–25%	Base	10.94	7.58	0%	8.52%	64	DLQ
CWHE0608	M9	–25%	–25%	21.81	7.71	0%	10.57%	Never	DLQ
CWHE0608	M9	Base	+25%	12.27	7.8	0%	8.62%	44	DLQ
CWHE0608	M9	Base	Base	19.88	7.88	0%	10.60%	Never	DLQ
CWHE0608	M9	Base	–25%	22.43	7.79	0%	13.04%	Never	DLQ
CWHE0608	M9	+25%	+25%	4.07	–44.08	100%	10.16%	Never	DLQ
CWHE0608	M9	+25%	Base	3.95	–3.19	73%	12.39%	Never	Both
CWHE0608	M9	+25%	–25%	3.88	1.2	0%	15.12%	Never	Both
HEAT0604	B1	–25%	+25%	3.77	7.42	0%	4.43%	37	DLQ
HEAT0604	B1	–25%	Base	4.05	7.31	0%	5.88%	45	DLQ
HEAT0604	B1	–25%	–25%	8.68	7.51	0%	7.85%	61	DLQ
HEAT0604	B1	Base	+25%	5.86	3.7	17%	5.58%	37	DLQ
HEAT0604	B1	Base	Base	10.5	7.68	0%	7.34%	44	DLQ
HEAT0604	B1	Base	–25%	20.46	7.77	0%	9.69%	Never	DLQ
HEAT0604	B1	+25%	+25%	3.12	–13.39	49%	6.61%	37	DLQ
HEAT0604	B1	+25%	Base	6.18	–19.82	100%	8.62%	Never	DLQ
HEAT0604	B1	+25%	–25%	5.03	–30.96	100%	11.26%	Never	DLQ
SAIL0604	M8	–25%	+25%	3.12	–64.84	100%	9.03%	Never	Both

EXHIBIT 11.20 (Continued)

		Default	Prepay	Wal.	Yield	Write-Down	Cum. Loss	Step-Down	1st Trig. Fail.
SAIL0604	M8	−25%	Base	3.13	−64.59	100%	11.17%	Never	Both
SAIL0604	M8	−25%	−25%	3.15	−64.09	100%	13.86%	Never	Both
SAIL0604	M8	Base	+25%	2.53	−83.24	100%	11.00%	Never	Both
SAIL0604	M8	Base	Base	2.56	−82.23	100%	13.43%	Never	Both
SAIL0604	M8	Base	−25%	2.59	−81.35	100%	16.42%	Never	Both
SAIL0604	M8	+25%	+25%	2.26	−94.27	100%	12.63%	Never	Both
SAIL0604	M8	+25%	Base	2.29	−92.98	100%	15.24%	Never	Both
SAIL0604	M8	+25%	−25%	2.32	−91.71	100%	18.38%	Never	Both
ACE06NC1	M9	−25%	+25%	6.32	7.98	0%	3.46%	359	DLQ
ACE06NC1	M9	−25%	Base	9.06	8.02	0%	4.64%	359	DLQ
ACE06NC1	M9	−25%	−25%	13.59	8.06	0%	6.17%	359	DLQ
ACE06NC1	M9	Base	+25%	6.5	8.03	0%	4.37%	359	DLQ
ACE06NC1	M9	Base	Base	8.9	8.06	0%	5.83%	359	DLQ
ACE06NC1	M9	Base	−25%	12.22	8.06	0%	7.71%	Never	DLQ
ACE06NC1	M9	+25%	+25%	7.05	8.12	0%	5.21%	359	DLQ
ACE06NC1	M9	+25%	Base	10.38	8.21	0%	6.91%	359	DLQ
ACE06NC1	M9	+25%	−25%	14.92	8.25	0%	9.06%	Never	DLQ
ARS06W01	M9	−25%	+25%	6.55	8.14	0%	6.41%	39	DLQ
ARS06W01	M9	−25%	Base	7.15	7.96	0%	8.14%	52	DLQ
ARS06W01	M9	−25%	−25%	10.08	8.03	0%	10.37%	65	DLQ
ARS06W01	M9	Base	+25%	3.42	−9.42	46%	7.90%	39	DLQ
ARS06W01	M9	Base	Base	5.49	−14.97	83%	9.90%	52	DLQ
ARS06W01	M9	Base	−25%	6.06	−5.47	91%	12.44%	Never	DLQ
ARS06W01	M9	+25%	+25%	3.01	−18.08	55%	9.18%	39	DLQ
ARS06W01	M9	+25%	Base	4.16	−41.36	100%	11.36%	Never	DLQ
ARS06W01	M9	+25%	−25%	3.91	−45.73	100%	14.09%	Never	DLQ
LBML0601	M9	−25%	+25%	5.8	−16.36	90%	7.97%	43	DLQ
LBML0601	M9	−25%	Base	12.72	2.16	77%	9.83%	Never	DLQ
LBML0601	M9	−25%	−25%	6.62	−7.68	99%	12.22%	Never	DLQ
LBML0601	M9	Base	+25%	4.17	−40.79	100%	9.66%	Never	Both
LBML0601	M9	Base	Base	3.83	−47.09	100%	11.73%	Never	Both
LBML0601	M9	Base	−25%	3.64	−50.89	100%	14.31%	Never	Both
LBML0601	M9	+25%	+25%	3.01	−65.76	100%	11.05%	Never	Both
LBML0601	M9	+25%	Base	2.92	−68.43	100%	13.22%	Never	Both
LBML0601	M9	+25%	−25%	2.86	−70.32	100%	15.87%	Never	Both
MSAB06H2	B3	−25%	+25%	6.31	4.61	18%	6.86%	39	DLQ
MSAB06H2	B3	−25%	Base	10.8	7.79	0%	8.97%	Never	DLQ
MSAB06H2	B3	−25%	−25%	15.23	7.84	0%	11.76%	Never	DLQ
MSAB06H2	B3	Base	+25%	10.92	3.56	50%	8.42%	Never	DLQ
MSAB06H2	B3	Base	Base	5.48	−25.46	100%	10.87%	Never	Both
MSAB06H2	B3	Base	−25%	4.59	−36.55	100%	14.03%	Never	Both

EXHIBIT 11.20 (Continued)

		Default	Prepay	Wal.	Yield	Write-Down	Cum. Loss	Step-Down	1st Trig. Fail.
MSAB06H2	B3	+25%	+25%	4.01	−43.92	100%	9.77%	Never	Both
MSAB06H2	B3	+25%	Base	3.61	−52.7	100%	12.45%	Never	Both
MSAB06H2	B3	+25%	−25%	3.41	−57.3	100%	15.83%	Never	Both
CMLT06N1	M9	−25%	+25%	4.84	8.14	0%	4.44%	37	DLQ
CMLT06N1	M9	−25%	Base	17.79	8.6	0%	5.88%	99	DLQ
CMLT06N1	M9	−25%	−25%	18.03	8.43	0%	7.81%	99	DLQ
CMLT06N1	M9	Base	+25%	4.35	8.07	0%	5.59%	37	DLQ
CMLT06N1	M9	Base	Base	12.3	8.46	0%	7.32%	99	DLQ
CMLT06N1	M9	Base	−25%	10.19	8.13	0%	9.62%	Never	DLQ
CMLT06N1	M9	+25%	+25%	8.75	8.49	0%	6.62%	37	DLQ
CMLT06N1	M9	+25%	Base	8.6	8.24	0%	8.58%	Never	DLQ
CMLT06N1	M9	+25%	−25%	12.98	8.38	0%	11.14%	Never	DLQ
FFML06F4	B1	−25%	+25%	5.37	8.3	0%	5.42%	40	DLQ
FFML06F4	B1	−25%	Base	5.74	8.11	0%	7.16%	54	DLQ
FFML06F4	B1	−25%	−25%	16.89	8.56	0%	9.49%	Never	DLQ
FFML06F4	B1	Base	+25%	3.62	−8.65	48%	6.76%	40	DLQ
FFML06F4	B1	Base	Base	14.1	3.98	65%	8.83%	Never	DLQ
FFML06F4	B1	Base	−25%	6.49	−16.55	100%	11.56%	Never	DLQ
FFML06F4	B1	+25%	+25%	3.01	−11.17	46%	7.95%	40	DLQ
FFML06F4	B1	+25%	Base	4.34	−37.6	100%	10.26%	Never	DLQ
FFML06F4	B1	+25%	−25%	4.01	−42.82	100%	13.26%	Never	DLQ
MAB06NC1	M9	−25%	+25%	3.56	7.64	0%	6.20%	38	DLQ
MAB06NC1	M9	−25%	Base	7.02	7.91	0%	7.76%	52	DLQ
MAB06NC1	M9	−25%	−25%	17.94	8.23	0%	9.73%	65	DLQ
MAB06NC1	M9	Base	+25%	4.95	2.45	21%	7.68%	38	DLQ
MAB06NC1	M9	Base	Base	20.07	8.47	0%	9.52%	Never	DLQ
MAB06NC1	M9	Base	−25%	23.79	8.4	0%	11.81%	Never	DLQ
MAB06NC1	M9	+25%	+25%	3.78	−27.12	77%	8.96%	39	DLQ
MAB06NC1	M9	+25%	Base	4.95	−30.64	100%	11.00%	Never	DLQ
MAB06NC1	M9	+25%	−25%	4.48	−36.8	100%	13.51%	Never	Both
MLHE06H1	B3A	−25%	+25%	5.1	7.73	0%	5.50%	37	DLQ
MLHE06H1	B3A	−25%	Base	7.79	7.61	0%	7.04%	169	DLQ
MLHE06H1	B3A	−25%	−25%	11.24	7.67	0%	9.02%	Never	DLQ
MLHE06H1	B3A	Base	+25%	5.63	7.83	0%	6.84%	37	DLQ
MLHE06H1	B3A	Base	Base	8.55	7.73	0%	8.70%	Never	DLQ
MLHE06H1	B3A	Base	−25%	11.56	7.77	0%	11.05%	Never	DLQ
MLHE06H1	B3A	+25%	+25%	6.5	3.71	26%	8.04%	37	DLQ
MLHE06H1	B3A	+25%	Base	10.77	7.94	0%	10.15%	Never	DLQ
MLHE06H1	B3A	+25%	−25%	17.49	8.05	0%	12.78%	Never	DLQ
RFC06NC2	M9	−25%	+25%	3.51	7.6	0%	6.21%	37	DLQ
RFC06NC2	M9	−25%	Base	4.64	7.54	0%	7.74%	53	DLQ

EXHIBIT 11.20 (Continued)

		Default	Prepay	Wal.	Yield	Write-Down	Cum. Loss	Step-Down	1st Trig. Fail.
RFC06NC2	M9	–25%	–25%	11.72	7.96	0%	9.71%	67	DLQ
RFC06NC2	M9	Base	+25%	3.81	–9.69	50%	7.68%	37	DLQ
RFC06NC2	M9	Base	Base	7.89	4.91	24%	9.49%	52	DLQ
RFC06NC2	M9	Base	–25%	18.1	6.21	30%	11.80%	Never	DLQ
RFC06NC2	M9	+25%	+25%	3.07	–20.31	58%	8.96%	37	DLQ
RFC06NC2	M9	+25%	Base	4.29	–39.54	100%	10.98%	Never	DLQ
RFC06NC2	M9	+25%	–25%	4.08	–42.82	100%	13.53%	Never	DLQ
RFC06KS3	M9	–25%	+25%	3.97	7.38	0%	6.42%	38	DLQ
RFC06KS3	M9	–25%	Base	6.2	7.47	0%	8.16%	51	DLQ
RFC06KS3	M9	–25%	–25%	16.55	7.81	0%	10.45%	Never	DLQ
RFC06KS3	M9	Base	+25%	4.17	–6.71	47%	7.90%	38	DLQ
RFC06KS3	M9	Base	Base	18.44	7.16	18%	9.96%	Never	DLQ
RFC06KS3	M9	Base	–25%	15.52	4.1	55%	12.63%	Never	DLQ
RFC06KS3	M9	+25%	+25%	7.46	–5.06	95%	9.20%	Never	Both
RFC06KS3	M9	+25%	Base	4.88	–32.5	100%	11.50%	Never	Both
RFC06KS3	M9	+25%	–25%	4.33	–40.16	100%	14.42%	Never	Both
SABR06O1	B3	–25%	+25%	2.81	7.01	0%	2.40%	37	Pass
SABR06O1	B3	–25%	Base	3.48	7	0%	3.48%	37	DLQ
SABR06O1	B3	–25%	–25%	9.63	7.32	0%	4.86%	57	DLQ
SABR06O1	B3	Base	+25%	3.51	7.19	0%	3.07%	37	Pass
SABR06O1	B3	Base	Base	5.4	7.31	0%	4.41%	37	DLQ
SABR06O1	B3	Base	–25%	12.69	7.44	0%	6.11%	Never	DLQ
SABR06O1	B3	+25%	+25%	5.49	4.42	17%	3.68%	37	Loss
SABR06O1	B3	+25%	Base	8.12	4.13	27%	5.26%	37	DLQ
SABR06O1	B3	+25%	–25%	16.07	7.59	0%	7.22%	Never	DLQ
SAS06WF2	M9	–25%	+25%	3.3	6.93	0%	3.79%	37	DLQ
SAS06WF2	M9	–25%	Base	4.41	6.93	0%	5.21%	44	DLQ
SAS06WF2	M9	–25%	–25%	6.27	6.97	0%	7.18%	62	DLQ
SAS06WF2	M9	Base	+25%	3.95	7.06	0%	4.84%	37	DLQ
SAS06WF2	M9	Base	Base	4.22	6.93	0%	6.61%	44	DLQ
SAS06WF2	M9	Base	–25%	5.83	6.96	0%	9.01%	61	DLQ
SAS06WF2	M9	+25%	+25%	5.83	2.48	28%	5.81%	37	DLQ
SAS06WF2	M9	+25%	Base	9.21	6.47	4%	7.86%	43	DLQ
SAS06WF2	M9	+25%	–25%	13.16	7.35	0%	10.62%	60	DLQ
BSHE06H3	M9	–25%	+25%	5.97	1.92	36%	7.62%	39	DLQ
BSHE06H3	M9	–25%	Base	15.93	8.08	0%	9.59%	Never	DLQ
BSHE06H3	M9	–25%	–25%	22.59	8.09	0%	12.10%	Never	DLQ
BSHE06H3	M9	Base	+25%	4.26	–36.64	97%	9.28%	38	DLQ
BSHE06H3	M9	Base	Base	5.16	–28.58	100%	11.50%	Never	DLQ
BSHE06H3	M9	Base	–25%	4.49	–37.46	100%	14.27%	Never	DLQ
BSHE06H3	M9	+25%	+25%	3.8	–47.83	100%	10.65%	Never	DLQ

EXHIBIT 11.20 (Continued)

		Default	Prepay	Wal.	Yield	Write-Down	Cum. Loss	Step-Down	1st Trig. Fail.
BSHE06H3	M9	+25%	Base	3.48	−55.07	100%	13.01%	Never	Both
BSHE06H3	M9	+25%	−25%	3.3	−59.24	100%	15.90%	Never	Both
GSA06HE3	M9	−25%	+25%	8.65	7.36	0%	8.45%	Never	DLQ
GSA06HE3	M9	−25%	Base	12.07	7.45	0%	10.59%	Never	DLQ
GSA06HE3	M9	−25%	−25%	16.71	7.5	0%	13.35%	Never	DLQ
GSA06HE3	M9	Base	+25%	13.22	5.89	26%	10.32%	Never	Both
GSA06HE3	M9	Base	Base	10.02	−0.56	82%	12.75%	Never	Both
GSA06HE3	M9	Base	−25%	5.62	−26.25	100%	15.83%	Never	Both
GSA06HE3	M9	+25%	+25%	4.44	−38.41	100%	11.89%	Never	Both
GSA06HE3	M9	+25%	Base	3.98	−46.86	100%	14.51%	Never	Both
GSA06HE3	M9	+25%	−25%	3.73	−51.6	100%	17.74%	Never	Both
MSAB06W2	B3	−25%	+25%	5.04	−30.66	100%	9.76%	Never	Both
MSAB06W2	B3	−25%	Base	4.47	−38.64	100%	12.32%	Never	Both
MSAB06W2	B3	−25%	−25%	4.17	−5.6	88%	15.54%	Never	Both
MSAB06W2	B3	Base	+25%	3.26	−61.52	100%	11.85%	Never	Both
MSAB06W2	B3	Base	Base	3.19	−63.28	100%	14.75%	Never	Both
MSAB06W2	B3	Base	−25%	3.15	−64.31	100%	18.32%	Never	Both
MSAB06W2	B3	+25%	+25%	2.78	−74.93	100%	13.59%	Never	Both
MSAB06W2	B3	+25%	Base	2.77	−75.33	100%	16.69%	Never	Both
MSAB06W2	B3	+25%	−25%	2.76	−75.62	100%	20.43%	Never	Both
SVHE06O5	M9	−25%	+25%	5.34	7.35	0%	5.94%	38	DLQ
SVHE06O5	M9	−25%	Base	4.74	7.08	0%	7.87%	52	DLQ
SVHE06O5	M9	−25%	−25%	9.85	7.4	0%	10.41%	66	DLQ
SVHE06O5	M9	Base	+25%	3.68	−7.41	44%	7.40%	38	DLQ
SVHE06O5	M9	Base	Base	5.96	3.48	14%	9.68%	51	DLQ
SVHE06O5	M9	Base	−25%	9.77	2.35	28%	12.62%	Never	DLQ
SVHE06O5	M9	+25%	+25%	3.3	−16.64	57%	8.67%	38	DLQ
SVHE06O5	M9	+25%	Base	4.6	−36.78	100%	11.21%	Never	DLQ
SVHE06O5	M9	+25%	−25%	4.2	−42.78	100%	14.42%	Never	DLQ
JPA06FR1	M9	−25%	+25%	6.06	7.85	0%	6.98%	177	DLQ
JPA06FR1	M9	−25%	Base	8.93	7.97	0%	8.87%	Never	DLQ
JPA06FR1	M9	−25%	−25%	14.83	8.13	0%	11.28%	Never	DLQ
JPA06FR1	M9	Base	+25%	7.66	8.04	0%	8.46%	Never	DLQ
JPA06FR1	M9	Base	Base	15.2	7.21	21%	10.63%	Never	DLQ
JPA06FR1	M9	Base	−25%	7.24	−6.76	97%	13.32%	Never	DLQ
JPA06FR1	M9	+25%	+25%	9.65	2.38	59%	9.72%	Never	DLQ
JPA06FR1	M9	+25%	Base	4.89	−30.56	100%	12.06%	Never	Both
JPA06FR1	M9	+25%	−25%	4.13	−42.53	100%	14.90%	Never	Both

Source: UBS, Intex, and CPR and CDR.

EXHIBIT 11.21   Summary of Model Output Trigger

What percentage of deals stepped down?

Never stepped down	57.22%
Step-down delayed	31.11%
Stepped down on or before month 37	11.67%

Which trigger inhibited step-down?

	Delinquency	Loss	Both
Never stepped down	56.31%	0.00%	43.69%
Step-down delayed	100.00%	0.00%	0.00%

Of the deals that stepped down on of before month 37, which trigger was eventually hit first?

	Neither	Delinquency	Loss	Both
Stepped down on or before month 37	9.52%	85.71%	4.76%	0.00%

Source: UBS, Intex, and CPR and CDR.

Exhibit 11.21 shows the performance of triggers under the model. Compared with history, the model predicts a generally harder time passing triggers going forward. These projections show 57% of the deals in ABX.HE 06-2 never stepping down, versus only 29% failing to step-down in 2001 (worst year in recent history). Only 12% step-down on or before month 37, whereas between 2000 and 2003 (years in which we have complete step-down statistics) that number is 50% to 60%. A large contributor is the great moderation in speeds predicted by the model relative to speeds experienced by those vintages. Breaking down the trigger types, we see that delinquency triggers have an ephemeral effect, delaying step-downs, and affecting deals after the first step-down. Loss triggers have a more permanent effect, making their contribution by permanently inhibiting deal step-down.

The major interpretation is that the model indicates that triggers will not pass as liberally as before, a welcome development given the challenging credit environment predicted.

The Data: Write-Downs versus Cumulative Losses

In the upper right cube in Exhibit 11.22, ARS06WO1 shows the pattern we expect in the scenario cubes—losses always rise from top to bottom, and from left to right. We also see write-downs rising with losses.

EXHIBIT 11.22 Contrasting the Write-Down Performance of Two Deals

ARS06W01 Performance

Prepays	Defaults: Low			Base			High		
High	Cum. Loss 6.41%	Write-down 0.00%	WAL 6.55	Cum. Loss 7.90%	Write-down 45.94%	WAL 3.42	Cum. Loss 9.18%	Write-down 55.06%	WAL 3.01
Base	Cum. Loss 8.14%	Write-down 0.00%	WAL 7.15	Cum. Loss 9.90%	Write-down 82.66%	WAL 5.49	Cum. Loss 11.36%	Write-down 100.00%	WAL 4.16
Low	Cum. Loss 10.37%	Write-down 0.00%	WAL 10.08	Cum. Loss 12.44%	Write-down 90.93%	WAL 6.06	Cum. Loss 14.09%	Write-down 100.00%	WAL 3.91

SAS06WF2 Performance

Prepays	Defaults: Low			Base			High		
High	Cum. Loss 3.79%	Write-down 0.00%	WAL 3.3	Cum. Loss 4.84%	Write-down 0.00%	WAL 3.9	Cum. Loss 5.81%	Write-down 28.49%	WAL 5.83
Base	Cum. Loss 5.21%	Write-down 0.00%	WAL 4.41	Cum. Loss 6.61%	Write-down 0.00%	WAL 4.2	Cum. Loss 7.86%	Write-down 4.17%	WAL 9.21
Low	Cum. Loss 7.18%	Write-down 0.00%	WAL 6.27	Cum. Loss 9.01%	Write-down 0.00%	WAL 5.83	Cum. Loss 10.62%	Write-down 0.00%	WAL 13.8

ARS06W01 Triggers

Prepays	Defaults: Low		Base		High	
High	Trigger Reason Step-down	Delay / DLQ / 39	Trigger Reason Step-down	Delay / DLQ / 39	Trigger Reason Step-down	Delay / DLQ / 39
Base	Trigger Reason Step-down	Delay / DLQ / 52	Trigger Reason Step-down	Delay / DLQ / 52	Trigger Reason Step-down	Fail / DLQ / Never
Low	Trigger Reason Step-down	Delay / DLQ / 65	Trigger Reason Step-down	Fail / DLQ / Never	Trigger Reason Step-down	Fail / DLQ / Never

SAS06WF2 Triggers

Prepays	Defaults: Low		Base		High	
High	Trigger Reason Step-down	Pass / — / 37	Trigger Reason Step-down	Pass / — / 37	Trigger Reason Step-down	Pass / — / 37
Base	Trigger Reason Step-down	Delay / DLQ / 44	Trigger Reason Step-down	Delay / DLQ / 44	Trigger Reason Step-down	Delay / DLQ / 43
Low	Trigger Reason Step-down	Delay / DLQ / 62	Trigger Reason Step-down	Delay / DLQ / 61	Trigger Reason Step-down	Delay / DLQ / 60

Expectation Legend

Prepays	Low	Base	High
High	Expectation: Low Losses Low Write-downs		
Base		Base Case	
Low			Expectation: High Losses High Write-downs

Source: UBS, Intex, and CPR and CDR.

233

However, in the lower left cube (SAS06WF2), this pattern is disturbed. The three high-loss scenarios (circled) show losses increasing as prepayments decline (as expected) from 5.8% to 10.6%. However, the direction of write-downs moves in the opposite direction, from 28% in the high prepayment scenario to 0% in the low prepayment scenario. In other words, in this set of scenarios, write-downs are decreasing (considerably so, from 6% to 11%), even as losses are increasing.

To gain insight into what is happening, we look at the two bonds' trigger behavior in those scenarios (the rightmost cubes in Exhibit 11.22). In the ARSI deal, the trigger is delayed in the high prepay scenario due to delinquencies, and fails completely in the other scenarios. The effect on the deal is to go from a delayed step-down to a sequential payment structure. Contrast this with the SASC deal's triggers. In this case, they never completely fail, but progressively delay the step-down. The progression is from 37 months, to 43, then to 60 months. The deal structure is actively managing cashflows to protect the BBB– bond.

The conclusion is that while losses are a function of pricing curves, write-downs are a function of losses and structure.

ABX VALUATION

We have shown summaries of write-downs and cumulative losses for each set of scenarios; we need cash flows to value the index. We do this by modeling ABCDS cash flows for each of the index components. To do so, we generate the cash bond cash flows and use monthly balance and write-down of the bonds in the index. The ABCDS consists of a [Premium leg + Loss coverage leg]. The premium coupon for the ABCDS is used with the notional balance to calculate monthly premia. Monthly write-downs make up the loss coverage leg. Monthly ABCDS cash flows are depicted in Exhibit 11.23. All values are shown as a percentage of the tranche original balance. Cash flows begin at month 12 because of the example deal's seasoning.

Exhibit 11.23 illustrates timing of ABCDS cash flows to the protection seller. For the first few years the seller receives premia, which declines as notional balance declines. In 2009, the deal steps down, pays principal to the BBB– cash bond, reducing its balance by 50%. Six years into the deal, the tranche starts to take write-downs, but approximately 12 years into the deal, excess interest is sufficient to cover losses and the bond stops taking write-downs while there is still outstanding balance (write-downs are less than 100%). In many deals, write-downs can be reversed once all bonds are paid down. In this example, about 26 years into the deal all certificates are paid, so the collateral's principal and interest are available to cover unpaid

EXHIBIT 11.23 ABCDS Cash Flow

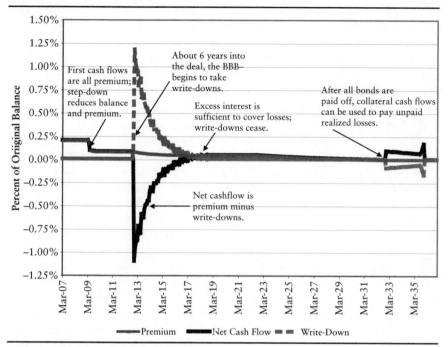

Source: UBS, Intex, CPR and CDR

realized loss amounts in seniority order. Thus the bond receives cash flow; write-downs are partly reversed.

The ABCDS cash flow is levered with respect to collateral performance. In some circumstances, there are no write-downs; and cash flows are all positive to the protection seller. In scenarios where there are write-downs, the write-downs typically occur four or more years into the deal. In this case, there are several years of positive cash flows and several years of negative cash flows.

When the swap is written, the premium coupon is set such that the expected present value of the premium leg equals the expected present value of the loss coverage leg; that is the swap's *net present value* (NPV) is zero. The protection seller is being compensated at fair value for the write-downs he is expected to owe.

The ABX.HE 06-2 BBB– fixed rate was set to 242 bps on 7/19/2006. (We use this rate as the premium for each of the 20 ABCDS in the index.) Since credit spreads widened dramatically since that rate was fixed, the stream of premia at 242 bps is too small to cover expected write-downs.

Marking that swap to market, the value of the premium leg is less than the value of the loss coverage leg, leading to a negative NPV. Given that the average of all index components of the ABX at time of writing March 2007 is negative, the index is priced below par by that amount.

What discount rate is appropriate to value the cash flows? Let's revisit Exhibit 11.23 and consider the shape of the cash flows. We expect to receive a stream of cash flows for the first six years, followed by owing cash flows for six years (or so) thereafter. (We ignore the relatively small postwrite-down flows.)

If the cash flows were certain, this transaction would be tantamount to borrowing cash now and repaying it six years later. Given this perspective, what is the right discount factor to use? Clearly, some discount factor must be specified to reflect the time value of six years of cash flow difference.

Let's add another variable by relaxing our stipulation that cash flows are certain. They are anything but certain, especially in the loss coverage leg, which will frequently be zero (no write-downs) or the full tranche balance (100% write-down). Is the knee-jerk reaction to slap a heavy discount rate onto these cashflows reasonable?

Using a high discount rate (say, [LIBOR + 1000]) is equivalent to borrowing money at 15% annually in our example. This might be a good credit card rate, but not otherwise attractive as a financial proposition. Furthermore, if perceived risk rise, and discount rates were increased to reflect that new risk, how would that change the premium? If the swap were previously 0 NPV, the increased discounting would reduce the value of the longer-dated loss coverage leg more than it does on the short-dated premium leg. In order to keep the swap 0 NPV, the premium leg would have to be reduced, by reducing the premium coupon. Reducing the premium coupon as a reaction to increased risk is clearly incorrect.

Because of our dissatisfaction with a 0 discount rate, and even greater reluctance to use a high risk premium discount rate, we take an agnostic approach and use LIBOR flat as the discount rate.

A second question goes back to the expected cash flows from the write-down. With relatively small changes in assumptions, it is not difficult to maneuver write-downs to be 0% and 100%. Are base-case cash flows sufficient to value the index? Can we get a better idea of expected value? Is there any way to capture the value of the uncertainty? At this point we punt again, and take as the value the average price over all nine scenarios.

Each of the nine scenarios is a column in Exhibit 11.24, showing the combinations of 25% shifts of default and prepayment curves. Each index component and scenario intersects to produce a BBB– write-down and present value of the ABCDS with 242 bps premium. The present values are averaged across scenarios and index component. At the bottom of Exhibit

EXHIBIT 11.24 ABX.HE 06-2 BBB– Valuation Using Our Assumptions.

	Premium	All Avg.		Benign		2		3		4	
		Write-Down	Present Value	Default 75% Write-Down	Prepayment 125% Present Value	Default 75% Write-Down	Prepayment 100% Present Value	Default 75% Write-Down	Prepayment 75% Present Value	Default 100% Write-Down	Prepayment 125% Present Value
CWL 2006-8	242	18%	-11%	0%	8%	0%	8%	0%	11%	16%	-14%
HEAT 2006-4	242	27%	-15%	0%	7%	0%	8%	0%	9%	35%	-21%
SAIL 2006-4	242	93%	-81%	38%	-26%	100%	-78%	100%	-78%	100%	-82%
ACE 2006-NC1	242	0%	8%	0%	5%	0%	7%	0%	10%	0%	6%
ARSI 2006-W1	242	35%	-23%	3%	6%	0%	10%	0%	11%	32%	-20%
LBMLT 2006-1	242	78%	-58%	35%	-20%	42%	-23%	48%	-2%	81%	-61%
MSC 2006-HE2	242	65%	-47%	27%	-15%	22%	-7%	0%	19%	34%	-24%
CARR 2006-NC1	242	0%	15%	0%	8%	0%	11%	0%	29%	0%	8%
FFML 2006-FF4	242	36%	-21%	4%	6%	0%	10%	0%	10%	34%	-22%
MABS 2006-NC1	242	27%	-13%	0%	7%	0%	7%	0%	12%	31%	-17%
MLMI 2006-HE1	242	4%	9%	0%	7%	0%	10%	0%	16%	0%	7%
RAMP 2006-NC2	242	32%	-19%	0%	8%	0%	8%	0%	10%	33%	-19%
RASC 2006-KS3	242	34%	-19%	0%	7%	0%	8%	0%	11%	38%	-23%
SABR 2006-OP1	242	8%	5%	0%	5%	0%	6%	0%	9%	0%	6%
SASC 2006-WF2	242	6%	4%	0%	6%	0%	7%	0%	10%	0%	8%
BSABS 2006-HE3	242	47%	-30%	26%	-12%	27%	-8%	0%	24%	35%	-23%
GSAMP 2006-HE3	242	38%	-20%	0%	11%	0%	14%	0%	20%	42%	-28%
MSAC 2006-WMC2	242	91%	-76%	35%	-11%	88%	-62%	100%	-70%	100%	-76%
SVHE 2006-OPT5	242	31%	-20%	2%	8%	0%	9%	0%	10%	37%	-24%
JPMAC 2006-FRE1	242	22%	-7%	0%	9%	0%	11%	0%	16%	35%	-23%
	242	35%	-21%	9%	1%	14%	-2%	12%	4%	34%	-22%
Price			78.97		101.35		97.75		104.37		78.00

EXHIBIT 11.24 (Continued)

	Premium	Base Default 100% Write-Down	Base Prepayment 100% Present Value	6 Default 100% Write-Down	6 Prepayment 75% Present Value	7 Default 125% Write-Down	7 Prepayment 125% Present Value	8 Default 125% Write-Down	8 Prepayment 100% Present Value	Severe Default 125% Write-Down	Severe Prepayment 75% Present Value
CWL 2006-8	242	0%	6%	0%	30%	45%	-31%	59%	-41%	47%	-57%
HEAT 2006-4	242	24%	-12%	0%	17%	37%	-25%	49%	-34%	100%	-63%
SAIL 2006-4	242	100%	-82%	100%	-82%	100%	-84%	100%	-84%	100%	-83%
ACE 2006-NC1	242	0%	7%	0%	9%	0%	8%	0%	9%	0%	9%
ARSI 2006-W1	242	42%	-26%	44%	-24%	41%	-29%	55%	-39%	100%	-71%
LBMLT 2006-1	242	100%	-69%	100%	-73%	100%	-76%	100%	-78%	100%	-79%
MSC 2006-HE2	242	100%	-72%	100%	-65%	100%	-78%	100%	-73%	100%	-76%
CARR 2006-NC1	242	0%	10%	0%	22%	2%	9%	0%	12%	0%	17%
FFML 2006-FF4	242	46%	-29%	56%	-13%	35%	-24%	48%	-33%	100%	-71%
MABS 2006-NC1	242	19%	-11%	0%	30%	37%	-24%	55%	-38%	100%	-67%
MLMI 2006-HE1	242	0%	10%	0%	17%	20%	-7%	15%	0%	0%	20%
RAMP 2006-NC2	242	38%	-20%	10%	8%	45%	-31%	57%	-40%	100%	-69%
RASC 2006-KS3	242	45%	-24%	8%	25%	37%	-25%	82%	-59%	100%	-68%
SABR 2006-OP1	242	0%	7%	0%	12%	21%	-10%	17%	-2%	30%	9%
SASC 2006-WF2	242	0%	8%	0%	10%	30%	-16%	24%	-6%	0%	15%
BSABS 2006-HE3	242	45%	-30%	100%	-64%	30%	-20%	61%	-45%	100%	-76%
GSAMP 2006-HE3	242	0%	18%	55%	-16%	42%	-29%	100%	-66%	100%	-72%
MSAC 2006-WMC2	242	100%	-77%	100%	-78%	100%	-80%	100%	-80%	100%	-80%
SVHE 2006-OPT5	242	45%	-27%	6%	-1%	36%	-24%	50%	-34%	100%	-69%
JPMAC 2006-FRE1	242	0%	13%	7%	21%	38%	-28%	21%	4%	100%	-68%
	242	35%	-20%	34%	-11%	45%	-31%	55%	-36%	74%	-50%
Price			80.00		89.27		68.76		63.61		50.03

Source: UBS, Intex, CPR and CDR.

11.24, prices for the index are backed out of the present values. The average of all scenarios gives a price of $78.97; this is where our model fair values the ABX.HE 06-2 BBB–. We note, too, that the best case scenario is $101.35 and the worst case scenario is $50.

In this section, we have illustrated how an econometric model can be used to value the ABX 06-2 BBB–. At the time, we did this work our model produced a value of $79 for this subindex. By early 2008, the subindex was trading at around $15. Hence, this is an illustration not only of our econometric approach but of how much the subprime world has changed since March 2007.

THE "SIMPLE" OR DO-IT-YOURSELF APPROACH TO ABX VALUATION

The second approach we use for ABX valuation can be described as a simple or do-it-yourself ABX valuation model because if you have access to Intex, you can replicate our results. That stands in sharp contrast to the econometric approach which requires access to an elaborate prepayment and default model.

In this approach our collateral loss projections come from our simple subprime loss projection model described in Chapter 10 of this book. The basic principle is to take the loans in the serious delinquency buckets, and assume a roll rate to estimate how many of these loans default (the pipeline default). We use a historical default timing curve (and historical cumulative loss) to extrapolate the pipeline defaults into total defaults and then multiply by severity to calculate the total cumulative loss for the deal. Column 2 (Proj Cum Loss) in Exhibits 11.25 to 11.27 summarize our projections of each deal in the three ABX indices. Note that for ABX 06-1, we increased projected cumulative loss by 20% to account for potentially back-loaded losses due to payment shock and lack of refinance alternatives.

For each deal in each index, we then calculate breakeven losses (Columns 3, 6, and 9). Break-even loss for a given tranche is the deal cumulative loss at the point where the tranche begins to take write-downs. A break-even loss for a tranche is higher than its original credit support, because break-even accounts for excess interest generated by the loans and applied against losses. Calculating break-even losses requires running a structured cash flow model (such as Intex).

We then calculate the ratio of break-even loss to projected cumulative loss (Columns 5, 8, and 11) which we will use to estimate the timing of write-downs. Note that these three columns are only populated by bonds expected to suffer write-down. Using ABX07-1 (Exhibit 11.27) as an exam-

EXHIBIT 11.25 ABX 06-1 Projected Cumulative Loss: Breakeven and Expected Write-Downs

ABX 06-1	Proj. Cum. Loss	Breakeven (BBB−)	Difference (BBB−)	Breakeven/Proj. Cum. Loss (BBB−)	Breakeven (BBB)	Difference (BBB)	Breakeven/Proj. Cum. Loss (BBB)	Breakeven (A)	Difference (A)	Breakeven/Proj. Cum. Loss (A)
ACE 2005-HE7	10.40	9.97	−0.43	0.96	11.04	0.64		15.09	4.69	
AMSI 2005-R11	4.47	7.94	3.47		8.74	4.27		12.16	7.69	
ARSI 2005-W2	8.01	9.15	1.14		9.78	1.77		13.45	5.44	
BSABS 2005-HE11	9.14	9.93	0.79		11.02	1.88		15.33	6.19	
CWL 2005-BC5	5.10	7.49	2.39		8.41	3.31		12.44	7.34	
FFML 2005-FF12	6.28	8.93	2.65		9.66	3.38		13.41	7.13	
GSAMP 2005-HE4	7.34	9.98	2.64		11.26	3.92		15.44	8.10	
HEAT 2005-8	8.21	9.05	0.84		9.90	1.69		13.41	5.20	
JPMAC 2005-OPT1	4.82	8.57	3.75		9.53	4.71		13.54	8.72	
LBMLT 2005-WL2	6.69	8.40	1.71		9.43	2.74		12.97	6.28	
MABS 2005-NC2	7.76	7.64	−0.12	0.98	8.67	0.91		12.18	4.42	
MLMI 2005-AR1	6.48	8.34	1.86		9.30	2.82		12.49	6.01	
MSAC 2005-HE5	6.91	9.13	2.22		9.93	3.02		13.78	6.87	
NCHET 2005-4	6.47	8.99	2.52		10.07	3.60		14.08	7.61	
RAMP 2005-EFC4	6.09	9.38	3.29		10.58	4.49		14.74	8.65	
RASC 2005-KS11	8.24	8.98	0.74		9.81	1.57		13.84	5.60	
SABR 2005-HE1	7.03	9.29	2.26		10.37	3.34		14.37	7.34	
SAIL 2005-HE3	8.21	6.98	−1.23	0.85	7.82	−0.39	0.95	10.45	2.24	
SASC 2005-WF4	3.76	7.57	3.81		8.36	4.60		11.04	7.28	
SVHE 2005-4	8.03	9.39	1.36		10.50	2.47		14.92	6.89	
Average	6.97	8.76	1.78	0.93	9.71	2.74	0.95	13.46	6.48	
Original loss timing				68.00			70.00			
Current age				24.00			24.00			24.00
Time remaining to loss				44.00			46.00			
Number of bonds written down				3.00			1.00			0.00

Source: UBS and Intex.

EXHIBIT 11.26 ABX 06-2 Projected Cumulative Loss: Breakeven and Expected Write-Downs

ABX 06-2	Proj. Cum. Loss	Breakeven (BBB–)	Difference (BBB–)	Breakeven/Proj. Cum. Loss (BBB–)	Breakeven (BBB)	Difference (BBB)	Breakeven/Proj. Cum. Loss (BBB)	Breakeven (A)	Difference (A)	Breakeven/Proj. Cum. Loss (A)
ACE 2006-NC1	5.95	8.44	2.49		9.38	3.43		13.43	7.48	
ARSI 2006-W1	9.18	8.66	-0.52	0.94	9.65	0.47		14.06	4.88	
BSABS 2006-HE3	10.15	9.33	-0.82	0.92	10.46	0.31		14.96	4.81	
CARR 2006-NC1	6.62	8.90	2.28		9.89	3.27		13.79	7.17	
CWL 2006-8	11.13	8.06	-3.07	0.72	8.93	-2.20	0.80	12.74	1.61	
FFML 2006-FF4	8.44	7.80	-0.64	0.92	8.68	0.24		12.62	4.18	
GSAMP 2006-HE3	11.80	10.47	-1.33	0.89	11.66	-0.14	0.99	15.97	4.17	
HEAT 2006-4	7.47	8.19	0.72		8.92	1.45		12.54	5.07	
JPMAC 2006-FRE1	11.66	10.39	-1.27	0.89	11.50	-0.16	0.99	15.82	4.16	
LBMLT 2006-1	12.51	8.74	-3.77	0.70	9.58	-2.93	0.77	13.42	0.91	
MABS 2006-NC1	8.46	8.59	0.13		9.45	0.99		13.49	5.03	
MLMI 2006-HE1	8.16	10.13	1.97		11.07	2.91		15.84	7.68	
MSAC 2006-WMC2	16.21	8.73	-7.48	0.54	9.52	-6.69	0.59	12.98	-3.23	0.80
MSC 2006-HE2	10.80	9.06	-1.74	0.84	9.87	-0.93	0.91	13.68	2.88	
RAMP 2006-NC2	8.78	8.36	-0.42	0.95	9.39	0.61		12.98	4.20	
RASC 2006-KS3	9.80	9.19	-0.61	0.94	10.23	0.43		14.22	4.42	
SABR 2006-OP1	3.81	6.96	3.15		7.70	3.89		10.42	6.61	
SAIL 2006-4	12.85	6.63	-6.22	0.52	7.42	-5.43	0.58	10.65	-2.20	0.83
SASC 2006-WF2	5.07	8.83	3.76		10.22	5.15		13.43	8.36	
SVHE 2006-OPT5	9.75	9.29	-0.46	0.95	10.44	0.69		14.50	4.75	
Average	9.43	8.74	-0.69	0.82	9.70	0.27	0.80	13.58	4.15	0.81
Original loss timing				61.00			59.00			60.00
Current age				19.00			19.00			19.00
Time remaining to loss				42.00			40.00			41.00
Number of bonds written down				13.00			7.00			2.00

Source: UBS and Intex.

EXHIBIT 11.27 ABX 07-1 Projected Cumulative Loss: Breakeven and Expected Write-Downs

ABX 07-1	Proj. Cum. Loss	Breakeven (BBB–)	Difference (BBB–)	BreakEven/Proj Cum Loss (BBB–)	Breakeven (BBB)	Difference (BBB)	Breakeven/Proj. Cum. Loss (BBB)	Breakeven (A)	Difference (A)	Breakeven/Proj. Cum. Loss (A)
ABFC 2006-OPT2	10.56	9.68	–0.88	0.92	10.48	–0.08	0.99	14.31	3.75	0.80
ACE 2006-NC3	16.33	8.65	–7.68	0.53	9.58	–6.75	0.59	12.99	–3.34	
BSABS 2006-HE10	14.07	10.04	–4.03	0.71	11.04	–3.03	0.78	14.63	0.56	
CARR 2006-NC4	12.27	9.24	–3.03	0.75	10.66	–1.61	0.87	14.34	2.07	
CBASS 2006-CB6	7.15	9.41	2.26		10.73	3.58		13.99	6.84	
CMLTI 2006-WH3	6.78	9.28	2.50		10.34	3.56		13.37	6.59	
CWL 2006-18	11.30	9.12	–2.18	0.81	10.12	–1.18	0.90	13.68	2.38	0.81
FFML 2006-FF13	10.78	8.27	–2.51	0.77	9.07	–1.71	0.84	12.54	1.76	
FHLT 2006-3	17.12	9.52	–7.60	0.56	10.66	–6.46	0.62	13.86	–3.26	
GSAMP 2006-HE5	13.98	9.58	–4.40	0.69	10.72	–3.26	0.77	15.06	1.08	0.89
HEAT 2006-7	14.69	8.59	–6.10	0.58	9.35	–5.34	0.64	13.06	–1.63	
JPMAC 2006-CH2	3.06	7.92	4.86		8.66	5.60		11.80	8.74	0.82
LBMLT 2006-6	16.76	8.89	–7.87	0.53	9.78	–6.98	0.58	13.69	–3.07	0.99
MABS 2006-NC3	14.40	9.83	–4.57	0.68	11.05	–3.35	0.77	14.28	–0.12	
MLMI 2006-HE5	12.95	9.68	–3.27	0.75	10.52	–2.43	0.81	14.56	1.61	0.80
MSAC 2006-HE6	16.85	9.17	–7.68	0.54	10.14	–6.71	0.60	13.49	–3.36	0.90
RASC 2006-KS9	15.71	9.14	–6.57	0.58	9.99	–5.72	0.64	14.13	–1.58	
SABR 2006-HE2	11.74	8.55	–3.19	0.73	9.84	–1.90	0.84	12.52	0.78	
SASC 2006-BC4	11.85	8.15	–3.70	0.69	9.18	–2.67	0.77	12.03	0.18	
SVHE 2006-EQ1	7.68	10.02	2.34		11.27	3.59		14.66	6.98	
Average	12.30	9.14	–3.16	0.68	10.16	–2.14	0.75	13.65	1.35	0.86
Original loss timing				52.00			56.00			63.00
Current age				12.00			12.00			12.00
Time remaining to loss				40.00			44.00			51.00
Number of bonds written down				16.00			16.00			7.00

Source: UBS and Intex.

ple, the average ratio for BBB– bonds is 0.68. Put differently, ABX07-1 will start to incur write-downs when the underlying bonds reach 68% of their respective cumulative loss. Historically, we reach 68% of cumulative loss by month (age) 52. Given the current WALA of 12, we expect ABX07-1 BBB– to write-down in 40 months, and the number of bonds to be written down is 16. We can do similar calculations for ABX 06-1, 06-2, BBB, and A tranches.

Connecting Write-Down Timing and Prices

How do our loss projections and write-down timing connect to market price? We do this with the aid of an ABX price/write-down table which shows the relationship between price and the number of bonds written down and their timing. (At the end of this section, we describe the assumptions that are used in the construction of these tables.) Using ABX 07-1 BBB– as an example of the data in Exhibit 11.28, we demonstrate that given 16 bonds expected to be written down in 40 months, the theoretical price should be approximately 46 (see the circle). Similarly, we present theoretical prices of BBB–, BBB, and A of all three indices, with theoretical prices circled (Exhibits 11.28 to 11.36). The border of the shaded areas in these exhibits reflects market ABX prices.

Note 07-1 BBB gives us a price lower than that of the BBB–. This anomaly is because the breakevens of the BBB flats are only 100 bps higher than BBB–, and the same 16-bond write-down. The estimated time of write-down is marginally longer, which reflects in a slightly smaller write-down PV. However, the 389 coupon versus the 224 coupon makes the BBB– premium leg more valuable.

The 07-1 A's breakevens are sufficiently higher that only 11 bonds are written down, which yields a higher price. In Exhibit 11.34, the 06-1 single A, even with the increased losses, there were no projected write-downs, and the index ended up pricing the value of the premium stream.

Our simple model does reasonably well with the 07-1 series, but progressively less well with 06-2 and 06-1. How do we reconcile that our theoretical prices for ABX 06-1, 06-2 and all single-A tranches are higher than market prices?

First, the market could be expecting a more back loaded default timing curve (more defaults after deals are seasoned) than the one we are using. This could happen if we believe that ARM resets, payment shock, and lack of refinance opportunities will render 40% or more *remaining* borrowers to default. On 06-1, if we increase the projected cumulative loss by 50%, then we would break eight BBB– bonds and bring the price down to 75.

EXHIBIT 11.28 ABX 07-1 BBB– Pricing Matrix (coupon 389 bps)

ABX Price (Months to Loss)	Number of Bonds Written Down																				
	0	1	2	3	4	5	6	7	8	9	10	11	12	13	14	15	16	17	18	19	20
0	100.0	95.0	90.0	85.0	80.0	75.0	70.0	65.0	60.0	55.0	50.0	45.0	40.0	35.0	30.0	25.0	20.0	15.0	10.0	5.0	0.0
6	101.9	97.0	92.2	87.3	82.4	77.6	72.7	67.8	63.0	58.1	53.2	48.4	43.5	38.6	33.7	28.9	24.0	19.1	14.3	9.4	4.5
12	103.8	99.0	94.3	89.6	84.8	80.1	75.3	70.6	65.8	61.1	56.4	51.6	46.9	42.1	37.4	32.7	27.9	23.2	18.4	13.7	8.9
18	105.6	101.0	96.4	91.7	87.1	82.5	77.9	73.3	68.7	64.0	59.4	54.8	50.2	45.6	41.0	36.3	31.7	27.1	22.5	17.9	13.2
24	107.4	102.9	98.4	93.9	89.4	84.9	80.4	75.9	71.4	66.9	62.4	57.9	53.4	48.9	44.4	39.9	35.4	30.9	26.4	21.9	17.4
30	109.1	104.7	100.3	96.0	91.6	87.2	82.8	78.4	74.1	69.7	65.3	60.9	56.5	52.2	47.8	43.4	39.0	34.7	30.3	25.9	21.5
36	110.8	106.5	102.2	98.0	93.7	89.4	85.2	80.9	76.7	72.4	68.1	63.9	59.6	55.3	51.1	46.8	42.5	38.3	34.0	29.7	25.5
42	112.4	108.2	104.1	99.9	95.8	91.6	87.5	83.3	79.2	75.0	70.9	66.7	62.6	58.4	54.3	50.1	46.0	41.8	37.7	33.5	29.4
48	114.0	109.9	105.9	101.9	97.8	93.8	89.7	85.7	81.6	77.6	73.6	69.5	65.5	61.4	57.4	53.3	49.3	45.2	41.2	37.2	33.1
54	115.5	111.6	107.7	103.7	99.8	95.8	91.9	88.0	84.0	80.1	76.2	72.2	68.3	64.3	60.4	56.5	52.5	48.6	44.7	40.7	36.8
60	117.0	113.2	109.4	105.5	101.7	97.9	94.0	90.2	86.4	82.5	78.7	74.9	71.0	67.2	63.4	59.5	55.7	51.9	48.0	44.2	40.4
66	118.5	114.8	111.0	107.3	103.6	99.8	96.1	92.4	88.6	84.9	81.2	77.4	73.7	70.0	66.2	62.5	58.8	55.0	51.3	47.6	43.8
72	119.9	116.3	112.7	109.0	105.4	101.8	98.1	94.5	90.9	87.2	83.6	79.9	76.3	72.7	69.0	65.4	61.8	58.1	54.5	50.9	47.2
78	121.3	117.8	114.3	110.7	107.2	103.6	100.1	96.6	93.0	89.5	85.9	82.4	78.8	75.3	71.8	68.2	64.7	61.1	57.6	54.1	50.5
84	122.7	119.2	115.8	112.3	108.9	105.5	102.0	98.6	95.1	91.7	88.2	84.8	81.3	77.9	74.4	71.0	67.5	64.1	60.6	57.2	53.7

Note: LIBOR 5.32%.

Source: UBS.

EXHIBIT 11.29   ABX 07-1 BBB Pricing Matrix (coupon 224 bps)

Months to Loss	ABX Price	Number of Bonds Written Down																			
		0	1	2	3	4	5	6	7	8	9	10	11	12	13	14	15	16	17	18	19	20
0		100.0	95.0	90.0	85.0	80.0	75.0	70.0	65.0	60.0	55.0	50.0	45.0	40.0	35.0	30.0	25.0	20.0	15.0	10.0	5.0	0.0
6		101.1	96.2	91.4	86.5	81.6	76.8	71.9	67.0	62.2	57.3	52.4	47.5	42.7	37.8	32.9	28.1	23.2	18.3	13.5	8.6	3.7
12		102.2	97.4	92.7	88.0	83.2	78.5	73.7	69.0	64.2	59.5	54.8	50.0	45.3	40.5	35.8	31.1	26.3	21.6	16.8	12.1	7.3
18		103.2	98.6	94.0	89.4	84.8	80.1	75.5	70.9	66.3	61.7	57.0	52.4	47.8	43.2	38.6	34.0	29.3	24.7	20.1	15.5	10.9
24		104.2	99.7	95.2	90.8	86.3	81.8	77.3	72.8	68.3	63.8	59.3	54.8	50.3	45.8	41.3	36.8	32.3	27.8	23.3	18.8	14.3
30		105.2	100.9	96.5	92.1	87.7	83.3	79.0	74.6	70.2	65.8	61.4	57.1	52.7	48.3	43.9	39.6	35.2	30.8	26.4	22.0	17.7
36		106.2	101.9	97.7	93.4	89.1	84.9	80.6	76.4	72.1	67.8	63.6	59.3	55.0	50.8	46.5	42.2	38.0	33.7	29.4	25.2	20.9
42		107.1	103.0	98.8	94.7	90.5	86.4	82.2	78.1	73.9	69.8	65.6	61.5	57.3	53.2	49.0	44.9	40.7	36.6	32.4	28.2	24.1
48		108.1	104.0	100.0	95.9	91.9	87.8	83.8	79.8	75.7	71.7	67.6	63.6	59.5	55.5	51.4	47.4	43.4	39.3	35.3	31.2	27.2
54		108.9	105.0	101.1	97.1	93.2	89.3	85.3	81.4	77.4	73.5	69.6	65.6	61.7	57.8	53.8	49.9	45.9	42.0	38.1	34.1	30.2
60		109.8	106.0	102.1	98.3	94.5	90.6	86.8	83.0	79.1	75.3	71.5	67.6	63.8	60.0	56.1	52.3	48.5	44.6	40.8	37.0	33.1
66		110.7	106.9	103.2	99.5	95.7	92.0	88.3	84.5	80.8	77.1	73.3	69.6	65.9	62.1	58.4	54.7	50.9	47.2	43.4	39.7	36.0
72		111.5	107.8	104.2	100.6	96.9	93.3	89.7	86.0	82.4	78.8	75.1	71.5	67.8	64.2	60.6	56.9	53.3	49.7	46.0	42.4	38.8
78		112.3	108.7	105.2	101.7	98.1	94.6	91.0	87.5	84.0	80.4	76.9	73.3	69.8	66.3	62.7	59.2	55.6	52.1	48.5	45.0	41.5
84		113.1	109.6	106.2	102.7	99.3	95.8	92.4	88.9	85.5	82.0	78.6	75.1	71.7	68.2	64.8	61.3	57.9	54.4	51.0	47.6	44.1

Note: LIBOR 5.32%.

Source: UBS.

EXHIBIT 11.30   ABX 07-1 A Pricing Matrix (coupon 64 bps)

ABX Price	Number of Bonds Written Down																				
(Months to Loss)	0	1	2	3	4	5	6	7	8	9	10	11	12	13	14	15	16	17	18	19	20
0	100.0	95.0	90.0	85.0	80.0	75.0	70.0	65.0	60.0	55.0	50.0	45.0	40.0	35.0	30.0	25.0	20.0	15.0	10.0	5.0	0.0
6	100.3	95.4	90.6	85.7	80.8	76.0	71.1	66.2	61.4	56.5	51.6	46.8	41.9	37.0	32.1	27.3	22.4	17.5	12.7	7.8	2.9
12	100.6	95.9	91.1	86.4	81.7	76.9	72.2	67.4	62.7	57.9	53.2	48.5	43.7	39.0	34.2	29.5	24.8	20.0	15.3	10.5	5.8
18	100.9	96.3	91.7	87.1	82.5	77.8	73.2	68.6	64.0	59.4	54.7	50.1	45.5	40.9	36.3	31.7	27.0	22.4	17.8	13.2	8.6
24	101.2	96.7	92.2	87.7	83.2	78.7	74.2	69.7	65.2	60.7	56.2	51.8	47.3	42.8	38.3	33.8	29.3	24.8	20.3	15.8	11.3
30	101.5	97.1	92.7	88.4	84.0	79.6	75.2	70.8	66.5	62.1	57.7	53.3	49.0	44.6	40.2	35.8	31.4	27.1	22.7	18.3	13.9
36	101.8	97.5	93.2	89.0	84.7	80.5	76.2	71.9	67.7	63.4	59.1	54.9	50.6	46.3	42.1	37.8	33.5	29.3	25.0	20.8	16.5
42	102.0	97.9	93.7	89.6	85.4	81.3	77.1	73.0	68.8	64.7	60.5	56.4	52.2	48.1	43.9	39.8	35.6	31.5	27.3	23.1	19.0
48	102.3	98.3	94.2	90.2	86.1	82.1	78.0	74.0	70.0	65.9	61.9	57.8	53.8	49.7	45.7	41.6	37.6	33.6	29.5	25.5	21.4
54	102.6	98.6	94.7	90.7	86.8	82.9	78.9	75.0	71.1	67.1	63.2	59.2	55.3	51.4	47.4	43.5	39.6	35.6	31.7	27.7	23.8
60	102.8	99.0	95.1	91.3	87.5	83.6	79.8	76.0	72.1	68.3	64.5	60.6	56.8	53.0	49.1	45.3	41.5	37.6	33.8	29.9	26.1
66	103.0	99.3	95.6	91.8	88.1	84.4	80.6	76.9	73.2	69.4	65.7	62.0	58.2	54.5	50.8	47.0	43.3	39.6	35.8	32.1	28.4
72	103.3	99.6	96.0	92.4	88.7	85.1	81.5	77.8	74.2	70.6	66.9	63.3	59.6	56.0	52.4	48.7	45.1	41.5	37.8	34.2	30.6
78	103.5	100.0	96.4	92.9	89.3	85.8	82.3	78.7	75.2	71.6	68.1	64.6	61.0	57.5	53.9	50.4	46.9	43.3	39.8	36.2	32.7
84	103.7	100.3	96.8	93.4	89.9	86.5	83.0	79.6	76.1	72.7	69.3	65.8	62.4	58.9	55.5	52.0	48.6	45.1	41.7	38.2	34.8

Note: LIBOR 5.32%.

Source: UBS.

EXHIBIT 11.31 ABX 06-2 BBB– Pricing Matrix (Coupon 242 bps)

ABX Price	Number of Bonds Written down																				
Months to Loss	0	1	2	3	4	5	6	7	8	9	10	11	12	13	14	15	16	17	18	19	20
0	100.0	95.0	90.0	85.0	80.0	75.0	70.0	65.0	60.0	55.0	50.0	45.0	40.0	35.0	30.0	25.0	20.0	15.0	10.0	5.0	0.0
6	101.2	96.3	91.5	86.6	81.7	76.8	72.0	67.1	62.2	57.4	52.5	47.6	42.8	37.9	33.0	28.2	23.3	18.4	13.5	8.7	3.8
12	102.4	97.6	92.9	88.1	83.4	78.6	73.9	69.2	64.4	59.7	54.9	50.2	45.5	40.7	36.0	31.2	26.5	21.7	17.0	12.3	7.5
18	103.5	98.9	94.2	89.6	85.0	80.4	75.8	71.2	66.5	61.9	57.3	52.7	48.1	43.5	38.8	34.2	29.6	25.0	20.4	15.8	11.1
24	104.6	100.1	95.6	91.1	86.6	82.1	77.6	73.1	68.6	64.1	59.6	55.1	50.6	46.1	41.6	37.1	32.6	28.1	23.6	19.2	14.7
30	105.7	101.3	96.9	92.5	88.1	83.8	79.4	75.0	70.6	66.2	61.9	57.5	53.1	48.7	44.4	40.0	35.6	31.2	26.8	22.5	18.1
36	106.7	102.4	98.2	93.9	89.6	85.4	81.1	76.8	72.6	68.3	64.1	59.8	55.5	51.3	47.0	42.7	38.5	34.2	29.9	25.7	21.4
42	107.7	103.6	99.4	95.3	91.1	87.0	82.8	78.6	74.5	70.3	66.2	62.0	57.9	53.7	49.6	45.4	41.3	37.1	33.0	28.8	24.7
48	108.7	104.7	100.6	96.6	92.5	88.5	84.4	80.4	76.4	72.3	68.3	64.2	60.2	56.1	52.1	48.0	44.0	40.0	35.9	31.9	27.8
54	109.7	105.7	101.8	97.9	93.9	90.0	86.0	82.1	78.2	74.2	70.3	66.4	62.4	58.5	54.5	50.6	46.7	42.7	38.8	34.9	30.9
60	110.6	106.8	102.9	99.1	95.3	91.4	87.6	83.8	79.9	76.1	72.3	68.4	64.6	60.8	56.9	53.1	49.3	45.4	41.6	37.7	33.9
66	111.5	107.8	104.0	100.3	96.6	92.8	89.1	85.4	81.6	77.9	74.2	70.4	66.7	63.0	59.2	55.5	51.8	48.0	44.3	40.6	36.8
72	112.4	108.8	105.1	101.5	97.9	94.2	90.6	87.0	83.3	79.7	76.0	72.4	68.8	65.1	61.5	57.9	54.2	50.6	47.0	43.3	39.7
78	113.3	109.7	106.2	102.7	99.1	95.6	92.0	88.5	84.9	81.4	77.9	74.3	70.8	67.2	63.7	60.2	56.6	53.1	49.5	46.0	42.5
84	114.1	110.7	107.2	103.8	100.3	96.9	93.4	90.0	86.5	83.1	79.6	76.2	72.7	69.3	65.8	62.4	58.9	55.5	52.0	48.6	45.2

Libor   5.32%

Source: UBS.

EXHIBIT 11.32 ABX 06-2 BBB Pricing Matrix (coupon 133 bps)

		Number of Bonds Written Down																			
ABX Price		0	1	2	3	4	5	6	7	8	9	10	11	12	13	14	15	16	17	18	19	20
Months to Loss	0	100.0	95.0	90.0	85.0	80.0	75.0	70.0	65.0	60.0	55.0	50.0	45.0	40.0	35.0	30.0	25.0	20.0	15.0	10.0	5.0	0.0
	6	100.7	95.8	90.9	86.0	81.2	76.3	71.4	66.6	61.7	56.8	52.0	47.1	42.2	37.4	32.5	27.6	22.8	17.9	13.0	8.1	3.3
	12	101.3	96.6	91.8	87.1	82.3	77.6	72.8	68.1	63.4	58.6	53.9	49.1	44.4	39.7	34.9	30.2	25.4	20.7	15.9	11.2	6.5
	18	101.9	97.3	92.7	88.1	83.4	78.8	74.2	69.6	65.0	60.4	55.7	51.1	46.5	41.9	37.3	32.7	28.0	23.4	18.8	14.2	9.6
	24	102.5	98.0	93.5	89.0	84.5	80.0	75.5	71.0	66.5	62.1	57.6	53.1	48.6	44.1	39.6	35.1	30.6	26.1	21.6	17.1	12.6
	30	103.1	98.7	94.3	90.0	85.6	81.2	76.8	72.5	68.1	63.7	59.3	54.9	50.6	46.2	41.8	37.4	33.0	28.7	24.3	19.9	15.5
	36	103.7	99.4	95.2	90.9	86.6	82.4	78.1	73.8	69.6	65.3	61.0	56.8	52.5	48.2	44.0	39.7	35.5	31.2	26.9	22.7	18.4
	42	104.2	100.1	95.9	91.8	87.6	83.5	79.3	75.2	71.0	66.9	62.7	58.6	54.4	50.3	46.1	42.0	37.8	33.7	29.5	25.3	21.2
	48	104.8	100.7	96.7	92.7	88.6	84.6	80.5	76.5	72.4	68.4	64.3	60.3	56.3	52.2	48.2	44.1	40.1	36.0	32.0	28.0	23.9
	54	105.3	101.4	97.4	93.5	89.6	85.6	81.7	77.7	73.8	69.9	65.9	62.0	58.1	54.1	50.2	46.2	42.3	38.4	34.4	30.5	26.6
	60	105.8	102.0	98.2	94.3	90.5	86.7	82.8	79.0	75.2	71.3	67.5	63.6	59.8	56.0	52.1	48.3	44.5	40.6	36.8	33.0	29.1
	66	106.3	102.6	98.9	95.1	91.4	87.7	83.9	80.2	76.5	72.7	69.0	65.3	61.5	57.8	54.1	50.3	46.6	42.9	39.1	35.4	31.6
	72	106.8	103.2	99.5	95.9	92.3	88.6	85.0	81.4	77.7	74.1	70.5	66.8	63.2	59.5	55.9	52.3	48.6	45.0	41.4	37.7	34.1
	78	107.3	103.8	100.2	96.7	93.1	89.6	86.0	82.5	79.0	75.4	71.9	68.3	64.8	61.3	57.7	54.2	50.6	47.1	43.6	40.0	36.5
	84	107.8	104.3	100.9	97.4	94.0	90.5	87.1	83.6	80.2	76.7	73.3	69.8	66.4	62.9	59.5	56.0	52.6	49.1	45.7	42.2	38.8

Note: LIBOR 5.32%.

Source: UBS.

EXHIBIT 11.33 ABX 06-2 A Pricing Matrix (coupon 44 bps)

ABX Price (Months to Loss)	Number of Bonds Written Down																				
	0	1	2	3	4	5	6	7	8	9	10	11	12	13	14	15	16	17	18	19	20
0	100.0	95.0	90.0	85.0	80.0	75.0	70.0	65.0	60.0	55.0	50.0	45.0	40.0	35.0	30.0	25.0	20.0	15.0	10.0	5.0	0.0
6	100.2	95.3	90.5	85.6	80.7	75.9	71.0	66.1	61.3	56.4	51.5	46.7	41.8	36.9	32.1	27.2	22.3	17.4	12.6	7.7	2.8
12	100.4	95.7	90.9	86.2	81.5	76.7	72.0	67.2	62.5	57.8	53.0	48.3	43.5	38.8	34.0	29.3	24.6	19.8	15.1	10.3	5.6
18	100.6	96.0	91.4	86.8	82.2	77.5	72.9	68.3	63.7	59.1	54.5	49.8	45.2	40.6	36.0	31.4	26.8	22.1	17.5	12.9	8.3
24	100.8	96.3	91.8	87.3	82.8	78.4	73.9	69.4	64.9	60.4	55.9	51.4	46.9	42.4	37.9	33.4	28.9	24.4	19.9	15.4	10.9
30	101.0	96.6	92.3	87.9	83.5	79.1	74.8	70.4	66.0	61.6	57.2	52.9	48.5	44.1	39.7	35.3	31.0	26.6	22.2	17.8	13.5
36	101.2	97.0	92.7	88.4	84.2	79.9	75.6	71.4	67.1	62.8	58.6	54.3	50.1	45.8	41.5	37.3	33.0	28.7	24.5	20.2	15.9
42	101.4	97.3	93.1	88.9	84.8	80.6	76.5	72.3	68.2	64.0	59.9	55.7	51.6	47.4	43.3	39.1	35.0	30.8	26.7	22.5	18.4
48	101.6	97.5	93.5	89.5	85.4	81.4	77.3	73.3	69.2	65.2	61.1	57.1	53.1	49.0	45.0	40.9	36.9	32.8	28.8	24.8	20.7
54	101.8	97.8	93.9	89.9	86.0	82.1	78.1	74.2	70.3	66.3	62.4	58.4	54.5	50.6	46.6	42.7	38.8	34.8	30.9	26.9	23.0
60	101.9	98.1	94.3	90.4	86.6	82.8	78.9	75.1	71.3	67.4	63.6	59.7	55.9	52.1	48.2	44.4	40.6	36.7	32.9	29.1	25.2
66	102.1	98.4	94.6	90.9	87.2	83.4	79.7	76.0	72.2	68.5	64.8	61.0	57.3	53.6	49.8	46.1	42.3	38.6	34.9	31.1	27.4
72	102.3	98.6	95.0	91.3	87.7	84.1	80.4	76.8	73.2	69.5	65.9	62.3	58.6	55.0	51.3	47.7	44.1	40.4	36.8	33.2	29.5
78	102.4	98.9	95.3	91.8	88.2	84.7	81.2	77.6	74.1	70.5	67.0	63.5	59.9	56.4	52.8	49.3	45.8	42.2	38.7	35.1	31.6
84	102.6	99.1	95.7	92.2	88.8	85.3	81.9	78.4	75.0	71.5	68.1	64.6	61.2	57.7	54.3	50.8	47.4	43.9	40.5	37.1	33.6

Note: LIBOR 5.32%.

Source: UBS.

249

EXHIBIT 11.34 ABX 06-1 BBB– Pricing Matrix (coupon 267 bps)

ABX Price	Number of Bonds Written Down																				
	0	1	2	3	4	5	6	7	8	9	10	11	12	13	14	15	16	17	18	19	20
0	100.0	95.0	90.0	85.0	80.0	75.0	70.0	65.0	60.0	55.0	50.0	45.0	40.0	35.0	30.0	25.0	20.0	15.0	10.0	5.0	0.0
6	101.3	96.4	91.6	86.7	81.8	77.0	72.1	67.2	62.4	57.5	52.6	47.8	42.9	38.0	33.1	28.3	23.4	18.5	13.7	8.8	3.9
12	102.6	97.9	93.1	88.4	83.6	78.9	74.1	69.4	64.7	59.9	55.2	50.4	45.7	41.0	36.2	31.5	26.7	22.0	17.2	12.5	7.8
18	103.8	99.2	94.6	90.0	85.4	80.8	76.1	71.5	66.9	62.3	57.7	53.1	48.4	43.8	39.2	34.6	30.0	25.3	20.7	16.1	11.5
24	105.1	100.6	96.1	91.6	87.1	82.6	78.1	73.6	69.1	64.6	60.1	55.6	51.1	46.6	42.1	37.6	33.1	28.6	24.1	19.6	15.1
30	106.2	101.9	97.5	93.1	88.7	84.3	80.0	75.6	71.2	66.8	62.5	58.1	53.7	49.3	44.9	40.6	36.2	31.8	27.4	23.0	18.7
36	107.4	103.1	98.9	94.6	90.3	86.1	81.8	77.5	73.3	69.0	64.7	60.5	56.2	52.0	47.7	43.4	39.2	34.9	30.6	26.4	22.1
42	108.5	104.4	100.2	96.1	91.9	87.7	83.6	79.4	75.3	71.1	67.0	62.8	58.7	54.5	50.4	46.2	42.1	37.9	33.8	29.6	25.5
48	109.6	105.6	101.5	97.5	93.4	89.4	85.3	81.3	77.3	73.2	69.2	65.1	61.1	57.0	53.0	48.9	44.9	40.9	36.8	32.8	28.7
54	110.7	106.7	102.8	98.9	94.9	91.0	87.0	83.1	79.2	75.2	71.3	67.4	63.4	59.5	55.5	51.6	47.7	43.7	39.8	35.9	31.9
60	111.7	107.9	104.0	100.2	96.4	92.5	88.7	84.9	81.0	77.2	73.4	69.5	65.7	61.9	58.0	54.2	50.3	46.5	42.7	38.8	35.0
66	112.7	109.0	105.2	101.5	97.8	94.0	90.3	86.6	82.8	79.1	75.4	71.6	67.9	64.2	60.4	56.7	53.0	49.2	45.5	41.8	38.0
72	113.7	110.1	106.4	102.8	99.1	95.5	91.9	88.2	84.6	81.0	77.3	73.7	70.1	66.4	62.8	59.1	55.5	51.9	48.2	44.6	41.0
78	114.6	111.1	107.6	104.0	100.5	96.9	93.4	89.9	86.3	82.8	79.2	75.7	72.2	68.6	65.1	61.5	58.0	54.4	50.9	47.4	43.8
84	115.6	112.1	108.7	105.2	101.8	98.3	94.9	91.4	88.0	84.5	81.1	77.6	74.2	70.7	67.3	63.9	60.4	57.0	53.5	50.1	46.6

Months to Loss

Note: LIBOR 5.32%.

Source: UBS.

EXHIBIT 11.35 ABX 06-1 BBB Pricing Matrix (coupon 154 bps)

ABX Price	Number of Bonds Written Down																				
	0	1	2	3	4	5	6	7	8	9	10	11	12	13	14	15	16	17	18	19	20
0	100.0	95.0	90.0	85.0	80.0	75.0	70.0	65.0	60.0	55.0	50.0	45.0	40.0	35.0	30.0	25.0	20.0	15.0	10.0	5.0	0.0
6	100.8	95.9	91.0	86.2	81.3	76.4	71.5	66.7	61.8	56.9	52.1	47.2	42.3	37.5	32.6	27.7	22.9	18.0	13.1	8.2	3.4
12	101.5	96.8	92.0	87.3	82.5	77.8	73.0	68.3	63.6	58.8	54.1	49.3	44.6	39.9	35.1	30.4	25.6	20.9	16.1	11.4	6.7
18	102.2	97.6	93.0	88.4	83.7	79.1	74.5	69.9	65.3	60.7	56.0	51.4	46.8	42.2	37.6	33.0	28.3	23.7	19.1	14.5	9.9
24	102.9	98.4	93.9	89.4	84.9	80.4	75.9	71.4	66.9	62.4	58.0	53.5	49.0	44.5	40.0	35.5	31.0	26.5	22.0	17.5	13.0
30	103.6	99.2	94.8	90.5	86.1	81.7	77.3	72.9	68.6	64.2	59.8	55.4	51.1	46.7	42.3	37.9	33.5	29.2	24.8	20.4	16.0
36	104.3	100.0	95.7	91.5	87.2	82.9	78.7	74.4	70.2	65.9	61.6	57.4	53.1	48.8	44.6	40.3	36.0	31.8	27.5	23.2	19.0
42	104.9	100.8	96.6	92.5	88.3	84.1	80.0	75.8	71.7	67.5	63.4	59.2	55.1	50.9	46.8	42.6	38.5	34.3	30.2	26.0	21.9
48	105.5	101.5	97.5	93.4	89.4	85.3	81.3	77.2	73.2	69.1	65.1	61.1	57.0	53.0	48.9	44.9	40.8	36.8	32.8	28.7	24.7
54	106.2	102.2	98.3	94.3	90.4	86.5	82.5	78.6	74.7	70.7	66.8	62.8	58.9	55.0	51.0	47.1	43.1	39.2	35.3	31.3	27.4
60	106.7	102.9	99.1	95.2	91.4	87.6	83.7	79.9	76.1	72.2	68.4	64.6	60.7	56.9	53.1	49.2	45.4	41.6	37.7	33.9	30.1
66	107.3	103.6	99.9	96.1	92.4	88.7	84.9	81.2	77.5	73.7	70.0	66.3	62.5	58.8	55.1	51.3	47.6	43.9	40.1	36.4	32.6
72	107.9	104.3	100.6	97.0	93.4	89.7	86.1	82.4	78.8	75.2	71.5	67.9	64.3	60.6	57.0	53.4	49.7	46.1	42.4	38.8	35.2
78	108.4	104.9	101.4	97.8	94.3	90.7	87.2	83.7	80.1	76.6	73.0	69.5	66.0	62.4	58.9	55.3	51.8	48.3	44.7	41.2	37.6
84	109.0	105.5	102.1	98.6	95.2	91.7	88.3	84.8	81.4	77.9	74.5	71.1	67.6	64.2	60.7	57.3	53.8	50.4	46.9	43.5	40.0

Months to Loss

Note: LIBOR 5.32%.

Source: UBS.

EXHIBIT 11.36 ABX 06-1 A Pricing Matrix (coupon 54 bps)

ABX Price / Months to Loss	Number of Bonds Written Down																				
	0	1	2	3	4	5	6	7	8	9	10	11	12	13	14	15	16	17	18	19	20
0	100.0	95.0	90.0	85.0	80.0	75.0	70.0	65.0	60.0	55.0	50.0	45.0	40.0	35.0	30.0	25.0	20.0	15.0	10.0	5.0	0.0
6	100.3	95.4	90.5	85.7	80.8	75.9	71.1	66.2	61.3	56.4	51.6	46.7	41.8	37.0	32.1	27.2	22.4	17.5	12.6	7.8	2.9
12	100.5	95.8	91.0	86.3	81.6	76.8	72.1	67.3	62.6	57.9	53.1	48.4	43.6	38.9	34.1	29.4	24.7	19.9	15.2	10.4	5.7
18	100.8	96.2	91.5	86.9	82.3	77.7	73.1	68.5	63.8	59.2	54.6	50.0	45.4	40.8	36.1	31.5	26.9	22.3	17.7	13.0	8.4
24	101.0	96.5	92.0	87.5	83.0	78.5	74.0	69.5	65.1	60.6	56.1	51.6	47.1	42.6	38.1	33.6	29.1	24.6	20.1	15.6	11.1
30	101.3	96.9	92.5	88.1	83.7	79.4	75.0	70.6	66.2	61.9	57.5	53.1	48.7	44.3	40.0	35.6	31.2	26.8	22.4	18.1	13.7
36	101.5	97.2	93.0	88.7	84.4	80.2	75.9	71.6	67.4	63.1	58.9	54.6	50.3	46.1	41.8	37.5	33.3	29.0	24.7	20.5	16.2
42	101.7	97.6	93.4	89.3	85.1	81.0	76.8	72.7	68.5	64.4	60.2	56.0	51.9	47.7	43.6	39.4	35.3	31.1	27.0	22.8	18.7
48	101.9	97.9	93.9	89.8	85.8	81.7	77.7	73.6	69.6	65.6	61.5	57.5	53.4	49.4	45.3	41.3	37.2	33.2	29.2	25.1	21.1
54	102.2	98.2	94.3	90.3	86.4	82.5	78.5	74.6	70.7	66.7	62.8	58.8	54.9	51.0	47.0	43.1	39.2	35.2	31.3	27.3	23.4
60	102.4	98.5	94.7	90.9	87.0	83.2	79.4	75.5	71.7	67.9	64.0	60.2	56.4	52.5	48.7	44.8	41.0	37.2	33.3	29.5	25.7
66	102.6	98.8	95.1	91.4	87.6	83.9	80.2	76.4	72.7	69.0	65.2	61.5	57.8	54.0	50.3	46.6	42.8	39.1	35.4	31.6	27.9
72	102.8	99.1	95.5	91.9	88.2	84.6	81.0	77.3	73.7	70.0	66.4	62.8	59.1	55.5	51.9	48.2	44.6	41.0	37.3	33.7	30.0
78	103.0	99.4	95.9	92.3	88.8	85.3	81.7	78.2	74.6	71.1	67.6	64.0	60.5	56.9	53.4	49.8	46.3	42.8	39.2	35.7	32.1
84	103.2	99.7	96.3	92.8	89.4	85.9	82.5	79.0	75.6	72.1	68.7	65.2	61.8	58.3	54.9	51.4	48.0	44.5	41.1	37.6	34.2

Note: LIBOR 5.32%.

Source: UBS.

Second, the market could also anticipate some extreme events (with small probability) that certain deals may have very high losses and expose higher parts of the capital structure to write-downs. A static analysis such as ours will not be able to price those events, since it only has a single path of projected losses. For this reason, we did not even attempt to run AA and AAA bonds; we know that the model will return no write-downs. Our static approach also leads to the discontinuity of pricing in the 07-1 BBB flats and minuses. While the data shows the 07-1 BBB minus breakevens are closer to the projected losses than the BBB flat breakevens, our model has no mechanism for capturing the higher probability of default.

Finally, our extrapolation along the default timing curve implicitly assumes that deals which have been performing well so far will continue to do so, while worse-performing deals will continue to underperform. Such an assumption will generate a relatively wide dispersion of losses across deals, which we observe historically. However, if the market believes that in a low HPA and distressed environment even good deals will have trouble going forward (a high correlation and low dispersion across deals), then more bonds may suffer write-down, hence the lower prices of certain tranches.

ABX Price/Write-Down Tables

An ABX price/write-down table implies a combination of principal write-down percentage and write-down timing. The value is the present value of the monthly stream of fixed coupon payments versus the present value of the expected write-downs. We can illustrate this relationship by making certain simplifying assumptions. First, we model the index only looking at principal write-downs, ignoring interest and principal shortfalls. We assume that write-downs for any given bond happen all in a single month and that write-downs for all 20 bonds happen at the same time. We assume no step-down takes place, which in turn implies that premium coupons will be constant until the write-down month. We assume a flat yield curve, and discount all cash flows using one-month LIBOR.

This leaves us with two degrees of freedom: (1) the magnitude of the write-down payment and (2) the number of months until the write-down occurs. As the number of bonds expected to write-down increases, the value of the ABX decreases. As time to write-down increases (if we believe losses are back-loaded), the value of ABX increases. Define n as the number of bonds that will be written down, and t as the time when the write-down occurs. The cash flows will consist of t premium payments, each 1/12th of the fixed coupon, and a single recovery payment at time t, where the payment is $n/20$ of the notional.

Exhibit 11.37 shows a two-way table of ABX prices (for the 07-1 BBB–, 389 bp coupon) by numbers of bonds written down and months to loss, using our simple model. The highlighted area reflects the Friday's (7/13/2007) closing price of 48.97.

One phenomenon to note is the natural tendency of the ABX to drop in price over time even with no change of assumptions. The ABX should converge in price to the value of the bonds not written down. Hence, if we assume 10 bonds written down in 48 months, and do not change this assumption, the price will drop from 74 down to 50 in four years, about one-half point per month.

A separate price/write-down table can be constructed for each of the 20 ABX subindices. As time passes. the tables must be updated to reflect the changes in the timing of the cash flows

ABX AFTER SUBPRIME SHUTDOWN

With the virtual shutdown of the subprime mortgage market in July–August 2007, it became increasingly clear that the loss projections from either of our ABX pricing approaches were seriously underestimating likely losses. In addition, the ABX prices implied by our simple model became further and further removed from actual ABX pricing. In order to incorporate this new reality into our valuations, we incorporated a shutdown adjustment to our basic model. The adjustment was based on the degree to which prepayment speeds on the individual subprime bonds had declined because of the subprime industry shutdown. These adjustments increased our loss forecasts by 40% to 50%.

In Exhibits 11.38 to 11.40, we present the base (prior to shutdown adjustments) projected cumulative losses under each exhibits second column, labeled Base Proj. Cum. Loss. Note that the ABX 06-1 losses include a 120% stress multiplier; the average of the unstressed losses from the model is 5.81%. Under the third column, Shutdown Proj. Cum. Loss, we show cumulative loss projection given the shutdown scenario appropriate for each vintage. In each exhibit, we compare the shutdown losses against break-even losses to determine loss coverage and write-downs.

In Exhibits A11.1 to A11.9 in the appendix to this chapter, we show both our original base pricing (and number of bonds written down) and the new shutdown estimates. Because we always come up with more conservative loss projections by considering the market shutdown effect, the ABX prices derived from the shutdown loss projections are always lower than our original base projections. From the exhibits in the appendix, we see that ABX prices estimated from the loss projection with subprime shutdown

EXHIBIT 11.37 ABX 07-1 BBB– Price/Write-Down Table

ABX Price	\multicolumn{21}{c}{Number of Bonds Written Down}

ABX Price	0	1	2	3	4	5	6	7	8	9	10	11	12	13	14	15	16	17	18	19	20
0	100	95	90	85	80	75	70	65	60	55	50	45	40	35	30	25	20	15	10	5	0
12	104	99	94	90	85	80	75	71	66	61	56	52	47	42	37	33	28	23	18	14	9
18	106	101	96	92	87	83	78	73	69	64	59	55	50	46	41	36	32	27	22	18	13
24	107	103	98	94	89	85	80	76	71	67	62	58	53	49	44	40	35	31	26	22	17
30	109	105	100	96	92	87	83	78	74	70	65	61	57	52	48	43	39	35	30	26	22
36	111	107	102	98	94	89	85	81	77	72	68	64	60	55	51	47	43	38	34	30	25
42	112	108	104	100	96	92	87	83	79	75	71	67	63	58	54	50	46	42	38	34	29
48	114	110	106	102	98	94	90	86	82	78	74	70	65	61	57	53	49	45	41	37	33
54	116	112	108	104	100	96	92	88	84	80	76	72	68	64	60	56	53	49	45	41	37
60	117	113	109	106	102	98	94	90	86	83	79	75	71	67	63	60	56	52	48	44	40
66	119	115	111	107	104	100	96	92	89	85	81	77	74	70	66	63	59	55	51	48	44
72	120	116	113	109	105	102	98	94	91	87	84	80	76	73	69	65	62	58	54	51	47
78	121	118	114	111	107	104	100	97	93	89	86	82	79	75	72	68	65	61	58	54	51
84	123	119	116	112	109	105	102	99	95	92	88	85	81	78	74	71	68	64	61	57	54

(ABX Price rows correspond to *Months to Loss*.)

Source: UBS.

EXHIBIT 11.38 ABX 06-1 A/BBB/BBB−

ABX 06-1	Base Proj. Cum. Loss	Shutdown Proj. Cum. Loss	Breakeven (BBB−)	Difference (BBB−)	Breakeven/Proj. Cum. Loss (BBB−)	Breakeven (BBB)	Difference (BBB)	Breakeven/Proj. Cum. Loss (BBB)	Breakeven (A)	Difference (A)	Breakeven/Proj. Cum. Loss (A)
ACE 2005-HE7	10.40	10.06	9.97	−0.09	0.99	11.04	0.98		15.09	5.03	
AMSI 2005-R11	4.47	4.55	7.94	3.39		8.74	4.19		12.16	7.61	
ARSI 2005-W2	8.01	9.59	9.15	−0.44	0.95	9.78	0.19		13.45	3.86	
BSABS 2005-HE11	9.14	9.92	9.93	0.01		11.02	1.10		15.33	5.41	
CWL 2005-BC5	5.10	7.75	7.49	−0.26	0.97	8.41	0.66		12.44	4.69	0.99
FFML 2005-FF12	6.28	13.60	8.93	−4.67	0.66	9.66	−3.94	0.71	13.41	−0.19	
GSAMP 2005-HE4	7.34	8.28	9.98	1.70		11.26	2.98		15.44	7.16	
HEAT 2005-8	8.21	11.73	9.05	−2.68	0.77	9.90	−1.83	0.84	13.41	1.68	
JPMAC 2005-OPT1	4.82	5.49	8.57	3.08		9.53	4.04		13.54	8.05	
LBMLT 2005-WL2	6.69	10.01	8.40	−1.61	0.84	9.43	−0.58	0.94	12.97	2.96	
MABS 2005-NC2	7.76	14.93	7.64	−7.29	0.51	8.67	−6.26	0.58	12.18	−2.75	0.82
MLMI 2005-AR1	6.48	6.85	8.34	1.49		9.30	2.45		12.49	5.64	
MSAC 2005-HE5	6.91	7.14	9.13	1.99		9.93	2.79		13.78	6.64	
NCHET 2005-4	6.47	9.29	8.99	−0.30	0.97	10.07	0.78		14.08	4.79	
RAMP 2005-EFC4	6.09	11.26	9.38	−1.88	0.83	10.58	−0.68	0.94	14.74	3.48	
RASC 2005-KS11	8.24	10.96	8.98	−1.98	0.82	9.81	−1.15	0.89	13.84	2.88	
SABR 2005-HE1	7.03	7.43	9.29	1.86		10.37	2.94		14.37	6.94	
SAIL 2005-HE3	8.21	8.43	6.98	−1.45	0.83	7.82	−0.61	0.93	10.45	2.02	
SASC 2005-WF4	3.76	4.62	7.57	2.95		8.36	3.74		11.04	6.42	
SVHE 2005-4	8.03	11.00	9.39	−1.61	0.85	10.50	−0.50	0.95	14.92	3.92	
Average	6.97	9.14	8.76	−0.39	0.83	9.71	0.56	0.85	13.46	4.31	0.90
Original loss timing					61.00			62.00			66.00
Current age					24.00			24.00			24.00
Time remaining to loss					37.00			38.00			42.00
Number of bonds written down					12.00			8.00			2.00

Source: UBS, Intex, and LoanPerformance.

EXHIBIT 11.39 ABX 06-2 A/BBB/BBB−

ABX 06-2	Base Proj. Cum. Loss	Shutdown Proj. Cum. Loss	Breakeven (BBB−)	Difference (BBB−)	Breakeven/ Proj. Cum. Loss (BBB−)	Breakeven (BBB)	Difference (BBB)	Breakeven/ Proj. Cum. Loss (BBB)	Breakeven (A)	Difference (A)	Breakeven/ Proj. Cum. Loss (A)
ACE 2006-NC1	5.95	7.36	8.44	1.08		9.38	2.02		13.43	6.07	
ARSI 2006-W1	9.18	12.11	8.66	−3.45	0.71	9.65	−2.46	0.80	14.06	1.95	
BSABS 2006-HE3	10.15	11.99	9.33	−2.66	0.78	10.46	−1.53	0.87	14.96	2.97	
CARR 2006-NC1	6.62	11.54	8.90	−2.64	0.77	9.89	−1.65	0.86	13.79	2.25	
CWL 2006-8	11.13	13.18	8.06	−5.12	0.61	8.93	−4.25	0.68	12.74	−0.44	0.97
FFML 2006-FF4	8.44	14.07	7.80	−6.27	0.55	8.68	−5.39	0.62	12.62	−1.45	0.90
GSAMP 2006-HE3	11.80	16.72	10.47	−6.25	0.63	11.66	−5.06	0.70	15.97	−0.75	0.96
HEAT 2006-4	7.47	10.92	8.19	−2.73	0.75	8.92	−2.00	0.82	12.54	1.62	
JPMAC 2006-FRE1	11.66	16.30	10.39	−5.91	0.64	11.50	−4.80	0.71	15.82	−0.48	0.97
LBMLT 2006-1	12.51	16.70	8.74	−7.96	0.52	9.58	−7.12	0.57	13.42	−3.28	0.80
MABS 2006-NC1	8.46	11.52	8.59	−2.93	0.75	9.45	−2.07	0.82	13.49	1.97	
MLMI 2006-HE1	8.16	14.37	10.13	−4.24	0.70	11.07	−3.30	0.77	15.84	1.47	
MSAC 2006-WMC2	16.21	17.38	8.73	−8.65	0.50	9.52	−7.86	0.55	12.98	−4.40	0.75
MSC 2006-HE2	10.80	11.46	9.06	−2.40	0.79	9.87	−1.59	0.86	13.68	2.22	
RAMP 2006-NC2	8.78	12.43	8.36	−4.07	0.67	9.39	−3.04	0.76	12.98	0.55	
RASC 2006-KS3	9.80	13.29	9.19	−4.10	0.69	10.23	−3.06	0.77	14.22	0.93	
SABR 2006-OP1	3.81	4.62	6.96	2.34		7.70	3.08		10.42	5.80	
SAIL 2006-4	12.85	14.53	6.63	−7.90	0.46	7.42	−7.11	0.51	10.65	−3.88	0.73
SASC 2006-WF2	5.07	7.65	8.83	1.18		10.22	2.57		13.43	5.78	
SVHE 2006-OPT5	9.75	12.08	9.29	−2.79	0.77	10.44	−1.64	0.86	14.50	2.42	
Average	9.43	12.51	8.74	−3.77	0.66	9.70	−2.81	0.74	13.58	1.07	0.87
Original loss timing					51.00			55.00			63.00
Current age					19.00			19.00			19.00
Time remaining to loss					32.00			36.00			44.00
Number of bonds written down					17.00			17.00			7.00

Source: UBS, Intex, and LoanPerformance.

257

EXHIBIT 11.40 ABX 07-1 A/BBB/BBB−

ABX 07-1	Base Proj. Cum. Loss	Shutdown Proj. Cum. Loss	Breakeven (BBB−)	Difference (BBB−)	Breakeven/Proj. Cum. Loss (BBB−)	Breakeven (BBB)	Difference (BBB)	Breakeven/Proj. Cum. Loss (BBB)	Breakeven (A)	Difference (A)	Breakeven/Proj. Cum. Loss (A)
ABFC 2006-OPT2	10.56	12.66	9.68	-2.98	0.76	10.48	-2.18	0.83	14.31	1.65	0.80
ACE 2006-NC3	16.33	16.23	8.65	-7.58	0.53	9.58	-6.65	0.59	12.99	-3.24	0.96
BSABS 2006-HE10	14.07	15.21	10.04	-5.17	0.66	11.04	-4.17	0.73	14.63	-0.58	0.94
CARR 2006-NC4	12.27	15.29	9.24	-6.05	0.60	10.66	-4.63	0.70	14.34	-0.95	
CBASS 2006-CB6	7.15	9.22	9.41	0.19		10.73	1.51		13.99	4.77	
CMLTI 2006-WH3	6.78	11.31	9.28	-2.03	0.82	10.34	-0.97	0.91	13.37	2.06	
CWL 2006-18	11.30	12.88	9.12	-3.76	0.71	10.12	-2.76	0.79	13.68	0.80	
FFML 2006-FF13	10.78	19.47	8.27	-11.20	0.42	9.07	-10.40	0.47	12.54	-6.93	0.64
FHLT 2006-3	17.12	18.59	9.52	-9.07	0.51	10.66	-7.93	0.57	13.86	-4.73	0.75
GSAMP 2006-HE5	13.98	16.86	9.58	-7.28	0.57	10.72	-6.14	0.64	15.06	-1.80	0.89
HEAT 2006-7	14.69	18.09	8.59	-9.50	0.47	9.35	-8.74	0.52	13.06	-5.03	0.72
JPMAC 2006-CH2	3.06	10.12	7.92	-2.20	0.78	8.66	-1.46	0.86	11.80	1.68	0.72
LBMLT 2006-6	16.76	18.92	8.89	-10.03	0.47	9.78	-9.14	0.52	13.69	-5.23	0.91
MABS 2006-NC3	14.40	15.67	9.83	-5.84	0.63	11.05	-4.62	0.71	14.28	-1.39	0.91
MLMI 2006-HE5	12.95	17.98	9.68	-8.30	0.54	10.52	-7.46	0.59	14.56	-3.42	0.81
MSAC 2006-HE6	16.85	16.99	9.17	-7.82	0.54	10.14	-6.85	0.60	13.49	-3.50	0.79
RASC 2006-KS9	15.71	16.23	9.14	-7.09	0.56	9.99	-6.24	0.62	14.13	-2.10	0.87
SABR 2006-HE2	11.74	15.22	8.55	-6.67	0.56	9.84	-5.38	0.65	12.52	-2.70	0.82
SASC 2006-BC4	11.85	13.32	8.15	-5.17	0.61	9.18	-4.14	0.69	12.03	-1.29	0.90
SVHE 2006-EQ1	7.68	14.97	10.02	-4.95	0.67	11.27	-3.70	0.75	14.66	-0.31	0.98
Average	12.30	15.26	9.14	-6.12	0.60	10.16	-5.10	0.67	13.65	-1.61	0.83
Original loss timing					48.00			51.00			61.00
Current age					12.00			12.00			12.00
Time remaining to loss					36.00			39.00			49.00
Number of bonds written down					19.00			19.00			15.00

Source: UBS, Intex, and LoanPerformance.

replicate market prices much better than the projections from our original loss model. Under our shutdown projections, the only indices that still look attractive are the single As from 06-1 and 06-2. This undoubtedly reflects hedging activity that moved up the ABX capital structure once the BBB flat and minuses were trading at interest-only levels.

Since we developed the original shutdown approach subprime collateral performance has continued to deteriorate. This has led to higher loss estimates and even further adjustments to our simple model but actual prices on the ABX have fallen faster than those implied by our latest adjustments. Essentially market sentiment continues to outrun the losses implied by the actual performance of the bonds. This episode simply confirms our bias that all models are just a starting point. One needs to continuously monitor prepayment and default trends and make subjective adjustments to any model in order to keep up with rapidly evolving markets, especially the subprime market in the wake of the industry's demise and the worst housing collapse since the great depression.

SUMMARY

Our simple models and simplified assumptions allow us to combine delinquency information, some historical timing curves, and breakeven data, to produce prices for the ABX indices. Of this data, only the breakeven requires a cash flow model to calculate the losses. The other data are easily updated from remittance reports.

The models most closely agree with the market in the 07-1 BBB flat and minus indices. The model systematically overprices the single As, and is also biased to overprice the better vintage deals in 06-1 and 06-2. We suspect these may both be symptoms of the inability of the model to price in the probability distribution of the projected losses versus the break-even losses.

Nevertheless, this model can prove useful to make a deterministic prediction of which bonds will write-down, when the write-downs will happen, and given these events, it can price the indices. Best of all, the model needs only the most elementary of inputs, making it attractive to those who prefer to "do the driving" themselves. We have added adjustment factors to our simple model to account for the virtual shutdown of the subprime market. Those adjustments increased our projected losses by 40% to 50% and increased the number of bonds expected to be written down in several ABX subindices.

EXHIBIT A11.1 ABX 06-1 BBB– Pricing

ABX Price	Number of Bonds Written Down																				
	0	1	2	3	4	5	6	7	8	9	10	11	12	13	14	15	16	17	18	19	20
0	100.0	95.0	90.0	85.0	80.0	75.0	70.0	65.0	60.0	55.0	50.0	45.0	40.0	35.0	30.0	25.0	20.0	15.0	10.0	5.0	0.0
6	101.3	96.4	91.6	86.7	81.9	77.0	72.1	67.3	62.4	57.5	52.7	47.8	42.9	38.1	33.2	28.3	23.5	18.6	13.7	8.9	4.0
12	102.6	97.9	93.1	88.4	83.7	78.9	74.2	69.5	64.7	60.0	55.3	50.5	45.8	41.1	36.3	31.6	26.9	22.1	17.4	12.7	7.9
18	103.8	99.2	94.6	90.0	85.4	80.8	76.2	71.6	67.0	62.4	57.8	53.2	48.6	44.0	39.4	34.8	30.2	25.6	20.9	16.3	11.7
24	105.0	100.6	96.1	91.6	87.1	82.6	78.2	73.7	69.2	64.7	60.2	55.8	51.3	46.8	42.3	37.8	33.4	28.9	24.4	19.9	15.4
30	106.2	101.9	97.5	93.1	88.8	84.4	80.1	75.7	71.4	67.0	62.6	58.3	53.9	49.6	45.2	40.8	36.5	32.1	27.8	23.4	19.0
36	107.4	103.1	98.9	94.6	90.4	86.2	81.9	77.7	73.4	69.2	65.0	60.7	56.5	52.2	48.0	43.8	39.5	35.3	31.0	26.8	22.5
42	108.5	104.4	100.2	96.1	92.0	87.9	83.7	79.6	75.5	71.3	67.2	63.1	59.0	54.8	50.7	46.6	42.5	38.3	34.2	30.1	26.0
48	109.6	105.6	101.5	97.5	93.5	89.5	85.5	81.5	77.5	73.4	69.4	65.4	61.4	57.4	53.4	49.3	45.3	41.3	37.3	33.3	29.3
54	110.6	106.7	102.8	98.9	95.0	91.1	87.2	83.3	79.4	75.5	71.6	67.7	63.8	59.8	55.9	52.0	48.1	44.2	40.3	36.4	32.5
60	111.6	107.8	104.0	100.2	96.4	92.6	88.8	85.0	81.2	77.4	73.6	69.8	66.0	62.2	58.4	54.6	50.8	47.0	43.2	39.4	35.6
66	112.6	108.9	105.3	101.6	97.9	94.2	90.5	86.8	83.1	79.4	75.7	72.0	68.3	64.6	60.9	57.2	53.5	49.8	46.1	42.4	38.7
72	113.6	110.0	106.4	102.8	99.2	95.6	92.0	88.4	84.8	81.2	77.6	74.0	70.5	66.9	63.3	59.7	56.1	52.5	48.9	45.3	41.7
78	114.6	111.1	107.6	104.1	100.6	97.1	93.6	90.1	86.6	83.1	79.6	76.1	72.6	69.1	65.6	62.1	58.6	55.1	51.6	48.1	44.6
84	115.5	112.1	108.7	105.3	101.9	98.5	95.1	91.6	88.2	84.8	81.4	78.0	74.6	71.2	67.8	64.4	61.0	57.6	54.2	50.8	47.4

(Left axis label: Months to Loss)

Note: Coupon 267; LIBOR 5.50%; market middle 55.5.

Source: UBS and Markit Group (8/21/2007 pricing).

EXHIBIT A11.2 ABX 06-1 BBB Pricing

	ABX Price	Number of Bonds Written Down																				
		0	1	2	3	4	5	6	7	8	9	10	11	12	13	14	15	16	17	18	19	20
Months to Loss	0	100.0	95.0	90.0	85.0	80.0	75.0	70.0	65.0	60.0	55.0	50.0	45.0	40.0	35.0	30.0	25.0	20.0	15.0	10.0	5.0	0.0
	6	100.8	95.9	91.0	86.2	81.3	76.4	71.6	66.7	61.8	57.0	52.1	47.2	42.4	37.5	32.7	27.8	22.9	18.1	13.2	8.3	3.5
	12	101.5	96.8	92.0	87.3	82.6	77.8	73.1	68.4	63.6	58.9	54.2	49.4	44.7	40.0	35.2	30.5	25.8	21.0	16.3	11.6	6.8
	18	102.2	97.6	93.0	88.4	83.8	79.2	74.6	70.0	65.4	60.8	56.2	51.6	47.0	42.3	37.7	33.1	28.5	23.9	19.3	14.7	10.1
	24	102.9	98.4	93.9	89.5	85.0	80.5	76.0	71.5	67.1	62.6	58.1	53.6	49.1	44.7	40.2	35.7	31.2	26.7	22.3	17.8	13.3
	30	103.6	99.2	94.9	90.5	86.2	81.8	77.4	73.1	68.7	64.4	60.0	55.6	51.3	46.9	42.6	38.2	33.8	29.5	25.1	20.8	16.4
	36	104.3	100.0	95.8	91.5	87.3	83.0	78.8	74.6	70.3	66.1	61.8	57.6	53.4	49.1	44.9	40.6	36.4	32.2	27.9	23.7	19.4
	42	104.9	100.8	96.6	92.5	88.4	84.3	80.1	76.0	71.9	67.8	63.6	59.5	55.4	51.3	47.1	43.0	38.9	34.7	30.6	26.5	22.4
	48	105.5	101.5	97.5	93.5	89.5	85.4	81.4	77.4	73.4	69.4	65.4	61.4	57.3	53.3	49.3	45.3	41.3	37.3	33.3	29.2	25.2
	54	106.1	102.2	98.3	94.4	90.5	86.6	82.7	78.8	74.9	71.0	67.1	63.2	59.3	55.3	51.4	47.5	43.6	39.7	35.8	31.9	28.0
	60	106.7	102.9	99.1	95.3	91.5	87.7	83.9	80.1	76.3	72.5	68.7	64.9	61.1	57.3	53.5	49.7	45.9	42.1	38.3	34.5	30.7
	66	107.3	103.6	99.9	96.2	92.5	88.8	85.1	81.4	77.7	74.0	70.3	66.6	62.9	59.2	55.5	51.8	48.1	44.4	40.7	37.0	33.3
	72	107.9	104.3	100.7	97.1	93.5	89.9	86.3	82.7	79.1	75.5	71.9	68.3	64.7	61.1	57.5	53.9	50.3	46.7	43.1	39.5	35.9
	78	108.4	104.9	101.4	97.9	94.4	90.9	87.4	83.9	80.4	76.9	73.4	69.9	66.4	62.9	59.4	55.9	52.4	48.9	45.4	41.9	38.4
	84	108.9	105.5	102.1	98.7	95.3	91.9	88.5	85.1	81.7	78.3	74.9	71.5	68.1	64.7	61.3	57.9	54.4	51.0	47.6	44.2	40.8

Note: Coupon 154; LIBOR 5.50%; market middle 58.94.

Source: UBS and Markit Group (8/21/2007 pricing).

EXHIBIT A11.3 ABX 06-1 A Pricing

									Number of Bonds Written Down												
ABX Price	0	1	2	3	4	5	6	7	8	9	10	11	12	13	14	15	16	17	18	19	20
0	100.0	95.0	90.0	85.0	80.0	75.0	70.0	65.0	60.0	55.0	50.0	45.0	40.0	35.0	30.0	25.0	20.0	15.0	10.0	5.0	0.0
6	100.3	95.4	90.5	85.7	80.8	75.9	71.1	66.2	61.3	56.5	51.6	46.8	41.9	37.0	32.2	27.3	22.4	17.6	12.7	7.8	3.0
12	100.5	95.8	91.1	86.3	81.6	76.9	72.1	67.4	62.7	57.9	53.2	48.5	43.7	39.0	34.3	29.5	24.8	20.1	15.3	10.6	5.9
18	100.8	96.2	91.6	87.0	82.4	77.8	73.1	68.5	63.9	59.3	54.7	50.1	45.5	40.9	36.3	31.7	27.1	22.5	17.9	13.3	8.7
24	101.0	96.5	92.1	87.6	83.1	78.6	74.1	69.7	65.2	60.7	56.2	51.7	47.3	42.8	38.3	33.8	29.3	24.9	20.4	15.9	11.4
30	101.3	96.9	92.5	88.2	83.8	79.5	75.1	70.7	66.4	62.0	57.7	53.3	49.0	44.6	40.2	35.9	31.5	27.2	22.8	18.4	14.1
36	101.5	97.2	93.0	88.8	84.5	80.3	76.0	71.8	67.6	63.3	59.1	54.8	50.6	46.4	42.1	37.9	33.6	29.4	25.2	20.9	16.7
42	101.7	97.6	93.5	89.3	85.2	81.1	77.0	72.8	68.7	64.6	60.5	56.3	52.2	48.1	43.9	39.8	35.7	31.6	27.4	23.3	19.2
48	101.9	97.9	93.9	89.9	85.9	81.9	77.8	73.8	69.8	65.8	61.8	57.8	53.8	49.7	45.7	41.7	37.7	33.7	29.7	25.7	21.6
54	102.1	98.2	94.3	90.4	86.5	82.6	78.7	74.8	70.9	67.0	63.1	59.2	55.3	51.4	47.5	43.6	39.7	35.7	31.8	27.9	24.0
60	102.4	98.6	94.8	91.0	87.2	83.4	79.6	75.8	72.0	68.2	64.4	60.6	56.8	53.0	49.2	45.4	41.6	37.8	34.0	30.2	26.4
66	102.6	98.9	95.2	91.5	87.8	84.1	80.4	76.7	73.0	69.3	65.6	61.9	58.2	54.5	50.8	47.1	43.4	39.7	36.0	32.3	28.6
72	102.8	99.2	95.6	92.0	88.4	84.8	81.2	77.6	74.0	70.4	66.8	63.2	59.6	56.0	52.4	48.8	45.2	41.6	38.0	34.4	30.8
78	102.9	99.4	95.9	92.4	88.9	85.4	81.9	78.4	74.9	71.4	67.9	64.4	60.9	57.4	53.9	50.4	46.9	43.4	39.9	36.4	32.9
84	103.1	99.7	96.3	92.9	89.5	86.1	82.7	79.3	75.9	72.5	69.1	65.7	62.3	58.9	55.5	52.1	48.6	45.2	41.8	38.4	35.0

(Row labels 0–84 in the ABX Price column represent *Months to Loss*.)

Note: Coupon 54; LIBOR 5.50%; market middle 73.44.

Source: UBS and Markit Group (8/21/2007 pricing).

EXHIBIT A11.4 ABX 06-2 BBB– Pricing

ABX Price / Months to Loss	Number of Bonds Written Down																				
	0	1	2	3	4	5	6	7	8	9	10	11	12	13	14	15	16	17	18	19	20
0	100.0	95.0	90.0	85.0	80.0	75.0	70.0	65.0	60.0	55.0	50.0	45.0	40.0	35.0	30.0	25.0	20.0	15.0	10.0	5.0	0.0
6	101.2	96.3	91.5	86.6	81.7	76.9	72.0	67.1	62.3	57.4	52.5	47.7	42.8	37.9	33.1	28.2	23.4	18.5	13.6	8.8	3.9
12	102.3	97.6	92.9	88.2	83.4	78.7	74.0	69.2	64.5	59.8	55.0	50.3	45.6	40.8	36.1	31.4	26.6	21.9	17.2	12.4	7.7
18	103.5	98.9	94.3	89.7	85.1	80.5	75.8	71.2	66.6	62.0	57.4	52.8	48.2	43.6	39.0	34.4	29.8	25.2	20.6	16.0	11.4
24	104.6	100.1	95.6	91.1	86.7	82.2	77.7	73.2	68.7	64.3	59.8	55.3	50.8	46.3	41.8	37.4	32.9	28.4	23.9	19.4	15.0
30	105.6	101.3	96.9	92.6	88.2	83.8	79.5	75.1	70.8	66.4	62.1	57.7	53.3	49.0	44.6	40.3	35.9	31.5	27.2	22.8	18.5
36	106.7	102.4	98.2	94.0	89.7	85.5	81.2	77.0	72.8	68.5	64.3	60.0	55.8	51.5	47.3	43.1	38.8	34.6	30.3	26.1	21.9
42	107.7	103.6	99.4	95.3	91.2	87.1	82.9	78.8	74.7	70.6	66.4	62.3	58.2	54.0	49.9	45.8	41.7	37.5	33.4	29.3	25.2
48	108.7	104.7	100.6	96.6	92.6	88.6	84.6	80.6	76.6	72.5	68.5	64.5	60.5	56.5	52.5	48.5	44.4	40.4	36.4	32.4	28.4
54	109.6	105.7	101.8	97.9	94.0	90.1	86.2	82.3	78.4	74.5	70.6	66.7	62.8	58.9	54.9	51.0	47.1	43.2	39.3	35.4	31.5
60	110.6	106.8	103.0	99.2	95.4	91.6	87.8	84.0	80.2	76.4	72.6	68.8	65.0	61.2	57.4	53.6	49.8	46.0	42.2	38.4	34.6
66	111.5	107.8	104.1	100.4	96.7	93.0	89.3	85.6	81.9	78.2	74.5	70.8	67.1	63.4	59.7	56.0	52.3	48.6	44.9	41.2	37.5
72	112.3	108.7	105.1	101.6	98.0	94.4	90.8	87.2	83.6	80.0	76.4	72.8	69.2	65.6	62.0	58.4	54.8	51.2	47.6	44.0	40.4
78	113.2	109.7	106.2	102.7	99.2	95.7	92.2	88.7	85.2	81.7	78.2	74.7	71.2	67.7	64.2	60.7	57.2	53.7	50.2	46.7	43.2
84	114.0	110.6	107.2	103.8	100.4	97.0	93.6	90.2	86.8	83.4	80.0	76.6	73.2	69.8	66.4	63.0	59.5	56.1	52.7	49.3	45.9

Note: Coupon 242; LIBOR 5.50%; market middle 37.5.

Source: UBS and Markit Group (8/21/2007 pricing).

EXHIBIT A11.5 ABX 06-2 BBB Pricing

ABX Price / Months to Loss	Number of Bonds Written Down																				
	0	1	2	3	4	5	6	7	8	9	10	11	12	13	14	15	16	17	18	19	20
0	100.0	95.0	90.0	85.0	80.0	75.0	70.0	65.0	60.0	55.0	50.0	45.0	40.0	35.0	30.0	25.0	20.0	15.0	10.0	5.0	0.0
6	100.7	95.8	90.9	86.1	81.2	76.3	71.5	66.6	61.7	56.9	52.0	47.1	42.3	37.4	32.5	27.7	22.8	18.0	13.1	8.2	3.4
12	101.3	96.6	91.8	87.1	82.4	77.6	72.9	68.2	63.4	58.7	54.0	49.2	44.5	39.8	35.0	30.3	25.6	20.8	16.1	11.4	6.6
18	101.9	97.3	92.7	88.1	83.5	78.9	74.3	69.7	65.1	60.5	55.9	51.3	46.7	42.0	37.4	32.8	28.2	23.6	19.0	14.4	9.8
24	102.5	98.0	93.6	89.1	84.6	80.1	75.6	71.2	66.7	62.2	57.7	53.2	48.7	44.3	39.8	35.3	30.8	26.3	21.9	17.4	12.9
30	103.1	98.7	94.4	90.0	85.7	81.3	76.9	72.6	68.2	63.9	59.5	55.2	50.8	46.4	42.1	37.7	33.4	29.0	24.6	20.3	15.9
36	103.7	99.4	95.2	90.9	86.7	82.5	78.2	74.0	69.7	65.5	61.3	57.0	52.8	48.5	44.3	40.1	35.8	31.6	27.3	23.1	18.8
42	104.2	100.1	96.0	91.8	87.7	83.6	79.5	75.3	71.2	67.1	63.0	58.8	54.7	50.6	46.5	42.3	38.2	34.1	30.0	25.8	21.7
48	104.8	100.8	96.7	92.7	88.7	84.7	80.7	76.7	72.6	68.6	64.6	60.6	56.6	52.6	48.6	44.5	40.5	36.5	32.5	28.5	24.5
54	105.3	101.4	97.5	93.6	89.7	85.8	81.9	77.9	74.0	70.1	66.2	62.3	58.4	54.5	50.6	46.7	42.8	38.9	35.0	31.1	27.2
60	105.8	102.0	98.2	94.4	90.6	86.8	83.0	79.2	75.4	71.6	67.8	64.0	60.2	56.4	52.6	48.8	45.0	41.2	37.4	33.6	29.8
66	106.3	102.6	98.9	95.2	91.5	87.8	84.1	80.4	76.7	73.0	69.3	65.6	61.9	58.2	54.5	50.8	47.1	43.4	39.7	36.0	32.4
72	106.8	103.2	99.6	96.0	92.4	88.8	85.2	81.6	78.0	74.4	70.8	67.2	63.6	60.0	56.4	52.8	49.2	45.6	42.0	38.4	34.8
78	107.3	103.8	100.3	96.8	93.3	89.8	86.3	82.8	79.3	75.8	72.3	68.8	65.3	61.8	58.3	54.8	51.3	47.8	44.3	40.8	37.3
84	107.7	104.3	100.9	97.5	94.1	90.7	87.3	83.9	80.5	77.1	73.7	70.3	66.8	63.4	60.0	56.6	53.2	49.8	46.4	43.0	39.6

Note: Coupon 133; LIBOR 5.50%; market middle 42.78.

Source: UBS and Markit Group (8/21/2007 pricing).

264

EXHIBIT A11.6 ABX 06-2 A Pricing

ABX Price	Number of Bonds Written Down																				
Months to Loss	0	1	2	3	4	5	6	7	8	9	10	11	12	13	14	15	16	17	18	19	20
0	100.0	95.0	90.0	85.0	80.0	75.0	70.0	65.0	60.0	55.0	50.0	45.0	40.0	35.0	30.0	25.0	20.0	15.0	10.0	5.0	0.0
6	100.2	95.4	90.5	85.6	80.8	75.9	71.0	66.2	61.3	56.4	51.6	46.7	41.8	37.0	32.1	27.2	22.4	17.5	12.7	7.8	2.9
12	100.4	95.7	91.0	86.2	81.5	76.8	72.0	67.3	62.6	57.8	53.1	48.4	43.6	38.9	34.2	29.4	24.7	20.0	15.2	10.5	5.8
18	100.6	96.0	91.4	86.8	82.2	77.6	73.0	68.4	63.8	59.2	54.6	50.0	45.4	40.8	36.2	31.6	27.0	22.3	17.7	13.1	8.5
24	100.8	96.4	91.9	87.4	82.9	78.4	73.9	69.5	65.0	60.5	56.0	51.5	47.1	42.6	38.1	33.6	29.1	24.7	20.2	15.7	11.2
30	101.0	96.7	92.3	87.9	83.6	79.2	74.9	70.5	66.2	61.8	57.4	53.1	48.7	44.4	40.0	35.6	31.3	26.9	22.6	18.2	13.8
36	101.2	97.0	92.7	88.5	84.3	80.0	75.8	71.5	67.3	63.0	58.8	54.6	50.3	46.1	41.8	37.6	33.4	29.1	24.9	20.6	16.4
42	101.4	97.3	93.1	89.0	84.9	80.8	76.6	72.5	68.4	64.3	60.1	56.0	51.9	47.8	43.6	39.5	35.4	31.3	27.1	23.0	18.9
48	101.6	97.6	93.5	89.5	85.5	81.5	77.5	73.5	69.5	65.4	61.4	57.4	53.4	49.4	45.4	41.4	37.3	33.3	29.3	25.3	21.3
54	101.8	97.8	93.9	90.0	86.1	82.2	78.3	74.4	70.5	66.6	62.7	58.8	54.9	51.0	47.1	43.2	39.3	35.3	31.4	27.5	23.6
60	101.9	98.1	94.3	90.5	86.7	82.9	79.1	75.3	71.5	67.7	63.9	60.1	56.3	52.5	48.7	44.9	41.1	37.3	33.5	29.7	25.9
66	102.1	98.4	94.7	91.0	87.3	83.6	79.9	76.2	72.5	68.8	65.1	61.4	57.7	54.0	50.3	46.6	42.9	39.2	35.5	31.8	28.1
72	102.2	98.6	95.0	91.5	87.9	84.3	80.7	77.1	73.5	69.9	66.3	62.7	59.1	55.5	51.9	48.3	44.7	41.1	37.5	33.9	30.3
78	102.4	98.9	95.4	91.9	88.4	84.9	81.4	77.9	74.4	70.9	67.4	63.9	60.4	56.9	53.4	49.9	46.4	42.9	39.4	35.9	32.4
84	102.6	99.1	95.7	92.3	88.9	85.5	82.1	78.7	75.3	71.9	68.5	65.1	61.7	58.3	54.9	51.5	48.1	44.7	41.3	37.9	34.4

Note: Coupon 44; LIBOR 5.50%; market middle 53.14.

Source: UBS and Markit Group (8/21/2007 pricing).

EXHIBIT A11.7 ABX 07-1 BBB– Pricing

ABX Price	Number of Bonds Written Down																				
Months to Loss	0	1	2	3	4	5	6	7	8	9	10	11	12	13	14	15	16	17	18	19	20
0	100.0	95.0	90.0	85.0	80.0	75.0	70.0	65.0	60.0	55.0	50.0	45.0	40.0	35.0	30.0	25.0	20.0	15.0	10.0	5.0	0.0
6	101.9	97.0	92.2	87.3	82.5	77.6	72.7	67.9	63.0	58.1	53.3	48.4	43.5	38.7	33.8	28.9	24.1	19.2	14.3	9.5	4.6
12	103.8	99.0	94.3	89.6	84.8	80.1	75.4	70.6	65.9	61.2	56.4	51.7	47.0	42.2	37.5	32.8	28.0	23.3	18.6	13.8	9.1
18	105.6	101.0	96.4	91.8	87.2	82.6	78.0	73.4	68.7	64.1	59.5	54.9	50.3	45.7	41.1	36.5	31.9	27.3	22.7	18.1	13.5
24	107.4	102.9	98.4	93.9	89.4	84.9	80.5	76.0	71.5	67.0	62.5	58.1	53.6	49.1	44.6	40.1	35.7	31.2	26.7	22.2	17.7
30	109.1	104.7	100.3	96.0	91.6	87.3	82.9	78.6	74.2	69.8	65.5	61.1	56.8	52.4	48.0	43.7	39.3	35.0	30.6	26.2	21.9
36	110.7	106.5	102.3	98.0	93.8	89.5	85.3	81.0	76.8	72.6	68.3	64.1	59.8	55.6	51.4	47.1	42.9	38.6	34.4	30.2	25.9
42	112.4	108.2	104.1	100.0	95.9	91.7	87.6	83.5	79.3	75.2	71.1	67.0	62.8	58.7	54.6	50.5	46.3	42.2	38.1	34.0	29.8
48	113.9	109.9	105.9	101.9	97.9	93.9	89.9	85.8	81.8	77.8	73.8	69.8	65.8	61.7	57.7	53.7	49.7	45.7	41.7	37.7	33.6
54	115.5	111.6	107.7	103.8	99.9	95.9	92.0	88.1	84.2	80.3	76.4	72.5	68.6	64.7	60.8	56.9	53.0	49.1	45.2	41.3	37.4
60	117.0	113.2	109.4	105.6	101.8	98.0	94.2	90.4	86.6	82.8	79.0	75.2	71.4	67.6	63.8	60.0	56.2	52.4	48.6	44.8	41.0
66	118.4	114.7	111.0	107.3	103.6	99.9	96.2	92.5	88.8	85.1	81.5	77.8	74.1	70.4	66.7	63.0	59.3	55.6	51.9	48.2	44.5
72	119.8	116.2	112.6	109.0	105.5	101.9	98.3	94.7	91.1	87.5	83.9	80.3	76.7	73.1	69.5	65.9	62.3	58.7	55.1	51.5	47.9
78	121.2	117.7	114.2	110.7	107.2	103.7	100.2	96.7	93.2	89.7	86.2	82.7	79.2	75.7	72.2	68.7	65.2	61.7	58.2	54.7	51.2
84	122.6	119.2	115.7	112.3	108.9	105.5	102.1	98.7	95.3	91.9	88.5	85.1	81.7	78.3	74.9	71.5	68.1	64.7	61.3	57.9	54.5

Note: Coupon 389; LIBOR 5.50%; market middle 32.25.

Source: UBS and Markit Group (8/21/2007 pricing).

EXHIBIT A11.8 ABX 07-1 BBB Pricing

ABX Price (Months to Loss)	ABX Price	Number of Bonds Written Down 0	1	2	3	4	5	6	7	8	9	10	11	12	13	14	15	16	17	18	19	20
0	100.0	100.0	95.0	90.0	85.0	80.0	75.0	70.0	65.0	60.0	55.0	50.0	45.0	40.0	35.0	30.0	25.0	20.0	15.0	10.0	5.0	0.0
6	101.1	101.1	96.2	91.4	86.5	81.6	76.8	71.9	67.0	62.2	57.3	52.5	47.6	42.7	37.9	33.0	28.1	23.3	18.4	13.5	8.7	3.8
12	102.2	102.2	97.4	92.7	88.0	83.2	78.5	73.8	69.0	64.3	59.6	54.8	50.1	45.4	40.6	35.9	31.2	26.4	21.7	17.0	12.2	7.5
18	103.2	103.2	98.6	94.0	89.4	84.8	80.2	75.6	71.0	66.4	61.8	57.2	52.6	48.0	43.4	38.7	34.1	29.5	24.9	20.3	15.7	11.1
24	104.2	104.2	99.8	95.3	90.8	86.3	81.8	77.4	72.9	68.4	63.9	59.4	54.9	50.5	46.0	41.5	37.0	32.5	28.1	23.6	19.1	14.6
30	105.2	105.2	100.9	96.5	92.1	87.8	83.4	79.1	74.7	70.3	66.0	61.6	57.3	52.9	48.6	44.2	39.8	35.5	31.1	26.8	22.4	18.0
36	106.2	106.2	101.9	97.7	93.5	89.2	85.0	80.7	76.5	72.3	68.0	63.8	59.5	55.3	51.0	46.8	42.6	38.3	34.1	29.8	25.6	21.4
42	107.1	107.1	103.0	98.9	94.7	90.6	86.5	82.4	78.2	74.1	70.0	65.9	61.7	57.6	53.5	49.3	45.2	41.1	37.0	32.8	28.7	24.6
48	108.0	108.0	104.0	100.0	96.0	92.0	88.0	83.9	79.9	75.9	71.9	67.9	63.9	59.9	55.8	51.8	47.8	43.8	39.8	35.8	31.7	27.7
54	108.9	108.9	105.0	101.1	97.2	93.3	89.4	85.5	81.6	77.7	73.8	69.9	65.9	62.0	58.1	54.2	50.3	46.4	42.5	38.6	34.7	30.8
60	109.8	109.8	106.0	102.2	98.4	94.6	90.8	87.0	83.2	79.4	75.6	71.8	68.0	64.2	60.4	56.6	52.8	49.0	45.2	41.4	37.6	33.8
66	110.6	110.6	106.9	103.2	99.5	95.8	92.1	88.4	84.7	81.0	77.3	73.6	69.9	66.2	62.5	58.8	55.1	51.5	47.8	44.1	40.4	36.7
72	111.4	111.4	107.8	104.2	100.6	97.0	93.4	89.8	86.2	82.6	79.0	75.5	71.9	68.3	64.7	61.1	57.5	53.9	50.3	46.7	43.1	39.5
78	112.2	112.2	108.7	105.2	101.7	98.2	94.7	91.2	87.7	84.2	80.7	77.2	73.7	70.2	66.7	63.2	59.7	56.2	52.7	49.2	45.7	42.2
84	113.0	113.0	109.6	106.2	102.8	99.4	96.0	92.6	89.2	85.7	82.3	78.9	75.5	72.1	68.7	65.3	61.9	58.5	55.1	51.7	48.3	44.9

Note: Coupon 224; LIBOR 5.50%; market middle 34.11.

Source: UBS and Markit Group (8/21/2007 pricing).

EXHIBIT A11.9 ABX 07-1 A Pricing

ABX Price	Number of Bonds Written Down																				
	0	1	2	3	4	5	6	7	8	9	10	11	12	13	14	15	16	17	18	19	20
0	100.0	95.0	90.0	85.0	80.0	75.0	70.0	65.0	60.0	55.0	50.0	45.0	40.0	35.0	30.0	25.0	20.0	15.0	10.0	5.0	0.0
6	100.3	95.5	90.6	85.7	80.9	76.0	71.1	66.3	61.4	56.5	51.7	46.8	41.9	37.1	32.2	27.3	22.5	17.6	12.8	7.9	3.0
12	100.6	95.9	91.2	86.4	81.7	77.0	72.2	67.5	62.8	58.0	53.3	48.6	43.8	39.1	34.4	29.6	24.9	20.2	15.4	10.7	6.0
18	100.9	96.3	91.7	87.1	82.5	77.9	73.3	68.7	64.1	59.5	54.9	50.3	45.7	41.1	36.5	31.8	27.2	22.6	18.0	13.4	8.8
24	101.2	96.7	92.2	87.8	83.3	78.8	74.3	69.8	65.4	60.9	56.4	51.9	47.4	43.0	38.5	34.0	29.5	25.0	20.6	16.1	11.6
30	101.5	97.1	92.8	88.4	84.1	79.7	75.3	71.0	66.6	62.3	57.9	53.5	49.2	44.8	40.5	36.1	31.7	27.4	23.0	18.7	14.3
36	101.8	97.5	93.3	89.0	84.8	80.6	76.3	72.1	67.8	63.6	59.4	55.1	50.9	46.6	42.4	38.2	33.9	29.7	25.4	21.2	16.9
42	102.0	97.9	93.8	89.7	85.5	81.4	77.3	73.1	69.0	64.9	60.8	56.6	52.5	48.4	44.3	40.1	36.0	31.9	27.8	23.6	19.5
48	102.3	98.3	94.3	90.2	86.2	82.2	78.2	74.2	70.2	66.2	62.1	58.1	54.1	50.1	46.1	42.1	38.1	34.0	30.0	26.0	22.0
54	102.5	98.6	94.7	90.8	86.9	83.0	79.1	75.2	71.3	67.4	63.5	59.6	55.7	51.8	47.9	44.0	40.1	36.1	32.2	28.3	24.4
60	102.8	99.0	95.2	91.4	87.6	83.8	80.0	76.2	72.4	68.6	64.8	61.0	57.2	53.4	49.6	45.8	42.0	38.2	34.4	30.6	26.8
66	103.0	99.3	95.6	91.9	88.2	84.5	80.8	77.1	73.5	69.8	66.1	62.4	58.7	55.0	51.3	47.6	43.9	40.2	36.5	32.8	29.1
72	103.3	99.7	96.1	92.5	88.9	85.3	81.7	78.1	74.5	70.9	67.3	63.7	60.1	56.5	52.9	49.3	45.7	42.1	38.5	34.9	31.3
78	103.5	100.0	96.5	93.0	89.5	86.0	82.5	79.0	75.5	72.0	68.5	65.0	61.5	58.0	54.5	51.0	47.5	44.0	40.5	37.0	33.5
84	103.7	100.3	96.9	93.5	90.1	86.7	83.3	79.9	76.5	73.1	69.7	66.3	62.8	59.4	56.0	52.6	49.2	45.8	42.4	39.0	35.6

Months to Loss (row labels)

Note: Coupon 64; LIBOR 5.50%; market middle 43.78.

Source: UBS, Markit Group (8/21/2007 pricing).

CHAPTER 12

ABS CDO Losses and Valuation

In this chapter, we predict mortgage bond losses within the portfolios of ABS CDOs. We look at 420 CDOs and their 20,797 underlying mortgage bonds from 4,259 underlying mortgage loan securitizations. Given the high collateral losses we predict for ABS CDOs, relative value among CDO tranches is dependent on structural idiosyncrasies. Structural terms control when collateral cash flow is cut off to subordinate CDO tranches and how much cash flow is diverted to senior CDO tranches. We find:

- Collateral losses will affect the very top of mezzanine ABS CDO capital structures. We predict that 86% of senior AAA tranches from 2006–2007 vintage subprime mezzanine ABS CDOs will default. Among BBB tranches, we predict 99% will default. These figures are horrific from a ratings and risk management point of view and indicative of the greatest ratings and credit risk management failure ever.
- Losses on mortgage loans underlying bonds owned by ABS CDOs vary greatly by vintage. Subprime loans originated 2006–2007 will have twice the losses of subprime loans originated in 2005. The effect follows through to the mortgage bond level. 2006 subprime mortgage bonds in the CDOs we study will have almost three times the losses of 2005 subprime mortgage bonds.
- The single best predictor of ABS CDO losses is the amount of 2006–2007 collateral they contain. After accounting for this variable, no other objective attribute of CDO collateral quality improves the prediction of collateral losses.
- In the generalized wreckage of subprime and ABS CDOs, there are few relative value opportunities arising from differences in collateral credit quality. But as more ABS CDOs experience event of default, the relative rights of senior and subordinate tranche holders have greater effect on remaining tranche value.

In this chapter, we first look at mortgage loan losses; then, mortgage bond losses; finally, ABS CDO losses. We next discuss patterns of CDO losses, looking at relationships with mortgage bond vintage, CDO closing date, and mortgage loan seasoning. We rely on the methodology discussed in Chapters 2 and 3 to predict underlying mortgage loan losses. Finally, we discuss differences in cash flow structure that drive relative value results.

THE MORTGAGE LOAN-MORTGAGE BOND-ABS CDO CHAIN

To put this chapter in context, it is necessary to understand the relationship among mortgage loans, mortgage bonds, and ABS CDOs. Exhibit 12.1 does just that. At the top left, subprime mortgage loans are made to borrowers with relatively bad credit quality and/or low down payments. These loans are securitized into subprime mortgage bonds; that is, the subprime mortgage loans are the securitization's assets and subprime mortgage bonds are the securitization's liabilities.

Note that the subprime mortgage bonds have various ratings and make up different percentages of the securitization's capital structure. The exhibit simplifies the subprime structure in that multiple tranches actually make up each rating band in the exhibit. For example, there are usually four AAA tranches of varying expected maturities in the securitization. In the other broad rating categories, there are usually tranches rated "plus," "minus," and "plain."

Exhibit 12.1 shows subprime mortgage bonds rated AAA, AA, and A going into high-grade ABS CDOs and BBB subprime bond going into mezzanine ABS CDOs. At various times, so-called "high-grade" ABS CDOs were comprised of higher rated collateral and mezzanine ABS CDOs were comprised of collateral rated A through BB. The exhibit shows typical ABS CDO collateral of 2006–2007 vintages. Finally, A and AA mezzanine ABS CDO tranches sometimes find their way into CDO squareds.

MORTGAGE DEAL LOSSES

The 420 ABS CDOs we study hold mortgage bonds from 4,259 separate mortgage loan securitizations issued from 1997 to 2007. In the top panel of Exhibit 12.2, these securitizations are broken out by deal type: subprime (high LTV and/or B and C rated borrowers), Alt-A, second liens, and prime; and by vintage, 1997–2007. About half (45%) of the mortgage deals in the ABS CDOs we study are subprime, 34% are Alt-A, 5% are seconds, and 17% are prime. Deals are predominately (57%) 2005–2006 vintage.

EXHIBIT 12.1 Flow Chart: Subprime Loans, ABS, CDOs, CDO^2

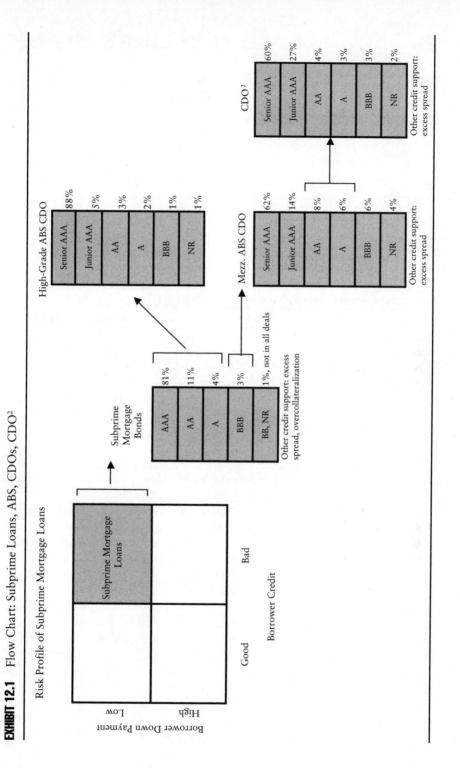

EXHIBIT 12.2   Residential Mortgage Deals in 420 ABS CDOs

Number of Deals by Vintage and Mortgage Loan Type

Vintage	Subprime	Alt-A	Seconds	Prime	Total
1997–2002	175	31	2	43	251
2003	215	71	7	136	429
2004	368	259	27	182	836
2005	483	473	64	191	1,211
2006	516	497	72	135	1,220
2007	150	115	21	26	312
Total	1,907	1,446	193	713	4,259

Average Predicted Losses by Vintage and Mortgage Type

Vintage	Subprime	Alt-A	Seconds	Prime	Average
1997–2002	5.0	0.7	4.7	0.3	3.7
2003	2.9	0.4	4.5	0.0	1.6
2004	3.0	0.5	6.5	0.1	1.7
2005	7.5	1.5	17.8	0.2	4.5
2006	19.5	4.6	46.9	0.3	12.9
2007	22.8	6.2	65.1	0.6	17.7
Average	10.3	2.7	31.6	0.2	7.0

Source: Intex and UBS CDO Research calculations.

The lower panel of Exhibit 12.2 shows average predicted losses over the life of the mortgage loan pool by mortgage type and vintage. As seen in the bottom row, and as one would expect, seconds have the highest predicted losses, followed by subprime, Alt-A, and then prime. More interesting are relative losses by vintage. Losses on 2006–2007 vintage mortgage deals are significantly higher than on earlier vintages; two and three times those of 2005.

The reasons for this loss pattern are well known and discussed earlier in this book. High U.S. home price appreciation led to decreased mortgage loan defaults and losses. Homeowners who became unable to keep up payments could refinance their loans or even sell their homes at a profit. Loan servicers foreclosing on properties could realize defaulted principal and interest on loans that were well cushioned by homeowner's equity. As the risk of mortgage lending became less tangible and as lending competition increased, underwriting standards declined. To qualify more borrowers for ever more expensive homes, "affordability" products were created. All of these new loans embed either payment shock or high *loan-to-value* (LTV) or both. Furthermore, runaway home price appreciation and easy funds encouraged fraudulent home speculation.

Beginning in 2006, homeowners were faced with payment shock from the end-of-low teaser rates. But tightening lending standards meant they could not readily refinance their mortgages. Low homeowner equity in homes, due to low down payments, interest only loans, and the lack of home price appreciation meant less of a cushion to protect lenders from losses.

SUBPRIME MORTGAGE BOND LOSSES

Having predicted losses on underlying mortgage loan portfolios, we now assess losses on the 20,797 mortgage bonds supported by those same mortgage loan portfolios. The top panel of Exhibit 12.3 shows the 11,557 subprime mortgage bonds held by the 420 ABS CDOs in our sample, broken out by original Moody's rating and vintage. The greatest concentration is in the A2 to Baa3 rating categories and the 2005 and 2006 vintages.

The second panel of Exhibit 12.3 shows bond losses using deal-by-deal mortgage loan losses. Note that we do not use the average loan losses presented in Exhibit 12.2, but the deal-specific loan losses that underlie those averages. Underlying loan losses are compared to breakpoints, or the amount of loan loss that causes a bond to default, for each of 11,557 subprime bonds. Our subprime loss predictions represent the principal writedowns that will occur sometime over the bond's life. Following the pattern of loan losses, subprime bond losses generally increase in later vintages.

One might notice in Exhibit 12.3 that sometimes higher-rated bonds have higher predicted losses than lower-rated bonds of the same vintage. This is because we are only looking at subprime mortgage bonds purchased by ABS CDOs, not the entire subprime bond market. ABS CDOs have invested in some higher-rated bonds destined to default without buying lower-rated bonds from those same mortgage deals. Also, sometimes very few bonds underlie a particular cell of the exhibit.

In the 2006–2007 vintages of Baa bonds, our estimates of losses range from 72% to 91%. This level of loss is unprecedented for bonds originally-rated investment grade. The table also shows losses for some bonds up into the Aaa rating category. Again, such losses are unprecedented in rating history. However, most of the Aaa bonds for which we predict default are from scratch and dent, or reperforming subprime mortgage deals.

The third panel of Exhibit 12.3 gives an idea of the sensitivity of our results. It answers the question "What happens to subprime bond losses as subprime loan losses vary?" We take 90% and 110% of our subprime

EXHIBIT 12.3 Subprime Mortgage Bonds in 420 ABS CDOs

Number of Subprime Mortgage Bonds by Vintage and Rating

Vintage	Aaa	Aa1	Aa2	Aa3	A1	A2	A3	Baa1	Baa2	Baa3	BIG	NA	All Ratings
1997–2002	24		24			55	1	10	76	24	5	28	247
2003	22	75	42	2	5	100	42	69	122	73	1	15	493
2004	117		204	87	92	270	176	274	326	279	61	43	2,004
2005	269	294	416	332	314	425	382	420	409	405	198	121	3,985
2006	174	253	416	378	391	460	435	448	444	403	195	127	4,124
2007	62	30	81	61	59	73	88	82	84	57	8	19	704
All vintages	668	652	1,183	860	861	1,383	1,124	1,303	1,461	1,241	468	353	11,557

Predicted Losses of Subprime Mortgage Bonds by Vintage and Rating

Vintage	Aaa	Aa1	Aa2	Aa3	A1	A2	A3	Baa1	Baa2	Baa3	BIG	NA	All Ratings
1997–2002	12%		28%			17%	0%	8%	11%	8%	60%	48%	19%
2003	6%	6%	19%	41%	12%	18%	22%	12%	14%	18%	71%	12%	16%
2004	12%		9%	7%	17%	11%	10%	10%	12%	20%	30%	36%	13%
2005	10%	4%	8%	7%	11%	14%	20%	30%	41%	53%	69%	35%	24%
2006	22%	30%	47%	59%	66%	69%	80%	83%	89%	91%	97%	88%	70%
2007	27%	55%	57%	74%	77%	72%	80%	84%	84%	72%	88%	89%	71%
All vintages	15%	17%	26%	35%	41%	35%	46%	46%	48%	56%	76%	57%	41%

EXHIBIT 12.3 (Continued)

90%–110% Range of Losses of Subprime Mortgage Bonds by Vintage and Rating

Vintage	Aaa	Aa1	Aa2	Aa3	A1	A2	A3	Baa1	Baa2	Baa3	BIG	NA	All Ratings
1997–2002	0%	0%	1%	0%	0%	1%	0%	1%	1%	3%	0%	0%	1%
2003	0%	0%	0%	2%	1%	0%	1%	2%	3%	5%	1%	4%	2%
2004	1%	1%	0%	0%	0%	1%	2%	1%	4%	8%	14%	13%	3%
2005	1%	0%	2%	4%	4%	6%	11%	12%	13%	16%	16%	15%	8%
2006	8%	15%	15%	13%	13%	14%	12%	10%	7%	4%	2%	5%	10%
2007	15%	21%	18%	16%	9%	8%	5%	3%	3%	0%	0%	0%	9%
All vintages	4%	7%	7%	8%	8%	7%	9%	8%	7%	9%	10%	9%	8%

Source: Intex and UBS CDO Research calculations.

loan loss estimates for each deal and reestimate mortgage bond losses. The exhibit shows the difference between the bond losses at 110% and 90% of loan loss, showing the sensitivity of bond losses to loan losses. There are two reasons why the range of bond losses in the panel might be narrow. First, mortgage loan losses might be so low in comparison to the bond's protection that increasing loan losses does not cause higher bond losses. Second, mortgage loan losses might be so high in comparison to the bond's protection that decreasing loan losses does not cause lower bond losses. By this theory, the greatest sensitivity of bond losses to loan losses occurs when loan losses are already close to a bonds' break point. We note a loose relationship between average bond losses being in the 30% to 70% range in the second panel of Exhibit 12.3 and the range of bond losses being wide in the same exhibit's third panel.

ALT-A, SECOND LIEN, AND PRIME MORTGAGE BOND LOSSES

Exhibits 12.4, 12.5, and 12.6 present similar analyses of Alt-A, second lien, and prime mortgage bonds in the sample of 420 ABS CDOs. Alt-A and prime bond losses are lower than those of subprime bonds, while second lien bond losses are much greater. The sensitivity of Alt-A, second lien, and prime bond losses to underlying mortgage loan losses is less than that of subprime bonds.

High loss levels for second lien mortgage bonds are a function of the investment choices of ABS CDO managers. Second mortgage bonds in ABS CDOs are typically not *home equity lines of credit* (HELOCs) extended to prime borrowers. Rather, they are usually closed end, amortizing loans made to finance the original home purchase. Often, they are the "20" of an 80–20 first and second lien loan package used to finance a home purchase without a down payment.

AGGREGATING MORTGAGE BOND LOSSES IN 2006–2007 MEZZANINE ABS CDOs

Of the 420 ABS CDOs we study, 165 of them are mezzanine ABS CDOs issued in 2006–2007. We exclude 10 CDOs whose portfolios consist primarily of prime and Alt-A bonds. These CDOs generally have lower predicted mortgage bond losses than CDOs collateralized predominantly with subprime bonds. For the remaining 155 CDOs, we calculate mortgage bond-by-mortgage bond losses and aggregate them to determine overall mortgage bond losses in each of the CDOs. The statistics we present are as of the por-

EXHIBIT 12.4 Alt-A Mortgage Bonds in 420 ABS CDOs

Number of Alt-A Mortgage Bonds by Vintage and Rating

Vintage	Aaa	Aa1	Aa2	Aa3	A1	A2	A3	Baa1	Baa2	Baa3	BIG	NA	All Ratings
1997–2002	1		3	1		11			6	2		14	38
2003	9		11		4	23	10	3	28	6	2	13	109
2004	84	9	132	18	16	123	33	31	148	47	34	99	774
2005	558	133	338	129	63	298	117	96	311	151	43	119	2,356
2006	672	311	319	180	163	282	155	153	233	160	31	109	2,768
2007	81	43	37	22	25	45	30	27	40	21	9	9	389
All vintages	1,405	496	840	350	271	782	345	310	766	387	119	363	6,434

Predicted Losses of Alt-A Mortgage Bonds by Vintage and Rating

Vintage	Aaa	Aa1	Aa2	Aa3	A1	A2	A3	Baa1	Baa2	Baa3	BIG	NA	All Ratings
1997–2002	2%		5%	8%		32%			3%	0%		1%	11%
2003	0%		5%		0%	6%	0%	6%	2%	0%	0%	2%	3%
2004	8%	3%	7%	2%	9%	9%	8%	12%	13%	11%	17%	22%	11%
2005	6%	14%	8%	9%	9%	13%	20%	26%	35%	31%	57%	46%	18%
2006	14%	20%	37%	42%	51%	57%	69%	60%	72%	74%	79%	73%	43%
2007	13%	20%	43%	54%	68%	65%	63%	59%	70%	64%	22%	84%	46%
All vintages	10%	18%	20%	29%	40%	31%	44%	44%	42%	47%	48%	45%	29%

EXHIBIT 12.4 (Continued)

90%–110% Range of Losses of Alt-A Mortgage Bonds by Vintage and Rating

Vintage	Aaa	Aa1	Aa2	Aa3	A1	A2	A3	Baa1	Baa2	Baa3	BIG	NA	All Ratings
1997–2002	0%	0%	1%	1%	0%	1%	0%	0%	0%	0%	0%	1%	1%
2003	0%	0%	0%	0%	0%	0%	0%	1%	1%	0%	0%	1%	0%
2004	1%	0%	0%	0%	1%	1%	0%	1%	3%	1%	6%	3%	2%
2005	1%	1%	1%	1%	3%	5%	8%	12%	10%	13%	4%	10%	5%
2006	3%	10%	8%	12%	15%	11%	8%	7%	5%	6%	3%	5%	7%
2007	4%	12%	9%	13%	4%	4%	6%	0%	3%	10%	0%	7%	6%
All vintages	2%	7%	4%	7%	10%	6%	7%	7%	6%	8%	4%	6%	5%

Source: Intex and UBS CDO Research calculations.

EXHIBIT 12.5 Second Lien Mortgage Bonds in ABS CDOs

Number of Second-Lien Mortgage Bonds by Vintage and Rating

Vintage	Aaa	Aa1	Aa2	Aa3	A1	A2	A3	Baa1	Baa2	Baa3	BIG	NA	All Ratings
1997–2002	1								1				2
2003						4			6	1			11
2004	1		5		1	7	6	11	24	16	5	2	78
2005	9	15	46	31	28	50	31	45	50	47	34	6	392
2006	17	32	46	39	28	43	39	44	36	28	3	4	359
2007	6	7	8	4	4	5	6	8	4	5		1	58
All vintages	34	54	105	74	61	109	82	108	121	97	42	13	900

EXHIBIT 12.5 (Continued)

Predicted Losses of Second Lien Mortgage Bonds by Vintage and Rating

Vintage	Aaa	Aa1	Aa2	Aa3	A1	A2	A3	Baa1	Baa2	Baa3	BIG	NA	All Ratings
1997–2002	0%								0%				0%
2003						0%			17%	0%			9%
2004	0%		58%		0%	24%	63%	9%	15%	11%	7%	17%	20%
2005	20%	7%	7%	10%	16%	22%	48%	63%	58%	65%	61%	96%	39%
2006	72%	78%	77%	91%	93%	95%	99%	99%	94%	93%	100%	100%	90%
2007	69%	71%	88%	75%	75%	60%	67%	63%	50%	60%		100%	69%
All vintages	53%	57%	46%	56%	55%	52%	75%	72%	58%	63%	57%	85%	59%

90%–110% Range of Losses of Second Lien Mortgage Bonds by Vintage and Rating

Vintage	Aaa	Aa1	Aa2	Aa3	A1	A2	A3	Baa1	Baa2	Baa3	BIG	NA	All Ratings
1997–2002	0%	0%	0%	0%	0%	0%	0%	0%	0%	0%	0%	0%	0%
2003	0%	0%	0%	0%	0%	0%	0%	0%	2%	0%	0%	0%	1%
2004	0%	0%	4%	0%	0%	1%	2%	0%	1%	6%	4%	20%	3%
2005	4%	0%	1%	11%	13%	15%	18%	10%	2%	8%	19%	13%	10%
2006	2%	14%	10%	9%	6%	5%	6%	2%	0%	0%	0%	0%	6%
2007	0%	1%	0%	0%	0%	0%	0%	0%	0%	0%	0%	0%	0%
All vintages	2%	9%	5%	10%	9%	9%	10%	5%	1%	5%	16%	9%	7%

Source: Intex and UBS CDO Research calculations.

EXHIBIT 12.6 Prime Mortgage Bonds in ABS CDOs

Number of Prime Mortgage Bonds by Vintage and Rating

Vintage	Aaa	Aa1	Aa2	Aa3	A1	A2	A3	Baa1	Baa2	Baa3	BIG	NA	All Ratings
1997–2002	7		2			4			11	6	1	22	53
2003	14		4	1		32	4	1	51	8	11	89	215
2004	46	10	44	2	2	79	2	2	94	4	48	119	452
2005	233	41	56	3	5	65	11	8	90	16	27	108	663
2006	213	34	18	1		19	3	4	24	1	10	120	447
2007	48	4	1	1	1	2	1	1	6	1		10	76
All vintages	561	89	125	8	8	201	21	16	276	36	97	468	1,906

Predicted Losses of Prime Mortgage Bonds by Vintage and Rating

Vintage	Aaa	Aa1	Aa2	Aa3	A1	A2	A3	Baa1	Baa2	Baa3	BIG	NA	All Ratings
1997–2002	0%		7%			0%			1%	0%	14%	1%	1%
2003	0%		1%	0%		0%	0%	0%	1%	0%	0%	4%	2%
2004	4%	5%	3%	0%	0%	2%	0%	0%	4%	0%	2%	5%	4%
2005	2%	6%	3%	0%	0%	6%	9%	0%	9%	10%	7%	12%	6%
2006	3%	0%	2%	0%		15%	33%	25%	28%	0%	0%	15%	8%
2007	3%	0%	18%	0%	0%	0%	100%	0%	50%	0%		0%	7%
All vintages	2%	4%	3%	0%	0%	4%	14%	6%	8%	5%	3%	9%	5%

EXHIBIT 12.6 (Continued)

90%–110% Range of Losses of Prime Mortgage Bonds by Vintage and Rating

Vintage	Aaa	Aa1	Aa2	Aa3	A1	A2	A3	Baa1	Baa2	Baa3	BIG	NA	All Ratings
1997–2002	0%	0%	1%	0%	0%	0%	0%	0%	1%	0%	2%	0%	0%
2003	0%	0%	0%	0%	0%	0%	0%	0%	0%	0%	0%	0%	0%
2004	0%	1%	0%	0%	0%	0%	0%	0%	1%	0%	0%	1%	1%
2005	0%	1%	0%	0%	0%	1%	1%	0%	2%	1%	2%	3%	1%
2006	0%	0%	3%	0%	0%	3%	0%	0%	7%	0%	1%	3%	2%
2007	0%	0%	0%	0%	0%	0%	0%	0%	0%	0%	0%	0%	0%
All vintages	0%	1%	0%	0%	0%	1%	1%	0%	2%	0%	1%	2%	1%

Source: Intex and UBS CDO Research calculations.

tion of the CDO's mortgage bonds we analyze. Note that we do not analyze nonresidential mortgage bonds held by these CDOs: their CDO and CMBS exposure. The loss statistics would apply to the CDO's entire portfolio only if the CDO's nonmortgage bond assets have the same loss experience. Given the quality of CDOs in ABS CDOs, we believe they will perform at least as bad as mortgage bonds.

Mortgage bond losses within these 155 CDOs range from 6% to 99%. Exhibit 12.7 shows the effect these collateral losses have on the CDO's liability tranches. The first row of the exhibit focuses on senior AAA tranches. This tranche would be at risk if collateral losses are 37% or more. 37% is the average subordination level of senior AAA tranches in a triggerless mezzanine ABS CDO. A mezzanine ABS CDO with overcollateralization and interest coverage triggers would usually have less subordination, but the potential diversion of excess interest would provide additional protection.

126, or 86% of the 155 2006–2007 mezzanine ABS CDOs we study have predicted collateral losses of 37% or more. Among the CDOs predicted

EXHIBIT 12.7 Estimated Defaults and Losses for 155 2006–2007 Subprime Mezzanine ABS CDOs

Base-Case Tranche Losses

Tranche	Threshold Collateral Losses that Threaten Tranche	% of CDOs Whose Predicted Losses Exceed Threshold	Loss Given Default	Tranche Expected Losses
Sr. AAA	37%+	86%	51%	43%
Jr. AAA	24%+	93%	97%	90%
AA	16%+	96%	99%	95%
A	12%+	97%	100%	96%
BBB	7%+	99%	99%	98%

Range of Tranche Losses

Tranche	Threshold Collateral Losses that Threaten Tranche	% of CDOs Whose Predicted Losses Exceed Threshold	Loss Given Default	Tranche Expected Losses
Sr. AAA	37%+	81%–90%	42%–57%	34%–51%
Jr. AAA	24%+	92%–95%	95%–98%	87%–93%
AA	16%+	95%–97%	98%–99%	93%–96%
A	12%+	96%–98%	99%–100%	96%–98%
BBB	7%+	98%–99%	99%–100%	97%–99%

to default on their super AAA tranche, the loss given default is 51%. Finally, across all 155 mezzanine ABS CDOs, the expected senior AAA tranche loss is 43%. As with mortgage bond losses, these figures represent principal loss sometime over the life of the CDO tranche. We perform a similar analysis on junior AAA CDO tranches in the next row of Exhibit 12.7. Collateral losses of 24% or more threaten junior AAA tranches. 93% of the 155 2006–2007 mezzanine ABS CDOs in our study fall into this category and junior AAA loss given default and expected loss across are 97% and 90%, respectively. Losses only get worse for lower tranches in Exhibit 12.7.

It is worth reflecting on the statistics in Exhibit 12.7. Aaa-rated securities are not supposed to default. Over the years, Moody's has rated 1,000 Aaa CDOs that are seasoned at least three years. None of these have suffered a loss. Only two have been downgraded to Caa1, and the next worse two have been downgraded to B2. Altogether, 1.2% of seasoned Aaa CDOs have been downgraded below investment grade. Yet, in the preceding paragraph, we predicted default rates of 86% and 93% for senior and junior AAA mezzanine ABS CDOs. Expected losses are 43% and 90%, respectively. This unprecedented level of default and loss make ABS CDOs are the biggest failure of ratings and credit risk management ever.

But things could be worse than our predictions. The uncertainties embedded in our predictions are all skewed toward the downside. Home price appreciation could be more negative than we implicitly assume and the U.S. economy could experience a recession and markedly higher unemployment. To show something of the sensitivity of CDO tranche losses to mortgage loan losses, we again look at cases where mortgage loan losses are 90% and 110% of expected. The results for CDO tranches, feeding through mortgage bond losses, are shown in the bottom panel of Exhibit 12.7. Notice that the expected loss ranges for tranches rated junior AAA and below are very tight. It is only in the senior AAA tranche where the outcome has significant uncertainty. For most ABS CDO tranches, there is little variability in their predicted results because so many of the mortgage bonds underlying these CDOs are so "deeply" in default.

AGGREGATING MORTGAGE BOND LOSSES IN 2005 MEZZANINE ABS CDOs

Exhibit 12.8 shows the equivalent analysis for 2005 vintage mezzanine ABS CDOs. Again, we exclude CDOs that invest predominantly in prime and Alt-A bonds. In the exhibit's top panel, losses are markedly lower than for the 2006–2007 vintage, especially at the senior AAA through A rated levels. In the exhibit's bottom panel, the sensitivity of tranche losses to mortgage

EXHIBIT 12.8 Estimated Defaults and Losses for 53 2005 Subprime Mezzanine ABS CDOs

Base-Case Tranche Losses

Tranche	Threshold Collateral Losses That Threaten Tranche	% of CDOs Whose Predicted Losses Exceed Threshold	Loss Given Default	Tranche Expected Losses
Sr. AAA	37%+	11%	24%	3%
Jr. AAA	24%+	40%	58%	23%
AA	16%+	68%	79%	54%
A	12%+	81%	92%	75%
BBB	7%+	98%	93%	91%

Range of Tranche Losses

Tranche	Threshold Collateral Losses That Threaten Tranche	% of CDOs Whose Predicted Losses Exceed Threshold	Loss Given Default	Tranche Expected Losses
Sr. AAA	37%+	9%–15%	18%–26%	2%–4%
Jr. AAA	24%+	28%–51%	48%–69%	14%–35%
AA	16%+	58%–81%	74%–81%	43%–66%
A	12%+	74%–91%	86%–98%	64%–89%
BBB	7%+	94%–98%	87%–98%	82%–96%

Source: Intex and UBS CDO Research calculations.

loan losses is also greater, even down to the BBB tranche. We will now explore some of the underlying portfolio attributes that cause these differences in CDO losses.

DRIVERS OF CDO LOSSES AND THE ROLE OF THE MANAGER

Ignoring the bottoms-up, loan-bond-CDO analysis we have shown, there are three objective indicators of mortgage loan quality that predict ABS CDO collateral losses. These are (1) the percent of 2006 and 2007 vintages among mortgage bonds in the CDO portfolio; (2) the WALA (weighted average loan age) of the mortgage loans underlying mortgage bonds in the CDO portfolio; and (3) the CDO's closing date. The relationships between these three explanatory variables and subprime mezzanine ABS CDO collateral losses are shown graphically in Exhibits 12.9, 12.10, and 12.11. The correlation of each of the three variables to collateral losses is high: the

EXHIBIT 12.9 Collateral WALA and Mezzanine ABS CDO Losses

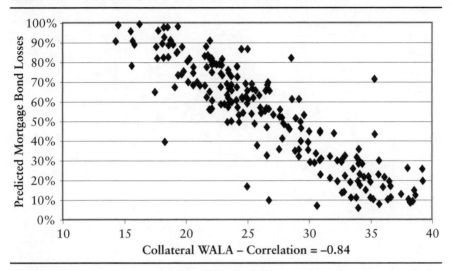

Collateral WALA – Correlation = –0.84

EXHIBIT 12.10 CDO Closing Date and Mezzanine ABS CDO Losses

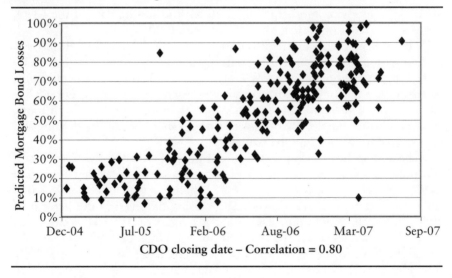

CDO closing date – Correlation = 0.80

EXHIBIT 12.11   Percent of 2006–2007 Vintage Collateral and Mezzanine ABS CDO Losses

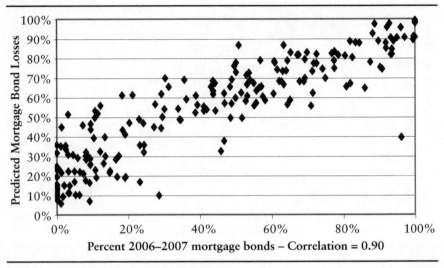

Percent 2006–2007 mortgage bonds – Correlation = 0.90

WALA of underlying mortgage loans, –0.84; the closing date of the CDO, 0.80.; and percent of 2006 and 2007 vintages, 0.90.

These three variables are also correlated with one another. Intuitively, a CDO with a more recent closing date is more likely to own 2006 or 2007 vintage mortgage bonds with low mortgage loan WALAs. Mathematically, the absolute value of their correlations with each other ranges from 0.82 to 0.86. All three variables merely track the real underlying causes of mortgage loan losses: the decline of underwriting standards and the slowing and reversing of home price appreciation.

The strong relationship between the percent of 2006–2007 collateral and predicted CDO collateral losses begs the question: "What is a good CDO manager?" An obvious answer is "a manager who avoids 2006–2007 collateral." Exhibit 12.12 shows CDO closing date versus the percent of 2006–2007 collateral in the CDO. Some managers of ABS CDOs closing as late as 2007 had less than 50% of their portfolio in 2006–2007 vintage collateral. But for most, the later the CDO's closing date, the more 2006–2007 collateral the CDO contains. Many CDO managers used ABCDS not to gain exposure to older mortgage bond vintages, but to gain more exposure to the current vintage.

We also see a couple of CDOs issued in 2005 that have high percentages of 2006–2007 vintage collateral. This occurs as the CDO's original portfolio amortizes and the CDO reinvests principal proceeds. As 2005 ABS

EXHIBIT 12.12   Closing Date and Percent of 2006–2007 Collateral

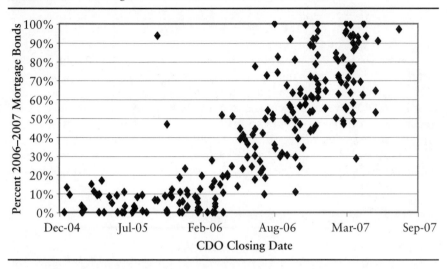

Source: Intex and UBS CDO Research calculations.

CDOs were almost always all cash structures, they must invest in what is available in the cash market, which is usually current issue.

But note that even in Exhibit 12.11, where predicted loss is correlated 0.90 to the percent of 2006–2007 collateral in the mezzanine ABS CDO, there is variability in predicted loss. For example, at the figure's right, where the percentage of 2006–2007 collateral is 95% or greater, predicted losses range from 39% to 100%. Meanwhile, regressing predicted collateral losses upon percent of 2006–2007 collateral predicts 92% to 100% collateral losses. Note that this 92%–100% based on 2006–2007 collateral is a "prediction of a prediction." Our regression formula is

Predicted CDO loss = 23% + 0.73 × Percent of 2006–2007 collateral

Clearly, the percent of 2006–2007 collateral a CDO has does not fully explain predicted losses. We know this anyway, because the R^2 of the regression of predicted losses upon 2006–2007 collateral is 0.81. Given that 2006–2007 collateral does not perfectly predict losses, what is the problem? We tried adding other variables to the regression, but that had little effect. WALA, CDO closing date, and the percent of the CDO's portfolio made up of subprime, second lien, Alt-A, and prime do not add to the ability of 2006–2007 collateral to predict losses. Despite the thoughts of some CDO investors, neither did the presence or absence of overcollateralization triggers. If these objective collateral attributes cannot explain predicted losses, perhaps differences in predicted losses are due to manager ability.

Unfortunately, we cannot confirm this hypothesis. When we look at the degree to which our bottom's up prediction of CDO losses are lower than those predicted by our percent of 2006–2007 collateral regression, we cannot reject the hypothesis that anything is happening other than the workings of chance. However, for one manager, with a large number of underperforming CDOs, we can reject the hypothesis that their performance is due to chance. In other words, we cannot say there are any managers who meaningfully *outperform* the percentage of 2006–2007 collateral in their CDOs, but we can point to one who *underperforms* the percentage of 2006–2007 collateral in their CDOs.

ABS CDO VALUATION AND CDO STRUCTURE

The high collateral losses we predict for ABS CDOs make valuation of their tranches dependent upon structural features. In other words, because collateral cash flow is too small to satisfy every CDO claimant, the division of cash flow among tranches by the CDO structure is crucial to valuation.

Two structural features divert collateral cash flow from lower tranches and direct it to senior tranches: (1) overcollateralization and interest coverage tests and (2) *event of default* (EoD) tests. The problem in making generalization about ABS CDO cash flows and hence tranche valuation is that not every CDO has these tests and the terms of EoD tests vary greatly from CDO to CDO. In fact, not only are EOD tests idiosyncratic, in some cases they are ambiguous due to poor document drafting. In such cases, ABS CDO valuation requires legal rather than credit skills.

ABS CDOs generally have three or more sets of overcollateralization and interest coverage tests. Generally, *overcollateralization* (OC) tests are failed before the interest coverage tests. When a test is failed, collateral interest is diverted from lower ranking CDO tranches and instead used to pay down principal of higher-rated tranches. An OC test takes the following form:

$$\frac{\text{Haircut par amount of the CDO's collateral}}{\text{Par amount of relevant CDO tranches}} < X\%$$

The relevant tranches included in the bottom of the ratio might be those initially rated AAA and AA for the "AA test" or those rated AAA, AA, A, and BBB for the "BBB test." The $X\%$ that the ratio must be greater than might be 108% for the AA test and 103% for the BBB test. Finally, the haircut in the numerator of the ratio is a reduction of collateral par exacted if collateral bonds have been downgraded below investment grade. This last factor makes the distribution of CDO cash flow dependent upon an exogenous factor, namely the actions taken upon the CDO's assets by its rating agencies. This places collateral downgrades and negative watches into the analysis of CDO tranche valuation. As we have mentioned, not all ABS CDOs have OC and interest coverage tests.

An EoD trigger is similar to an ordinary OC test, and trips if the OC ratio on AAA CDO liabilities falls below a specified amount (usually 100%, although we have seen deals as high as 102% and as low as 98%). However, not all CDOs have EoD OC tests and not all that do have tests that provide for ratings-based collateral haircuts.

If an EoD occurs due to a breach of the junior AAA OC test, the *controlling class holder* (or the majority of the controlling class holders) has the right to declare an acceleration. In the overwhelming majority of outstanding deals, the *controlling class* is the super-senior tranche; less frequently it also includes the junior AAA and the AA tranches.

In most cases, acceleration means that the reinvestment period is terminated (if this has not already occurred as a result of the static test, discussed below) and all cash flows (both principal and interest) are diverted to the controlling class holder. In many cases, once acceleration is declared, the BBB, A, and probably AA classes no longer receive interest cash flows.

Acceleration increases the attractiveness of super-senior tranches and decreases the attractiveness of lower rated tranches via the redirection of cash flows. Senior tranche acceleration can be very powerful. To illustrate this, assume a deal's capital structure is 63% unfunded super-senior and 37% lower-rated cash tranches. Further assume that the synthetic portion of the CDO portfolio is also 63% (which makes the math easy, without any conceptual loss). Assume that the ABS CDO receives LIBOR + 250 bps on its $37 cash portfolio and 250 bps on the $63 of its portfolio where it sold synthetic protection. Thus, the super-senior is entitled to the entire cash flow of $2.50\% \times \$63 + (LIBOR + 2.50) \times \$37$.

If LIBOR is assumed to be 4.75%, then the cash flow to the super-senior is $4.26. This cash flow goes to pay the super-senior coupon and into the deal's reserve fund to defease the super-senior notional amount. If the coupon is 25 bps, then $0.16 ($0.0025 \times \$63$) is needed to pay the coupon. The remaining $4.10 is used to amortize the $63 notional amount of the super-senior bond, for a 6.51% annual amortization rate.

An EoD due to breaching the junior AAA OC test also allows the controlling class(es) to liquidate the deal by selling collateral. Given the price of CDO collateral versus the cash flow that collateral can be reasonably expected to generate, we would not normally expect to see that right exercised. There might be cases, however, where the controlling class would have an incentive to simultaneously order liquidation and bid for the collateral. This incentive would exist in the cases where acceleration does not cut off cash flows to subordinate CDO tranches.

To value the various tranches of a given CDO, an investor must first determine what cash flow triggers are in place as well as whether ratings haircuts are applied to downgraded collateral in calculating the relevant ratios. In Exhibit 12.13, we diagram the process and show the relative length of time that interest payments will be paid to subordinate CDO tranches. We assume that the CDO's collateral is so distressed that tranches below the junior AAA are never going to receive principal. Therefore, the valuation question is how long they are going to receive interest payments. This implicitly answers the question of how much collateral cash flow will be diverted to the senior AAA tranche.

At the top of the figure, we ask if there are OC tests. In deals which have OC tests, the levels are set to trip well in advance of the EoD trigger (if there is one), should there be collateral write-downs or downgrades. Thus, deals

EXHIBIT 12.13   ABS CDO Cash Flow Decision Tree

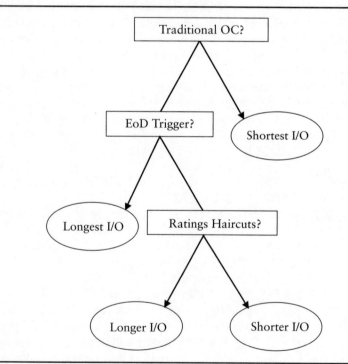

Source: UBS CDO Research.

with traditional OC triggers will be quickest to switch to sequential payment, leading to the shortest interest only period for subordinate tranches.

For deals with OC triggers, one should check whether any of the triggers have been tripped. If the test for a given tranche fails, cash flows to subordinate tranches are cut off until the outstanding par value of the senior tranches is reduced to a level that passes the test (i.e., by reducing the denominator of the OC ratio). Thus, predicting how OC ratios will behave, particularly those in the neighborhood of trigger levels, is critical in estimating the risk of cash flows going forward. Is an OC trigger going to be tripped soon? If so, will the collateral remain stable enough for the ratio to recover? Answering these questions requires assumptions about timing and severity of future collateral downgrades and write-downs.

Following the diagram in Exhibit 12.13 downward, again from the perspective of a subordinate tranche investor, we show that the next step in valuing interest payments involves EoD: is there a collateral test, and if so, does it apply ratings haircuts? Subordinate tranches can survive significantly longer in deals where ratings haircuts are not applied to the EoD, since downgrades generally precede write-downs. Of course, the subordinate tranches in deals without any OC tests, traditional or EoD, will have the longest IO period.

Subordinate CDO investors also have to consider the reaction of the controlling class. If an EoD'ed CDO still leaks cash flow to subordinate tranches, the controlling class has a greater incentive to liquidate the CDO portfolio if they have that control, which they do not always have.

SUMMARY

We looked at CDO collateral losses from the bottom up: within 4,259 mortgage loan portfolios, 20,797 mortgage bonds, and finally, 420 ABS CDOs. Predicted losses on mortgage loans and mortgage bonds are much greater for 2006–2007 vintages than for earlier vintages. ABS CDO losses depend heavily on how much 2006–2007 collateral they contain. Mezzanine ABS CDOs losses reach all the way up to their senior AAA tranches. Given these losses, CDO valuation depends upon structural features that distribute collateral cash flow among the CDO's tranches. These vary greatly from CDO to CDO.

The results of our tranche by tranche analysis are depressing from a credit standpoint. Subprime mortgage bonds and ABS CDOs are the biggest credit and risk management failure ever.

Subprime Meltdown

CHAPTER 13

The Great Subprime Meltdown of 2007

This chapter provides a brief survey of the subprime mortgage market that existed in the United States from 2000 to 2007. It is a story of how a small, inconsequential part of the mortgage market grew into a monster large enough to shake the very foundations of the U.S. financial system. It is a story with some elements that are old (all bull markets share common traits) and some that are new (credit default swaps, mezzanine CDOs, ABX, etc.), and it is a story that is not over.

A "new" subprime industry is evolving from the ashes of the old, but its final shape is not yet known. We know that the industry that prevailed from 2000 to 2007 no longer exists. We do not know precisely what will take its place. It will be a much smaller industry; it will consist of largely portfolio-based lending by large financial institutions; and it will be mainly subprime loans that have few of the layered risk elements (explained here in detail) that came to dominate the industry in recent years. As of this writing (September 2007), the industry is struggling to find the right type of loan that borrowers can afford and still meet the new bank regulations. If and when subprime loans are securitized again, the new loans will also have to accommodate much tougher enhancement levels demanded by the rating agencies and be a product that investors will once again accept. Developing a product that meets all of those constraints will not be easy.

The subprime crisis has triggered a repricing of risk and leverage across world markets and created a liquidity crisis that has impacted many financial institutions. To describe the full complexity of this episode would take us far afield and require a much larger survey than the one envisioned for this chapter. Therefore, we shall limit our comments to developments within the subprime market and broader U.S. mortgage market, and leave a discussion of the further impact of this credit and liquidity saga for later.

AN EARLIER SUBPRIME CRISIS

The meltdown of 2007 was not the first crisis in the subprime market. In 1998 and 1999, many of the then-leading subprime lenders went out of business. This included such names as The Money Store, UCFC, AMRESCO, and Conti-Mortgage. In the early 1990s, these firms first began using the securitized markets to grow their lending business to subprime customers. Since commercial banks preferred not to lend to subprime customers, it fell to these independent specialty finance companies to pick up the slack left by the demise of the thrift industry in the late 1980s, the banking sector that had previously provided loans to credit-challenged homeowners. While playing a useful role in the housing market, these specialty finance companies soon discovered the benefits of gain-on-sale accounting. This accounting technique allowed a mortgage originator to book the entire gain from a new loan in the month the loan was originated, rather than over the term of the loan. Through the judicious choice of prepayment speed and loss assumptions, the subprime firms in the early to mid-1990s were able to exaggerate their profitability via gain-on-sale accounting. This led to a rapid increase in their stock prices and handsome payouts for the owners. However, investors began to understand the gain-on-sale process just as the 1998 liquidity crisis hit. Credit lines were pulled, the specialty finance subprime lenders that were the heart of the business were no longer able to warehouse new loans, and they did not have the capital to add newly created loans to their balance sheets. The resulting credit squeeze led to many bankruptcies or forced mergers with larger, better-capitalized firms.

Exhibit 13.1 shows the major subprime issuers in 1998 and those in 2000. The issuers in 1998 that went out of business by 2000 represented about 40% of the issuance volume in 1998.

The subprime market that self-destructed in 1998 and 1999 was markedly different from the one that blew up in 2007. The borrower was different, the loans were different, and the capital markets were different. We chose to review that earlier period because the "new" subprime loans that will dominate the industry in the coming years will look a lot more like the loans from that earlier period than those from the recent period.

The typical subprime loan in 1998 was a cash-out refi, 30-year fixed rate loan or a 30-year, six-month LIBOR floater. The borrower was, on average, a middle-aged homeowner who had been in his home for 10 years and wanted to take some equity out of his home in order to put an addition on the house, send a child to college, or buy a new car. Very few subprime borrowers used these mortgages to purchase a home. Relatively little borrower/loan information was available to investors in the early subprime deals. For example, few loans had FICO scores. Rather, the loans were categorized as A, B, or C. About 50% of loans were A or A−, the rest were B and C.

EXHIBIT 13.1 Reorganization of Home Equity Industry ($ Millions)

Issuer	1998	1999	2000	2000–1999 % Change
Group 1				
Aames	1,575	793	928	17%
Advanta	3,925	2,043	1,050	–49%
Alliance Funding	1,665	2,375	785	–67%
American Business	499	842	960	14%
Ameriquest	0	0	1,359	—
Associates	235	0	0	0%
Block Financial	436	558	0	–100%
Centex	804	1,266	1,460	15%
Champion	300	1,150	0	–100%
Chase Manhattan	925	1,695	3,180	88%
CountrryWide	1,549	3,211	5,540	73%
Delta	1,720	1,495	1,040	–30%
EQCC	2,228	2,651	0	–100%
Fremont	0	1,411	0	–100%
GE Capital	349	1,215	0	–100%
GMAC	310	555	1,750	215%
Green Tree/Conseco	900	4,625	3,584	–23%
Long Beach	0	0	1,000	—
IndyMac	871	194	1,015	424%
New Century	0	1,147	1,020	–11%
New South	0	667	0	–100%
Novastar	615	160	564	253%
Ocwen	1,326	145	0	–100%
Option One	0	707	779	10%
Provident	1,243	2,398	1,289	–46%
RFC	4,069	5,630	6,438	14%
Saxon	1,964	2,503	2,332	–7%
Subtotal	27,508	39,436	36,072	–9%

EXHIBIT 13.1 (Continued)

Issuer	1998	1999	2000	2000–1999 % Change
Group 2 (broker/dealers)				
Bear Stearns	—	510	535	5%
CSFB	635	929	1,000	8%
Goldman Sachs	—	—	513	—
Lehman	425	—	6,339	—
Morgan Stanley	—	—	547	—
PaineWebber	—	—	200	—
Salomon SB	4,732	5,032	1,096	–78%
Subtotal	5,792	6,471	10,230	58%
Group 3 (No longer originating home equity loans)				
Amresco	3,000	200	0	–100%
ContiMortgage	6,599	2,000	0	–100%
First Alliance	430	426	0	–100%
IMC	5,100	0	0	0%
Money Store	3,406	0	0	0%
Southern Pacific	1,310	0	0	0%
UCFC	3,053	0	0	0%
Subtotal	22,898	2,626	0	–100%
Total	56,198	48,533	46,302	–5%

Note: Includes subprime home equities and HELOCs, but not high-LTVs.

In the early subprime market these loans were referred to as *home equity* loans because in most cases the borrower was indeed taking equity out of his home. Of course, lenders preferred to use "home equity" rather than "subprime" because of the latter's unfavorable connotation. The use of the term home equity for subprime led to endless explanations of how a subprime home equity loan was not a traditional home equity loan, that is, it was not a revolving *home equity line of credit* (HELOC) that most Americans were familiar with. It didn't help that many data services that reported mortgage origination volume by sector included both subprime and HELOC in a broad category of loans labeled "home equity." In recent years, as the product became distributed worldwide, the more investor-friendly term *home equity* was superseded by the more accurate term *subprime*. For example, in 2007 one probably never saw a headline proclaiming the dire impact of the "home equity" crisis. While the term *home equity* has pretty much faded from the picture, other terms from that earlier period still persist. The term *B&C* is still used in some instances to refer to subprime loans, as in the CDO market, where the term is *resi B&C*, and in the mortgage publications, where the term is *B&C lending*.

In what other ways did the old home equity market differ from the recent subprime market? At that time credit default swaps and ABX indices did not exist, so there was no mechanism to short mortgage credit. Also, very little credit and default analysis was done in the mid-1990s. In fact, as the delinquency and loss rates began to rise in 1996 and 1997, there was very little comment from Wall Street because few research groups were tracking performance data at the time. And of course there was no Loan-Performance or Intex data to chart the deterioration in credit. In many ways the industry that ended in 1998 was a totally different market from the one that blew up in 2007.

So how did this tiny, parochial market transform itself into the headline-grabbing monster of 2006–2007? Simple—by riding a classic runaway credit cycle fueled by low interest rates, a laissez-faire attitude on the part of government officials and regulators, a securitization process that separated the origination process from ultimate credit risk, and new derivatives that brought tens of billions of dollars of speculative capital into this part of the mortgage market.

THE VIRTUOUS CYCLE

At the heart of the 2000–2007 subprime story is what has been termed the *virtuous subprime cycle* illustrated in Exhibit 13.2. ("Virtuous" in the sense that it helped push home prices ever higher.) The cycle began with the greatest period of home price appreciation in U.S. history. The extent of that price increase since 1890 has been well documented by Shiller.[1] The recent cycle surpassed the great increase in home prices associated with the end of World War II and made the major housing cycles of the 1980s and the 1990s look insignificant. As prices advanced, affordability dropped and many Americans were priced out of the housing market. To address that problem, mortgage lenders began to develop an array of "affordability" products, such as *interest only* (IO), pay option ARMS, piggybacked sec-

---

[1] Robert J. Shiller, *Irrational Exuberance*, 2nd ed. (Princeton, NJ: Princeton University Press, 2000).

EXHIBIT 13.2   "Virtuous" Mortgage/Housing Cycle

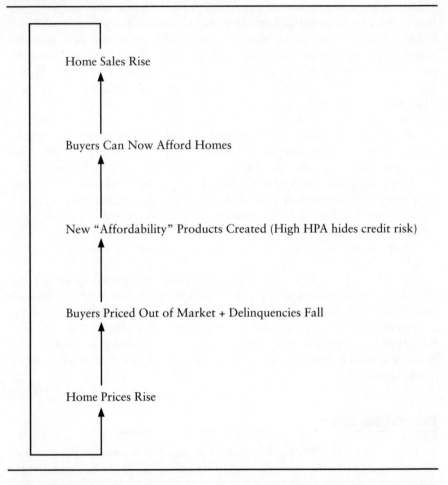

onds, stated income, and the like. These affordability products helped the advance of *home price appreciation* (HPA), and after another round of HPA yet another affordability product was introduced, and so forth in an endless spiral until the bubble finally burst.

We put the word "affordability" in quotes because, in essence, all affordability products are cut from the same cloth. They all allow a homeowner, with a given income and given credit history, to purchase a more expensive home than he could with a traditional loan. In other words, "affordability" equals greater credit risk. During this great run-up in home prices, some Wall Street research departments and some real estate associations (California's, for example) switched from a 30-year fixed rate to a hybrid ARM rate to measure housing affordability. They did this because that was the type of loan many homeowners were opting to use. We always stuck with the 30-year fixed rate loan in our affordability calculations on the premise that, if we shifted to an ARM rate, we were implicitly assuming a higher level of credit risk, a risk level inconsistent with our historical affordability series stretching back to the 1970s. (Changing the affordability benchmark is just one example of how the world accommodated itself to rapidly rising home prices.)

One of the key aspects of this virtuous cycle was that it camouflaged the performance of high-risk loans. With HPA increasing at double-digit rates, it was almost impossible to create a loan type that would produce losses. Defaults yes; losses no. A classic example from that period relates to the introduction of the *interest-only loan* (IO) into the subprime space. For a year or so after the IO loan had become common in subprime, Ameriquest, the largest subprime lender, refused to offer IOs on the grounds that the loans were too risky. Then, after a year of watching other lenders grow their business with IOs, Ameriquest announced that since the IO had performed very well the past year, it too would begin offering the IO product. Yes, IOs performed very well, but so did every other affordability product that year. (Here is a cautionary tale for the CMBS and leveraged loan markets: Do not set your loss expectations on the basis of performance in the best of all credit environments.) So the virtuous cycle not only helped push home prices to unsustainable levels, it also made high-risk mortgage loans appear to have little risk.

EARLY PAY DEFAULTS: THE FIRST HINT THINGS WERE CHANGING

An increase in *early pay defaults* (EPDs) in first quarter 2006 was the first hint that the subprime bull market was beginning to falter. In early 2006, lenders began to complain about the rising level of EPDs. But at that point it was too early to detect serious problems with the 2006 vintage. That would not come for several months. And those who now look back on the subprime debacle and say we all should have been aware of the coming deluge were conspicuously absent in early to mid-2006. As far as we know, no one had a clue in mid-2006 just how bad the 2006 vintage would ultimately turn out to be. The rise in EPDs was a warning, but no one projected from that increase that 2006 would turn out to be the worst vintage in subprime history.

EXHIBIT 13.3   Questions Investors Ask (from 01/05 UBS Mortgage Seminar)

- Isn't the rapid growth in subprime unsustainable and highly risky?
- Aren't underwriting standards dropping (higher LTVs and larger number of no docs)?
- Aren't the new loan types (IOs, 80/20s, etc.) raising the risk profile?
- Won't the housing bubble collapse and carry us all with it?
- With spreads so tight, does it make sense to play in the market at all?

Source: Reproduced from "Subprime Home Equities: On the Brink or Safe for Another Year," Thomas Zimmerman, UBS Securitized Seminar, January 21, 2005.

This is not to say we did not see a major problem developing in the mortgage market centered in the subprime sector. Exhibit 13.3 is the first page from a presentation one of the authors of this book gave in January 2005. Clearly, at that time many investors and analysts were asking pointed questions about subprime and the health of the overall housing market. At that point, we were aware of two things: Underwriting standards had deteriorated sharply, and once the housing boom faded foreclosures and losses would accelerate sharply. During 2002–2005, a series of articles showing the relationship between home price appreciation and housing credit were written by the UBS ABS Research team.[2] It was clear from the data that default rates and losses are directly and highly correlated to HPA. The UBS ABS research team was convinced that the United States was experiencing a housing bubble, and once it broke, defaults and foreclosures would increase sharply. What that team did not foresee was the sharp deterioration that would evolve in underwriting standards in 2006 among subprime and Alt-A mortgage lenders and the sharp increase in defaults that poor underwriting would create.

One of the first (possibly the very first) articles warning about the problems with the 2006 vintage was written in an August 2006 UBS publication prepared by its ABS Research team.[3] In that article, it was shown that the 60+-day delinquencies on the 2006 subprime deals were worse than the 60+-

---

[2] UBS Mortgage Strategist articles on mortgage credit and housing prices include: "Mortgage Credit and the Economic Environment" (July 30, 2002); "Impact of 0% Housing Inflation" (September 24, 2002); "Impact of Rising Rates and Lower Unemployment on Subprime Losses" (May 14, 2004); "Home Price Inflation and Mortgage Credit" (September 4, 2004); "The Key to Subprime Mortgage Credit—Prepayment Speeds and Housing Prices" (September 13, 2005); "Has the U.S. Housing Bubble Begun to Lose Air?" (November 1, 2005); and "Weaker Housing Markets—Implications for Mortgage Losses" (December 12, 2005).

[3] "Early Warning Signs in Mortgage Credit," *Mortgage Strategist*, UBS, August 22, 2006, p. 30.

day delinquencies on 2005 vintage loans, which were already worse than the 2004 vintage. Within the next several months, the data for 2006 vintage became unquestionably bad. The authors of that article described that deterioration in an infamous conference call on November 21, 2006, a call on which there were more than 800 investors on the line. As a result of that conference call and the articles written in late 2006, the UBS ABS Research team quickly became known for one of the most bearish outlooks on the Street. But as it turned out the UBS ABS Research team was not bearish enough.

THE 2006 CONUNDRUM

By now the whole world knows that the 2006 vintage subprime loans were the worst ever created by man (except for 2007). What is less well known is that we still do not have the complete answer as to why they are so bad. To use an old Greenspan cliché: The 2006 subprime vintage is a conundrum. Why do we say that when we know the types of loans that caused the problem? As shown in Exhibit 13.4, it was the layered risk loans that caused

EXHIBIT 13.4   The Unbearable Weight of Risk Layering

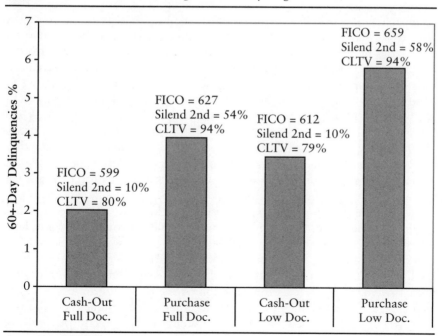

Source: LoanPerformance and UBS.

EXHIBIT 13.5   Subprime 60+-Day Delinquencies, by Vintage Year

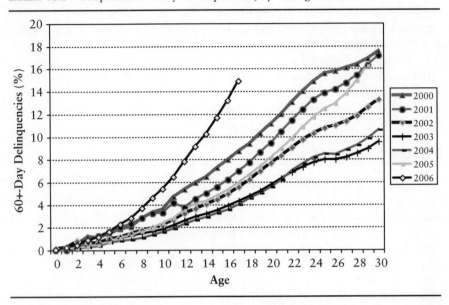

the problem. It was the short-rest hybrid ARM (2/28), simultaneous silient second mortgages (0% down), stated income (liar's) loan that created all the havoc. In a normal world, such loans would never have been created. No one in the subprime industry believes that type of loan should have been the mainstay of the market. Everyone knew it was an accident waiting to happen. They just did not comprehend the magnitude of the coming crackup. But if we know the characteristics of the loans that went bad, why the conundrum? It is because the loans from 2006 with the same characteristics are defaulting at about twice the rate of their 2005 cousins. We know that the 2005 loans had more home price appreciation to buffer them; but that alone does not explain the enormous difference between the delinquency rates on the two vintages shown in Exhibit 13.5.

There are two possible explanations for this conundrum. One, suggested by Standard & Poor's, is that the loan and borrower attributes normally used to set enhancement levels on mortgage deals lost all relevance in 2006. FICO credit scores, *loan-to-value ratios* (LTV), stated income, and the like, were all corrupted, either by the borrowers who deliberately committed fraud, or by a general corruption of the underwriting process that led to exaggerated incomes and appraisals, and new techniques that allowed borrowers to inflate their FICO scores. Whatever the precise mechanism, the traditional relationship among FICO, LTV, mortgage document type or *doc type, debt-to-income ratios* (DTI), and defaults failed to hold for the 2006 book of business.[4]

We also have a second possible explanation for the conundrum. When a lender underwrites a loan he looks at numerous variables on the loan documents, many of them in addition to the eight or so that appear on term sheets. Such things as time since last bankruptcy, time on job, length of time at the same residence, and the like are all important elements in mortgage credit, but those secondary items are not disclosed on a term sheet, and dealers, rating agencies, and investors seldom have access to that information. Historically, when lenders eased standards to keep volume up they first loosened these secondary attributes (lending criteria) before lowering their required minimum FICO scores or other major attributes. We suspect this was a major reason the 2006 vintage performed so much worse than 2005, even though the main attributes (such as FICO, CLTV, etc.) were similar. (CLTV is a combined loan-to-value ratio taking a first and second mortgage into account.) In truth, it was probably a combination of the two—a degradation of the main attributes as well as a loosening of the secondary attributes (along with lower HPA). But neither of those two critical changes was obvious to investors, analysts, or rating agencies in mid-2006. So when the pundits proclaim they knew all along the subprime lending practices would lead to a crisis, we wonder how they were so perceptive when those in the industry missed it. By late 2006, it was becoming clear that problems loomed. But it was not so clear in mid-2006, or from the loan attributes themselves, that a disaster was looming. Also, even in late 2006, when it looked like subprime mortgages from 2006 would be a very serious problem, no one could conceive that credit losses in this sector could literally cause a seizure of credit in the entire U.S. capital market.

Another way of thinking about this is to note that the losses on 2005-vintage subprime loans, as bad as they are, will not cause write-downs on very many bonds from subprime MBS securities. That is, the enhancement levels in the deals protected most of the subordinated bonds from 2005. That suggests that if the subprime industry had maintained the relatively loose underwriting standards they were using in 2005 and not loosened them even further in 2006, the subprime industry might still be alive today.

We can show this with the help of a simple subprime loss model we developed at UBS and the deals referenced by the ABX indices. In Exhibit 13.6, we show projected losses for the 20 subprime deals referenced by two of the ABX indices, 06-1 and 07-1. We also show which of the subordinated

---

[4] Mortgage documentation type is a risk-based pricing factor that affects the overall interest rate for which the borrower qualifies. The major categories of mortgage loan documentation are: Full Income Verified Asset (FIVA), Stated Income Verified Asset (SIVA), No Ratio, and No Doc.

EXHIBIT 13.6 ABX 06-1 and 07-1: Projected Loss, Breakeven, and Expected Write-Downs

ABX 06-1	Proj. Cum. Loss	Breakeven (BBB–)	Difference (BBB–)	Breakeven/ Proj. Cum. Loss (BBB–)	Breakeven (BBB)	Difference (BBB)	Breakeven/ Proj. Cum. Loss (BBB)	Breakeven (A)	Difference (A)	Breakeven Proj. Cum. Loss (A)
ACE 2005-HE7	10.40	9.97	–0.43	0.96	11.04	0.64		15.09	4.69	
AMSI 2005-R11	4.47	7.94	3.47		8.74	4.27		12.16	7.69	
ARSI 2005-W2	8.01	9.15	1.14		9.78	1.77		13.45	5.44	
BSABS 2005-HE11	9.14	9.93	0.79		11.02	1.88		15.33	6.19	
CWL 2005-BC5	5.10	7.49	2.39		8.41	3.31		12.44	7.34	
FFML 2005-FF12	6.28	8.93	2.65		9.66	3.38		13.41	7.13	
GSAMP 2005-HE4	7.34	9.98	2.64		11.26	3.92		15.44	8.10	
HEAT 2005-8	8.21	9.05	0.84		9.90	1.69		13.41	5.20	
JPMAC 2005-OPT1	4.82	8.57	3.75		9.53	4.71		13.54	8.72	
LBMLT 2005-WL2	6.69	8.40	1.71		9.43	2.74		12.97	6.28	
MABS 2005-NC2	7.76	7.64	–0.12	0.98	8.67	0.91		12.18	4.42	
MLMI 2005-AR1	6.48	8.34	1.86		9.30	2.82		12.49	6.01	
MSAC 2005-HE5	6.91	9.13	2.22		9.93	3.02		13.78	6.87	
NCHET 2005-4	6.47	8.99	2.52		10.07	3.60		14.08	7.61	
RAMP 2005-EFC4	6.09	9.38	3.29		10.58	4.49		14.74	8.65	
RASC 2005-KS11	8.24	8.98	0.74		9.81	1.57		13.84	5.60	
SABR 2005-HE1	7.03	9.29	2.26		10.37	3.34		14.37	7.34	
SAIL 2005-HE3	8.21	6.98	–1.23	0.85	7.82	–0.39	0.95	10.45	2.24	
SASC 2005-WF4	3.76	7.57	3.81		8.36	4.60		11.04	7.28	
SVHE 2005-4	8.03	9.39	1.36		10.50	2.47		14.92	6.89	
Average	6.97	8.76	1.78	0.93	9.71	2.74	0.95	13.46	6.48	
Original loss timing				68.00			70.00			
Current age				24.00			24.00			24.00
Time remaining to loss				44.00			46.00			
Number of bonds written down				3.00			1.00			0.00

ABX 06-1	Proj. Cum. Loss	Breakeven (BBB–)	Difference (BBB–)	Breakeven/ Proj. Cum. Loss (BBB–)	Breakeven (BBB)	Difference (BBB)	Breakeven/ Proj. Cum. Loss (BBB)	Breakeven (A)	Difference (A)	Breakeven/ Proj. Cum. Loss (A)
ABFC 2006-OPT2	10.56	9.68	−0.88	0.92	10.48	−0.08	0.99	14.31	3.75	
ACE 2006-NC3	16.33	8.65	−7.68	0.53	9.58	−6.75	0.59	12.99	−3.34	0.80
BSABS 2006-HE10	14.07	10.04	−4.03	0.71	11.04	−3.03	0.78	14.63	0.56	
CARR 2006-NC4	12.27	9.24	−3.03	0.75	10.66	−1.61	0.87	14.34	2.07	
CBASS 2006-CB6	7.15	9.41	2.26		10.73	3.58		13.99	6.84	
CMLTI 2006-WH3	6.78	9.28	2.50		10.34	3.56		13.37	6.59	
CWL 2006-18	11.30	9.12	−2.18	0.81	10.12	−1.18	0.90	13.68	2.38	
FFML 2006-FF13	10.78	8.27	−2.51	0.77	9.07	−1.71	0.84	12.54	1.76	
FHLT 2006-3	17.12	9.52	−7.60	0.56	10.66	−6.46	0.62	13.86	−3.26	0.81
GSAMP 2006-HE5	13.98	9.58	−4.40	0.69	10.72	−3.26	0.77	15.06	1.08	
HEAT 2006-7	14.69	8.59	−6.10	0.58	9.35	−5.34	0.64	13.06	−1.63	0.89
JPMAC 2006-CH2	3.06	7.92	4.86		8.66	5.60		11.80	8.74	
LBMLT 2006-6	16.76	8.89	−7.87	0.53	9.78	−6.98	0.58	13.69	−3.07	0.82
MABS 2006-NC3	14.40	9.83	−4.57	0.68	11.05	−3.35	0.77	14.28	−0.12	0.99
MLMI 2006-HE5	12.95	9.68	−3.27	0.75	10.52	−2.43	0.81	14.56	1.61	
MSAC 2006-HE6	16.85	9.17	−7.68	0.54	10.14	−6.71	0.60	13.49	−3.36	0.80
RASC 2006-KS9	15.71	9.14	−6.57	0.58	9.99	−5.72	0.64	14.13	−1.58	0.90
SABR 2006-HE2	11.74	8.55	−3.19	0.73	9.84	−1.90	0.84	12.52	0.78	
SASC 2006-BC4	11.85	8.15	−3.70	0.69	9.18	−2.67	0.77	12.03	0.18	
SVHE 2006-EQ1	7.68	10.02	2.34		11.27	3.59		14.66	6.98	
Average	12.30	9.14	−3.16	0.68	10.16	−2.14	0.75	13.65	1.35	0.86
Original loss timing				52.00			56.00			63.00
Current age				12.00			12.00			12.00
Time remaining to loss				40.00			44.00			51.00
Number of bonds written down				16.00			16.00			7.00

bonds would be wiped out if our model losses came to pass. We chose the 06-1 and 07-1 indices because they are representative of subprime under-writing standards of 2005 and 2006, respectively. The loans in ABX 06-1 are mainly from Q2 and Q32005. The loans in ABX 07-1 are mainly from Q2 and Q3 2006.

Using our simple loss model, we estimate that cumulative losses on the 20 subprime deals that ABX 06-1 references will average 6.97% and range from 3.76% to 10.40%. As shown in Exhibit 13.6, for this amount of losses the following number of bonds in the 06-1 index will be wiped out: three bonds that are rated BBB–, one rated BBB, and zero rated A. In contrast, our simple loss model projects average losses of 12.30% for ABX 07-1 with a range of 3.06% to 17.12%. For 07-1, 16 BBB– bonds will be wiped out, as well as 15 BBBs and 11 As. This is the difference between a problem and a disaster. If subprime losses had been restrained to the levels of the 2005 vintage, much of the carnage we have witnessed over the past eight months would not have occurred. We have recently rerun our loss estimates follow-ing the virtual shutdown of the subprime industry. We now estimate 06-1 losses at 11.7% and 07-2 losses at 22.5%. This causes more BBB– and BBBs from 06-1 to be written down, but 06-1 continues to far outperform 07-1 in this much tougher credit environment.

BANKING REGULATORS: NOT TOO LITTLE BUT TOO LATE

When the definitive history of the 2007 subprime crisis is written, bank regulators will come in for part of the blame, as will the politicians and other government authorities. In retrospect, everyone now agrees that the short reset loan should never have formed the core of the subprime market. Never mind the other attributes that would make these loans so lethal—pig-gybacked seconds, low or no documentation, first-time home owners, and so on—the basic short-reset hybrid was not an appropriate loan for a hom-eowner who had already proven to be a poor credit risk.

The basic subprime loan was a hybrid 2/28. This means a loan with a fixed rate for two years followed by an adjustable rate for 28 years. Depend-ing on the shape of the yield curve, the reset from fixed to adjustable could mean a very large increase in the monthly payment or it might mean a decrease. Since the typical adjustable margin on a 2/28 subprime loan was 6.00% and the index was six-month LIBOR, only in a very low short-term rate environment would the monthly payment rate decline at reset. More likely there would be a very large increase at reset. This would force the subprime borrower to refinance his mortgage after two years. The rationale for this product was that many subprime borrowers would cure their credit in the two-year fixed period and they would then be eligible to refinance into a conforming (Freddie/Fannie eligible) loan with a lower rate. In point of fact, some subprime borrowers did cure their credit and move out of the subprime sector. However, many others did not cure their credit and they were confronted with an unpleasant choice. They could let their loan rate rise sharply (to six-month LIBOR + 6.00%, which is now around 11.50%) or they could refinance into another subprime 2/28 that might have a higher fixed two-year rate and certainly would entail additional closing costs.

Exhibit 13.7 graphs the relationship between the average two-year fixed rate on subprime loans and the ARM reset rate, which is equal to six-month LIBOR + 6.00%. The data in Exhibit 13.7 are actual rates through August 2007 and forecasts thereafter. The two-year fixed rate is shown twice, once when it occurs and once with a two-year lag. The lagged rate allows the reader to see the choice open to the borrower at any point in time. For example, in March 2007, the 2/28 borrower who took out his loan in March 2005 at 7.30% could have refinanced into another 2/28 at 8.50% or allowed the loan to reset to around 11.25%. Either choice at that time would have been painful. In contrast, in 2002–2004, a period of high HPA and low rates, subprime borrowers had wonderful options. As Exhibit 13.7 shows, they could refinance into a lower two-year loan rate and take equity out of their homes. That was truly a golden period not just for subprime lenders but also for subprime borrowers. However, as you can see from the options available to the subprime borrower in 2006 and 2007, that golden age did not last forever. In fact this graph is now obsolete, since the 2/28

EXHIBIT 13.7   2/28 Refis: No Easy Choice

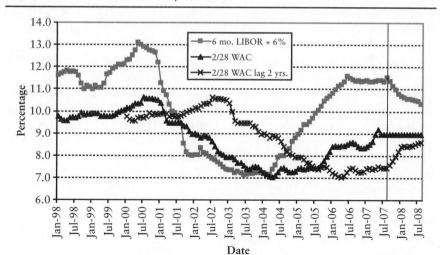

subprime loan is no longer an option. The bank regulators and the capital markets have effectively turned it into a historic relic. The whole world now sees that for most subprime borrowers a 2/28 is not an appropriate loan. Fixed rate loans or hybrids with long initial reset periods (such as five years) are much better suited for the subprime borrower.

So how did the bank regulators miss this? It is always a tough call for a regulator to restrict lending to the American consumer. There have been many credit cycles in the United States. All of them have been based on aggressive lending behavior. And most of the companies that ultimately have paid the price for poor underwriting have known they were writing high risk loans. This was true of the credit card companies in 1996 and 1997, the manufactured housing lenders from 1998 to 2000, the 125 lenders (remember First Plus?) in 1998, and on and on. A common element in all of these cycles is the need to sustain issuance volume in a competitive environment. At an industry conference in mid-2006, I heard an executive from one of the leading subprime lenders describe the layered risk loans that made up much of his company's lending. When an investor questioned him on whether this was a sound policy, he admitted that if he had suggested such a loan several years earlier he would have been fired, but since all of his competitors were using those loose standards he could either go along with it or he could see his volume plummet. He chose to meet the lowest common denominator in the marketplace. So it was not a secret that the subprime (and Alt-A) loans created in the final blow-off phase of this cycle were high risk.

During this period, the mantra of Congress and the Administration was pro business, pro home ownership, and laissez-faire. When the Fed Chairman gives his blessing to the new affordability loans and the President and Congressional leaders brag about the increase in home ownership, it takes a tough bank regulator to take away the source of so much happiness.

In late 2005, bank regulators were discussing what to do about the growing risk in the mortgage market. They were aware of the 2/28 risk, but they were mainly concerned about the interest-only and negative amortization (pay-option ARMS) features of the new affordability loans. For a while it seemed that the 2/28s would be included in the proposal for non-traditional mortgage products, but the proposal released in December 2005 and implemented on September 29, 2006 focused solely on IOs and pay-option ARMs. The main concept behind the guidelines was that lenders should qualify borrowers at a "fully indexed, fully amortized" rate. The rules were not meant to ban a particular product, but rather require rational underwriting if the product were offered. In the case of the 2/28 subprime loan, this would have meant qualifying the borrower at six-month LIBOR + 6.00%, a rate that would have disqualified the vast majority of subprime borrowers.

The new guidelines not only did not address subprime loans but contained a specific carve out for "traditional hybrid ARMs." When the compliance officer from a major subprime lender saw that language, he said that the subprime industry was free to continue qualifying 2/28 borrowers at the two-year teaser rate rather than the fully indexed ARM rate. If that September guidance had contained language about 2/28s, it probably would have not stopped the ensuing crisis; but it would have lessened the impact because the regulators did not issue their guidance on subprime 2/28s until June 2007. In retrospect, including 2/28s in the September 2006 guidance would have been a smart move, but no one knew in September what lay ahead.

One of the reasons that most investors in early 2007 did not believe the bank regulators would put 2/28s under the "fully indexed, fully amortized" guidance was that to do so would effectively shutdown the subprime lending business. As late as the ABS Barcelona conference in June 2007, investors could not believe that the U.S. bank regulators would do this. However, what appeared to us to be likely in late 2006 became a certainty in early 2007 when Senator Dodd and Representative Frank began to pummel bank regulators for not acting sooner to stop what they viewed as high-risk subprime lending. Some in Congress even threatened to the Federal Reserve that if it didn't use the powers given to it under the 1994 Home Ownership and Equity Protection Act (HOEPA) legislation, then it would be taken away and given to another bank regulator that would in fact use that power to prevent another subprime disaster from developing a few years hence.

The heads of the Congressional banking committees, when asked if they believed the bank regulators should stop the worst of the high-risk subprime lending if it meant that many existing homeowners with 2/28s would be forced into foreclosure, replied that it made no sense to protect existing homeowners at the cost of putting even more borrowers at risk. The Congressional banking committees effectively gave the bank regulators an ultimatum: stop the worst of the current lending practices, and if possible come up with a plan to help those already in 2/28 loans. The proposed subprime guidelines were released in February. The final rules were published in June. This was probably a record for bank regulators turning a proposal in to final guidance.

Following the release of the final guidelines, what was still left of the subprime industry began to shutdown. By July virtually all subprime lenders had gone out of business, or if they were still alive had stopped making subprime loans. The homeowners who had taken out 2/28s or 3/27s in prior years were now trapped in their loans with few options for where to refinance when their loans reset.

WHO WILL RESCUE THE SUBPRIME BORROWER?

Much has been written about the various plans being established to help the subprime borrower who is now effectively trapped in his subprime loan. The problem is acute since an enormous number of the subprime and Alt-A loans written in 2005 and 2006 will come up for reset in the next year or so. Exhibit 13.8 shows the number of subprime loans that will reach their reset dates over that period. It averages around $20 billion or 100,000 loans per month. The concern is that because almost all subprime originators have gone out of business or have shutdown their subprime lending, these homeowners will have very little option when their loans reset. Unless their loans are modified or they find subsidized lenders (such as the FHA), they will either have to pay up for much higher fixed rate loans being offered by the banks still making subprime loans, or they will have to pay the adjustable rate which is set to go to six-month LIBOR + 6.00% = 11.50%.

The programs to help these trapped borrowers range from modifications by servicers, to refinance loans from Freddie/Fannie, to the traditional FHA programs, to the new FHA program announced in February 2008 by President Bush. We have examined each of these programs and found they have a common flaw. They target the upper end of the subprime sector, that is, the subprime homeowners who are the least strapped. In a recent study, it was shown that about 50% of the subprime borrowers could qualify for a Freddie/Fannie loan under the new GSE subprime programs.[5] The President's FHA program is limited to homeowners "with a good payment history" or those who were current until their hybrid ARM reset upwards. That is, if you are in trouble before your loan reset or in trouble with a fixed rate loan you are not eligible for this new FHA program. Our feeling is that all of these programs will help the subprime crisis from becoming a total disaster because they will help the top 50% of the subprime borrowers find a way out, but none of these programs addresses the more difficult problem of the borrowers who probably should never have bought homes or are facing financial difficulties that preclude them for meeting even subsidized monthly payments. Also, we know that a large number of the subprime loans written in 2006 were either fraudulent or were used to speculate on the housing market. None of those loans will be made good by any public or private program announced to date, and they are the source of losses that have devastated the subprime market.

IS SECURITIZATION THE VILLAIN?

One of the major themes coming out of the Congressional hearings on subprime was the role played by securitization in perpetuating and, perhaps,

---

[5] "GSE's Role in Return to Normalcy," *Mortgage Strategist*, August 14, 2007, p. 16.

EXHIBIT 13.8 Amount of Subprime Resetting ($ billions)

Product Type	Current Outstanding Balance	Outstanding Adj. × 1.2	Sep-2007	Oct-2007	Nov-2007	Dec-2007	Jan-2008	Feb-2008	Mar-2008	Apr-2008	May-2008	Jun-2008	Jul-2008	Aug-2008	Sep-2008	Oct-2008	Nov-2008	Dec-2008
1-yr. hybrid	0.20	0.24	0.01	0.01	0.01	0.01	0.00	0.01	0.00	0.00	0.00	0.00	—	—	—	—	—	—
2-yr. hybrid	304.13	364.96	12.59	12.91	11.99	13.14	14.65	12.47	13.15	17.58	15.30	16.49	18.34	16.84	18.76	15.85	16.03	13.30
3-yr. hybrid	60.89	73.07	1.20	1.28	1.40	1.48	1.58	1.12	1.35	1.80	1.83	1.74	1.91	2.05	2.39	2.37	2.30	2.22
5-yr. hybrid	10.07	12.08	0.01	0.02	0.03	0.02	0.03	0.03	0.03	0.04	0.04	0.05	0.04	0.04	0.06	0.07	0.06	0.05
7-yr. hybrid	0.11	0.14	—	—	0.00	—	—	—	—	—	—	—	—	—	—	—	—	0.00
10-yr. hybrid	0.72	0.86	—	—	—	0.01	—	—	—	—	—	—	—	—	—	—	—	—
1-yr. hybrid	0.15	0.18	0.01	0.00	0.01	0.01	0.00	0.00	0.00	0.00	—	—	—	—	—	—	—	—
2-yr. hybrid	98.78	118.53	8.52	8.33	6.74	5.58	4.54	3.16	3.49	4.57	3.98	4.41	4.63	3.94	4.27	3.71	3.89	3.24
3-yr. hybrid	23.67	28.40	0.51	0.72	0.44	0.66	0.73	0.58	0.78	1.25	1.45	1.31	1.63	1.63	1.96	1.62	1.31	1.00
5-yr. hybrid	8.36	10.04	0.00	0.00	0.00	0.00	0.01	0.01	0.01	0.00	0.01	0.01	0.02	0.02	0.03	0.04	0.02	0.03
7-yr. hybrid	0.17	0.21	—	—	—	—	—	—	—	—	—	—	—	—	0.00	—	—	—
Total without prepay assumption	507.26	608.71	22.85	23.28	20.63	20.91	21.52	17.38	18.82	25.25	22.61	24.01	26.57	24.52	27.48	23.65	23.62	19.84
Total with prepay assumption	507.26	608.71	22.02	22.01	19.15	19.05	19.25	15.25	16.21	21.36	18.78	19.57	21.26	19.25	21.18	17.89	17.54	14.46
Total number of loans resetting in 000s[a]			109	111	98	100	102	83	90	120	108	114	127	117	131	113	112	94

[a] Based on average loan sizes for the last few years of 210,000.
Source: CPRCDR and UBS.

exaggerating the debacle. The premise is that because the link between loan originator and loan risk was broken by the process of securitization, the lender no longer had a major stake in minimizing losses. A corollary to that is that the emergence of the ABS CDS and the CDO market funneled a large amount of capital into the subprime market and kept it running at full tilt longer than it would have in the absence of the funds flowing from investors via CDOs. There probably is some truth to this but, as they say, "it comes with the territory." If we want the blessings that come with more efficient capital markets, we have to put up with the risks.

Not that long ago mortgage lending in the United States was a local affair. Local banks and thrifts were the main providers of loans to home-owners, and homeowners were the chief source of funds via savings accounts held in local banks and thrifts. We have come a long way from that—first with nationwide banking and then with securitization, beginning with the *government-sponsored enterprises* (GSEs) that created a secondary market for residential mortgages in the mid-1980s. Once mortgages became securi-tized the entire range of capital market institutions—insurance companies, mutual funds, pension funds, and eventually overseas investors—provided funding to the U.S. residential mortgage market. American homeowners are no longer the source of funds for mortgages provided by their local banks and thrifts. It is doubtful if anyone wants to go back to those days, so secu-ritization will remain.

But didn't subprime lenders adopt a very cavalier attitude toward underwriting? Was that because they could off-load the risk to investors? Well, while subprime lenders securitized a large percentage of their loans or sold them to Street firms that securitized them, they did not eliminate all of the risk associated with those loans. On the loans they securitized most of the rated bonds were sold to investors, but the lenders often retained a part of the residual—the first loss piece on a securitization. Many of the subprime lenders that converted to REIT status in 2004 and 2005 retained a large amount of residuals on their books so they had a large stake in loan credit quality. And even if a subprime lender sold most of its residual risk from its own securitizations and eliminated most of the rest via whole loan sales to the Street, it still had institutional risk if its loans performed poorly. If investors became disillusioned with a particular issuer's deals, its future securitizations would be hard to sell. Of course, in the heated environment of 2002–2006, virtually any subprime bond was eagerly snapped up by investors looking for yield. In that low-yield, tight-spread world, there was little tiering by issuer and very little penalty for producing ugly collateral. It was the classic bull market behavior of investors, not securitization, that drove the subprime market to extremes. In a more rational world an issuer that produced high-risk collateral would not remain in business for long, even if a large percentage of its credit risk had been shifted to others.

On the other hand, securitization did open the door to derivatives and structured products that would not have come into existence in the absence of securitization. In particular the mezzanine and high-grade CDOs created from subprime and Alt-A MBS attracted investors from around the world. There are many varieties of CDOs. Those backed largely by mezzanine subprime MBS are referred to as *mezzanine* or *mezz* CDOs. Mezzanine subprime bonds account for 85% to 95% of the collateral in these CDOs. The ratings on this collateral have varied from largely AA to BBB+ several years ago to virtually all BBBs in 2005 and 2006. In fact, in 2005 and 2006, mezzanine CDOs absorbed virtually all BBB subprime bonds created in those years. High-grade CDOs use mainly AA and A bonds from subprime and Alt-A deals for collateral. Subprime comprises roughly 50% of the bonds in high-grade CDOs.

Without this influx of capital, the subprime MBS deals would not have been priced as aggressively as they were, and subprime lenders would not have been able to offer their loans at such low interest rates. It appears to most that the existence of the CDO market allowed the subprime bull market to roll on longer than it would have otherwise and perhaps the collapse was greater because it endured longer. One of the reasons the CDO market could attract such interest was that it offered higher yields than most other similarly rated fixed income securities, partly because the transparency of these deals was less than on most other fixed income securities. In the following section we discuss why these securities were so difficult to model and evaluate.

Securitization also allowed the creation of ABS CDS and the ABX indices, a type of credit default swap that references individual subprime securities. ABS CDS and the ABX were vehicles the mortgage industry could use to hedge credit risk, but they also allowed a large number of hedge funds that had never participated in the fixed income mortgage market to short mortgage credit on a massive scale. The large shorts put on by the hedge funds also helped CDO managers create a large volume of synthetic mezzanine CDOs, a much larger number of CDOs than would have been created just from cash subprime MBS. In this way CDS also contributed to the creation of an even larger number of mezzanine CDOs that would ultimately run into problems and to further extend the subprime bull market. Hence, it appears that these derivative and structured products helped exaggerate the swings in the subprime market even though they themselves were not the source of the underlying credit problem.

LACK OF TRANSPARENCY

One legitimate complaint about subprime securities and their mezzanine CDO offshoots is the lack of transparency in many deals. This issue arises first with the subprime securities and is then further compounded when those securities are used to support other structured products such as CDOs. MBS securities in the United States use two main structures: the so-called "six-pack" structure or the "excess spread/overcollateralization" structure. The "six-pack" structure gets its name from the six subordinated classes ranging from AA to unrated that are used for enhancement in the deal. In such a deal the amount of collateral losses a particular bond can withstand is relatively simple to calculate. Note that we said "calculate," not "forecast." It is never easy to forecast the amount of losses a nonagency MBS is likely to generate. But at least on a six-pack, once you have a loss estimate, you can fairly easily calculate how far up the capital structure the losses will go.

Most subprime deals, and in recent years many Alt-A deals as well, use what is termed an *excess spread/overcollateralization* (ES/OC) structure. This structure is used with higher-risk loans that generate a large amount of excess spread in the deal, where excess spread is the difference between the average loan rate on the assets (loans securitized in the deal) less the average loan rate on the liabilities (bonds issued from the securitization). The excess spread is used to cover losses as they occur on a month-to-month basis. An overcollateralization amount is also used to cover losses. Only after the excess spread and OC are exhausted will the lower-rated bonds begin to experience write-downs. The ES/OC structure also incorporates a trigger test at three years that allows the deal to release extra enhancement if the deal has been performing well. The existence of triggers and the complicated cash flow mechanics make it difficult to calculate how far up the capital structure a given amount of collateral losses will go in a subprime deal. To further complicate matters, the interaction of prepayment speeds and default rates can create nonintuitive write-down scenarios on many subprime MBS. So not only is it difficult to estimate future collateral losses on a subprime deal, once that is done it is no simple matter to estimate which bonds will be written down given that loss amount.

This problem is only compounded when subprime securities are used in CDOs. As we've noted, it is difficult to estimate which bonds (tranches) will be written down on a single subprime deal. Mezzanine CDOs contain or reference (if synthetic) hundreds of individual subprime bonds and often contain CDOs of other CDOs. Calculating expected bond losses on mezzanine CDOs is a complex, highly data-intensive task that requires access to a large database and a large amount of computing power, as well as knowledgeable analysts. Hence, it is difficult for the average investor to forecast how a specific level of subprime losses will impact a mezzanine CDO.

SPILLOVER

As the subprime market imploded, the shock waves were felt across world capital markets. In particular, the institutions and vehicles that had purchased subprime MBS or mezzanine CDOs began to feel the impact of sharply reduced valuations. The first to get hit were the owners of the lower part of the capital structure, the holders of equity tranches and residuals on subprime securities and CDOs. Then came the sharp decline in valuation on the BB/BBB subprime and mezzanine bonds. The last to feel the shockwaves were the AAA holders who had used large amounts of leverage. A relatively small decline in price multiplied by 10 or 20 times leverage suddenly brought about a sharp decline in asset valuation that threatened to wipe out the underlying capital in many leveraged funds and vehicles. As this chapter is being written the market is placing odds on the possible liquidation of large amounts of AAA securities from *asset-backed securities, commercial paper* (ABCP) conduits, and *structured investment vehicles* (SIVs). Many other parts of the capital markets are feeling the impact of this spreading crisis. As we mentioned earlier, how far this crisis goes and its further ramifications are beyond the scope of this chapter.

The one area that we will briefly discuss is the immediate impact on the housing market. In July and August 2007, the nonagency mortgage market effectively shutdown. All lenders except the banks had ceased originating subprime and Alt-A loans, and to a large extent prime jumbo loans. This shutdown will have a devastating impact on an already reeling housing market. Because this shutdown has just occurred, it has not been reflected in housing market data. We suspect that in the next several months existing home sales and other indicators will paint a grim picture of the U.S. housing market.

FUTURE FOR SUBPRIME

At the moment, only commercial banks are offering subprime loans and then only on a limited basis—no more 80/20s, no more liar loans, no more layered risk, just good old fashioned full documentation, 80 LTV loans. Most are either fixed rate or 5/1 ARMs. It is difficult to predict issuance volume in the next several quarters as the industry tries to recover. Since it will be virtually impossible to securitize and sell subprime securities for the foreseeable future (at least at a spread that can support a viable loan rate) most new subprime loans will go onto someone's balance sheet. Ultimately we see this market recovering, but it will never (in our lifetime) return to the $500 billion market of 2005–2006. It will be more like a $150–$200 billion market—say, 8% to 10% of the U.S. new issuance mortgages instead of 20%—and the loans will look a lot more like those of subprime market of 1992–2000 than those created in 2000–2007.

Index